Integrated Developmental & Life-Course Theories of Offending

Integrated Developmental & Life-Course Theories of Offending

Advances in Criminological Theory
Volume 14

Edited by
David P. Farrington

Transaction Publishers
New Brunswick (U.S.A.) and London (U.K.)

Library of Congress Catalog Number: 2004066079
ISBN: 0-7658-0280-5
Printed in the United States of America

Library of Congress Cataloging-in-Publication Data

Integrated developmental and life-course theories of offending / David P. Farrington, editor.
    p. cm.—(Advances in criminological theory ; v. 14)
Includes bibliographical references and index.
ISBN 978-1-4128-0799-9 (cloth : alk. paper)
    1. Juvenile delinquency. 2. Deviant behavior. 3. Criminal behavior.
4. Developmental psychology. I. Farrington, David P. II. Series.

HV9069.I64 2005
364.36'01'9—dc22   2004066079

Contents

Foreword

The Urgency to Improve Developmental Theories

This volume fills a glaring gap in the literature on criminological theories. Written in response to "classical theories" of crime (strain theory, differential association theory, and control theory), the principal issue is whether these and more recent theories address developmental and life-course aspects of crime. These developmental aspects include the transition between antisocial behavior and delinquency, the age-crime curve, a wide range of and developmental shifts in the putative causal factors in the individual, family, peer, school, and neighborhood, and an emphasis on protective factors as they affect individuals' development of offending over time. Another expansion has taken place in the life periods studied, which now cover childhood to old age. In contrast to the earlier theories, both escalation and desistance processes are nowadays within the scope of criminological theorists. To varying degrees these topics are discussed in the chapters that follow, which present the major theories by Lahey and Waldman, Piquero and Moffitt, Farrington himself, Catalano and his colleagues, Le Blanc, Sampson, and Laub, Thornberry and Krohn, and Wikström.

A few important volumes on theories have appeared in recent years. They are worthy of mention here, because they have helped to develop the theme for this book and the types of chapters included in the current volume. Thornberry edited a volume entitled, *Developmental Theories of Crime and Delinquency* (Transaction, 1997), and more recently (with M. D. Krohn) *Taking Stock of Delinquency* (Kluwer/Plenum, 2003), while Lahey, Moffitt, and Caspi ambitiously edited *Causes of Conduct Disorder and Juvenile Delinquency* (Guilford, 2003). Each of these volumes contains specially commissioned chapters by researchers who carefully conducted longitudinal studies spanning many years. Even though each volume had several purposes, the integration of the chapters does not appear to have been the primary consideration, nor whether each author would address the same key theoretical questions. These three volumes can be contrasted with two other collective initiatives, that is the two OJJDP study groups led by David P. Farrington and myself, which culminated in the publication of *Serious and Violent Juvenile Offenders: Risk Factors and Successful Interventions* (Sage, 1998), and *Child Delinquents: Development, Intervention and Service Needs* (Sage, 2001). Although these edited volumes were more coordinated by the editors, they are limited in their theoretical coverage, other than expounding a public health approach to crime.

Why yet another volume on criminological theories? The editor of the present volume, David P. Farrington, rightly recognized that theories often "pass like ghosts in the night" (not his quote) or miscommunicate among themselves because they address very different outcomes, life periods, and processes. They often have limited ranges of explanatory factors and do not necessarily address processes that account for individuals' escalation from minor to serious forms of delinquency, or their de-escalation from serious to minor delinquency, or even more interesting, their transition to non-offending. As another example, the theories also vary in their ability to focus on selection processes in which certain populations of youth (and not others) move into to high-risk experiences or settings, such as gang involvement or drug dealing.

The present volume is a welcome and timely addition to the aforementioned books because its editor challenges the theorist contributors to address a common set of key developmental questions. Farrington masterly draws from his decades of experience in research on delinquency and crime to formulate these key questions (see his list in the first chapter of the book). He then challenged each author to expand on the issues, which he/she usually has addressed (and incorporated in his/her theory) and requested that he/she addresses, perhaps for the first time in criminological theory, the common set of key questions. Knowing Farrington a bit, it is his way of provoking answers from his colleagues on matters that they, in a less obvious manner, have been able to avoid for a long time. The ways that each of the contributors dealt with the common questions (or chose to highlight some questions over others) should be of great relevance to anyone working in criminology.

The results of this exercise in collective questioning are startling. For the first time in criminology, theories that appeared to be distinct now are moving closer together into more general, shared themes. The theories also advanced by becoming more explicit and comprehensive in the developmental matters they cover. At the same time, some theories have moved into more oppositional or contrasting positions to other theories. These movements all are characteristic of increasing sophistication of theories and, importantly, lead to improved comparability, and, hopefully, eventual improved verification or falsification. In the process of formulating their chapters, the authors also address several other key points, particularly whether a single theory can account for gender, race, secular, and neighborhood differences in crime. In several ways, this volume sets a new standard for iterations of present theories and the formulation of the next generation of theories. It should be of enormous interest to scholars, practitioners, and students of crime.

Rolf Loeber

Preface

The idea for this book arose from my address on receiving the Sutherland Award of the American Society of Criminology (Farrington, 2003). In recognition of Edwin H. Sutherland's great theoretical contributions to criminology, I focused on developmental and life-course (DLC) theories. After reviewing key empirical issues in developmental and life-course criminology, I described my own DLC theory, summarized several other important DLC theories, and compared assumptions and predictions from the various theories.

There was a limit, however, to what I could cover in a short article. Therefore, I thought that it would be much more satisfactory to invite the authors of the most fully developed DLC theories to present the latest version of their theory in a book chapter and to explain how it addresses key theoretical and empirical issues in developmental and life-course criminology. I was delighted that everyone who was invited agreed to do this. Hopefully, this book will make it possible to compare and contrast the leading DLC theories and to assess their importance in explaining key empirical findings.

DLC theories are more wide-ranging than previous theories because they integrate knowledge about individual, family, peer, school, neighborhood, community, and situational factors, and also integrate key elements of earlier theories. Several DLC theories aim to explain both the development of offenders and the commission of offenses. Prior to the development of these theories, developmental, ecological, and situational scholars tended to be highly compartmentalized and rarely influenced each other's work.

I am particularly grateful to Freda Adler and Bill Laufer for sharing my enthusiasm for this venture and for agreeing to publish the results in their highly prestigious series on *Advances in Criminological Theory*. I am also greatly indebted to Maureen Brown for her speedy and efficient secretarial assistance.

Reference

Farrington, D. P. (2003). Developmental and Life-Course Criminology: Key Theoretical and Empirical Issues—The 2002 Sutherland Award address. *Criminology* 41: 221-255.

1

Introduction to Integrated Developmental and Life-Course Theories of Offending

David P. Farrington

Developmental and life-course criminology (DLC) is concerned with three main issues: the development of offending and antisocial behavior, risk and protective factors at different ages, and the effects of life events on the course of development. DLC is especially concerned to document and explain within-individual changes in offending throughout life. The main aim of this volume is to advance knowledge about DLC theories, which have been developed only in the last twenty years. These recent theories aim to integrate knowledge about individual, family, peer, school, neighborhood, community, and situational influences on offending, and to integrate key elements of earlier theories such as strain, social learning, control, and differential association.

Criminological Theories

Traditionally, criminological theories have aimed to explain between-individual differences in offending, such as why lower-class boys commit more offenses than upper-class boys. Hence, most classic criminological theories are essentially static theories. This is true of, for example, strain theory (Agnew, 1992; Cloward & Ohlin, 1960), social disorganization theory (Shaw & McKay, 1969), differential association theory (Sutherland & Cressey, 1974) and social control or bonding theory (Hirschi, 1969). Often, these theories were concerned with between-individual differences because they were trying to explain results obtained in cross-sectional surveys. For example, *Causes of Delinquency* (Hirschi, 1969) tested social control or bonding theory using a cross-sectional survey and was one of the most frequently cited works in criminology in the next twenty-five years (Cohn & Farrington, 1996; Cohn et al., 1998). Nevertheless, it is possible that some of these theories could be adapted to explain within-individual variations in offending over time (e.g., Agnew, 1997).

Some criminological theories are more dynamic in nature, such as labelling theory (Lemert, 1972) and social learning theory (Akers, 1998). However, these more dynamic theories rarely address many of the key DLC issues (see later), and the same is true of theories that aim to explain why offenses are committed rather than differences between offenders and non-offenders, such as rational choice theory (Clarke & Cornish, 1985) or routine activities theory (Cohen & Felson, 1979). Also, some of the more recent integrated theories do not address many of the key DLC issues, such as the integration of strain, control, and learning theories by Elliott et al. (1985, 1989) and the reintegrative shaming theory of Braithwaite (1989). As a final example, Tittle (1995: 241-249) discusses how control balance theory explains variations in offending at different ages but otherwise does not address many of the key DLC issues.

In my theoretical exposition a decade ago (Farrington, 1992b), I complained that previous criminological theories tended to neglect the overlap between offending and antisocial behavior, the continuity from childhood to adulthood in offending and antisocial behavior, and the importance of biological and psychological factors. Previous theories focused primarily on offending during the teenage years when it is most prevalent, and hence emphasized constructs that are particularly applicable to the teenage years, such as status frustration (Cohen, 1955) and the strain between aspirations and what can be achieved by legitimate means (Cloward & Ohlin, 1960). In short, while they have made important contributions to knowledge, many previous criminological theories were not developmental.

Gottfredson and Hirschi's (1990) self-control theory is interesting because in many ways it is explicitly anti-developmental. They deny the need to address many of the key DLC issues and the need for prospective longitudinal research. Their crucial argument is that the relative ordering of people on their key underlying construct of self-control is established in childhood (depending primarily on socialization processes) and is then largely stable throughout life. Hence, they say, the causes of offending (when these are based on between-individual correlations between risk factors and offending) are the same at all ages and can be studied cross-sectionally at any age. This argument depends on the implicit assumption that within-individual correlations between risk factors and offending are the same as between-individual correlations between risk factors and offending, which is not necessarily true (Farrington et al., 2002). To the extent that within-individual correlations are different from between-individual correlations, or to the extent that between-individual correlations vary with age, longitudinal studies are needed. Correlations between low self-control and offending are greater in cross-sectional than in longitudinal studies (Pratt & Cullen, 2000).

Gottfredson and Hirschi (1990) argue that it is unnecessary to investigate why people start, continue or stop offending, because all criminal career parameters reflect their underlying theoretical construct of self-control. Hence, the predictors and correlates of onset, continuation, frequency, seriousness, and desistance are the same. They also argue that since the age-crime curve is universal in all places and times, it essentially reflects universal biological processes associated with ageing (e.g., maturational reform in the twenties). Hence, life events such as getting married and getting a satisfying job have no effect on offending, and events following the commission of a crime (e.g., reinforcement or stigmatization) do not change the propensity to commit crimes in the future. They argue that offending is essentially a rational decision and that whether people commit offenses depends on opportunities and routine activities. All of these arguments are discussed in this chapter and illuminated by empirical evidence.

Developmental and Life-Course Criminology

Developmental and life-course criminology (DLC) is a further elaboration of the criminal career paradigm that became prominent in the 1980s (Blumstein et al., 1986), by adding in the study of risk factors and life events. This paradigm enormously advanced knowledge about the measurement of criminal career features such as onset, continuation, and desistance, but it paid less attention to risk factors and life events that influenced these features, or to theories that might explain development, risk factors, and life events (see Piquero et al., 2003). To some extent, the DLC theories were a reaction to what was perceived as a largely atheoretical criminal career paradigm.

DLC incorporates three other paradigms with slightly different emphases that became prominent during the 1990s. The risk factor prevention paradigm focuses on identifying the key risk factors for offending and implementing prevention methods to tackle these risk factors (Farrington, 2000; Hawkins & Catalano, 1992; Loeber & Farrington, 1998). Developmental criminology focuses especially on the development of offending but also on risk factors (Le Blanc & Loeber, 1998; Loeber & Le Blanc, 1990). Life-course criminology focuses especially on the effects of life events and life transitions on offending but also on development and risk factors (Sampson & Laub, 1993). Since all four paradigms (including the criminal career paradigm) are essentially concerned with the same interlinked set of issues, I will incorporate them all under the heading of "developmental and life-course criminology," in the hope of including everyone. This book focuses mainly on fundamental theoretical issues, but there are also important policy implications of DLC, such as risk/needs assessment or risk-focused prevention.

The main reason why DLC paradigms became important during the 1990s was because of the enormous volume and significance of longitudinal research on offending that was published during this decade. Particularly influential were the three Causes and Correlates studies originally mounted by OJJDP in

Denver, Pittsburgh, and Rochester (Huizinga et al., 2003; Loeber et al., 2003; Thornberry et al., 2003). Other important longitudinal projects that came to prominence in the 1990s were the Seattle Social Development Project (Hawkins et al., 2003), the Dunedin study in New Zealand (Moffitt et al., 2001), the important Montreal surveys by Le Blanc (1996) and Tremblay et al. (2003), and the further analyses by Sampson and Laub (1993) of the classic Gluecks' study.

DLC theories are more wide-ranging than previous theories because they integrate knowledge about individual, family, peer, school, neighborhood, community, and situational influences on crime, and also integrate key elements of earlier theories. Many DLC theories aim to explain both the development of offenders and the commission of offenses. Before the integrative efforts of researchers such as Per-Olof Wikström (Farrington et al., 1993; Wikström et al., 1995), developmental, ecological, and situational scholars tended to be highly compartmentalized and rarely influenced each other's work.

At the outset, I should say that I do not expect any DLC theory to be proved or disproved as a result of comparing its predictions with key existing and future DLC findings. However, I do hope that this comparison will encourage researchers to modify their theories to make them more adequate in explaining a wider range of DLC findings. Like Tittle (1995: 270), I am more than willing to modify my own theory (see chapter 4) if any part of it appears to conflict with existing or future DLC findings.

Typically in the past, researchers have proposed their own theories and then investigated the adequacy of these theories in explaining their own and other people's empirical results (see Moffitt, 2003, for an excellent example). However, I believe that a great deal can be learned from comparing several theories with each other and with empirical results. This book is intended to facilitate such comparisons, which are also made in chapter 10. In future, these comparisons may lead to a widespread consensus about key elements that should be included in any DLC theory.

DLC theories aim to explain offending by individuals (as opposed to crime rates of areas, for example). "Offending" refers to the most common crimes of theft, burglary, robbery, violence, vandalism, minor fraud, and drug use, and to behavior that in principle might lead to a conviction in Western industrialized societies such as the United States and the United Kingdom. These theories should explain results on offending obtained from both official records and self-reports. Generally, DLC findings and theories apply particularly to offending by lower-class urban males in Western industrialized societies in the last eighty years or so. How far they apply to other types of persons (e.g., middle-class rural females) or offenses (e.g., white collar crime or sex offenses against children) are important empirical questions that generally are not addressed in this book (see e.g., Weisburd et al., 2001).

What Do We Know?

I begin with ten widely accepted conclusions about the development of offending that any DLC theory must be able to explain. First, the prevalence of offending peaks in the late teenage years—between ages 15 and 19 (Farrington, 1986; Wolfgang et al., 1987). Second, the peak age of onset of offending is between 8 and 14, and the peak age of desistance from offending is between 20 and 29 (Farrington, 1992a). Third, an early age of onset predicts a relatively long criminal career duration and the commission of relatively many offenses (Farrington et al., 1998; Le Blanc and Frechette, 1989).

Fourth, there is marked continuity in offending and antisocial behavior from childhood to the teenage years and to adulthood (Farrington, 1989, 1992a; Tracy and Kempf-Leonard, 1996). What this means is that there is relative stability of the ordering of people on some measure of antisocial behavior over time, and that people who commit relatively many offenses during one age range have a high probability of also committing relatively many offenses during another age range. However, neither of these statements is incompatible with the assertion that the prevalence of offending varies with age or that many antisocial children become conforming adults. Between-individual stability in antisocial ordering is perfectly compatible with within-individual change in behavior over time (Farrington, 1990; Verhulst et al., 1990). For example, people may graduate from cruelty to animals at age 6 to shoplifting at age 10, burglary at age 15, robbery at age 20, and eventually spouse assault and child abuse later in life. Generally, continuity in offending reflects persistent heterogeneity (the persistence of between-individual differences) more than state dependence (a facilitating effect of earlier offending on later offending), although both processes can occur (Nagin & Farrington, 1992b; Nagin & Paternoster, 2000).

Fifth, a small fraction of the population (the "chronic" offenders) commit a large fraction of all crimes (Farrington & West, 1993; Wolfgang et al., 1972). In general, these chronic offenders have an early onset, a high individual offending frequency, and a long criminal career. Sixth, offending is versatile rather than specialized. For example, violent offenders are indistinguishable from frequent offenders in childhood, adolescent, and adult risk factors (Capaldi & Patterson, 1996; Farrington, 1991b; Piquero, 2000). Seventh, the types of acts defined as offenses are elements of a larger syndrome of antisocial behavior, including heavy drinking, reckless driving, sexual promiscuity, bullying, and truancy. Offenders tend to be versatile not only in committing several types of crimes but also in committing several types of antisocial behavior (Farrington, 1991a).

Eighth, most offenses up to the late teenage years are committed with others, whereas most offenses from age 20 onwards are committed alone (McCord & Conway, 2002; Reiss & Farrington, 1991). This aggregate change is not caused by dropping out processes, or group offenders desisting earlier than lone offenders. Instead, there is change within individuals; people change from group offending to lone offending as they get older. Ninth, the reasons given for offending up to the late teenage years are quite variable, including utilitarian ones (e.g., to obtain material goods or for revenge), for excitement or enjoyment (or to relieve boredom), or because people get angry (in the case of violent crimes). In contrast, from age 20 onwards, utilitarian motives become increasingly dominant (Farrington, 1993; Le Blanc, 1996). Tenth, different types of offenses tend to be first committed at distinctively different ages. For example, shoplifting is typically committed before burglary, which in turn is typically committed before robbery (Le Blanc & Frechette, 1989). In general, there is increasing diversification of offending up to age 20; as each new type of crime is added, previously committed crimes continue to be committed. Conversely, after age 20, diversification decreases and specialization increases (Piquero et al., 1999).

The main risk factors for the early onset of offending before age 20 are well known (Farrington, 2004; Hawkins et al., 1998): individual factors (low intelligence, low school achievement, hyperactivity-impulsiveness and risk-taking, antisocial child behavior including aggression and bullying), family factors (poor parental supervision, harsh discipline and child physical abuse, inconsistent discipline, a cold parental attitude and child neglect, low involvement of parents with children, parental conflict, broken families, criminal parents, delinquent siblings), socioeconomic factors (low family income, large family size), peer factors (delinquent peers, peer rejection and low popularity), school factors (a high delinquency rate school) and neighborhood factors (a high crime neighborhood).

The main life events that encourage desistance after age 20 are getting married, getting a satisfying job, moving to a better area, and joining the military (Horney et al., 1995; Laub & Sampson, 2001). The distinction between risk factors and life events is not clear-cut, since some life events may be continuing experiences whose duration is important (e.g., marriage or a job), while some risk factors may occur at a particular time (e.g., loss of a parent). Other life events (e.g., converting to religion) may be important but have been studied less.

While the focus in DLC is on the development of offenders, it is important not to lose sight of factors that influence the commission of offenses. It is plausible to assume that offenses arise out of an interaction between the person (with a certain degree of criminal potential) and the environment (including opportunities and victims). Existing evidence suggests that people faced with criminal opportunities take account of the perceived benefits and costs of offending (compared with other possible activities) in deciding whether or not to offend (Clarke & Cornish, 1985). DLC theories should explain the commission of offenses as well as the development of offenders.

Contentious DLC Issues

I now turn to some more contentious issues. First, while it is clear that the prevalence of offending peaks in the late teenage years, it is far less clear how the individual offending frequency (that is, the frequency of offending by those who offend) varies with age. Some studies suggest that the individual offending frequency accelerates to a peak in the late teenage years and then decelerates in the twenties, whereas others suggest that the individual offending frequency does not change with age (Farrington, 1997; Loeber & Snyder, 1990). Second, it is not clear whether the seriousness of offending escalates up to a certain age and then de-escalates, or whether it does not change with age (Piquero et al., 2003; Tracy et al., 1990).

Third, while it is clear that an early age of onset of offending predicts a long career duration and many offenses, it is far less clear whether an early age of onset predicts a high individual offending frequency or a high average seriousness of offending (Tarling, 1993). Nor is it clear whether early onset offenders differ in degree or in kind from later onset offenders, or how much there are distinctly different behavioral trajectories (Moffitt, 1993; Nagin & Tremblay, 1999). Fourth, while chronic offenders commit more offenses than others, it is not clear whether their offenses are more serious on average (Farrington & West, 1993). Nor is it clear whether chronic offenders differ in degree or in kind from nonchronic offenders.

Fifth, as mentioned, it is clear that certain types of offenses occur on average before other types, and hence that onset sequences can be identified. However, it is not clear whether these onset sequences are merely age-appropriate behavioral manifestations of some underlying theoretical construct (e.g., criminal potential) or whether the onset of one type of behavior facilitates or acts as a stepping stone towards the onset of another. In other words, onset sequences could reflect persistent heterogeneity or state dependence (Nagin & Farrington, 1992a). Similarly, little is known about onset sequences in which childhood antisocial behavior has some kind of influence on later offending, which might suggest opportunities for early prevention.

Sixth, while the main risk factors for the early onset of offending are well known, to what extent these risk factors have causal effects on offending is not clear. A major problem is that knowledge about these risk factors is based on between-individual differences. For example, it is demonstrated that children who receive poor parental supervision are more likely to offend than other children who receive good parental supervision, after controlling for other between-individual factors that influence both parental supervision and offending. However, within-individual variations are more relevant to the concept of cause, as well as to DLC and to prevention or intervention research (which requires within-individual change). For example, if it is demonstrated that children are more likely to offend during time periods when they are receiving poor parental supervision than during time periods when they are receiving good parental supervision, this would be more compelling evidence that poor parental supervision caused offending. In the Pittsburgh Youth Study, Farrington et al. (2002) found that poor parental supervision predicted a boy's delinquency both between and within individuals, but peer delinquency predicted a boy's delinquency between individuals but not within individuals. They speculated that peer delinquency might not be a cause of a boy's delinquency but instead might be measuring the same underlying theoretical construct (perhaps reflecting co-offending).

Seventh, many risk factors could either be causes of offending or indicators of the same underlying construct, or even both. For example, heavy drinking could reflect the same underlying construct as offending (e.g., antisocial potential) in comparisons between individuals, but could be a cause of offending in comparisons within individuals (e.g., if people committed more offenses while drinking than while not drinking). In other words, heavy drinking could be a factor that influenced short-term within-individual variations in offending: why people commit offenses in some times and places but not in others.

There are many other unresolved issues concerning risk factors for offending. While a great deal is known about family risk factors (especially) and individual risk factors, far less is known about biological, peer, school, or neighborhood risk factors. Little is known about risk factors for continuation of offending after onset, for later onsets after age 20, or for persistence or desistance of offending after age 20. Little is known about risk factors for the duration of criminal careers. Little is known about the causal processes that intervene between risk factors and offending. And little is known about protective factors, whether defined as factors that are opposite to risk factors (e.g., high school achievement compared with low school achievement) or as factors that interact with and counteract the effects of risk factors (Losel & Bender, 2003).

While the main life events that encourage desistance are well known, far less is known about life events that influence onset or continuation after onset. Also, the effect of the criminal justice system (police, courts, prison, and probation) on desistance is highly controversial. The labelling effects of convictions, in increasing the probability, frequency, variety, or seriousness of subsequent offending, are also controversial (Paternoster & Iovanni, 1989). Few DLC theories include specific postulates about the effects of interventions.

The final complication is that there may be intermittency in criminal careers (Barnett et al., 1989). Rather than the straightforward model of onset followed by continuation followed by desistance, people may cease offending and then restart after a gap of some years, perhaps because of changes in life events (e.g., losing a job, separating from a spouse, starting heavy drinking).

The challenge to DLC theories is to make predictions about these contentious issues and then see—when these issues are resolved and become part of the conventional wisdom—how far their predictions are correct. (For reviews of knowledge about these more and less contentious issues, see Piquero et al., 2003.)

Key DLC Issues to be Addressed

The key empirical issues that need to be addressed by any DLC theory are as follows:

1. Why do people start offending?
2. How are onset sequences explained?
3. Why is there continuity in offending from adolescence to adulthood?
4. Why do people stop offending?
5. Why does prevalence peak in the teenage years?
6. Why does an early onset predict a long criminal career?
7. Why is there versatility in offending and antisocial behavior?
8. Why does co-offending decrease from adolescence to adulthood?
9. Why are there between-individual differences in offending?
10. What are the key risk factors for onset and desistance, and how can they be explained?
11. Why are there within-individual differences in offending?
    (a) long-term (over life)
    (b) short-term (over time and place)
12. What are the main motives and reasons for offending?
13. What are the effects of life events on offending?

The key theoretical issues that need to be addressed in any DLC theory are as follows:

1. What is the key construct underlying offending?
2. What factors encourage offending?
3. What factors inhibit offending?
4. Is there a learning process?
5. Is there a decision-making process?
6. What is the structure of the theory?
7. What are operational definitions of theoretical constructs?
8. What does the theory explain?
9. What does the theory not explain?
10. What findings might challenge the theory? (Can the theory be tested?)
11. Crucial tests: How much does the theory make different predictions from another DLC theory?

Bernard (1990) argued that criminology has failed to make scientific progress because no criminological theory has ever been falsified; all that happens over time is that new theories are added. Following Popper (1968), he argued that it was important to derive falsifiable propositions from theories and to test these empirically. A theory might be considered to have been verified if, after much testing of its falsifiable predictions, it has not been falsified. In chapter 10, I will attempt to respond to these arguments by highlighting different implications that can be derived from different DLC theories.

Aims of This Book

In constructing this book, I invited the authors of some of the most important DLC theories to present the latest version of their theory and to explain how it addresses the key theoretical and empirical issues raised in this chapter. The authors have varied in how far they have slavishly followed this template. Nevertheless, the expositions in all the chapters are interesting and provocative, and I hope that this book will stimulate and advance knowledge about the formulation and testing of integrated developmental and life-course theories of offending.

References

Agnew, R. (1992). Foundation for a general strain theory of crime and delinquency. *Criminology*, 30: 47-87.

Agnew, R. (1997). Stability and change in crime over the life course: A strain theory explanation. In T. P. Thornberry (Ed.), *Developmental Theories of Crime and Delinquency* (pp. 101-132). Advances in Criminological Theory, Vol. 7. New Brunswick, NJ: Transaction Publishers.

Akers, R. L. (1998). *A Social Learning Theory of Crime*. Boston, MA: Northeastern University Press.

Akers, R. L. (2000). *Criminological Theories: Introduction, Evaluation, and Application* (3rd ed.). Los Angeles, CA: Roxbury.

Barnett, A., Blumstein, A. & Farrington, D. P (1989). A prospective test of a criminal career model. *Criminology,* 27: 373-388.

Bernard, T. J. (1990). Twenty years of testing theories: What have we learned and why? *Journal of Research on Crime and Delinquency,* 27: 325-347.

Blumstein, A., Cohen, J., Roth, J. A. & Visher, C. A. (Eds.). (1986). *Criminal Careers and "Career Criminals."* Washington, DC: National Academy Press.

Braithwaite, J. (1989). *Crime, Shame and Reintegration.* Cambridge: Cambridge University Press.

Capaldi, D. M. & Patterson, G. R. (1996). Can violent offenders be distinguished from frequent offenders? Prediction from childhood to adolescence. *Journal of Research in Crime and Delinquency,* 33: 206-231.

Clarke, R. V. & Cornish, D. B. (1985). Modeling offenders' decisions: A framework for research and policy. In M. Tonry & N. Morris (Eds.), *Crime and Justice,* Vol. 6 (pp. 147-185). Chicago: University of Chicago Press.

Cloward, R. A. & Ohlin, L. E. (1960). *Delinquency and Opportunity*. New York: Free Press.

Cohen, A. K. (1955). *Delinquent Boys: The Culture of the Gang.* Glencoe, IL: Free Press.

Cohen, L. E. & Felson, M. (1979) Social change and crime rate trends: A routine activity approach. *American Sociological Review,* 44: 588-608.

Cohn, E. G. & Farrington, D .P. (1996) "Crime and Justice" and the criminal justice and criminology literature. In M. Tonry (Ed.), *Crime and Justice*, Vol. 20 (pp. 265-300). Chicago: University of Chicago Press.

Cohn, E. G., Farrington, D. P. & Wright, R. A. (1998). *Evaluating Criminology and Criminal Justice*. Westport, CT: Greenwood Press.

Elliott, D. S., Huizinga, D. & Ageton, S. S. (1985). *Explaining Delinquency and Drug Use*. Beverly Hills, CA: Sage.

Elliott, D. S., Huizinga, D. & Menard, S. (1989). *Multiple Problem Youth: Delinquency, Substance Use, and Mental Health Problems.* New York: Springer-Verlag.

Farrington, D. P. (1986). Age and crime. In M. Tonry & N. Morris (Eds.), *Crime and Justice,* Vol. 7 (pp. 189-250). Chicago: University of Chicago Press.

Farrington, D. P. (1989). Self-reported and official offending from adolescence to adulthood. In M. W. Klein (Ed.), *Cross-National Research in Self-Reported Crime and Delinquency* (pp. 399-423). Dordrecht, Netherlands: Kluwer.

Farrington, D. P. (1990). Age, period, cohort, and offending. In D. M. Gottfredson & R. V. Clarke (Eds.), *Policy and Theory in Criminal Justice: Contributions in Honor of Leslie T. Wilkins* (pp. 51-75). Aldershot, England: Avebury.

Farrington, D. P. (1991a). Antisocial personality from childhood to adulthood. *The Psychologist,* 4: 389-394

Farrington, D. P. (1991b). Childhood aggression and adult violence: Early precursors and later life outcomes. In D. J. Pepler & K. H. Rubin (Eds.), *The Development and Treatment of Childhood Aggression* (pp. 5-29). Hillsdale, NJ: Erlbaum.

Farrington, D. P. (1992a). Criminal career research in the United Kingdom. *British Journal of Criminology,* 32: 521-536.

Farrington, D. P. (1992b). Explaining the beginning, progress, and ending of antisocial behavior from birth to adulthood. In J. McCord (Ed.), *Facts, Frameworks and Forecasts.* Advances in Criminological Theory, Vol. 3 (pp. 253-286). New Brunswick, NJ: Transaction Publishers.

Farrington, D. P. (1993). Motivations for conduct disorder and delinquency. *Development and Psychopathology,* 5: 225-241.

Farrington, D. P. (1997). Human development and criminal careers. In M. Maguire, R. Morgan & R. Reiner (Eds.), *The Oxford Handbook of Criminology* (2nd ed., pp. 361-408). Oxford, England: Clarendon Press.

Farrington, D. P. (2000). Explaining and preventing crime: The globalization of knowledge—The American Society of Criminology 1999 Presidential Address. *Criminology,* 38: 1-24.

Farrington, D. P. (2004). Conduct disorder, aggression, and delinquency. In R. M. Lerner & L. Steinberg (Eds.), *Handbook of Adolescent Psychology* (2nd ed., pp. 627-664). New York: Wiley.

Farrington, D. P., Lambert, S. & West, D. J. (1998). Criminal careers of two generations of family members in the Cambridge Study in Delinquent Development. *Studies on Crime and Crime Prevention,* 7: 85-106.

Farrington, D. P., Loeber, R., Yin, Y. & Anderson, S. J. (2002). Are within-individual causes of delinquency the same as between-individual causes? *Criminal Behavior and Mental Health,* 12: 53-68.

Farrington, D. P., Sampson, R. J. & Wikström, P-O. H. (Eds.). (1993). *Integrating Individual and Ecological Aspects of Crime.* Stockholm, Sweden: National Council for Crime Prevention.

Farrington, D. P. & West, D. J. (1993) Criminal, penal, and life histories of chronic offenders: Risk and protective factors and early identification. *Criminal Behavior and Mental Health,* 3, 492-523.

Gottfredson, M. R. & Hirschi, T. (1990). *A General Theory of Crime.* Stanford, CA: Stanford University Press.

Hawkins, J. D. & Catalano, R. F. (1992). *Communities That Care.* San Francisco: Jossey-Bass.

Hawkins, J. D., Herrenkohl, T., Farrington, D. P., Brewer, D., Catalano, R. F. & Harachi, T. W. (1998). A review of predictors of youth violence. In R. Loeber & D. P. Farrington (Eds.), *Serious and Violent Juvenile Offenders: Risk Factors and Successful Interventions* (pp. 106-146). Thousand Oaks, CA: Sage.

Hawkins, J. D., Smith, B. H., Hill, K. G., Kosterman, R., Catalano, R. F. & Abbott, R. D. (2003). Understanding and preventing crime and violence: Findings from the Seattle Social Development Project. In T. P. Thornberry & M. D. Krohn (Eds.), *Taking Stock of Delinquency: An Overview of Findings from Contemporary Longitudinal Studies* (pp. 255-312). New York: Kluwer/Plenum.

Hirschi, T. (1969). *Causes of Delinquency*. Berkeley, CA: University of California Press.

Horney, J., Osgood, D. W. & Marshall, I. H. (1995). Criminal careers in the short-term: Intra-individual variability in crime and its relation to local life circumstances. *American Sociological Review*, 60: 655-673.

Huizinga, D., Weiher, A. W., Espiritu, R. & Esbensen, F. (2003). Delinquency and crime: Some highlights from the Denver Youth Survey. In T. P. Thornberry & M. D. Krohn (Eds.), *Taking Stock of Delinquency: An Overview of Findings from Contemporary Longitudinal Studies* (pp. 47-91). New York: Kluwer/Plenum.

Laub, J. H. & Sampson, R. J. (2001). Understanding desistance from crime. In M. Tonry (Ed.), *Crime and Justice*, Vol. 28 (pp. 1-69). Chicago: University of Chicago Press.

Le Blanc, M. (1996). Changing patterns in the perpetration of offenses over time: Trajectories from early adolescence to the early 30s. *Studies on Crime and Crime Prevention*, 5: 151-165.

Le Blanc, M. & Frechette, M. (1989). *Male Criminal Activity from Childhood through Youth*. New York: Springer-Verlag.

Le Blanc, M. & Loeber, R. (1998). Developmental criminology updated. In M. Tonry (Ed.), *Crime and Justice*, Vol. 23 (pp. 115-198). Chicago: University of Chicago Press.

Lemert, E. M. (1972). *Human Deviance, Social Problems and Social Control* (2nd ed.). Englewood Cliffs, NJ: Prentice-Hall.

Loeber, R. & Farrington, D. P. (Eds.). (1998). *Serious and Violent Juvenile Offenders: Risk Factors and Successful Interventions*. Thousand Oaks, CA: Sage.

Loeber, R., Farrington, D. P., Stouthamer-Loeber, M., Moffitt, T. E., Caspi, A., White, A. W., Wei, E. H. & Beyers, J. M. (2003). The development of male offending: Key findings from fourteen years of the Pittsburgh Youth Study. In T. P. Thornberry & M. D. Krohn (Eds.), *Taking Stock of Delinquency: An Overview of Findings from Contemporary Longitudinal Studies* (pp. 93-136). New York: Kluwer/Plenum.

Loeber, R. & Le Blanc, M. (1990) Toward a developmental criminology. In M. Tonry and N. Morris (Eds.), *Crime and Justice*, Vol. 12 (pp. 375-473). Chicago: University of Chicago Press.

Loeber, R. & Snyder, H. N. (1990). Rate of offending in juvenile careers: Findings of constancy and change in lambda. *Criminology*, 28: 97-109.

Lösel, F. & Bender, D. (2003). Protective factors and resilience. In D. P. Farrington & J. W. Coid (Eds.), *Early Prevention of Adult Antisocial Behaviour* (pp. 130-204). Cambridge: Cambridge University Press.

McCord, J. & Conway, K. (2002). Patterns of juvenile delinquency and co-offending. In E. Waring & D. Weisburd (Eds.), *Crime and Social Disorganization* (pp. 15-30). Advances in Criminological Theory, Vol.10. New Brunswick, NJ: Transaction Publishers.

Moffitt, T. E. (1993). Adolescence-limited and life-course-persistent antisocial behavior: A developmental taxonomy. *Psychological Review*, 100: 674-701.

Moffitt, T. E. (2003). Life-course persistent and adolescence-limited antisocial behavior: A 10-year research review and a research agenda. In B. B. Lahey, T. E. Moffitt & A. Caspi (Eds.), *Causes of Conduct Disorder and Juvenile Delinquency* (pp. 49-75). New York: Guilford.

Moffitt, T. E., Caspi, A., Rutter, M. & Silva, P. A. (2001). *Sex Differences in Antisocial Behavior: Conduct Disorder, Delinquency, and Violence in the Dunedin Longitudinal Study.* Cambridge: Cambridge University Press.

Nagin, D. S. & Farrington, D. P. (1992a). The onset and persistence of offending. *Criminology,* 30: 501-523.

Nagin, D. S. & Farrington, D. P. (1992b). The stability of criminal potential from childhood to adulthood. *Criminology,* 30: 235-260.

Nagin, D. S. & Paternoster, R. (2000). Population heterogeneity and state dependence: State of the evidence and directions for future research. *Journal of Quantitative Criminology,* 16: 117-144.

Nagin, D. S. & Tremblay, R. E. (1999). Trajectories of boys' physical aggression, opposition, and hyperactivity on the path to physically violent and nonviolent juvenile delinquency. *Child Development,* 70: 1181-1196.

Paternoster, R. & Iovanni, L. (1989). The labeling perspective and delinquency: An elaboration of the theory and assessment of the evidence. *Justice Quarterly,* 6: 359-394.

Piquero, A. (2000). Frequency, specialization and violence in offending careers. *Journal of Research in Crime and Delinquency,* 37: 392-418.

Piquero, A., Farrington, D .P. & Blumstein, A. (2003). The criminal career paradigm. In M. Tonry (Ed.), *Crime and Justice,* Vol. 30 (pp. 359-506). Chicago: University of Chicago Press.

Piquero, A., Paternoster, R., Mazerolle, P., Brame, R. & Dean, C. W. (1999). Onset age and offense specialization. *Journal of Research in Crime and Delinquency,* 36: 275-299.

Popper, K. (1968. *The Logic of Scientific Discovery.* New York: Harper and Row.

Pratt, T. C. & Cullen, F. T. (2000). The empirical status of Gottfredson and Hirschi's general theory of crime: A meta-analysis. *Criminology,* 38: 931-964.

Reiss, A. J. & Farrington, D. P. (1991) Advancing knowledge about co-offending: Results from a prospective longitudinal survey of London males. *Journal of Criminal Law and Criminology,* 82: 360-395.

Sampson, R. J. & Laub, J. H. (1993). *Crime in the Making: Pathways and Turning Points Through Life.* Cambridge, MA: Harvard University Press.

Shaw, C. R. & McKay, H. D. (1969). *Juvenile Delinquency and Urban Areas* (rev. ed.). Chicago: University of Chicago Press.

Sutherland, E. H. & Cressey, D. R. (1974). *Criminology* (9th ed.). Philadelphia: Lippincott.

Tarling, R. (1993). *Analyzing Offending: Data, Models and Interpretations.* London: Her Majesty's Stationery Office.

Thornberry, T. P., Lizotte, A. J., Krohn, M. D., Smith, D. A. & Porter, P. K. (2003). Causes and consequences of delinquency: Findings from the Rochester Youth Development Study. In T. P. Thornberry & M. D. Krohn (Eds.), *Taking Stock of Delinquency: An Overview of Findings from Contemporary Longitudinal Studies* (pp. 11-46). New York: Kluwer/Plenum.

Tittle, C. R. (1995). *Control Balance: Toward a General Theory of Deviance.* Boulder, CO: Westview.

Tracy, P. E. & Kempf-Leonard, K. (1996). *Continuity and Discontinuity in Criminal Careers.* New York: Plenum.

Tracy, P. E., Wolfgang, M. E. & Figlio, R. M. (1990). *Delinquency Careers in Two Birth Cohorts.* New York: Plenum.

Tremblay, R. E., Vitaro, F., Nagin, D., Pagani, L. & Seguin, J. R. (2003). The Montreal Longitudinal and Experimental study: Rediscovering the power of descriptions. In T. P. Thornberry & M. D. Krohn (Eds.), *Taking Stock of Delinquency: An Overview of Findings from Contemporary Longitudinal Studies* (pp. 205-254). New York: Kluwer/Plenum.

Verhulst, F. C., Koot, H. M. & Berden, G.F.M.G. (1990). Four-year follow-up of an epidemiological sample. *Journal of the American Academy of Child and Adolescent Psychiatry,* 29: 440-448.

Weisburd, D., Waring, E. & Chayet, E. F. (2001). *White Collar Crime and Criminal Careers.* Cambridge: Cambridge University Press.

Wikström, P-O. H., Clarke, R. V. & McCord, J. (Eds.). (1995). *Integrating Crime Prevention Strategies: Propensity and Opportunity.* Stockholm, Sweden: National Council for Crime Prevention.

Wolfgang, M. E., Figlio, R. M. & Sellin, T. (1972). Delinquency in a Birth Cohort. Chicago: University of Chicago Press.

Wolfgang, M. E., Thornberry, T. P. & Figlio, R. M. (1987). *From Boy to Man, from Delinquency to Crime.* Chicago: University of Chicago Press.

2

A Developmental Model of the Propensity to Offend during Childhood and Adolescence*

Benjamin B. Lahey and Irwin D. Waldman

The goal of our psychological model of juvenile offending (Lahey & Waldman, 2003) is to provide a set of testable causal hypotheses that attempt to explain the development of delinquency and related mental health problems. Our causal model is developmental in two ways. First, it describes causal processes that begin in early childhood and continue at least through adolescence. Second, our model highlights the importance of distinguishing among differing developmental trajectories of child and adolescent offending for the purpose of identifying causal influences on offending.

To unify the chapters in this volume around a common theme, David Farrington challenged the chapter authors to offer explanations for ten "widely accepted conclusions about the development of offending" (Farrington, 2003). In its present form, our model does not address offending during adulthood and does not include hypotheses related to the impact of the criminal justice system on future offending. Nonetheless, our model addresses most of the ten "widely accepted" conclusions and a number of the "contentious issues" about the development of antisocial behavior outlined by Farrington (2003).

The focus of this chapter is on juvenile offending, but we believe that juvenile offending cannot be fully understood without viewing it as part of a broader syndrome of dysfunctional behavior. In this chapter, we use the term "conduct problems" to refer to a range of correlated antisocial behaviors that includes crimes against persons and property offenses (theft, robbery, vandalism, forced sex, etc.), status offenses (running away from home and truancy), and behaviors that are considered to be symptoms of conduct disorder in DSM-IV and ICD-10 that typically do not result in arrest (lying, bullying, fighting, cruelty to animals, violating family curfew, etc.). Moreover, this broad syndrome of conduct

*Writing this chapter was supported in part by grants R01-MH42529, R01-MH53554, R01-MH51091, and K01-MH01818 to the authors from the National Institute of Mental Health.

problems is only one part of a broader spectrum of correlated maladaptive behaviors, which includes substance abuse and risky behavior (reckless driving, high risk sexual behavior, etc.). In addition, youth who engage in the most serious and persistent offending tend to meet diagnostic criteria for a range of mental health problems, including attention-deficit/hyperactivity disorder, oppositional defiant disorder, depression, and anxiety disorders. Because the diagnosis of conduct disorder is defined by engaging in a variety of conduct problems, many youth who engage in serious and persistent offending also meet diagnostic criteria for CD, of course.

For two reasons, we believe that it is not possible to develop an adequate developmental model of juvenile offending without considering the full range of antisocial behavior. First, the critically important early development of juvenile offending is seen in conduct problems that are less serious than arrestable criminal offenses. Not considering these conduct problems to be part of the same syndrome would make it impossible to study the earliest parts of developmental trajectories. Second, minor conduct problems, juvenile offenses, substance abuse, risky behavior, and several types of mental health problems are correlated because they *share some of their causal influences*. In this chapter, we will focus on the subset of maladaptive behaviors that we have defined as conduct problems. We will briefly address substance abuse, risky behaviors, and mental health problems to advance hypotheses for why they tend to co-occur in the same youth (i.e., hypotheses regarding their shared causal influences).

Overview of the Developmental Model

Our primary goal is to advance testable hypotheses regarding the causal processes that link risk factors to juvenile offending. In this section, we provide a brief overview of the structure of the causal model. In the sections that follow, we provide more detailed causal hypotheses.

Social Learning and Child Characteristics

One overarching goal of our model is to *integrate* the most useful constructs from previous causal models. We attempt to build on this integrated foundation by elaborating key concepts that have not been fully developed and by adding new elements to the model. In general terms, our model is as an extension of the social learning model (Patterson, 1982; Patterson, Reid, & Dishion, 1992). That is, we view reinforcement, modeling, persuasion, and other forms of social influence as fundamental causal processes. Our model is also a developmental model of criminology (Loeber, 1988; Loeber & LeBlanc, 1990; Moffitt, 1993) in its emphases on both processes of change in behavior over time and the importance of heterogeneity among differing developmental trajectories of antisocial behavior.

Like Moffitt (1993), we place special emphasis on the characteristics of the child that are associated with differing trajectories of conduct problems. We adopt Gottfredson and Hirschi's (1990) term "antisocial propensity" to refer to individual differences in youth's net predisposition to offend that derive from characteristics of the youth that transact over developmental time with social and situational influences. Antisocial propensity is often simply inferred from antisocial behavior, but to avoid circularity, it must be defined independently of the behavior that it explains (Farrington, 1991, 1995). In our model, the child's temperament and cognitive abilities are the key elements of antisocial propensity.

Recent statements of the social learning model have acknowledged the importance of child characteristics in the development of conduct problems (Snyder, Reid & Patterson, 2003). Our model offers more detailed hypotheses regarding the child characteristics that play a profoundly important role in the social learning process. In addition, because our model also reflects important influences from the fields of developmental psychopathology (e. g., Keenan & Shaw, 2003; Rutter, 1988; Olson, Bates, Sandy, & Lanthier, 2000; Sanson & Prior, 1999), developmental epidemiology (Rutter, 1997), and behavior genetics (Plomin, DeFries, & Loehlin, 1977; Rutter et al., 1997), we offer hypotheses regarding both environmental and genetic influences on antisocial propensity.

Cairns (1979) borrowed the concept of "epigenesis" from developmental biology to describe behavioral development. Just as simple cells develop into complex organs over time, behavior develops from the simple and undifferentiated into the complex. This occurs through a process of interactions between behavior and the environment. Likewise, we posit a developmental sequence from the undifferentiated dimensions of temperament that have substantial genetic influences into complex behaviors, including antisocial behaviors, through transactions with the environment.

Children enter the world with a wide range of temperamental characteristics and capacities to develop complex cognitive skills. At birth, these individual differences are the product of genetic influences and any prenatal environmental influences. From the moment of birth on, however, the child engages in reciprocal interactions (transactions) with his or her post-natal environment that shape his or her abilities, temperament, and adaptive or maladaptive behavior. In some cases, the non-specific behaviors that we refer to as temperament are literally shaped into conduct problems. In other cases, individual differences in temperament influence the likelihood that the child will develop conduct problems by altering the social learning environment and by influencing the child's reaction to it.

Developmental Trajectories of Conduct Problems

It is now clear that youth who commit juvenile offenses do not all follow the same developmental trajectory (Farrington, 1991; Loeber, 1988). *Developmen-*

tal trajectories of conduct problems are defined both by the youth's intercept (the level of conduct problems at the youngest age at which conduct problems are measured) and by the youth's slope (increasing or decreasing trends over time). Like others, we take the position that variations in developmental trajectories are central to understanding the causes of juvenile offending (Hinshaw, Lahey, & Hart, 1993; Moffitt, 1993; Patterson, Reid, & Dishion, 1992). In contrast to Moffitt's (1993) "developmental taxonomy," however, we posit there is a continuum of developmental trajectories, rather than two distinct trajectories with qualitatively different causes. The continuum of developmental trajectories results from variations across the full continua of each element of antisocial propensity and social influence.

Developmental types of conduct problems. In order to understand developmental trajectories, we believe that it is necessary to distinguish between two types of conduct problems based on their individual developmental trajectories in the general population. *Developmentally-early* conduct problems are behaviors like lying and minor aggression (bullying, fighting, and hurting animals) that are highly prevalent in children at the time of school entry, but become less prevalent in most youth with increasing age through adolescence. In contrast, *developmentally-late* conduct problems are nonaggressive conduct problems (e.g., stealing, running away from home, truancy, breaking and entering) and serious forms of aggression (e.g., robbery, use of a weapon, and forced sex) that are very uncommon during early childhood, but become more prevalent with increasing age, reaching a peak during adolescence.

Most theorists have differentiated among developmental trajectories at least partly in terms of the "age of onset" of antisocial behavior. It is meaningful to measure the age of onset of some developmentally-late conduct problems that never occur in early childhood (e.g., automobile theft) or the age of the youth's first criminal conviction. In contrast, as noted by Tremblay (Tremblay et al., 1996, 1999), attempting to measure the "age of onset" of developmentally-early conduct problems is problematic. He has shown that nearly half of all toddlers hit, kick, intentionally break things, take other children's toys, state untruths, and resist the authority of adults from the time they can walk and talk (Tremblay et al., 1999). Over the course of development, most children become less likely to engage in these problem behaviors, but others do not. Thus, although it may be meaningful to think of youth learning new behaviors such as drug sales or burglary, it may be more accurate to think of children as sometimes failing to "unlearn" developmentally-early behaviors such as fighting when it is normative for them to do so (Tremblay, 2000). This implies differences in the mix of causal influences on developmentally-early and developmentally-late conduct problems. We will offer detailed hypotheses regarding this point later in this chapter.

Varying developmental trajectories. At school entry, levels of developmentally-early conduct problems vary tremendously. A small group of children already exhibit high levels of conduct problems that seriously impair their social and academic functioning, another small group exhibits no conduct problems at school entry, and most children fall between these extremes. Slopes of conduct problems vary in every possible direction from these varying starting points at school entry through adolescence. In general, however, it is possible to predict future trajectories of conduct problems from school entry through late adolescence reasonably well from the level of developmentally-early conduct problems at school entry (Lahey & Loeber, 1994). Children with higher levels of developmentally-early conduct problems at school entry are more likely than other children to show high levels of conduct problems that persist (at least) through adolescence (Brame et al., 2001; Nagin & Tremblay, 1999). On the other hand, nearly half of all children who engage in high levels of conduct problems at school entry show considerable improvement by early adolescence (Fergusson, Lynskey, & Horwood, 1996; Moffitt, Caspi, Dickson, Silva, & Stanton, 1996; Nagin & Tremblay, 1999). Thus, a comprehensive model of conduct problems must explain not only why some children have high initial levels of conduct problems at school entry, but explain why some children persist (or worsen) when other children desist.

Over time, the youth whose high initial levels of developmentally-early conduct problems do not desist are more likely than other youth to add developmentally-late conduct problems to their repertoires during late childhood and adolescence (Brame et al., 2001; Sampson & Laub, 1992). These developmentally-late conduct problems are likely to include serious and violent behaviors (Haemaelaeinen & Pulkkinen, 1996). In addition, some youth with histories of low to moderate levels of developmentally-early conduct problems during childhood show increasing levels of developmentally-late conduct problems during late childhood or adolescence. They mostly (but not always) engage in less serious and non-violent offenses, such as truancy and theft (Brame et al., 2001).

Components of Antisocial Propensity

The focus of our model is on the individual components of antisocial propensity. Our goal is to describe them, give them independent operational definitions, and advance hypotheses regarding how they contribute to the development of conduct problems.

Dimensions of Temperament That Contribute to Antisocial Propensity

We hypothesize that three independent dimensions of temperament each contribute to the risk of conduct problems in our developmental model. Like others (Allport, 1937, Buss & Plomin, 1984; Goldsmith, Losoya, Bradshaw, & Campos, 1994), we define temperament as broad aspects of socioemotional functioning. Some variations in temperament are evident in infancy, whereas others emerge later in early childhood. Individual differences in temperament tend to persist into adolescence and adulthood and constitute the socioemotional core of "personality traits" across the life span (Caspi, 1998, 2000; Clark & Watson, 1999; Rothbart & Ahadi, 1994; Rutter, 1987).

Our measurement-based model differs from existing models of temperament and personality in two ways. First, we developed a new measure of child and adolescent temperament, termed the Child and Adolescent Dispositions Scale (CADS) (Lahey, Waldman, Applegate, Rowe, Urbano, & Chapman, 2005) by searching the existing literature for temperament-like characteristics that had been shown to be related to conduct problems. Second, because our goal was to use the CADS in studies that examined relations between temperament and conduct problems (and other mental health problems), we were careful to exclude items from the CADS if they could be considered to be synonyms or antonyms to conduct problems or symptoms of mental health problems. If the CADS had not been constructed in this way, any correlations of temperament with conduct problems or mental health problems could reflect the overlapping items (Sanson, Prior, & Kyrios, 1990). This is important as all existing temperament and personality scales are contaminated by items such as "angry," "aggressive," "impulsive," "untrustworthy," "anxious," "nervous,' "fearful," and "depressed." Recent studies that "purified" existing temperament measures by eliminating common items (Lengua, West, & Sandler, 1998; Lemery, Essex, & Smider, 2002) suggest that not all of the association between temperament and conduct problems is an artifact of overlapping items, however, supporting our decision to develop a model and measure of dispositions that does not include such items.

In an earlier paper (Lahey & Waldman, 2003), we provided a detailed discussion of the similarities between these three putative dimensions of dispositions and two of the three dimensions consistently identified in three-factor models of personality (Eysenck, 1947; Clark & Watson, 1999; Tellegen, 1982) and three of the factors in the robust five-factor model of personality (Costa & McCrae, 1987, 1995; Goldberg & Rosolack, 1994). We do not repeat this detailed discussion in the present chapter, but we briefly summarize it to place our model of dispositions in the context of contemporary models of temperament and personality.

The CADS was developed by first conducting exploratory factor analyses of a pool of relevant items in a population-based sample to refine the hypothesized factor structure. Then, the CADS model was tested against alternative models using confirmatory factor analysis in a second population-based sample. The model was strongly supported in these stringent tests (Lahey et al., 2003). The three CADS dimensions of dispositions are termed *prosociality*, *daring*, and *negative emotionality*.

Prosociality. Based in part on Eisenberg and Mussen's (1991) construct of "dispositional sympathy," a hypothesized dimension of prosociality is defined in the CADS by frequent manifestations of concern for the feelings of others, such as spontaneous sharing and helping. Several concurrent and longitudinal studies suggest that sympathy and concern for others is inversely correlated with youth conduct problems (e.g., Cohen & Strayer, 1996; Eisenberg, Fabes, Murphy, Karbon, Smith, & Maszk, 1996; Graziano, 1994; Graziano & Ward, 1992; Haemaelaeinen & Pulkkinen, 1996; Hastings, Zahn-Waxler, Robinson, Usher, & Bridges, 2000; Hughes, White, Sharpen, & Dunn, 2000; John, Caspi, Robins, Moffitt, & Stouthamer-Loeber, 1994; Luengo, Otero, Carrillo-de-la-Pena, & Miron, 1994).

Daring. The second hypothesized dimension distinguished in the CADS is defined by daring, adventurousness, and enjoyment of loud, rough, and risky activities (Lahey & Waldman, 2003). We labeled this hypothesized dimension as *daring* based on Farrington and West's (1993) finding that children rated on the single item of "daring" were markedly more likely to be chronic criminal offenders during adolescence and adulthood. This dimension bears a strong resemblance to aspects of "sensation seeking" (Zuckerman, 1996) and "novelty seeking" (Cloninger, 1987), which have been found to be positively correlated with conduct problems (Arnett, 1996; Daderman, 1999; Daderman, Wirsen, & Hallman, 2001; Goma-I-Freixnet, 1995; Greene, Krcmar, Walters, Rubin, & Hale, 2000; Luengo, et al., 1994; Newcomb & McGee, 1991; Schmeck & Poustka, 2001). For this reason, some items that were included in the CADS to reflect *daring* were based on our earlier measure of sensation seeking in children (Russo et al., 1993).

It is also seems likely that *daring* represents the inverse of Kagan, Reznick, and Snidman's (1988) construct of "behavioral inhibition." In a series of studies, young children were classified as "behaviorally inhibited" if they were fretful, slow to respond to persons and objects, and slow to vocalize when exposed to challenging laboratory situations, (e.g., meeting an unfamiliar adult and having a robot emerge from behind a curtain and speak to them (Garcia-Coll, Kagan, & Reznick, 1987; Kagan, Reznick, Snidman, Gibbons, & Johnson, 1988; Schwartz, Snidman, & Kagan, 1999). Children who displayed the opposite pattern in these situations were classified as "behaviorally disinhibited." Behavioral disinhibition has been found to predict behavior problems (Biederman et al., 2001; Hirshfeld et al., 1992; Hirshfeld-Becker et al., in press; Kerr, Tremblay, Pagani, & Vitaro, 1997; Raine, Reynolds, Venables, Mednick, & Farrington, 1998; Schwartz, Snidman, & Kagan, 1996; Shaw, Gilliom, Ingoldsby, & Nagin, 2003). Other studies suggest that behavioral inhibition predicts anxiety disorders (Biederman, Hirshfeld-Becker, Rosenbaum, Herot, Friedman, Snidman, Kagan, & Faraone, 2001; Muris, Merckelbach, Schmidt, Gadet, & Bogie, 2001). These findings suggest the hypothesis that the CADS dimension of *daring* will be positively related to conduct problems and inversely related to anxiety disorders.

Negative emotionality. Youth who are given high ratings on the CADS dimension of negative emotionality experience negative emotions frequently, intensely, and out of proportion to the circumstances. The items that define this dimension in the CADS mostly do not refer to specific emotions, but to negative emotions in general. The only specificity in the CADS *negative emotionality* dimension is that the items of "jealous" and "easily bored" loaded uniquely on this dimension. Based on the nonspecific nature of the *negative emotionality* dimension, we hypothesize that it measures a general tendency to react to situations with negative emotions, similar to Gray and McNaughton's (1996) conceptualization of the "fight-or-flight" system. A dimension similar to CADS *negative emotionality* has been identified in all major temperament and personality measures, variously termed neuroticism (Bouchard & Loehlin, 2001; Digman, 1989; Digman & Inouye, 1986; Eysenck, 1947; Goldberg, 1993), negative affectivity, or negative emotionality (Rothbart, Ahadi, Hersey, & Fisher, 2001; Watson, Clark, & Tellegen, 1988; Zuckerman, Kuhlman, Joireman, Teta, & Kraft, 1993).

Consistent with our view of *negative emotionality* as a non-specific tendency to respond to threat or fustration with a range of negative emotions, previous studies have found similar negative affect dimensions to be related to a wide range of mental health problems, including anxiety disorders, depression, and antisocial behavior across the life span (Anthony, Lonigan, Hooe, & Phillips, 2002; Barlow, 2000; Caspi, Moffitt, Silva, Stouthamer-Loeber, Schmutte, & Krueger, 1994; Eysenck & Eysenck, 1970; Farmer, Redman, Harris, Mahmood, Sadler, Pickering, & McGuffin, 2002; Gershuny & Sher, 1998; Gjone & Stevenson, 1997; Goodyer et al., 1993; Goma-I-Freixnet, 1995; Krueger, 1999; Moffitt, Caspi, Dickson, Silva, & Stanton, 1996; Roberts, & Kendler, 1999; Shiner, Masten, & Tellegen, 2002). Not all previous studies of children and adolescents found *negative emotionality* to be significantly correlated with conduct problems, however (e.g., Heaven, 1996; John et al., 1994; Powell & Stewart, 1983; Tranah, Harnett, & Yule, 1998). This raises important empirical questions about the conditions under which *negative emotionality* is and is not associated with antisocial behavior.

Note on "difficult temperament." Developmental theorists have used the construct of "difficult temperament." Prospective studies have shown that children who are classified as exhibiting a difficult temperament during infancy and toddlerhood are at increased risk for serious conduct problems (Kingston & Prior, 1995; Olson et al., 2000; Sanson & Prior, 1999). The relation between the construct of difficult temperament and the CADS model, if any, has not yet been defined. It seems likely, however, that young children who are classified as difficult exhibit deviant levels of one or more of the CADS dimensions of temperament, particularly *negative emotionality*.

Contribution of Cognitive Abilities to Antisocial Propensity

Based on evidence that cognitive abilities, particularly verbal abilities, inversely predict the development of conduct problems (Elkins, Iacono, Doyle,

& McGue, 1997; Giancola, Martin, Tarter, Pelham, & Moss, 1996; Ge, Donnellan, & Wenk, 2000; Kratzer & Hodgins, 1999; Lynam, Moffitt, & Stouthamer-Loeber, 1993; Moffitt & Silva, 1988; Seguin et al., 1999; Stattin & Klackenberg-Larsson, 1993), we hypothesize that lower cognitive ability and slow language development also increase risk for conduct problems. A series of studies have provided evidence that this inverse correlation cannot be explained by differences in SES associated with cognitive abilities, the greater likelihood that more intelligent delinquent youth will avoid detection, or differences in motivation to perform well on cognitive tests (Lynam et al., 1993; Moffitt & Silva, 1988). A range of constructs has been used to refer to the cognitive deficits associated with conduct problems, including verbal intelligence, language delays, neuropsychological dysfunction, and executive functioning. It is not presently clear which construct or constructs are most defensible, but this is an area of active inquiry (e.g., Nigg & Huang-Pollock, 2003).

Genetic and Environmental Influences on Antisocial Propensity

In this section, we summarize existing evidence for genetic and environmental influences on the development of conduct problems. We first address evidence for these casual influences on conduct problems, *per se*. Second, we discuss evidence for causal influences on personality and cognitive abilities. Third, we discuss the complex interplay between genetic and environmental influences in general terms. Finally, we integrate these topics in the context of our causal model.

Rhee and Waldman (2002, 2003) recently reviewed the body of evidence from twin and adoption studies and concluded that there is convincing evidence of both substantial genetic and substantial environmental influences on child and adolescent conduct problems (see also Lahey & Waldman, 2003). Other evidence suggests that this includes genetic influences on both the origins of child conduct problems and on their persistence over time (O'Connor, Neiderhiser, Reiss, Hetherington, & Plomin, 1998; Robinson et al., 1992; Saudino et al., 1996).

There is also strong and consistent evidence that dimensions of personality that appear to be similar to the three CADS dimensions have both genetic and environmental influences. Studies of traits like *negative emotionality* using other measures have found evidence of both moderate genetic and environmental influences from toddlerhood through adulthood (Cyphers, Phillips, Fulker, & Mrazek, 1990; Emde et al., 1992; Gjone & Stevenson, 1997; Goldsmith, Buss, & Lemery, 1997; McGue, Bacon, Lykken, 1993; Pedersen, Plomin, McClearn, & Friberg, 1988; Phillips & Matheny, 1997; Saudino, Plomin, & DeFries, 1996; Tellegen et al., 1988). Similarly, studies of sympathy and prosocial behavior have shown modest to moderate genetic influences across the life span (Davis, Luce, & Kraus, 1994; Emde et al., 1992; Matthews, Batson,

Horn, & Rosenman, 1981; Zahn-Waxler et al., 1992). The same has been found for the construct of behavioral inhibition in toddlers and children (Cyphers et al., 1990; DiLalla, Kagan, & Reznick, 1994; Emde et al., 1992; Goldsmith et al., 1997; Phillips & Matheny, 1997; Robinson, Kagan, Reznick, & Corley, 1992), which we believe to be related to *daring* in our model. It is also very clear that there are both genetic and environmental influences on cognitive ability and language development from toddlerhood on (Eley, Dale, & Bishop, 2001; Emde et al., 1992; Petrill et al., 1997; Plomin & Petrill, 1997). Based on this evidence, we hypothesize that the four elements of antisocial propensity in the CADS model (cognitive ability and the three dispositional dimensions) will each have substantial genetic and environmental influences.

Interplay of Genetic and Environmental Influences

There are genetic and environmental influences on conduct problems. Because genetic and environmental influences are ubiquitous on all significant aspects of human behavior, this information is of little importance by itself. It is the nature of the complex *interplay* between genetic and environmental influences that is important. In this section, we discuss this interplay in general terms to lay a foundation for more specific hypotheses. In particular, it is essential to consider environmental influences in the context of their interplay with genetic influences to fully understand them and to harness their power in prevention and treatment. This is partly because the child's transactions with the environment that shape personality and behavior operate largely through both genotype-environment correlations and genotype-environment interactions (Rutter, 1997; Rutter et al., 1997).

Genotype-environment correlations. In many cases, genetic and environmental influences on the origins of conduct problems are correlated, rather than independent of one another. There are three types of genotype-environment correlations that appear to be relevant to the development of conduct problems: passive, evocative, and active (Plomin, DeFries, & Loehlin, 1977; Rutter, 1997; Rutter et al., 1997).

The interplay of genetic and environmental influences takes the form of *passive genotype-environment correlations* when characteristics of the child and the causally significant aspects of the family environment share the same genetic influences. Because parents and children share genetic influences, children with the most serious conduct problems tend to have antisocial fathers and tend to be raised by younger antisocial mothers with mental health problems (Klerman, 1993; Lahey et al., 1988, 1989; Nagin, Pogarsky, & Farrington, 1997; Wakschlag, Gordon, Lahey, Loeber, Green, & Leventhal, 2000; Wahler & Hann, 1987). Because such families are poorly prepared to provide the kinds of skilled childrearing that could prevent the development of conduct problems, this genotype-environment correlation fosters the development of conduct problems.

In the case of *evocative genotype-environment* correlations, the child's genetically influenced personality and cognitive characteristics impact aspects of the social environment that foster the development of conduct problems. Consistent with the social learning model (Patterson, 1982), we hypothesize that parenting plays the key role in the developmental transformation of antisocial predisposition into conduct problems. Cognitively and temperamentally predisposed children are less likely to develop conduct problems if they receive adaptive parenting. Unfortunately, we hypothesize that such predisposing child characteristics evoke exactly the kinds of coercive, harsh, nonresponsive, inconsistent, and negative parenting behaviors that foster conduct problems (Anderson, Lytton, & Romney, 1986; Ge et al., 1996; Loeber & Tengs, 1986; Patterson, 1982; Sanson & Prior, 1999).

In other cases, *active genotype-environment correlations* operate because genetic influences lead some children to actively seek out social environments that foster their development of conduct problems. For example, there is evidence that children with conduct problems tend to associate with delinquent peers (Fergusson & Horwood, 1999) and that associating with delinquent peers fosters the future development of delinquent behavior (Fergusson, Swain-Campbell, & Horwood, 2002; Keenan, Loeber, & Zhang, 1995). Furthermore, there is evidence of genetic influences on associating with delinquent peers (Rowe, & Osgood, 1984). Thus, we hypothesize that there is an active genotype-environment correction reflecting genetic influences on characteristics of children that lead to the selection of social environments that foster offending.

Genotype-environment interactions. These occur when the effects of genetic and environmental influences on a trait depend on one another (i.e., are not simply additive). For example, a number of adoption studies indicate that conduct problems in the adopted-away offspring of antisocial parents are less common when they are raised by well-adjusted adoptive parents than by adoptive parents with problems like their biological parents (Bohman, 1996; Cadoret, Yates, Troughton, Woodward, & Stewart, 1995). This suggests that genetic influences on conduct problems are muted by the favorable social learning environments of well-functioning adoptive families. Similarly, there is emerging evidence that individuals respond in different ways to social factors that encourage conduct problems partly because of genetic differences. For example, Caspi et al. (2002) provided striking evidence that maltreated children who have one particular version (allele) of the gene that controls levels of monoamine oxidase (MAO), which is an enzyme that inactivates the neurotransmitters serotonin, dopamine, and norepinephrine in the brain, are more likely to engage in antisocial behavior than maltreated children without this allele. The allele confers little increased risk for conduct problems in the absence of physical abuse. We expect that many such gene-environment interactions will need to be examined to understand the role of both genes and the environment. For example, we posit that genetic influences are one factor that increase or decrease the likelihood that youth will respond to the social influences on delinquent behavior.

Antisocial Propensity and the Mediation Hypothesis

It is likely that genetic influences (and any prenatal environmental influences) on conduct problems are *mediated* by the dispositional and cognitive components of antisocial propensity (Lahey, Waldman, & McBurnett, 1999; Rutter, 2003). That is, we hypothesize that there are genetic influences and possibly prenatal environmental influences on personality and cognitive ability, but there is little (if any) direct genetic influence on complex behaviors such as stealing and vandalism. Rather we hypothesize that genetic influences on conduct problems are *indirect*, operating through the four dimensions of antisocial propensity.

The mediation hypothesis is based in part on evidence that the genetic influences on conduct problems, ODD, and ADHD overlap substantially (Coolidge, Thede, & Young, 2000; Eaves, Rutter, Silberg, Shillady, Maes, & Pickles, 2000; Thapar, Harrington, & McGuffin, 2001; Waldman, Rhee, Levy, & Hay, 2001). In terms of the CADS model, we hypothesize that the dispositional and cognitive-verbal components of antisocial propensity (a) each have unique genetic influences, and (b) these components of propensity mediate the genetic influences on conduct problems (Lahey & Waldman, 2003).

A number of behavior genetic studies provide preliminary support for the mediation hypothesis. Schmitz et al. (1999) found that maternal ratings of negative emotionality measured at the ages of 14, 20, 24, and 36 months predicted a composite rating of oppositional, aggressive, and non-aggressive conduct problems at age 4 years. Consistent with the mediation hypothesis, 96 percent of the correlation between negative emotionality and conduct problems was explained by genetic influences common to both variables. In 270 pairs of twins, Lemery et al., (2002) found that temperament ratings at 5 years of age predicted conduct problems at age 7. Consistent with the mediation hypothesis, genetic influences on conduct problems were substantial and were entirely mediated by temperament. Although Lemery et al. did not use the CADS, two of the dimensions of temperament in her measure (negative affectivity and surgency) resemble *negative emotionality* and *daring* enough to lend plausibility to our mediation hypothesis.

Gjone and Stevenson (1997) followed a sample of 759 twin pairs who were 5-15 years old in the first assessment. Parent ratings of negative emotionality in the first assessment predicted both aggressive and nonaggressive conduct problems two years later. Genetic influences on *aggressive* conduct problems were mediated by *negative emotionality*. In contrast, neither common genetic nor shared environmental influences explained the prospective association between temperament and *nonaggressive* conduct problems. Although the CADS model would have predicted some shared causal influences on *negative emotionality* and nonaggressive conduct problems, this finding is consistent with our hypothesis that the conduct problems of youth who follow a trajectory of high and persistent conduct problems beginning in school entry, which include aggressive conduct problems, have stronger genetic influences that are mediated by the components of antisocial propensity than the conduct problems of youth with later ages of onset (whose conduct problems tend to be nonaggressive). In addition, there is preliminary evidence that "executive functioning" mediates a substantial proportion of the genetic influences on conduct problems (Coolidge, Thede, & Young, 2000). This is consistent with our hypothesis that genetic influences on conduct problems are mediated partly by deficits in cognitive ability.

Developmental Trajectories and Causal Influences

We posit that the same set of child characteristics and social factors influence conduct problems in children who follow all developmental trajectories, but differences in developmental trajectories result from different combinations of the same set of causal influences. Note that we speak of different developmental trajectories in this section as if they are discrete categories for the sake of clarity. We view them, however, as segments along the two continua of trajectories: (1) the continuum of initial levels of conduct problems (intercepts), and (2) the continuum of slopes from these initial levels.

When young children are deviant in the direction of increased risk on one or more components of antisocial propensity, their deviant temperament and/or slow verbal development foster high levels of developmentally-early conduct problems prior to school entry. The stronger the child's net propensity early in life, the more likely the child is to show a developmental trajectory characterized by high levels of developmentally-early conduct problems at school entry, little or no decline in these behaviors, and the rapid learning of developmentally-late conduct problems. Therefore, children with high levels of antisocial propensity tend to develop versatile repertoires of conduct problems, which tend to endure and sometimes worsen over time. Only a small proportion of children in the general population have extreme levels of antisocial propensity in early childhood, but these children commit a high proportion of crimes because they start early, are versatile, commit serious offenses, offend frequently, and persist in their offending over long periods of time.

Some children exhibit high levels of developmentally-early conduct problems at school entry, but improve over the course of childhood. Compared to children who exhibit persistent conduct problems, several studies suggest that children who improve have less extreme initial levels of childhood conduct problems, are more intelligent, have fewer delinquent friends, and come from families with higher socioeconomic status (SES) and fewer antisocial and mental health problems (Fergusson et al., 1996; Lahey, Loeber, Burke, & Rathouz, 2002; Nagin & Tremblay, 2001). Thus, we hypothesize that children who exhibit deviant but improving levels of early conduct problems at school entry improve both because they have less maladaptive personality and higher intelligence and because they live in more adaptive social environments. It seems likely that their social environments are more adaptive partly because of passive, evocative, and active genotype-environment correlations that are driven by genetic influences. In either case, we hypothesize that these youth who improve during childhood are not at high risk for adding developmentally-late conduct problems to their repertoires during adolescence. They lack both the extreme antisocial propensity and social environments that would place them at risk.

Youth whose personalities and cognitive abilities are in the average range during childhood are not likely to develop serious conduct problems. They can, and often do, become offenders, however, if social influences to offend are sufficiently strong. Such youth will tend to show normative levels of developmentally-early conduct problems at school entry, but will show increasing levels of developmentally-late conduct problems in late childhood or adolescence. They never exhibit high levels of developmentally-early conduct problems because they lack the temperamental and cognitive basis for acquiring them early in life. When peer influences become more powerful during late childhood and adolescence, they may acquire developmentally-late conduct problems. Because they lack the temperamental basis for the development of aggression, however, they mostly acquire less serious nonaggressive conduct problems (e.g., truancy and stealing).

Youth with little antisocial propensity (i.e., highly adaptive personalities and cognitive abilities) are unlikely to engage in conduct problems. This is because they lack the dispositional and cognitive basis for developmentally-early conduct problems and their adaptive traits protect them from social pressures to engage in delinquent acts during adolescence.

Specific Causal Mechanisms in the Development of Conduct Problems

Through what causal mechanisms do individual differences in antisocial propensity influence the social learning of conduct problems? The answer lies in the interplay between child characteristics (propensity) and the social environment (Keenan & Shaw, 1995, 2003; Lahey & Waldman, 2003). Social learning plays the key role for youth on all developmental trajectories, but in ways that reflect the characteristics of the child. In this section, we explicate our causal model in greater detail.

From temperament to conduct problems. Deviant levels of temperament influences how children and adolescents respond to the environmental demands that are placed on them, how they relate to peers and adults, and what activities are perceived as desirable. The three putative dispositional dimensions are hypothesized to operate in somewhat different ways.

Toddlers who are high in *negative emotionality* often become highly upset when they are frustrated or annoyed in even minor ways. The rules that adults place on children at home, in day care, and at school are a prime source of frustration. As a result, higher *negative emotionality* creates a press to oppose and circumvent adult rules by lying and acting covertly. In addition, the inevitable frustrations of daily social life in the home or preschool (e.g., having a sibling or classmate play take the toy they were playing with or bump into them) cause children who are higher in negative emotionality to react with intense, global negative affect. Very little is required from the social environment to shape these affective reactions into the more specific behaviors of hitting, shoving, biting, and destroying property. Because of the frequency and intensity of their negative affective responses, toddlers who are high in *negative emotionality* are more likely to push a child down or land a flailing blow that is reinforced by removing the frustration.

High levels of *negative emotionality* in children may also strain parent-child relationships (Rothbart & Ahadi, 1994) and lead to peer rejection (Maszk, Eisenberg, & Guthrie, 1999). These consequences may contribute to the development of conduct problems by disrupting parenting and isolating the child from well-behaved peers early in life. Likewise, high *negative emotionality* would be expected to promote the increasingly aversive parent-child exchanges that Patterson (1982) refers to as the "coercion cycle." Thus, *negative emotionality* contributes to the development of conduct problems largely through genotype-environment correlations.

In contrast, we hypothesize that *prosociality* and *daring* primarily contribute to the social learning of conduct problems mostly by influencing how different children will respond to the same environmental influences (i.e., genotype-environment interactions). Consider, for example, a toddler who accidentally pushes another child onto the floor during an argument over a toy. For a child who is low in *prosociality*, the victim's crying and acquiescence would tend to positively reinforce the aggression, but the victim's crying would tend to punish the same behavior in a child who is high in *prosociality*. That is, the same event would influence the likelihood of future aggression in opposite directions in toddlers who are high or low on *prosociality*. Similarly, if a child covertly took a toy from a classmate who became upset over its loss, the child's sadness would punish the act of stealing in a highly prosocial child, but not in a less prosocial child.

The dispositional dimension of *daring* alters the child's response to the social environment in similar ways. To a child who is high on *daring*, leaving the school building without permission would be exciting and positively reinforcing, but to a child who is low on *daring*, the same event would be punishing. Similarly, children high on *daring* would tend to enjoy being in physical fights and be more likely to fight in the future because of it. In contrast, children who are low on *daring* would be frightened by being in a fight and would be less likely to fight again. In addition, peers quickly learn who is game for risky ventures such as shoplifting or vandalism and seek them out for joint delinquent activities. In many such ways, the dispositional dimensions both influence the social environment (genotype-environment correlation) and influence the child's reaction to it (genotype-environment interaction).

Role of cognitive skills. Although much remains to be learned, we suspect that variations in cognitive abilities influence the development of conduct problems in multiple ways. For example, the extent to which children understand rules, appreciate the potential consequences of their behavior, and have adaptive options for success available to them are related to their cognitive ability. In addition, particularly in early childhood, individual differences in intelligence are manifested partly as differences in the development of communication skills (Sparks, Ganschow, & Thomas, 1996; Stattin & Klackenberg-Larsson, 1993). A number of cross-sectional and prospective studies have shown that children with slow language development in early childhood are more likely to develop conduct problems (Baker & Cantwell, 1987; Beitchman et al., 2001; Cohen et al., 1998; Dery et al., 1999; Klackenberg-Larsson, 1993; Pennington & Ozonoff, 1996). Following Keenan and Shaw (1997, 2003), we hypothesize that it is easier for parents and other caregivers to socialize young children who have better-developed communication skills. This is both because they can understand parental instructions better and because they can communicate their needs better (and hence are less likely to be frustrated during interactions with adults and peers).

Interactions among the components of antisocial propensity. We believe that it is likely that the temperamental and cognitive components of antisocial propensity operate both additively and interactively. This means that (1) deviance in the direction of increased risk on any component of antisocial propensity increases the risk of conduct problems, and (2) some combinations of deviance on the components antisocial propensity contribute to the likelihood of conduct problems in more than an additive manner. At this point, there is tentative evidence that the CADS dispositional dimensions may contribute to the likelihood of conduct problems interactively, rather than additively (Lahey et al., 2005), but this will be an important topic for future studies.

It also seems likely that interactions will be found between cognitive ability and at least some dispositional dimensions. For example, it is likely that children with lower cognitive abilities and delayed language will often experience failure in tasks and games. If they were also high on *negative emotionality*, these frustrations would elicit in a high rate of the kinds of negative affective reactions that promote the development of aggression and alienate both peers and adults (Hughes, Cutting, & Dunn, 2001). In addition, during elementary school, children with less well-developed cognitive skills are at increased risk for grade retention. A longitudinal study (Pagani, Tremblay, Vitaro, Boulerice, & McDuff, 2001) has shown that grade retention does not improve academic performance, but increases future conduct problems, particularly in boys. This might happen both because grade retention is frustrating and because it places children with a temperamental predisposition to aggression with younger and weaker classmates who are more likely to reinforce their aggression by cowering and complying. Because lower intelligence is the major reason for grade retention, lower intelligence also can contribute to this social opportunity for becoming more aggressive.

Personality and the Construct of Psychopathy

The construct of psychopathy is defined by callous disregard for others, irresponsibility, lack of guilt, sensation seeking, and impulsivity. Adults with psychopathic characteristics are known to be at greatly increased risk for serious and persistent offending (Hare, 1987, 1994). Studies using measures of psychopathy developed for children and adolescents have similarly found psychopathy to be correlated with conduct problems (Frick, O'Brien, Wootton, & McBurnett, 1994; Frick, Bodin, & Barry, 2000; Lynam, 1997). It is important that psychopathic characteristics have been found to be related to the five-factor model personality dimensions of low agreeableness and low conscientiousness in adults (Lynam & Widiger, 2001; Miller, Lynam, Widiger, & Leukefeld, 2001). Because these are two of the dimensions of the five-factor model that appear to be similar to the CADS dimensions, we will test the hypothesis that youth with psychopathic characteristics tend to exhibit high levels of daring and low levels of prosociality in the CADS model. If so, this would integrate the CADS model with a large and important literature.

Note on Situational Influences

We have not addressed the important topic of situational influences on offending, both because of lack of space and because this topic has been treated well by Wikström and Sampson (2003) and others. This is an exceptionally important topic for the prevention of offending. If we are correct that the most serious offenders are characterized by maladaptive personalities and cognitive abilities, it will be very difficult to control offending until methods of changing antisocial propensity have been developed. This is because we hypothesize a propensity-by-situation interaction, in which opportunities for offending will more often lead to actual offending in high propensity than low propensity youth. Until the field learns how to reduce antisocial propensity in youth, however, the most effective solutions would seem to lie in reducing opportunities for offending through increased adult supervision, such as by providing well-supervised, healthy, and engaging after-school programs.

Explaining the Co-Occurrence of Conduct and Other Problems

Youth who engage in conduct problems are very likely to meet diagnostic criteria for a wide range of mental health problems, including attention-deficit/hyperactivity disorder (ADHD), oppositional defiant disorder (ODD), anxiety disorders, and depression (Angold, Costello, & Erkanli, 1999; Lahey, Miller, Gordon, & Riley, 1999b). This high degree of co-occurrence is found primarily, but not exclusively, among youth who follow trajectories of high and stable levels of conduct problems from school entry through adolescence (Henry, Caspi, Moffitt, & Silva, 1996; Hinshaw, Lahey, & Hart, 1993; Lahey et al., 1998; Loeber, Green, Keenan, & Lahey, 1995; Lynam, 1998; Moffitt, 1990; Moffitt et al., 1996). This means that most youth who engage in serious and persistent juvenile offending also have serious mental health problems. Therefore, a satisfactory model of juvenile offending should be able to explain such frequent co-occurrence.

Co-occurrence with ADHD, ODD, Substance Abuse, and Risky Behavior

ADHD and ODD may share dispositional and cognitive profiles that are similar to conduct problems (Lahey et al., 2003). We have hypothesized that differences in the child's social environment are the primary cause of which children with high-risk levels of temperament and cognitive ability exhibit which combination of ADHD behaviors, ODD behaviors, and conduct problems (Lahey & Waldman, 2003). In addition, there may be somewhat different dispositional and ability profiles when these disorders occur separately or co-occur. Consistent with the latter possibility, children in the Australian Temperament Project with co-occurring conduct problems and ADHD were more likely to receive high ratings on a trait similar to *negative emotionality* from infancy onward than children with only conduct problems, only ADHD, or neither disorder (Sanson & Prior, 1999). In addition, there is consistent evidence from many studies (reviewed by Henry & Moffitt, 1997; Hinshaw, 1992; Hogan, 1999; and Waschbusch, 2002) that children with both conduct problems and ADHD tend to have lower verbal intelligence scores than children with only conduct problems, only ADHD, or neither disorder. Indeed, youth who exhibited only conduct problems and not ADHD did not differ from controls in verbal intelligence (Waschbusch, 2002).

Studies of adolescents and adults also suggest that three of the five-factor model dimensions of personality (agreeableness, conscientiousness, and negative emotionality) that appear to be related to the three CADS dimensions are correlated with alcohol and drug abuse (Flory, Lynam, Milich, Leukefeld, & Clayton, 2002; McCormick, Dowd, Quirk, & Zegarra, 1998; Wills, Sandy, & Yaeger, 2000) and with high risk behavior (Gullone & Moore, 2000). This suggests the possibility that juvenile offenders often abuse drugs and alcohol and engage in high risk behavior partly because the same dimensions of personality that increase the likelihood of the development of conduct problems also increase the likelihood of substance abuse and risky behavior. This hypothesis could be tested by determining if youth who engage in conduct problems and also abuse substances and engage in high-risk behaviors are lower, for example, in *prosociality* and higher in *daring* than youth who only engage in conduct problems. It should be noted that there is some evidence that substance use also increases the risk of offending over time (e.g., Van Kammen & Loeber, 1994). This could be because substance use creates a need for money to buy drugs, because intoxication temporarily increases antisocial propensity, or both. Much more research from longitudinal studies is needed on the possibility of bi-directional influences.

Co-occurrence with Anxiety and Depression

We have hypothesized that persistent conduct problems often co-occur with emotional disorders primarily because these mental health problems are also more common in youth with high levels of *negative emotionality* (Lahey & Waldman, 2003). For example, as noted earlier, many studies suggest that *negative emotionality* is positively correlated with conduct problems, ADHD, ODD, anxiety, and depression. This suggests that *negative emotionality* is a nonspecific dimension of personality that fosters the development of many types of problems and, therefore, increases the likelihood of co-occurring disorders.

In addition, there is strong evidence from longitudinal studies that childhood conduct problems predict the later emergence of depression, but not vice versa (Capaldi, 1992; Lahey et al., 2002; Patterson & Stoolmiller, 1991). There is evidence that some of this prospective association is mediated by the adverse effect of the youth's conduct problems on aspects of his or her social environment (e.g., rejection by peers and adults) that foster depression (Burke, Loeber, & Lahey, 2003; Capaldi, 2002).

The CADS model may be able to explain three well established, but seemingly paradoxical findings regarding the relation between conduct problems and anxiety. First, it is clear that anxiety disorders co-occur with conduct problems at greater than chance rates across the life span (Loeber & Keenan, 1994; Zoccolillo, 1992). Second, children with conduct problems who are characterized as "socially withdrawn" are at increased risk for persistent and serious conduct problems (Blumstein, Farrington, & Moitra, 1985; Kerr et al., 1997; Serbin, Moskowitz, Schwartzman, & Ledingham, 1991). Third, shyness and anxiety in young children without early conduct problems protect against the development of later conduct problems (Graham & Rutter, 1973; Kohlberg, Ricks, & Snarey, 1984; Mitchell & Rosa, 1981; Sanson, Pedlow, Cann, Prior, & Oberklaid, 1996) and juvenile offenders with high levels of anxiety have lower recidivism rates than other juvenile offenders (Quay & Love, 1977).

Thus, anxiety and shyness are sometimes associated with increased risk for conduct problems and are sometimes associated with decreased risk. We hypothesize that the difference depends on the profile of temperament associated with the shyness, anxiety, or social withdrawal. Specifically, we hypothesize that anxiety protects against serious conduct problems if it reflects low *daring* (i.e., high timidity). When anxiety reflects greater *negative emotionality*, however, anxiety will be positively correlated with conduct problems (because *negative emotionality* is also positively correlated with conduct problems). When children are socially withdrawn because they have little interest in other children due to low *prosociality*, their social withdrawal will be positively correlated with conduct problems because *prosociality* is inversely related to conduct problems. These hypotheses can be easily tested, shedding important light on this confusing pattern of associations among conduct and emotional problems.

Explaining Demographic Differences in Conduct Problems

Because there are large demographic differences in the prevalence of conduct problems (Lahey et al., 199b), a comprehensive causal model of conduct problems must be able to explain these differences.

Sex Differences

By school entry, boys are more likely than girls to engage in conduct problems (Keenan & Shaw, 1997; Moffitt et al., 2001; Lahey et al., 2000; Tremblay et al., 1996). We hypothesize that the causes of conduct problems are the same for girls and boys, with sex differences in conduct problems arising from a combination of sex differences in the *levels* of the components of antisocial propensity (Moffit et al., 2001; Rhee & Waldman, 2002; Rowe, Vazsonyi, & Flannery, 1995) and sex differences in socialization (Keenan & Shaw, 1997). For example, boys lag behind girls on average in the development of language communication during the crucial toddler years (Sanson, Smart, Prior, & Oberklaid, 1993). Keenan and Shaw (1997) suggested that girls are easier to socialize for this reason and that the resulting differences in socialization help create sex differences in conduct problems. To take a second example, girls show higher levels of empathy and guilt than boys from toddlerhood through adolescence (Keenan, Loeber, & Green, 1999; Keenan & Shaw, 1997; Zahn-Waxler et al., 1992). We posit that *prosociality* plays the same role in the development of conduct problems in girls and boys, but from an early age, boys are less prosocial. This difference may reflect inherent sex differences in prosociality, early sex differences in socialization that create differences in prosociality, or both. For this explanation of sex differences in conduct problems to be meaningful, however, it will be necessary to eventually explain why there are sex differences in personality, language development, and socialization.

It should be noted that there is some evidence that there could be more fundamental sex differences in genetic and environmental influences on conduct problems. Two studies suggest that genetic and environmental influences are similar for girls and boys on developmentally-early conduct problems, but are more distinct on developmentally-late conduct problems (Eley et al., 1999; Silberg et al., 1996). This could reflect sex differences in the magnitude of genetic influences, but it raises the possibility of unique causal influences on girls' conduct problems that are not included in the present model, such as genetic influences on pubertal timing. This seems plausible as some evidence suggest that early-maturing girls show an earlier and higher peak in conduct problems (Moffitt et al., 2001) and pubertal timing has strong genetic influences in girls (Pickles, Pickering, Simonoff, Silberg, Meyer, & Maes, 1998).

Socioeconomic and Race-Ethnic Differences

An inverse relation between SES and conduct problems has been found in many population-based studies (Lahey et al., 1999b). An important task for any general model of conduct problems is to explain why this is the case, and to explain why the great majority of children from low SES families do *not* engage in serious conduct problems. We hypothesize that multiple environmental factors associated with lower SES influence the developmental transition from antisocial propensity to conduct problems. These SES-linked environmental factors include living in high-crime neighborhoods, attending schools with delinquent peers, and the family's lack of economic resources—which affect access to day care, after-school care, mental health services, and the like (Harnish, Dodge, & Valente, 1995; Kilgore, Snyder, & Lentz, 2000). We hypothesize that these environmental circumstances foster the social learning of conduct problems (Caspi, Taylor, Moffitt, & Plomin, 2000). On the other hand, it seems likely that part of the correlation of lower SES with conduct problems reflects selection effects. There is evidence of downward socioeconomic mobility (or staying at the low SES of their family of origin) among parents who are antisocial and/or have mental health and substance abuse problems (Dohrenwend & Dohrenwend, 1974; Miech et al., 1999). In some instances, then, characteristics of persons lead them to live in adverse socioeconomic circumstances and these circumstances, in turn, influence their children.

Why do most children living in low SES circumstances not engage in serious antisocial behavior? Consistent with our general model, we hypothesize that children who are dispositionally and cognitively predisposed to develop conduct problems will be more influenced by the environmental factors associated with lower SES than other children. Because there are genetic influences on antisocial propensity, this means that the environmental influences associated with SES influence the child largely through genotype-environment interactions.

After controlling for SES and neighborhood factors, there is little or no difference in the prevalence of most conduct problems among African American, Hispanic, and non-Hispanic white youth (Bird et al., 2001; Loeber et al. 1998). It is likely that there are race-ethnic differences in the rates of some specific crimes, however, such as drug selling and assault with a deadly weapon (Blum et al., 2000). We hypothesize that these differences are mostly attributable to a marked difference in the tendency of youth in different race-ethnic groups to join antisocial gangs. Evidence is sparse for girls, but there is substantial evidence that the boys from all race-ethnic groups who join gangs had high and escalating levels of aggressive and nonaggressive conduct problems prior to gang entrance (Esbensen, Huizinga, & Weiher, 1993; Lahey, Gordon, Loeber, Stouthamer-Loeber, & Farrington, 1999a). Different race-ethnic groups have been more or less likely to join antisocial gangs at different times during the last 100 years. For example, Irish immigrant youth were most likely to join gangs around the turn of the twentieth century. Presently, however, misbehaving non-Hispanic white boys are much less likely to join gangs than misbehaving African American and Hispanic boys (Lahey et al., 1999a). There is also clear evidence from longitudinal studies that during the period of gang membership, gang members show marked increases in the frequency of drug-related and violent offenses (so that they account for ten times more assaults and drug sales than non-gang members), which declines after their period of gang membership ends (Esbensen et al., 1993; Gordon, Lahey, Kawai, Loeber, Stouthamer-Loeber, & Farrington, 2004; Thornberry, Krohn, Lizotte, & Chard-Wierschem, 1993). We posit that the powerful social influence of gang membership accounts for the race-ethnic difference in serious adolescent antisocial behavior.

Evaluating And Testing The CADS Model

"Nothing is new under the sun" —William Shakespeare

In general terms, our hypothesis that antisocial propensity is related to multiple dimensions of temperament is not original. The conceptual framework for our model was spelled out by Hippocrates around 400 B.C. and revived by Pavlov in the 1920s. Eysenck (1964) proposed thirty years ago that persons who commit crimes are high in neuroticism, psychoticism, and extraversion. In time, it became clear that there were both genetic and environmental influences on Eysenck's dimensions of personality (Eysenck, 1990). Thus, if the present model has value, it must derive from its specific hypotheses.

Potential Strengths and Weaknesses of the CADS Model

The measurement-based CADS model posits dimensions of personality that appear to be similar to dimensions identified in the five-factor model of personality, but they are operationalized in a way that is independent of the conduct and mental health problems. Thus, the CADS model will facilitate research on the temperamental foundations of juvenile offending and mental health problems. In addition, the CADS model includes cognitive deficits, which have been ignored in previous temperament/personality models. Our model also places antisocial propensity in developmental context, integrates the propensity model with the social learning model, and uses the concepts and methods of epidemiology and behavior genetics to frame and test our hypotheses regarding environmental and genetic influences.

The CADS model shares with other temperament models an important threat to its internal validity, however. The correlations between disposition and conduct problems that appear to support their validity may be circular. If a mother is asked if her child "gets upset easily," "cares about the feelings of others," and "likes risky activities," her responses may be influenced by her knowledge of her child's frequent fighting. Even if there is evidence to the contrary, the salience of the fighting may lead the mother to *infer* that her child is easily upset, unconcerned about others, and likes risky activities.

Therefore, it will be necessary to test the CADS model within a multi-method that avoids this potential circularity. There are two key ways in which this could be done. First, it would be useful to test the model using measures of disposition that were not obtained from the person who rates the youth's conduct problems. For example, studies using independent observers have found that preschoolers with conduct problems engage in less prosocial behavior and display more negative emotion during play (Hughes et al., 2000) and react more emotionally to failure in a competitive task (Hughes et al., 2001). Second, it would be possible to test the CADS model using laboratory tasks. For example, Canli et al. (2001) found striking correlations (in the $r = .70-.85$ range) between Eysenck's dimension of neuroticism and activity in frontal and limbic structures in response to negatively valenced stimuli using functional magnetic resonance imaging. If the CADS *negative emotionality* dimension showed similar physiological correlates, but the other two CADS dimensions did not, that would support the model.

The most important tests of any model, however, are assessments of its scientific and practical utility. The scientific utility of the CADS model will depend primarily on its ability to organize data and generate supported hypotheses. The CADS model can be evaluated by testing specific model-based a priori hypotheses. For example, we will test the hypothesis that the dispositional and cognitive-linguistic components of propensity mediate genetic influences on conduct problems. In addition, behavior genetic designs offer innovative and powerful ways of testing hypotheses about environmental influences and their interplay with genetic influences that have been very difficult to test in the past (e.g., Rutter, Pickles, Murray, & Eaves, 2001; Rose, Viken, Dick, Bates, Pulkkinen, & Kaprio, 2003).

The practical utility of the CADS model should be evaluated in at least two ways. First, the CADS model must be able to predict the future development of conduct problems. If preschool children with deviant levels of parent-rated dispositions and tested cognitive ability in early childhood fail to show high and persistent levels of youth-reported conduct problems through adolescence, the model would be disconfirmed. Second, the CADS model must eventually be able to inform prevention and perhaps intervention research. For example, the CADS model implies that one potentially successful method of prevention would be to modify the temperamental and cognitive elements of predisposition in early childhood. For example, it may be possible to influence *prosociality* and *negative emotionality* by teaching parents more adaptive methods of parenting (Eisenberg, & Mussen, 1991; Eisenberg, Fabes, & Murphy, 1996; Grusec, 1991; Keenan & Shaw, 2003). Another potentially useful preventive strategy might be to identify high-risk children based on their dispositional and ability profiles and design school- and home-based social learning interventions to reduce the likelihood that their antisocial propensity will lead to offending. This might include increased adult supervision to limit opportunities to offend.

References

Anderson, K. E., Lytton, H. & Romney, D. M. (1986). Mothers' interactions with normal and conduct-disordered boys: Who affects whom? *Developmental Psychology*, 22: 604-609.

Angold, A., Costello, E. J. & Erkanli, A. (1999). Comorbidity. *Journal of Child Psychology and Psychiatry*, 40: 57-87.

Arnett, J. J. (1996). Sensation seeking, aggressiveness, and adolescent reckless behavior. *Personality and Individual Differences*, 20: 693-702.

Baker, L. & Cantwell, D. P. (1987). A prospective psychiatric follow-up of children with speech/language disorders. *Journal of the American Academy of Child and Adolescent Psychiatry*, 26: 546-553.

Beitchman, J. H., Wilson, B., Johnson, C. J., Atkinson, L., Young, A., Adlaf, E., Escobar, M., Douglas, L. (2001). Fourteen-year follow-up of speech/language-impaired and control children: Psychiatric outcome. *Journal of the American Academy of Child and Adolescent Psychiatry*, 40: 75-82.

Biederman, J., Hirshfeld-Becker, D. R., Rosenbaum, J. F., Herot, C., Friedman, D., Snidman, N., Kagan, J., Faraone, S. V. (2001). Further evidence of association between behavioral inhibition and social anxiety in children. *American Journal of Psychiatry*, 158: 1673-1679.

Bird, H. R., Canino, G. J., Davies, M., Zhang, H., Ramirez, R. & Lahey, B. B. (2001). Prevalence and correlates of antisocial behaviors among three ethnic groups. *Journal of Abnormal Child Psychology*, 29: 465-478.

Blair, C. (2002). School readiness: Integrating cognition and emotion in a neurobiological conceptualization of children's functioning at school entry. *American Psychologist*, 57: 111-127.

Blum, R., W., Beuhring, T., Shew, M. L., Bearinger, L. H., Sieving, R. E. & Resnick, M. D. (2000). The effects of race/ethnicity, income, and family structure on adolescent risk behaviors. *American Journal of Public Health*, 90: 1879-1884.

Blumstein, A., Farrington, D. P. & Moitra, S. (1985). Delinquency careers: Innocents, desisters, and persisters. In M. Tonry & N. Morris (Eds.), *Crime and Justice*. Chicago: University of Chicago Press.

Bohman, M. (1996). Predispositions to criminality: Swedish adoption studies in retrospect. In G. R. Bock & J. A. Goode (Eds.), *Genetics of Criminal and Antisocial Behavior*. Chichester, England: Wiley.

Bouchard, T. J. & Loehlin, J. C. (2001). Genes, evolution, and personality. *Behavior Genetics*, 31: 243-273.

Brame, B., Nagin, D. S., Tremblay, R. E. (2001). Developmental trajectories of physical aggression from school entry to late adolescence. *Journal of Child Psychology and Psychiatry*, 42: 503-512.

Burke, J. D., Loeber, R. & Lahey, B. B. (2003). Mechanisms in the transition from disruptive behavior disorder to comorbid depression in young men. Manuscript under editorial review.

Buss, A. H. & Plomin, R. (1984). *Temperament: Early Developing Personality Traits*. Hillsdale, NJ: Lawrence Erlbaum.

Cadoret, R.J., Yates, W.R., Troughton, E., Woodward, G. & Stewart, M.A. (1995). Genetic-environmental interaction in the genesis of aggressivity and conduct disorders. *Archives of General Psychiatry*, 52: 916-924.

Cairns, R. B. (1979). *Social Development: The Origins and Plasticity of Social Interchanges*. San Francisco: Freeman.

Canli, T., Zhao, Z., Desmond, J. E., Kang, E., Gross, J., Gabrieli, J.D.E. (2001). An fMRI study of personality influences on brain reactivity to emotional stimuli. *Behavioral Neuroscience*, 115: 33-42.

Capaldi, D. M. (1992). Co-occurrence of conduct problems and depressive symptoms in early adolescent boys: II. A 2-year follow-up at grade 8. *Development & Psychopathology*, 4: 125-144.

Caspi, A. (1998). Personality development across the life course. In N. Eisenberg (Ed.), *Handbook of Child Psychology, Vol. 3* (5th ed.), (pp. 311-388). New York: Wiley.

Caspi, A. (2000). The child is father of the man: Personality continuities from childhood to adulthood. *Journal of Personality and Social Psychology*, 78: 158-172.

Caspi, A., McClay, J., Moffitt, T., Mill, J., Martin, J., Craig, I. W., Taylor, A. & Poulton, R. (2002). Role of genotype in the cycle of violence in maltreated children. *Science*, 297: 851-854.

Caspi, A., Moffitt, T. E., Silva, P. A., Stouthamer-Loeber, M., Schmutte, P. S. & Krueger, R. (1994). Are some people crime-prone? Replications of the personality-crime relation across nation, gender, race and method. *Criminology*, 32: 301-333.

Caspi, A., Lynam, D., Moffitt, T. E., Silva, P. A. (1993). Unraveling girls' delinquency: Biological, dispositional, and contextual contributions to adolescent misbehavior. *Developmental Psychology* 29: 19-30.

Caspi, A. & Roberts, B. W. (2001). Personality development across the life course: The argument for change and continuity. *Psychological Inquiry*, 12: 49-66.

Caspi, A., Taylor, Al., Moffitt, T. E. & Plomin, R. (2000). Neighborhood deprivation affects children's mental health: Environmental risks idenitified in a genetic design. *Psychological Science*, 11: 338-342.

Cloninger, C. R. (1987). A systematic method for clinical description and classification of personality variants: A proposal. *Archives of General Psychiatry*, 44: 573-588.

Cohen, D.C. & Strayer, J. (1996). Empathy in conduct-disordered and comparison youth. *Developmental Psychology*, 32: 988-998.

Cohen, N. J., Menna, R., Vallance, D. D., Barwick, M. A., Im, N. & Horodezky, N. B. (1998). Language, social cognitive processing, and behavioral characteristics of psychiatrically disturbed children with previously identified and unsuspected language impairments. *Journal of Child Psychology and Psychiatry*, 39: 853-864.

Coolidge, F. L., Thede, L. L. & Young, S. E. (2000). Heritability and the comorbidity of attention deficit hyperactivity disorder with behavioral disorders and executive function deficits: A preliminary investigation. *Developmental Neuropsychology*, 17: 273-287.

Costa, P. T. & McCrae, R. R. (1987). *NEO*. Odessa, FL: Psychological Assessment Resources.

Costa, P. T. & McCrae, R. R. (1995). Primary traits of Eysenck's P-E-N system: Three and

Cyphers, L. H., Phillips, K., Fulker, D. W. & Mrazek, D. A. (1990). Twin temperament during the transition from infancy to early childhood. *Journal of the American Academy of Child and Adolescent Psychiatry*, 29: 392-397.

Daderman, A. M. (1999). Differences between severely conduct-disordered juvenile males and normal juvenile males: The study of personality traits. *Personality and Individual Differences*, 26: 827-845.

Daderman, A. M., Wirsen M. A. & Hallman, J. (2001). Different personality patterns in non-socialized (juvenile delinquents) and socialized (air force pilot recruits) sensation seekers. *European Journal of Personality*, 15: 239-252.

Davidson, R. J., Putnam, K. M. & Larson, C. L. (2000). Dysfunction in the neural circuitry of emotion regulation—A possible prelude to violence. *Science*, 289: 591-594.

Davis, M. H., Luce, C. & Kraus, S. J. (1994). The heritability of characteristics associated with dispositional empathy. *Journal of Personality*, 62: 369-391.

Depue, R. A. & Collins, P. F. (1999). Neurobiology of the structure of personality: Dopamine facilitation of incentive motivation and extraversion. *Behavioral and Brain Sciences*, 22: 491–569.

Dery, M., Toupin, J., Pauze, R., Mercier, H. & Fortin, L. (1999). Neuropsychological characteristics of adolescents with conduct disorder: Association with attention-deficit-hyperactivity and aggression. *Journal of Abnormal Child Psychology*, 27: 225-236.

Digman, J. M. & Inouye, J. (1986). Further specification of the five robust factors of personality. *Journal of Personality and Social Psychology*, 50: 116-123.

DiLalla, L. F., Kagan, J. & Reznick, J. S. (1994). Genetic etiology of behavioral inhibition among 2-year-old children. *Infant Behavior and Development*, 17: 405-412.

Dohrenwend, B. P. & Dohrenwend, B. S. (1974). Social and cultural influences on psychopathology. *Annual Review of Psychology*, 25: 417-452.

Eaves, L., Rutter, M., Silberg, J. L., Shillady, L., Maes, H. & Pickles, A. (2000). Genetic and environmental causes of covariation in interview assessments of disruptive behavior in child and adolescent twins. *Behavior Genetics*, 30: 321-334.

Eisenberg, N., Fabes, R. A. & Murphy, B. C. (1996). Parents' reactions to children's negative emotions: Relations to children's social competence and comforting behavior. *Child Development*, 67: 2227-2247.

Eisenberg, N., Fabes, R. A., Murphy, B., Karbon, M., Smith, M. & Maszk, P. (1996). The relations of children's dispositional empathy-related responding to their emotionality, regulation, and social functioning. *Developmental Psychology*, 32: 195-209.

Eisenberg, N. & Mussen, P. H. (1991). *The Roots of Prosocial Behavior in Children*. New York: Cambridge University Press.

Eley, T. C., Dale, P. & Bishop, D. (2001). Longitudinal analysis of the genetic and environmental influences on components of cognitive delay in preschoolers. *Journal of Educational Psychology*, 93: 698-707.

Eley, T.C., Lichtenstein, P. & Stevenson, J. (1999). Sex differences in the etiology of aggressive and nonaggressive antisocial behavior: Results from two twin studies. *Child Development*, 70: 155-168

Elkins, I., Iacono, W., Doyle, A. & McGue, M. (1997). Characteristics associated with the persistence of antisocial behavior: Results from recent longitudinal research. *Aggression and Violent Behavior*, 2: 101-124.

Emde, R.N., Plomin, R., Robinson, J., Corley, R., et al. (1992). Temperament, emotion, and cognition at fourteen months: The MacArthur Longitudinal Twin Study. *Child Development*, 63: 1437-1455.

Eron, L.D. & Huesmann, L.R. (1984). The relation of prosocial behavior to the development of aggression and psychopathology. *Aggressive Behavior*, 10: 201-211.

Esbensen, F.-A., Huizinga, D. & Weiher, A.W. (1993). Gang and non-gang youth: Differences in explanatory factors. *Journal of Contemporary Criminal Justice*, 9: 94-116.

Eysenck, H. J. (1947). *Dimensions of Personality*. New York: Praeger.

Eysenck, H. J. (1964). *Crime and Personality*. New York: Houghton Mifflin.

Eysenck, H. J. (1990). Genetic and environmental contributions to individual differences: The three major dimensions of personality. *Journal of Personality*, 58: 245-261.

Eysenck, S. G. & Eysenck, H. J. (1970). Crime and personality: An empirical study of the three-factor theory. *British Journal of Criminology*, 10: 225-239.

Eysenck, S. B. & Eysenck, H. J. (1977). Personality differences between prisoners and controls. *Psychological Reports,* 40: 1023-1028.

Farrington, D. P. (1991). Antisocial personality from childhood to adulthood. *The Psychologist*, 4: 389-394.

Farrington, D. P. (1995). The development of offending and antisocial behaviour from childhood: Key findings from the Cambridge Study in Delinquent Development. *Journal of Child Psychology and Psychiatry*, 6: 929-964.

Farrington, D. P. (2003). Developmental and life-course criminology: Key theoretical and empirical issues. *Criminology*, 41: 221-255.

Farrington, D. P. & West, D. J. (1993). Criminal, penal and life histories of chronic offenders: Risk and protective factors and early identification. *Criminal Behaviour and Mental Health*, 3: 492-523.

Fergusson, D. M., Horwood, L. J. (1999) Prospective childhood predictors of deviant peer affiliations in adolescence. *Journal of Child Psychology and Psychiatry*, 40: 581-592.

Fergusson, D. M., Lynskey, M. T. & Horwood, L. J. (1996). Factors associated with continuity and change in disruptive behavior patters between childhood and adolescence. *Journal of Abnormal Child Psychology*, 24: 533-553.

Fergusson, D. M., Swain-Campbell, N. R. & Horwood, L. J. (2002). Deviant peer affiliations, crime and substance use: A fixed effects regression analysis. *Journal of Abnormal Child Psychology*, 30: 419-430.

Flory, K., Lynam, D., Milich, R., Leukefeld, C. & Clayton, R. (2002). The relations among personality, symptoms of alcohol and marijuana abuse, and symptoms of comorbid psychopathology: Results from a community sample. *Experimental and Clinical Psychopharmacology*, 10: 425-434.

Gabrys, J. B. (1983). Contrasts in social behavior and personality of children. Psychological Reports, 52, 171-178.

Garcia-Coll, C., Kagan, J., Reznick, J. S. (1984). Behavioral inhibition in young children. *Child Development*, 55: 1005-1019.

Ge, X., Donnellan, M. B. & Wenk, E. (2001). The development of persistent criminal offending in males. *Criminal Justice and Behavior*, 26: 731-755.

Gershuny, B. S. & Sher, K. J. (1998). The relation between personality and anxiety: Findings from a 3-year prospective study. *Journal of Abnormal Psychology*, 107: 252-262.

Giancola, P. R., Martin, C. S., Tarter, R. E., Pelham, W. E. & Moss, H. B. (1996). Executive cognitive functioning and aggressive behavior in preadolescent boys at high risk for substance abuse/dependence. *Journal of Studies on Alcohol*, 57: 352-359.

Gjone, H. & Stevenson, J. (1997). A longitudinal twin study of temperament and behavior problems: Common genetic or environmental influences? *Journal of the American Academy of Child and Adolescent Psychiatry*, 36: 1448-1456.

Goldberg, L.R. (1993). The structure of phenotypic personality traits. *American Psychologist*, 48: 26-34.

Goldberg, L. R. & Rosolack, T. K. (1994). The big five factor structure as an integrative framework: An empirical comparison with Eysenck's P-E-N model. In C. F. Halverson, G. A. Kohnstamm, & R. P. Martin (Eds.), *The Developing Structure of Temperament and Personality from Infancy to Adulthood* (pp. 7-35). Hillsdale, NJ: Lawrence Erlbaum.

Goldsmith, H. H., Buss, K. A. & Lemery, K. S. (1997). Toddler and childhood temperament: Expanded content, stronger genetic evidence, new evidence for the importance of environment. *Developmental Psychology*, 33: 891-905.

Goma-I-Freixnet, M. (1995). Prosocial and antisocial aspects of personality. *Personality and Individual Differences*, 19: 125-134.

Goodman, R. (2001). Psychometric properties of the Strengths and Difficulties Questionnaire. *Journal of the American Academy of Child and Adolescent Psychiatry*, 40: 1337-1345.

Gordon, R. A., Lahey, B. B., Kawai, E., Loeber, R., StouthamerLoeber, M. & Farrington, D. P. (2004). Antisocial behavior and youth gang membership: Selection and socialization. *Criminology*, 42: 55-87.

Gottfredson, M.R. & Hirschi, T. (1990). *A General Theory of Crime*. Stanford, CA: Stanford University Press.

Graham P. & Rutter, M. (1973). Psychiatric disorders in the young adolescent: A follow-up study. *Proceedings of the Royal Society of Medicine*, 66: 1226-1229.

Graziano, W. G. (1994). The development of agreeableness as a dimension of personality. In C. F. Halverson, G. A. Kohnstamm, & R. P. Martin (Eds.), *The Developing Structure of Temperament and Personality from Infancy to Adulthood* (pp. 339-354) Hillsdale, NJ: Lawrence Erlbaum.

Graziano, W. G., Eisenberg, N. (1997). Agreeableness: A dimension of personality. In R. Higan, J. Johnson, & S. Briggs (Eds.), *Handbook of Personality Psychology* (pp.795-824). San Diego, CA: Academic Press.

Greene, K., Krcmar, M., Walters, L. H., Rubin, D. L. & Hale, J. L. (2000). Targeting adolescent risk-taking behaviors: The contribution of egocentrism and sensation-seeking. *Journal of Adolescence*, 23: 439-461.

Grusec, J. E. (1991). Socializing concern for others in the home. *Developmental Psychology*, 27: 338-342.

Gullone, E. & Moore, S. (2000). Adolescent risk-taking and the five-factor model of personality. *Journal of Adolescence*, 23: 393-407.

Haemaelaeinen, M. & Pulkkinen, L. (1996). Problem behavior as a precursor of male criminality. *Development and Psychopathology*, 8: 443-455.

Harnish, J.D., Dodge, K.A. & Valente, E. (1995). Mother-child interaction quality as a partial mediator of the roles of maternal depressive symptomatology and socioeconomic status in the development of child conduct problems. *Child Development*, 66: 739-753.

Hastings, P. D., Zahn-Waxler, C., Robinson, J., Usher, B. & Bridges, D. (2000). The development of concern for others in children with behavior problems. *Developmental Psychology*, 36: 531-546.

Heaven, P. C. L. (1996). Personality and self-reported delinquency: A longitudinal analysis. *Journal of Child Psychology and Psychiatry*, 37: 747-751.

Henry, B., Caspi, A., Moffitt, T. E. & Silva, P.A. (1996). Temperamental and familial predictors of violent and nonviolent criminal convictions: Age 3 to age 18. *Developmental Psychology*, 32: 614-623.

Hinshaw, S. P., Lahey, B. B. & Hart, E. L. (1993). Issues of taxonomy and comorbidity in the development of conduct disorder. *Development and Psychopathology*, 5: 31-50.

Hirshfeld-Becker, D. R., Biederman, J., Faraone, S. V., Violette, H., Wrightsman, J. & Rosenbaum, J. F. (in press). Temperamental correlates of disruptive behavior disorders in young children: Preliminary findings. *Biological Psychiatry.*

Hirshfeld, D. R., Rosenbaum, J. F., Biederman, J., Bolduc, E. A., Faraone, S. V., Snidman, N., Reznick, J. S. & Kagan, J. (1992). Stable behavioral inhibition and its association with anxiety disorder. *Journal of the American Academy of Child and Adolescent Psychiatry*, 31: 103-111.

Hoffman, M. L. (1982). Development of prosocial motivation: Empathy and guilt. In N. Eisenberg (Ed.), *The Development of Prosocial Behavior* (pp. 281-313). New York: Academic Press.

Hogan, A. (1999). Cognitive functioning in children with oppositional defiant disorder and conduct disorder. In H.C. Quay & A.E. Hogan (Eds.), *Handbook of Disruptive Behavior Disorders* (pp. 317-335). New York: Kluwer Academic/Plenum.

Hughes, C., Cutting, A. L. & Dunn, J. (2001). Acting nasty in the face of failure? Longitudinal observations of "hard-to-manage" children playing a rigged competitive game with a friend. *Journal of Abnormal Child Psychology*, 29: 403-416.

Hughes, C., White, A., Sharpen, J. & Dunn, J. (2000). Antisocial, angry, and unsympathetic: "Hard-to-manage" preschoolers' peer problems and possible cognitive influences. *Journal of Child Psychology and Psychiatry*, 41: 169-179.

John, O. P., Caspi, A., Robins, R. W., Moffitt, T. E., Stouthamer-Loeber, M. (1994). The "little five": Exploring the nomological network of the five-factor model of personality in adolescent boys. *Child Development*, 65: 160-178.

Kagan, J. (1992). Stable behavioral inhibition and its association with anxiety disorder. *Journal of the American Academy of Child and Adolescent Psychiatry*, 31: 103-111.

Kagan, J., Reznick, J. S. & Snidman, N. (1988). Biological bases of childhood shyness. *Science*, 240: 167-171.

Kagan, J., Reznick, J. S., Snidman, N., Gibbons, J. & Johnson, M. O. (1988). Childhood derivatives of inhibition and lack of inhibition to the unfamiliar. *Child Development*, 59: 1580-1589.

Keenan, K., Loeber, R. & Green, S. (1999). Conduct disorder in girls: A review of the literature. *Clinical Child and Family Psychology Review*, 2: 3-19.

Keenan, K., Loeber, R. & Zhang, Q. (1995). The influence of deviant peers on the development of boys' disruptive and delinquent behavior: A temporal analysis. *Development and Psychopathology*, 7: 715-726.

Keenan, K. & Shaw, D. (1995). The development of coercive family processes: The interaction between aversive toddler behavior and parenting factors. In. J. McCord (Ed.), *Coercion and Punishment in Long-Term Perspectives* (pp. 165-180). New York: Cambridge University Press.

Keenan, K. & Shaw, D. (1997). Developmental and social influences on young girls' early problem behavior. *Psychological Bulletin*, 121: 95-113.

Keenan, K. & Shaw, D. (2003). Starting at the beginning: Exploring etiological factors of later antisocial behavior in the first years of life. In B. B. Lahey, T. E. Moffitt, & A. Caspi (Eds.), *Causes of Conduct Disorder and Juvenile Delinquency* (pp. 153-181). New York: Guilford Press.

Kerr, M., Tremblay, R. E., Pagani-Kurtz, L. & Vitaro, F. (1997). Boy's behavioral inhibition and the risk of later delinquency. *Archives of General Psychiatry*, 54: 809-816.

Kilgore, K., Snyder, J. & Lentz, C. (2000). The contribution of parental discipline, parental monitoring, and school risk to early-onset conduct problems in African American boys and girls. *Developmental Psychology*, 36: 835-845.

Kingston, L. & Prior, M. (1995). The development of patterns of stable, transient, and school-age onset aggressive behavior in young children. *Journal of the American Academy of Child and Adolescent Psychiatry*, 34: 348-358.

Klerman, L. V. (1993). The relationship between adolescent parenthood and inadequate parenting. *Children and Youth Services Review*, 15: 309-320.

Kohlberg, L., Ricks, D. & Snarey, J. (1984). Childhood development as a predictor of adaptation in adulthood. *Genetic Psychology Monographs*, 110: 91-172.

Kratzer, L. & Hodgins, S. (1999). A typology of offenders: A test of Moffitt's theory among males and females from childhood to age 30. *Criminal Behaviour and Mental Health*, 9: 57-73.

Krueger, R. F. (1999). Personality traits in late adolescence predict mental disorders in early adulthood: A prospective-epidemiologic study. *Journal of Personality*, 67: 39-65.

Krueger, R., Schmutte, P. S., Caspi, A., Moffitt, T. E., Campbell, K. & Silva, P. A. (1994). Personality traits are linked to crime among males and females: Evidence from a birth cohort. *Journal of Abnormal Psychology*, 103: 328-338.

Lahey, B.B., Applegate, B., Barkley, R.A., Garfinkel, B., McBurnett, K., Kerdyk, L., Greenhill, L., Hynd, G. W., Frick, P. J., Newcorn, J., Biederman, J., Ollendick, T., Hart, E. L., Perez, D., Waldman, I. & Shaffer, D. (1994). DSM-IV field trials for oppositional defiant disorder and conduct disorder in children and adolescents. *American Journal of Psychiatry*, 151: 1163-1171.

Lahey, B. B., Gordon, R. A., Loeber, R., Stouthamer-Loeber, M. & Farrington, D. P. (1999a). Boys who join gangs: A prospective study of predictors of first gang entry. *Journal of Abnormal Child Psychology*, 27: 261-276.

Lahey, B. B. & Loeber, R. (1994). Framework for a developmental model of oppositional defiant disorder and conduct disorder. In D.K. Routh (Ed.). *Disruptive Behavior Disorders in Childhood*. New York: Plenum.

Lahey, B. B., Loeber, R., Burke, J. & Rathouz, P. J. (2002). Adolescent outcomes of childhood conduct disorder among clinic-referred boys: Predictors of improvement. *Journal of Abnormal Child Psychology*, 30: 333-348.

Lahey, B. B., Loeber, R., Burke, J. D., Rathouz, P. & McBurnett, K. (2002). Waxing and waning in concert: Dynamic comorbidity of conduct disorder with other disruptive and emotional problems over seven years among clinic-referred boys. *Journal of Abnormal Psychology*, 111:556-567.

Lahey, B. B., Loeber, R., Quay, H. C., Applegate, B., Shaffer, D., Waldman, I., Hart, E. L., McBurnett, K., Frick, P J., Jensen, P., Dulcan, M., Canino, G. & Bird, H. (1998). Validity of DSM-IV subtypes of conduct disorder based on age of onset. *Journal of the American Academy of Child and Adolescent Psychiatry*, 37: 435-442.

Lahey, B.B., McBurnett, K. & Loeber, R. (2000). Are attention-deficit hyperactivity disorder and oppositional defiant disorder developmental precursors to conduct disorder? In A. Sameroff, M. Lewis, & S. Miller (Eds.), *Handbook of Developmental Psychopathology* (2nd ed.) (pp. 431-446). New York: Plenum.

Lahey, B. B., Miller, T. L., Gordon, R. A. & Riley, A. (1999b). Developmental epidemiology of the disruptive behavior disorders. In H. Quay & A. Hogan (Eds.), *Handbook of the Disruptive Behavior Disorders* (pp. 23-48). San Antonio: Academic Press.

Lahey, B. B. Russo, M. F., Walker, J. L. & Piacentini, J. C. (1989). Personality characteristics of the mothers of children with disruptive behavior disorders. *Journal of Consulting and Clinical Psychology*, 57: 512-515.

Lahey, B. B., Schwab-Stone, M., Goodman, S. H., Waldman, I. D., Canino, G., Rathouz, P. J., Miller, T. L., Dennis, K. D., Bird, H. & Jensen, P. S. (2000). Age and gender differences in oppositional behavior and conduct problems: A cross-sectional household study of middle childhood and adolescence. *Journal of Abnormal Psychology*, 109: 488-503.

Lahey, B. B. & Waldman, I. D. (2003). A developmental propensity model of the origins of conduct problems during childhood and adolescence. In B. B. Lahey, T. E. Moffitt, & A. Caspi (Eds.), *Causes of Conduct Disorder and Juvenile Delinquency* (pp. 76-117). New York: Guilford Press.

Lahey, B. B., Waldman, I. D. & McBurnett, K. (1999). The development of antisocial behavior: An integrative causal model. *Journal of Child Psychology and Psychiatry*, 40: 669-682.

Lahey, B. B., Waldman, I. D., Applegate, B., Rowe, D. C., Urbano, R. C. & Chapman, D. A. Emotional and social dispositions underlying conduct disorder. Manuscript under editorial review.

Lemery, K. S., Essex, M. J. & Smider, N. A. (2002). Revealing the relationship between temperament and behavior problems by eliminating measurement confounding: Expert ratings and factor analysis. *Child Development*, 73: 867-882.

Lenneberg, E. H. (1967). *Biological Foundations of Language*. New York: Wiley.

Loeber, R. (1982). The stability of antisocial and delinquent behavior: A review. *Child Development*, 53: 1431-1446.

Loeber, R. (1988). Natural histories of conduct problems, delinquency, and associated substance abuse: Evidence for developmental progressions. In B.B. Lahey & A.E. Kazdin (Eds.), *Advances in Clinical Child Psychology*, Volume 11. New York: Plenum.

Loeber, R., Farrington, D. P., Stouthamer-Loeber, M. & Van Kammen, W. (1998). *Antisocial Behavior and Mental Health Problems: Explanatory Factors in Childhood and Adolescence*. Mahwah, NJ: Lawrence Erlbaum.

Loeber, R., Green, S. M., Keenan, K. & Lahey, B. B. (1995). Which boys will fare worse? Early predictors of the onset of conduct disorder in a six-year longitudinal study. *Journal of the American Academy of Child and Adolescent Psychiatry*, 34: 499-509.

Loeber, R. & Keenan, K. (1994). Interaction between conduct disorder and its comorbid conditions: Effects of age and gender. *Clinical Psychology Review*, 14: 497-523.

Loeber, R. & LeBlanc, M. (1990). Toward a developmental criminology. In M. Tonry & N. Morris (Eds.), *Crime and Justice* (Vol. 12, pp. 375-473). Chicago: University of Chicago Press.

Loeber, R. & Tengs, T. (1986). The analysis of coercive chains between children, mothers, and siblings. *Journal of Family Violence*, 1: 51-70.

Luengo, M. A., Otero, J. M., Carrillo-de-la-Pena, M. T., Miron, L. (1994). Dimensions of antisocial behaviour in juvenile delinquency: A study of personality variables. *Psychology Crime and Law*, 1: 27-37.

Lynam, D. R. (1998). Early identification of the fledgling psychopath: Locating the psychopathic child in the current nomenclature. *Journal of Abnormal Psychology*, 107, 566-575.

Lynam, D., Moffitt, T. & Stouthamer-Loeber, M. (1993). Explaining the relation between IQ and delinquency: Class, race, test motivation, school failure or self-control? *Journal of Abnormal Psychology*, 102: 187-196.

Maszk, P., Eisenberg, N. & Guthrie, I. K. (1999). Relations of children's social status to their emotionality and regulation: A short-term longitudinal study. *Merrill-Palmer Quarterly*, 45: 468-492.

Matthews, K. A., Batson, C. D., Horn, J. & Rosenman, R. H. (1981). "Principles in his nature which interest him in the fortune of others...": The heritability of empathic concern for others. *Journal of Personality*, 49: 237-247.

McCormick, R. A., Dowd, E. T., Quirk, S. & Zegarra, J. H. (1998). The relationship of NEO-PI performance to coping styles, patterns of use, and triggers for use among substance abusers. *Addictive Behaviors*, 23: 497-507.

McGue, M., Bacon, S. & Lykken, D. T. (1993). Personality stability and change in early adulthood: A behavioral genetic analysis. *Developmental Psychology*, 29: 96-109.

McRae, R. R. & Costa, P. T. (1987). Validation of the five-factor model of personality across instruments and observers. *Journal of Personality and Social Psychology*, 52: 81-90.

Meltzer, H., Gatward, R., Goodman, R. & Ford, T. (2000). *Mental Health of Children and Adolescents in Great Britain*. London: Stationery Office.

Miech, R. A., Caspi, A., Moffitt, T. E., Wright, B.R.E. & Silva, P. A. (1999). Low socio-economic status and mental disorders: A longitudinal study of selection and causation during young adulthood. *American Journal of Sociology*, 104: 1096-1131.

Miller, J. D. & Lynam, D. R. (2001). Structural models of personality and their relation to antisocial behavior: A meta-analytic review. *Criminology*, 39: 765-792.

Miller, P. A. & Eisenberg, N. (1988). The relation of empathy to aggressive and external-izing/antisocial behavior. *Psychological Bulletin*, 103: 324-344.

Mitchell, S. & Rosa, P. (1981). Boyhood behaviour problems as precursors of criminality: A fifteen-year study. *Journal of Child Psychology and Psychiatry*, 22: 19-33.

Moffitt, T.E. (1990). Juvenile delinquency and attention deficit disorder: Boys' develop-mental trajectories from age 3 to 15. *Child Development*, 61: 893-910.

Moffitt, T. E. (1993). Adolescence-limited and life-course-persistent antisocial behavior: A developmental taxonomy. *Psychological Review*, 100: 674-701.

Moffitt, T. E., Caspi, A., Dickson, N., Silva, P. & Stanton, W. (1996). Childhood-onset versus adolescent-onset antisocial conduct problems in males: Natural history from ages 3 to 18 years. *Development and Psychopathology*, 8: 399-424.

Moffitt, T. E., Caspi, A., Harrington, H., Milne, B. J. (2002). Males on the life-course-persistent and adolescence-limited antisocial pathways: Follow-up at age 26 years. *Development and Psychopathology*, 14: 179-207.

Moffitt, T. E., Caspi, A., Rutter, M. & Silva, P. A. (2001). *Sex Differences in Antisocial Behaviour*. Cambridge: Cambridge University Press.

Moffitt, T. E. & Silva, P. A. (1988). IQ and delinquency: A direct test of the differential detection hypothesis. *Journal of Abnormal Psychology*, 97: 330-333.

Nagin, D. S., Pogarsky, G. & Farrington, D. P. (1997). Adolescent mothers and the criminal behavior of their children. *Law and Society Review*, 31: 137-162.

Nagin, D. & Tremblay, R. E. (1999). Trajectories of boys' physical aggression, opposition, and hyperactivity on the path to physically violent and non-violent delinquency. *Child Development*, 70: 1181–1196.

Nagin, D. S. & Tremblay, R. E. (2001). Parental and early childhood predictors of persis-tent physical aggression in boys from kindergarten to high school. *Archives of General Psychiatry*, 58: 389-394.

Newcomb, M. D. & McGee, L. (1991). Influence of sensation seeking on general deviance and specific problem behaviors from adolescence to young adulthood. *Journal of Personality and Social Psychology*, 61: 614-628.

Nigg, J. T. & Huang-Pollock, C. L. (2003). An early onset model of the role of executive functions and intelligence in conduct disorder/delinquency. In B. B. Lahey, T. Moffitt, & A. Caspi (Eds.), *Causes of Conduct Disorder and Juvenile Delinquency* (pp. 227-253). New York: Guilford Press.

O'Connor, T. G., Neiderhiser, J. M., Reiss, D., Hetherington, E. M. & Plomin, R. (1998). Genetic contributions to continuity, change, and co-occurrence of antisocial and depres-sive symptoms in adolescence. *Journal of Child Psychology and Psychiatry*, 39: 323-336.

Olson, S. L., Bates, J. E., Sandy, J. M. & Lanthier, R. (2000). Early developmental precursors of externalizing behavior in middle childhood and adolescence. *Journal of Abnormal Child Psychology*, 28: 119-133.

Pagani, L., Tremblay, R. E., Vitaro, F., Boulerice, B. & McDuff, P. (2001). Effects of grade retention on academic performance and behavioral development. *Development and Psychopathology*, 13: 297-315.

Patterson, G. R. (1982). *Coercive Family Process*. Eugene, OR: Castalia.

Patterson, G. R., Reid, J. B. & Dishion, T. J. (1992). *Antisocial Boys*. Eugene, OR: Castalia.

Patterson, G. R. & Stoolmiller, M. (1991). Replications of a dual failure model for boys' depressed mood. *Journal of Consulting and Clinical Psychology*, 59: 491-498.

Pedersen, N. L., Plomin, R., McClearn, G. E. & Friberg, L. (1988). Neuroticism, extraversion, and related traits in adult twins reared apart and reared together. *Journal of Personality and Social Psychology*, 55: 950-957.

Pennington, B. F. & Ozonoff, S. (1996). Executive functions and developmental psychopathology. *Journal of Child Psychology and Psychiatry*, 37: 51-87.

Petrill, S. A., Saudino, K., Cherny, S. S., Emde, R. N., Hewitt, J. K., Fulker, D. W. & Plomin, R. (1997). Exploring the genetic etiology of low general cognitive ability from 14 to 36 months. *Developmental Psychology*, 33: 544-548.

Phillips, K., & Matheny, A. P. (1997). Evidence for genetic influence on both cross-situation and situation-specific components of behavior. *Journal of Personality and Social Psychology*, 73: 129-138.

Pickles, A., Pickering, K., Simonoff, E., Silberg, J., Meyer, J. & Maes, H. (1998). Genetic "clocks" and "soft" events: A twin model for pubertal development and other recalled sequences of developmental milestones, transitions, or ages at onset. *Behavior Genetics*, 28: 243-253.

Plomin, R., DeFries, J. C. & Loehlin, J. C. (1977). Genotype-environment interaction and correlation in the analysis of human behavior. *Psychological Bulletin*, 84: 309-322.

Plomin, R. & Petrill, S. A. (1997). Genetics and intelligence: What's new? *Intelligence*, 24: 53-77.

Powell, G. E. & Stewart, R. A. (1983). The relationship of personality to antisocial and neurotic behaviours as observed by teachers. *Personality and Individual Differences*, 4: 97-100.

Presley, R. & Martin, R. P. (1994). Toward a structure of preschool temperament: Factor structure of the Temperament Assessment Battery for Children. *Journal of Personality*, 62: 415-448.

Quay, H. C. & Love, C. T. (1977). The effect of a juvenile diversion program on rearrests. *Criminal Justice and Behavior*, 4: 377-396.

Raine, A., Reynolds, C., Venables, P. H., Mednick, S. A. & Farrington, D. P. (1998). Fearlessness, stimulation-seeking, and large body size at age 3 years as early predispositions to childhood aggression at age 11 years. *Archives of General Psychiatry*, 55: 745-751.

Reid, J. B. & Patterson, G. R. (1989). The development of antisocial behavior patterns in childhood and adolescence. *European Journal of Personality*, 3: 107-119.

Rhee, S. H. & Waldman, I. D. (2002). Genetic and environmental influences on antisocial behavior: A meta-analysis of twin and adoption studies. *Psychological Bulletin*, 128: 490-529.

Roberts, S. & Kendler, K. S. (1999). Neuroticism and self-esteem as indices of the vulnerability to major depression in women. *Psychological Medicine*, 29: 1101-1109.

Robinson, J. L., Kagan, J., Reznick, J. S. & Corley, R. (1992). The heritability of inhibited and unihibited behavior: A twin study. *Developmental Psychology*, 28: 1030-1037.

Rose, R. J., Viken, R., J., Dick, D. M., Bates, J. E., Pulkkinen, L. & Kaprio, J. (2003). It does take a village: Nonfamilial environments and children's behavior. *Psychological Science*, 14: 273-277.

Rothbart, M. K. & Ahadi, S. A. (1994). Temperament and the development of personality. *Journal of Abnormal Psychology*, 103: 55-66.

Rothbart, M. K., Ahadi, S. A., Hershey, K. L. & Fisher, P. (2001). Investigations of temperament at three to seven years: The Children's Behavior Questionnaire. *Child Development*, 72:1394-1408.

Rowe, D. C., Almeida, D. M. & Jacobson, K. C. (1999). School context and genetic influences on aggression in adolescence. *Psychological Science*, 10: 277-280.

Rowe, D. C. & Flannery, D. J. (1994). An examination of environmental and trait influences on adolescent delinquency. *Journal of Research in Crime and Delinquency*, 31: 374-389.

Rowe, D. C. & Osgood, D. W. (1984). Heredity and sociology theories of delinquency: A reconsideration. American Sociological Review, 49: 526-540.

Rowe, D. C., Vazsonyi, A. T. & Flannery, D. J. (1995). Sex differences in crime: Do means and within-sex variation have similar causes? *Journal of Research in Crime and Delinquency*, 32: 84-100.

Russo, M. F., Lahey, B. B., Christ, M.A.G., Frick, P. J., McBurnett, K., Walker, J. L. Loeber, R., Stouthamer-Loeber, & Green, S. M. (1991). Preliminary development of a sensation seeking scale for children. *Journal of Personality and Individual Differences*, 12: 399-405.

Russo, M. F., Stokes, G. S., Lahey, B. B., Christ, M.A.G., McBurnett, K., Loeber, R., Stouthamer-Loeber, M. & Green, S.M. (1993). A sensation seeking scale for children: Further refinement and psychometric development. *Journal of Psychopathology and Behavioral Assessment*, 15: 69-86.

Rutter, M. (1987). Temperament, personality, and personality disorder. *British Journal of Psychiatry*, 150: 443–458.

Rutter, M. (1988). Epidemiological approaches to developmental psychopathology. *Archives of General Psychiatry*, 45: 486-495.

Rutter, M. L. (1997). Nature-nurture integration: The example of antisocial behavior. *American Psychologist*, 52: 390-398.

Rutter, M., Dunn, J., Plomin, R., Siminoff, E., Pickles, A., Maughan, B., Ormel, J., Meyer, J. & Eaves, L. (1997). Integrating nature and nuture: Implications of person-environment correlations and interactions for developmental psychopathology. *Development and Psychopathology*, 9: 335-364.

Rutter, M., Pickles, A., Murray, R. & Eaves, L. (2001). Testing hypotheses on specific environmental causal effects on behavior. *Psychological Bulletin*, 127: 291-324.

Sampson, R. J. & Laub, J. H. (1992). Crime and deviance. *Annual Review of Sociology*, 18: 63–84.

Sanson, A., Pedlow, R., Cann, W., Prior, M. & Oberklaid, F. (1996). Shyness ratings: Stability and correlates in early childhood. *International Journal of Behavioral Development*, 19: 705-724.

Sanson, A. & Prior, M. (1999). Temperament and behavioral precursors to oppositional defiant disorder and conduct disorder. In H. Quay & A. Hogan (Eds.), *Handbook of the Disruptive Behavior Disorders* (pp. 397-417). New York: Kluwer Academic/Plenum.

Sanson, A., Smart, D., Prior, M. & Oberklaid, F. (1993). Precursors of hyperactivity and aggression. *Journal of the American Academy of Child and Adolescent Psychiatry*, 32: 1207-1216.

Saudino, K. J., Plomin, R. & DeFries, J. C. (1996). Tester-rated temperament at 14, 20 and 24 months: Environmental change and genetic continuity. *British Journal of Developmental Psychology*, 14: 129-144.

Schmeck, K. & Poustka, F. (2001). Temperament and disruptive behavior disorders. *Psychopathology*, 4: 159-163.

Schmitz, S., Fulker, D. W., Plomin, R., Zahn-Waxler, C., Emde, R. N. & DeFries, J. C. (1999). Temperament and problem behavior during early childhood. *International Journal of Behavioral Development*, 23: 333-355.

Schwartz, C. E., Snidman, N. & Kagan, J. (1996). Early childhood temperament as a determinant of externalizing behavior in adolescence. *Developmental Psychopathology*, 8: 527-537.

Seguin, J. R., Boulerice, B., Harden, P. W., Tremblay, R. E., Pihl, R. O. (1999). Executive functions and physical aggression after controlling for attention deficit hyperactivity disorder, general memory and IQ. *Journal of Child Psychology and Psychiatry*, 40:1197-1208.

Serbin, L. A., Moskowitz, D. S., Schwartzman, A. E. & Ledingham, J. E. (1991). Aggressive, withdrawn, and aggressive/withdrawn children in adolescence: Into the next generation. In D. J. Pepler & K. H. Rubin (Eds.), *The Development and Treatment of Childhood Aggression*. Hillsdale, NJ: Lawrence Erlbaum.

Shaw, D. S., Gilliom, M., Ingoldsby, E. M. & Nagin, D. S. (2003). Trajectories leading to school-age conduct problems. *Developmental Psychology*, 39: 189-200.

Shiner, R. L., Masten, A. S. & Tellegen, A. (2002). A developmental perspective on personality in emerging adulthood: Childhood antecedents and concurrent adaptation. *Journal of Personality and Social Psychology*, 83: 1165-1177.

Silberg, J. L., Rutter, M., Meyer, J., Maes, H., Hewitt, J., Siminoff, E., Pickles, A., Loeber, R. & Eaves, L. (1996). Genetic and environmental influences on the covariation between hyperactivity and conduct disturbance in juvenile twins. *Journal of Child Psychology and Psychiatry*, 37: 803-816.

Silverthorn, P. & Frick, P. J. (1999). Developmental pathways to antisocial behavior: The delayed-onset pathway in girls. *Development and Psychopathology*, 11: 101-126.

Silverthorn, P., Frick, P. J. & Reynolds, R. (2001). Timing of onset and correlates of severe conduct problems in adjudicated girls and boys. *Journal of Psychopathology and Behavioral Assessment*, 23: 171-181.

Snyder, J., Reid, J. & Patterson, G. (2003). A social learning model of child and adolescent antisocial behavior. In B. B. Lahey, T. Moffitt, & A. Caspi (Eds.), *Causes of Conduct Disorder and Juvenile Delinquency*. New York: Guilford Press.

Sparks, R., Ganschow, L. & Thomas, A. (1996). Role of intelligence tests in speech/language referrals. *Perceptual and Motor Skills*, 83: 195-204.

Stattin, H. & Klackenberg-Larsson, I. (1993). Early language and intelligence development and their relationship to future criminal behavior. *Journal of Abnormal Psychology*, 102: 369-378.

Tellegen, A. (1982). *Brief Manual for the Multidimensional Personality Questionnaire*. Minneapolis: University of Minnesota.

Tellegen, A., Lykken, D. T., Bouchard, T. J., Wilcox, K. J., Segal, N. L. & Rich, S. (1988). Personality similarity in twins reared apart and together. *Journal of Personality and Social Psychology*, 54: 1031-1039.

Thornberry, T. P., Krohn, M. D., Lizotte, A. J. & Chard-Wierschem, D. (1993). The role of juvenile gangs in facilitating delinquent behavior. *Journal of Research in Crime and Delinquency*, 30: 55-87.

Tranah, T., Harnett, P. & Yule, W. (1998). Conduct disorder and personality. *Personality and Individual Differences*, 24: 741-745.

Tremblay, R. E. (2000). The development of aggressive behaviour during childhood: What have we learned in the past century? *International Journal of Behavioral Development*, 24:129-141.

Tremblay, R. E., Boulerice, B., Harden, P. W., McDuff, P., Perusse, D., Pihl, R. O. & Zoccolillo, M. (1996). Do children in Canada become more aggressive as they approach adolescence? In M. Cappe & I. Fellegi (Eds.), *Growing up in Canada*. Ottawa: Statistics Canada.

Tremblay, R.E., Pihl, R.O., Vitaro,F. & Dobkin, P.L. (1994). Predicting early onset of male antisocial behavior from preschool behavior. *Archives of General Psychiatry*, 51: 732-739.

Tremblay, R, E., Japel, C., Perusse, D., McDuff, P., Boivin, M., Zoccolillo, M. & Montplaisir, J. (1999). The search for the age of 'onset' of physical aggression: Rousseau and Bandura revisited. *Criminal Behaviour and Mental Health*, 9: 8-23.

Van Kammen, W. & Loeber, R. (1994). Are fluctuations in delinquent activities related to the onset and offset in juvenile illegal drug use and drug dealing? *Journal of Drug Issues*, 24: 9-24.

Wahler, R. G. & Hann, D. M. (1987). An interbehavioral approach to clinical child psychology: Toward an understanding of troubled families. In D.H. Ruben & D.J. Delpratto (Eds.), *New Ideas in Therapy: Introduction to an Interdisciplinary Approach*. New York: Greenwood Press.

Wakschlag, L. S., Gordon , R. A., Lahey, B. B., Loeber, R., Green, S. M. & Leventhal, B. L. (2000). Maternal age at first birth and boys' risk for conduct disorder. *Journal of Research on Adolescence*, 10: 417-441.

Waldman, I. D. (1996). Aggressive children's hostile perceptual and response biases: The role of attention and impulsivity. *Child Development*, 67: 1015-1033.

Waldman, I. D., Rhee, S. H., Levy, F. & Hay, D. A. (2001). Genetic and environmental influences on the covariation among symptoms of attention deficit hyperactivity disorder, oppositional defiant disorder, and conduct disorder. In D. A. Hay & F. Levy (Eds.), *Attention, Genes, and ADHD*. Hillsdale, NJ: Lawrence Erlbaum Associates.

Waschbusch, D. A. (2002). A meta-analytic examination of comorbid hyperactive-impulsive-attention problems and conduct problems. *Psychological Bulletin*, 128:118-150.

Watson, D., Clark, L. A., Tellegen, A. (1988). Development and validation of brief measures of positive and negative affect: The PANAS scales. *Journal of Personality and Social Psychology*, 54: 1063-1070.

Wikström, P.-O. H. & Sampson, R. J. (2003). Social mechanisms of community influences on crime and pathways in criminality. In B. B. Lahey, T. E. Moffitt, & A. Caspi (Eds.), *Causes of Conduct Disorder and Juvenile Delinquency* (pp. 118-148). New York: Guilford Press.

Wills, T. A., Sandy, J. M. & Yaeger, A. (2000). Temperament and adolescent substance use: An epigenetic approach to risk and protection. *Journal of Personality*, 68: 1127-1151.

Zahn-Waxler, C., Robinson, J.L. & Emde, R.N. (1992). The development of empathy in twins. *Developmental Psychology*, 28: 1038-1047.

Zhou, Q., Eisenberg, N., Losoya, S. H., Fabes, R. A., Reiser, M., Guthrie, I. K., Murphy, B. C., Cumberland, A. J. & Shepard, S. (2002). The relations of parental warmth and positive expressiveness to children's empathy-related responding and social functioning: A longitudinal study. *Child Development*, 73: 893-915.

Zoccolillo, M. (1992). Co-occurrence of conduct disorder and its adult outcomes with depressive and anxiety disorders: A review. *Journal of the American Academy of Child and Adolescent Psychiatry*, 31: 547-556.

Zuckerman, M. (1996). The psychobiological model for impulsive unsocialized sensation seeking: A comparative approach. *Neuropsychobiology*, 34:125-129.

Zuckerman, M., Kuhlman, D. M., Joireman, J., Teta, P. & Kraft, M. (1993). A comparison of three structural models for personality: The big three, the big five, and the alternative five. *Journal of Personality and Social Psychology*, 65: 757-768.

3

Explaining the Facts of Crime: How the Developmental Taxonomy Replies to Farrington's Invitation

Alex R. Piquero and Terrie E. Moffitt

Introduction

The relationship between age and crime has been one of the most well-documented (Quetelet, 1831; Hirschi and Gottfredson, 1983) and contentious (Steffensmeier et al., 1989; Britt, 1992) of all criminological facts. Researchers studying the relationship between age and crime have typically observed that the aggregate pattern is such that criminal activity tends to peak in the late teens through the mid-twenties, and then declines throughout adulthood.

At the same time that the aggregate relationship between age and crime has been reproduced, questions have been raised as to whether the *aggregate* pattern displayed in the age/crime curve is similar to–or different from–the pattern of *individual* careers and whether conclusions about individuals can be validly drawn from aggregate data (Piquero, Farrington, and Blumstein, 2003). For example, how far does the observed peak of the aggregate age/crime curve reflect changes within individuals as opposed to changes in the composition of offenders? In other words, is the peak in the age/crime curve a function of active offenders committing more crime, or is it a function of more individuals actively offending at those peak years? This is but just one of the many important questions that are addressed by developmental/life-course criminologists who attempt to understand the patterning of criminal activity over the life-course.

In his recent Sutherland Address to the American Society of Criminology, David Farrington (2003) reviewed the current state of developmental and life-course criminology by outlining the key theoretical and empirical issues endemic to this line of research. In particular, he listed the widely accepted findings from this line of research that all developmental/life-course theories have been designed to explain. Then, Farrington carefully reviewed the contentious and unresolved empirical issues that present challenges to developmental and life-course theories. After reviewing several prominent theories that examine criminal activity over the life-course, Farrington closed with an important recommendation: a detailed comparison of the key features of all developmental and life-course theories, of their answers to key empirical and theoretical questions, and of their predictions regarding key unresolved empirical developmental and life-course issues. This chapter responds to Farrington's invitation.

In this chapter, we take one particular developmental/life-course theory, namely Moffitt's developmental taxonomy of antisocial behavior, and address Farrington's questions and concerns. The chapter is broken down into four specific sections. First, we present a broad overview of Moffitt's theory and a brief review of the research that has been undertaken to study its central tenants. Second, we list out Farrington's widely accepted conclusions regarding crime over the life-course and then show how Moffitt's theory accounts for these conclusions. Third, we apply Moffitt's theory to several important empirical and theoretical issues listed by Farrington that every developmental/ life-course criminological theory must account for. Finally, we highlight the contentious issues raised by Farrington that emanate from research on developmental criminology, and highlight how Moffitt's theory may explain these issues.

Moffitt's Developmental Taxonomy

Moffitt's original taxonomy (1993) proposes two primary types of offenders, each of which possess a unique set of factors that cause criminal and antisocial activity, as well as a different patterning of criminal and antisocial activity over the life-course. A third group of individuals was also reported, the abstainers, a small, select group who refrain from antisocial and criminal activity throughout the life-course. Subsequent to the original publication of the taxonomy, a fourth group has emerged from empirical work, which appears to be made up of low-level offenders with particular mental health problems. Discussion of the latter two groups is beyond the scope of this chapter, but they are discussed in detail in Moffitt (2003).

The first group of offenders in Moffitt's theory, adolescence-limited, constrain their offending activity to the adolescent developmental period, occurring alongside puberty. The set of factors underlying adolescence-limited delinquency consists of the maturity gap and the peer social context. The maturity gap reflects the youngsters' experience of dysphoria during the relatively role-less years between their biological maturation and their access to mature privileges and responsibilities, while the peer social context reflects the observation that similarly situated adolescents biologically and socially "grow-up" together, and as a result, look to each other for support during the time period when they are not allowed to be adults. During the adolescent time period, then, delinquent coping is appealing and involvement in delinquency surfaces as a way to demonstrate autonomy from parents and teachers, win affiliation with peers, and hasten social maturation. Because adolescence-limited delinquency is typically social, offending takes on a group-oriented nature that is characterized by involvement in relatively minor and status-oriented offenses, but adolescence-limited delinquents should seldom initiate violence (although they may be drawn reluctantly into violent acts, for example as a result of altercations in drug deals). Importantly, because their pre-delinquent development is normal, most adolescence-limited delinquents are able to desist from crime when they age into real adult roles, returning gradually to a more conventional lifestyle. Individual variation in the timing of desistance (across the 20s) is expected within the group of adolescence-limited delinquents. Their recovery may be delayed because of snares, or experiences that can compromise the ability to make a successful transition to adulthood. Examples of such snares include a criminal record, incarceration, drug and alcohol addiction, truncated education, and for girls, unwanted pregnancy.

In contrast, the second group of offenders, life-course-persistent, begins their antisocial activity early in the life-course, offends more while active, commits all sorts of crimes, including violence, and is very unlikely to desist from criminal activity in adulthood. Many of the crimes committed by life-course-persistent offenders tend to be committed without the assistance of others, oftentimes referred to as "lone offending." Peer influence is not a necessary condition for life-course-persistent offending, although life-course-persistent offending may have some correlation with measures of peer delinquency, simply because life-course-persistent offenders serve as a role magnets, attracting adolescence-limited peers as co-offenders, in roles such as lookouts, offending apprentices, or girlfriends. According to the taxonomy, the child's risk for life-course-persistent offending emerges from inherited or acquired neuro-psychological variation, initially manifested as subtle cognitive deficits, difficult temperament, or hyperactivity. The environment in which the child is reared is also an important contributory factor as inadequate parenting, disrupted family bonds, poverty, etc. tend to compromise effective parenting efforts and in many cases exacerbate the child's individual differences. The environmental risk domain expands beyond the family as the child ages, to include poor relations with people such as peers and teachers. Over the first two decades of development, transactions between individual and environment gradually construct a disordered personality with hallmark features of physical aggression and antisocial behavior persisting to mid-life. The taxonomy anticipates that antisocial behavior will infiltrate multiple adult life domains including illegal activities, employment, marriage, and intimate victimization. As could be expected, this infiltration diminishes the possibility of reform such that life-course-persistent offenders have few (if any) opportunities to learn and practice prosocial behavior and limited opportunities for change, and this is especially the case since many LCPs become ensnared in an antisocial lifestyle by the consequences of offending, such as school drop-out, incarceration, and so forth (i.e., labeling effects). Fortunately, Moffitt anticipates that membership in this group is quite small, averaging about 5-8 percent of the population across representative research samples.

Several studies have sought to examine the viability of Moffitt's developmental taxonomy, and in particular have assessed some of the key hypotheses underlying the taxonomy. A number of the hypotheses associated with life-course-persistent offending have been examined with data from the Dunedin Multidisciplinary Health and Development Study, a thirty-year longitudinal study of a birth cohort of 1,000 New Zealanders. In general, these studies have examined childhood predictors measured early in life and examined their relation to criminal and antisocial activity measured via self-report, maternal reports, teacher reports, informant reports, and official records. These efforts have consistently shown that life-course-persistent offending is differentially predicted by individual risk factors including undercontrolled temperament measured by observers at age three, neurological abnormalities and delayed motor development at age three, low intellectual abilities, reading difficulties, poor scores on neuropsychological tests of memory, hyperactivity, and slow heart rate (see Bartusch et al., 1997; Moffitt and Caspi, 2001; Moffitt et al., 1994, 1996). In addition, life-course-persistent offending is also differentially predicted by parenting risk factors including teenaged single parents, mothers with poor mental health, mothers who were observed to be harsh or neglectful, as well as experiences of harsh and inconsistent discipline, much family conflict, many changes of the primary caretaker, low family SES, and rejection by peers in school (Moffitt and Caspi, 2001).

Importantly, the main findings regarding life-course-persistent offending uncovered with the Dunedin data have also been observed in other samples from different countries (see review in Moffitt, 2003). For example, using data from the Philadelphia portion of the National Collaborative Perinatal Project (NCPP), Tibbetts and Piquero (1999) examined how the biosocial interaction of low birth weight and disadvantaged environment predicted early onset offending. Their results indicated that the biosocial interaction was significantly related to early—but not late—onset of offending. Piquero and Tibbetts (1999) examined the interaction between pre/perinatal disturbances and disadvantaged familial environment in distinguishing between involvement in nonviolent and violent offending. Their analysis indicated that, consistent with Moffitt's expectation, the biosocial interaction was predictive of violent but not nonviolent offending (see also Arseneault et al., 2002). Piquero (2001) used the Philadelphia data to examine how neuropsychological variation, using cognitive test scores, was related to three different manifestations of life-course-persistent offending (early onset, chronic offending, and seriousness of offending) by age 18. His results indicated that poor neuropsychological test scores were predictive of all three measures of life-course-persistent offending in a manner consistent with Moffitt. Gibson et al. (2001) extended Piquero's analysis and found that neuropsychological risk also combines with poor familial environments to predict early onset of offending. Finally, Kratzer and Hodgins (1999) used data from a Swedish cohort to study how cognitive abilities related to offending from childhood to age thirty. Their results indicated that early start offenders (i.e., life-course-persistent offenders) committed more crimes and a greater diversity of crimes than other offending groups. Childhood problems and low global scores of intelligence distinguished these offenders from other offender types as well as non-offenders.

Because much of the research on Moffitt's taxonomy has tended to focus on life-course-persistent offending, only a few studies have examined adolescence-limited offending. Using a low SES sample from Minneapolis, Aguilar et al. (2000) found that adolescent-onset delinquents experienced elevated internalizing symptoms and perceptions of stress at age 16, which may be consistent with Moffitt's assertion that these adolescents experience dysphoria during the maturity gap. Data from the Dunedin study also indicates that the offending of adolescence-limiteds is strongly associated with delinquent peers, as compared to life-course-persistent offenders (Bartusch et al., 1997; Moffitt and Caspi, 2001). In addition, Caspi and his colleagues (1993) showed that an increase in young teens' awareness of peers' delinquency antedates and predicts onset of their own later delinquency. Piquero and Brezina (2001) used data from 2,000 males participating in the Youth in Transition Survey to test the hypothesis that a desire for autonomy promoted adolescent-onset offending. They found that the offenses committed by adolescence-limited delinquents were primarily rebellious in nature (i.e., not violent), and that this rebellious offending was predicted by the interaction between maturational timing and aspects of peer activities that were related to personal autonomy. However, one measure of youth autonomy did not yield a significant finding in their analysis.

We cannot finish our discussion of adolescence-limited delinquency without reviewing what we know about those adolescents who refrain from delinquency, that is, abstainers. This is an important issue because, if as the taxonomy says adolescence-limited delinquency is normative, then the existence of teenagers who abstain from delinquency requires explanation. Moffitt proffers four potential reasons for such abstinence. First, some youths may refrain from antisocial behavior because they do not sense the maturity gap, and therefore lack the hypothesized motivation for experimenting with crime, or they may skip the maturity gap altogether because of late puberty. Second, some adolescents incur early initiation into adult roles, or at the very least, they have access to prosocial roles. Third, some adolescents encounter few opportunities for mimicking life-course-persistent delinquent models. Fourth, and the "explanation most central to [Moffitt's] theory" is that abstainers are excluded from opportunities to mimic antisocial peers because of some personal characteristic(s) that cause(s) them to be excluded from the delinquent peer groups, which ascend to importance during adolescence (see also Moffitt et al., 1996: 419). Thus, under this hypothesis, some adolescents may possess certain personality characteristics that prevent them from being a part of the peer social context during adolescence.

Unfortunately, aside from a few exceptions (Moffitt et al., 1996; Shedler and Block, 1990), the developmental histories of adolescents who abstain from delinquency have not been examined in great detail. Only one study in fact, has tested Moffitt's "abstainer" hypothesis. Piquero, Brezina, and Turner (2005) used data from the National Longitudinal Survey of Youth (NLSY) to examine the abstainer hypothesis, and their results led to three main conclusions. First, adolescent abstainers were comprised of a small group of individuals. Second, the correlates of abstention primarily included situational and social characteristics, with social factors exhibiting central importance. Individuals who were not part of the peer social context and/or who spent less time with peers, were more likely to be abstainers. In contrast to Moffitt's expectations, the results also revealed little evidence of "psychopathology" in that many personality characteristics were not directly related to abstention. Third, bearing in mind the importance of access to the peer social context, Piquero et al. found that, consistent with Moffitt, several personality, emotional, structural, and situational characteristics were related to involvement in the peer social context, but in some cases in the direction opposite to that predicted.

The Taxonomy and Farrington's Widely Accepted Conclusions

Farrington (2003) offers ten widely accepted conclusions about the development of offending that any developmental/life-course theory must be able to explain. In this section, we outline these ten conclusions and then briefly outline how Moffitt's taxonomy accounts for them. The existence of these factors was known in the 1980s, and the taxonomy was originally developed to account for them; as such, Moffitt (1993) can be consulted for more detail than we can provide in this chapter.

First, the prevalence of offending peaks in the late teenage years (i.e., ages 15-19). Moffitt would argue that the total prevalence of offending peaks in the teenage years because of the increase of AL offenders (who overlap in offending activity with LCPs during this age period).

Second, the peak age of onset of offending is between 8 and 14 years of age, and the peak of desistance from offending is between ages 20 and 29. Because of its articulation of two groups of offenders, the developmental taxonomy would answer this question in a two-fold fashion. For both ALs and LCPs, onset peaks during the ages of 8-14 (with LCPs much earlier than ALs), with relatively few "onsets" in the late teens, and even fewer (if any) in early adulthood

(Moffitt et al., 2001). With regard to the peak age of desistance, most (if not all) ALs are expected to desist in their early 20s because of transitions into adult roles. Because ALs comprise the largest number of offenders, they alone will be responsible for much of the aggregate desistance observed in the age/crime curve. Nevertheless, a small number of offenders, LCPs, continue offending throughout adulthood and do not desist. Such an expectation does not square away perfectly with Farrington's "accepted conclusions" because few studies have studied criminal offending beyond the 20s and 30s (for a recent exception, see Sampson and Laub, 2003).

Third, an early age of onset predicts a relatively long criminal career duration and the commission of relatively many offenses. As the developmental taxonomy anticipates that early onset is a characteristic of LCPs only, Moffitt expects that among the small number of LCPs, early onset relates to a lengthy criminal career and the commission of a large number of offenses over the life-course.

Fourth, there is marked continuity in offending and antisocial behavior from childhood to the teenage years and to adulthood. In other words, there is relative stability of the ordering of people on some measure of antisocial behavior over time, and people who commit relatively many offenses during one age range have a high probability of also committing relatively many offenses during another age range. This "conclusion" may also be reached by Moffitt's taxonomy. LCPs are believed to be generally stable over the life-course with regard to their involvement in antisocial and criminal activity. To be sure, this involvement is likely to change in manifestation (i.e., few 3 year olds are convicted of assault, but many hit) over the life-course, but the point remains that LCPs are involved in high amounts of antisocial activity at all phases of the life-course. Because their scores on antisocial measures are extreme, high outliers, LCPs, though small in number, tend to sway temporal stability correlations, creating the impression of moderate stability in antisocial behavior for the entire population. The same is not true of ALs.

Fifth, a small fraction of the population (chronics) commit a large fraction of all crimes. Once again, this conclusion is relegated only to the small number of high-rate offenders in Moffitt's taxonomy, the LCPs. These individuals are believed to be a small fraction of the population (i.e., 5-8 percent) but engage in a large number of criminal acts. Although ALs offend during adolescence, and their offending activities *may* be indistinguishable from LCPs in the teenage years, looking back over their criminal careers, LCPs will represent the smallest fraction of the population but yet be involved in the most amount of crime.

Sixth, offending is versatile rather than specialized, and violent offenders are indistinguishable from frequent offenders on a variety of risk factors. This is a particularly interesting "conclusion" when viewed in the light of Moffitt's theory. For Moffitt, LCPs are versatile offenders, engaging in all sorts of antisocial and criminal activity over the life-course. These acts are committed with high frequency and will include run-of-the-mill crimes as well as violent acts. LCPs, then, tend not to specialize. On the other hand, ALs, are believed to engage predominantly in crimes that symbolize adult status, and are expected to have little motivation for person-oriented crimes.

Seventh, the types of acts defined as offenses are elements of a larger syndrome of antisocial behavior. Among both ALs and LCPs, antisocial behavior may encompass any number of antisocial and criminal acts. For example, the former group tends to engage in property- and status-oriented offenses such as drug use, truancy, sexual promiscuity, and so forth, while the latter group tends to engage in all of the aforementioned acts as well as more person-oriented acts. Thus, for both groups, the causal factors that implicate membership should relate similarly to all sorts of offenses and acts within each group's repertoire. However, for LCPs, the causal processes behind antisocial behavior continue longer across the life-course, and as a result antisocial behavior infiltrates more aspects of the adult lifestyle, including work life and family life.

Eighth, most offenses up to late teens are committed with others, whereas most offenses from age 20 onwards are committed alone. On this score, Moffitt implicates co-offending as a key risk factor for AL delinquency, but not LCP offending styles. Interestingly, as ALs begin to desist in early adulthood, the majority of offending activity that occurs in mid-life, past the early 20s, is committed by LCPs, who do not need co-offenders to offend. Thus, the developmental taxonomy predicts that co-offending follows much of the aggregate age-crime curve because this curve is dominated by AL-path offenders and not by LCP-path offenders. As crime drops in the early 20s, so, too, do co-offending patterns.

Ninth, the reasons given for offending up to the late teens are quite variable including utilitarian reasons, excitement, boredom, or anger, while from age 20 onwards, utilitarian motives become more dominant. Although the taxonomy does not directly speak to this issue—nor has research testing the taxonomy examined this "conclusion," we would anticipate that since offending through the late teens is dominated in the aggregate by AL-path offenders, their being situated in a maturity gap likely encapsulates many of the aforementioned explanations, especially excitement and boredom. LCPs, however, likely do not offend for many of the same reasons; instead, they are likely to suggest that their motives are more utilitarian *from their perspective*. Recall that ALs desist by early adulthood, so the offending population after that age is comprised by proportionately more LCP-type offenders. Thus, LCP offending tends to be motivated by an interest in monetary gains (burglary, robbery, drug selling) and by retaliatory considerations (revenge crimes such as assault and homicide). In adulthood, as in early childhood, the LCP's motive for antisocial behavior remains the same: to get what they want, when they want it.

Tenth, different types of offenses tend to be first committed at distinctively different ages (i.e., shoplifting before burglary). Diversification is key prior to adulthood, when crimes become more specialized (Piquero et al., 1999). This tenth fact is considered non-problematic by the taxonomy. In other words, there is nothing about the progression observation that requires empirical attention or theoretical explanation. Different kinds of antisocial acts tend to be committed at predictably different ages in a regular sequence for the same reasons that different kinds of every behavior tend to be committed at different ages in a sequence that is more or less predictable: thus, maturation brings changes in what people can do. Generally, one hits as soon as one can control one's arm, one truants only after enrolled in school, one shoplifts as soon as one is old enough to go to shops alone without mother/father, one steals cars after one learns to drive, one rapes after one begins to get reliable erections, and one commits embezzlement only after one secures a job where there is money. This fundamental principle of development is known as "heterotypic continuity." The taxonomy does not explain this natural progression, but rather it makes use of it, to explain how the acts of LCPs change across time, while remaining antisocial in essence and in function (Moffitt, 1993).

To provide a data-based example of this truism that the age of onset of an antisocial behavior is a function of opportunity to commit it successfully, consider the numerous longitudinal studies that have shown that girls begin to engage in drug- and alcohol-related delinquency on average eighteen months before boys. This sex difference in developmental progression can be readily explained by the fact that girls complete puberty on average eighteen months before boys, and thus girls look old enough to successfully gain access to illicit substances eighteen months before boys, on average (Moffitt et al., 2001). Once boys, too, complete puberty, they begin to commit as much drug- and alcohol-related crime as girls.

The Taxonomy's Answer to Key Empirical and Theoretical Issues

Key empirical questions are answered as follows:

Q1:   Why do people start offending?
A1:   Among ALs, offending occurs as a result of the interaction between the maturity gap and the peer social context.
A2:   Among LCPs, offending occurs as a result of the interaction between neuropsychological risk and disadvantaged environment.
Q2:   How are onset sequences explained?
A1:   Among ALs, onset sequences are not proposed. Offending for this group includes a myriad of property- and status-oriented offenses that occur with ready opportunities for such acts in adolescence.
A2:   Among LCPs, behavioral manifestations of the underlying interaction vary over time because of changes in opportunities and victims. Thus, as children, LCPs engage in grabbing, pushing, yelling, and lying; as adolescents and young adults, LCPs engage in property crimes, drug use, robbery, rape, *and* assault; as adults, LCPs engage in spouse abuse, income tax evasion, and so forth.

Q3:   Why is there continuity in offending?

A1:   Among most ALs, continuity in offending does not exist, save for a small number of ALs who become ensnared.

A2:   Among LCPs, continuity in offending occurs because the relative ordering of individuals on the interaction between neuropsychological risk and disadvantaged environment stays fairly consistent over time. Further, the continuity of LCP antisocial behavior is a function of a process known as "cumulative continuity" in which present antisocial behavior increases the probability of future antisocial behavior, by reducing possibilities for alternative kinds of behavior. For example, if conduct problems cause a young man to be expelled permanently from school, his lack of a degree reduces his chance to get a job, and crime remains for him the most feasible way to get money.

Q4:   Why do people stop offending?

A1:   Among ALs, desistance is the norm. Their strong cognitive abilities and prosocial skills should aid their desistance as aging into adulthood provides ready and legal access to once coveted prizes that signify adulthood social status. In general, ALs profit from opportunities for desistance because they retain the option of successfully resuming a conventional lifestyle.

A2:   Among LCPs, desistance is the exception. LCPs may make transitions into marriage or work, but their injurious childhoods make it less likely that they can leave their past behind; they should select jobs and spouses that support their antisocial style, and they should express antisocial behavior at home and at work.

Q5:   Why does prevalence peak in the teenage years?

A1:   The total prevalence of offending peaks in the teenage years because of the large influx of AL offenders. According to the taxonomy, crime ought to peak when the largest number of individuals experience the maturity gap between biological maturity (puberty) and social maturity (career commitment and family formation).

Q6:   Why does early onset predict a long criminal career?

A1:   Among ALs, lengthy criminal careers do not exist because ALs do not exhibit early onset.

A2:   Among LCPs, early onset predicts lengthy criminal careers because both early onset and long career duration are linked manifestations of LCP-type offending that is a function of the interaction between neuropsychological risk and disadvantaged environment. The construction of an LCP antisocial personality is gradual over the first two decades of life, but once constructed, the style is relatively enduring.

Q7:   Why is there versatility in offending and antisocial behavior?

A1:   Among ALs, offending should be more specialized and organized around crimes that symbolize adult privilege or that demonstrate autonomy from parental control such as vandalism, public order offenses, substance use, theft, and running away. ALs however, should not engage in person-oriented offenses.

A2:   Among LCPs, offending should be highly versatile including person-oriented crimes as well as crimes that are often committed by lone offenders.

Q8:   Why does co-offending decrease from adolescence to adulthood?

A1:   Among ALs, for whom co-offending is relevant to their involvement in delinquency as adolescents, adulthood brings on desistance and thus, co-offending ceases.

A2:   Among LCPs, for whom co-offending is largely irrelevant, adulthood brings continued crime without the need for co-offenders.

Q9:   Why are there between-individual differences in offending?

A1:   There are between-individual differences in offending because the hypothesized risk factors for offending are qualitatively different for both groups of offenders.

Q10:   What are the key risk factors for onset and desistance, and how can they be explained?

A1:   Among ALs, the key risk factor for onset is the interaction between the maturity gap and the peer social context, while for desistance, the key factors are aging into adulthood, recognition that once coveted "things" are now legally available, and strong cognitive abilities and prosocial skills.

A2:   Among LCPs, the key risk factor for onset is the interaction between neuropsychological risk and disadvantaged environment, while for desistance, there is no such factor(s) because LCPs rarely desist. Of course, the taxonomic theory did not assert that LCP offenders would carry on committing crimes, especially street crimes, at the same rate from age 18 until they dropped into the grave at old age. Such so called "absolute stability" was already known to be implausible before the taxonomy was developed, because published age distributions of official crime (arrests) showed that very few individuals are engaged in official crime after age 50. Rather than positing "absolute stability," the taxonomy predicted that LCP offenders would be characterized by "individual-difference stability" which means that throughout the life-course, LCP offenders would continue to manifest more antisocial activities than other men their age. Moreover, the original taxonomy invoked the aforementioned principle of "heterotypic continuity" in which age-graded changes in opportunities will alter the expression of antisocial tendencies. Although virtually everyone gives up street crime as they age, LCPs would be expected to maintain antisocial attitudes as long as they live, and to take advantage of even meager opportunities for antisocial activity late in life, such as hitting their wives, cheating at cards, kicking the dog, or falling over drunk.

Q11:   Why are there within-individual differences in offending?

A1:   Among ALs, changes in risk factors and life events over time are assumed to cause changes in offending.

A2:   Among LCPs, because the interaction between neuropsychological risk and disadvantaged environment is played out early in the life-course and is reinforced over time as a result of cumulative continuity, there should be little (if any) within-individual differences in offending. This is so because LCPs rarely desist.

Q12:   What are the main motives and reasons for offending?

A1:   Among ALs, the main motive for offending occurs for the first time when they enter adolescence. For them, an emerging appreciation of desirable adult privileges is met with an awareness that those privileges are yet forbidden. After observing their antisocial peers' effective solution to the modern dilemma of the maturity gap, youths mimic that delinquent solution. Perversely, the consequences of delinquency reinforce and sustain their efforts, but only until aging brings a subjective shift in the valence of the consequences of crime.

A2:   Among LCPs, offending has its origins in neuropsychological problems that interact with disadvantaged environments. Beginning in childhood, discipline problems and academic failures accumulate increasing momentum, knifing off opportunities to practice prosocial behavior. As time passes, recovery is precluded by maladaptive individual dispositions and narrowing life options, and LCPs are channeled into antisocial adult lifestyles. Thus, unlike the motives for AL-path offenders, which tend to be reactionary to situated historical periods (i.e., adolescence), LCP motives are a much more internalized integral part of adult personality structure.

Q13: What are the effects of life events on offending?

A1: According to the taxonomy, transition events in the life-course are *not* unconditional determinants of desistance. Events such as marriage, employment, or military service can provide opportunities for desistance, but such events can also provide opportunities for continuity. In particular, individual's reactions to life transition events will vary predictably, depending on their personal antisocial histories.

A2: Among ALs, major life transitions likely aid in the desistance process.

A3: Among LCPs, major life transitions bear little impact on the desistance process because LCPs rarely desist. In fact, some life transitions may provide new opportunities for the expression of antisocial motivations.

Key theoretical questions are answered as follows:

Q1: What is the key construct underlying offending?

A1: Among ALs, it is the interaction between the maturity gap and the peer social context.

A2: Among LCPs, it is the interaction between neuropsychological risk and disadvantaged environment.

Q2: What factors encourage offending?

A1: Among ALs, situational factors such as delinquent peers provide the strongest pro-offending factor.

A2: Among LCPs, aside from the interaction between neuropsychological risk and disadvantaged environment, opportunities and victims provide the strongest pro-offending factors.

Q3: What factors inhibit offending?

A1: Among ALs, ensuing adulthood, strong cognitive abilities, and ready prosocial skills inhibit offending.

A2: Among LCPs, other than lack of opportunities or ready access to victims, few (if any) factors inhibit offending.

Q4: Is there a learning process?

A1: Among ALs, the effects of antisocial models (i.e., delinquent peers) could involve learning as well as imitation.

A2: Among LCPs, the socialization process of parents in child-rearing is the most prominent learning process.

Q5: Is there a decision-making process?

A1: Among ALs, the decision-making process is a fairly rational one as they undertake acts that provide temporary relief from the strains of the maturity gap (i.e., benefits outweigh costs).

A2: Among LCPs, behavioral repertoires, expectancies, and attitudes constructed and stored since early life inform the decision-making process, which may by adulthood be so automatic as to require little mental deliberation and weight of risks/benefits.

Q6: What is the structure of the theory?

A1: Among ALs, the interaction between the maturity gap and the peer social context should relate to AL-type delinquency including theft, vandalism, drug use, and running away.

A2: Among LCPs, the interaction between neuropsychological risk and disadvantaged environment should relate to LCP-type delinquency that subsumes AL-type delinquency and expands the behavioral repertoire to include solo- and person-oriented offenses.

A3: Aside from these two prototypes, the theory specifies two other groups, an abstainer group and a low-level chronic group (see Moffitt, 2003 for information about these two groups).

Q7: What are the operational definitions of theoretical constructs?

A1: Among ALs, the maturity gap may be measured by individual perceptions of their biological and social maturity and by desire for autonomy. The peer social context may be measured by knowledge of peer attitudes toward delinquency, knowledge of peer involvement in delinquency, time spent with peers in both structured and unstructured activities, as well as general peer influence (i.e., it's important to me what my friends say, think about me, etc.).

A2: Among LCPs, neuropsychological risk may be measured by tests of cognitive ability, neuropsychological functioning and impairment, observational measures of difficult infant temperament, toddler overactivity and undercontrol, and even genetic risk as measured via behavioral or molecular genetic methods. Disadvantaged environments could be measured via any number of ways including familial make-up, socioeconomic status of families, neighborhoods, etc., as well as observations of parent-child interactions, measures of unskilled parenting, child maltreatment, and child neglect.

Q8: What does the theory explain?

A1: The taxonomy is designed to explain the patterning of criminal activity over the life-course, with explicit recognition that there are multiple groups of offenders, some of whom offend transitorily and temporarily and others who offend at higher rates and for longer duration. The taxonomy does anticipate differences across historical periods and national cultures in the salience and duration of the maturity gap. For example, the original statement described evidence that the maturity gap has widened and grown during this century, paralleling the emergence and growth of the adolescent peak in offending. The taxonomy also explains the findings listed in the "key conclusions" section.

Q9: What does the theory not explain?

A1: The taxonomy is not designed to explain variations in crime rates at the macro level (i.e., between countries, states, neighborhoods, etc.). It does not necessarily explain gang development and gang criminality.

Q10: What findings might challenge the theory?

A1: The taxonomy proposes that there are two qualitatively distinct types of offenders, who offend for different reasons, for different periods of time, and who engage in different types of crimes. If evidence documents less or more groups of offenders who do not mimic the causal structure and sequence as articulated by the taxonomy, then the taxonomy may be questioned (see Moffitt, 2003).

A2: The processes that link past to future offending across the two groups differ. Among ALs, the taxonomy assumes that state dependence is the rule (i.e., that criminal activity materially transforms conditions in the offender's life, thus increasing the probability of future offending), while among LCPs the taxonomy assumes that persistent heterogeneity is the rule (i.e., that continuity in criminal activity over time is due to stable differences between individuals in factors that influence crime). If one or both of these is found to be incorrect, then the taxonomy may be questioned.

A3: Among ALs, the taxonomy assumes that violent and person-oriented offenses are not prominent features of the offending repertoire, while among LCPs the taxonomy assumes that all sorts of offenses are committed. If one or both of these is found to be incorrect, then the taxonomy may be questioned.

A4:   Among ALs, the taxonomy assumes that most (if not all) will desist as adulthood ensues, while among LCPs the taxonomy assumes that desistance is rare (though see earlier discussion of "absolute stability" versus "individual-difference stability"). If one or both of these is found to be incorrect, then the taxonomy may be questioned.

Q11:   How much does the theory make different predictions from other theories?

A1:   Similar to other taxonomic/developmental theories (i.e., Patterson, Loeber, etc.), the taxonomy assumes that the offending population is comprised of more than one group of offenders, each of whom offends for distinct reasons. The taxonomy differs from other developmental theories that assume that the offending population is comprised by a single group of offenders having a unitary, single causal process (i.e., Gottfredson and Hirschi, Sampson and Laub, Thornberry and Krohn, etc.).

A2:   Unlike other developmental/life-course theories (i.e., Sampson and Laub), the taxonomy allows for the important effect of biology and personality.

A3:   Unlike other developmental/life-course theories (i.e., Farrington; Thornberry and Krohn), the taxonomy suggests that early-onset offenders are different in kind from later-onset offenders.

A4:   Unlike other developmental/life-course theories (i.e., Sampson and Laub), the taxonomy suggests that informal social control does not mediate risk factors such as impulsivity, neuropsychological risk, and disadvantaged familial and socioeconomic environments.

The Taxonomy and Farrington's Contentious Issues

Farrington's essay nicely identifies a number of contentious issues within the developmental/life-course criminology area. In this section, we list these contentious issues, and then describe how the taxonomy would predict the outcome of these issues.

First, it is not clear how individual offending frequencies (i.e., the frequency of offending among those who offend) vary with age. There is mixed evidence on this front with some research showing that individual offending frequency does not change with age (Farrington et al., 2003; Loeber and Snyder, 1990). The taxonomy would predict that the individual offending frequency of LCPs would exhibit little variation with age (at least while crime is a feature of the human population, i.e., up until mid-life), while the individual offending frequency of ALs would show a decrease (to a stable rate near or at zero) in early adulthood.

Second, it is not clear whether the seriousness of offending escalates up to a certain age and then de-escalates or whether it does not change with age. Among ALs, the taxonomy would predict escalation in offense seriousness because such offenders engage in relatively minor forms of criminal and antisocial acts, but among LCPs, the taxonomy would expect there to be little de-escalation in the seriousness of antisocial behavior over the life-course.

Third, it is not clear whether an early age of onset predicts a high individual offending frequency or a high average seriousness of offending. Among LCPs only, an early age of onset of offending predicts a high individual offending frequency and a high average seriousness of offending because both reflect the interaction between neuropsychological risk and disadvantaged environment. An early age of onset indicates a relatively high level of this interaction, and the ordering of individuals on this interaction remains relatively consistent over time with few LCPs recovering (see Moffitt et al., 1996). As ALs do not exhibit an early onset, they are unlikely to similarly experience high individual offending frequency and high average seriousness of offending.

Fourth, are the offenses committed by chronic offenders more serious on average? Chronic offenders should have both a high frequency and a high seriousness of offending over the life-course, though the outward manifestations of these acts may change over the life-course. Because LCPs make up the majority of chronic offenders, we would not expect ALs to be chronic and engaging in serious acts because they are seldom expected to engage in serious, person-oriented offenses.[1]

Fifth, it is not clear whether onset sequences are merely age-appropriate behavioral manifestations of some underlying theoretical construct (i.e., criminal potential–persistent heterogeneity) or whether the onset of one type of behavior facilitates or acts as a stepping stone towards the onset of another (i.e., state dependence). LCP-path offenders are believed to follow an age-appropriate behavioral manifestation of an underlying theoretical construct that conforms with the notion of persistent heterogeneity. Once the interaction between neuropsychological risk and disadvantaged environment is played out, LCPs begin with antisocial acts as children, graduate to more juvenile-type crimes in adolescence, including person-oriented offenses, then continue into adulthood engaging in all sorts of criminal and antisocial acts such as spouse abuse, income tax evasion, pilfering from the workplace, and so forth. There is some room for state dependence because by the very nature of their experiences, LCPs may become incarcerated, fail to finish school, and so forth such that these negative experiences cut off avenues toward prosocial activities. By and large however, their stepping-stone toward serious criminal activity is due to persistent heterogeneity. On the other hand, ALs tend not to follow any sort of stepping-stone approach. Their involvement in antisocial activity starts in the teenage years largely as a result of the interaction between the maturity gap and the peer social context (i.e., state dependence). Since ALs stop as adulthood ensues, their criminal activity ceases and does not graduate to a more serious level (i.e., person-oriented offenses). However, it should be noted that for some small sub-sample of ALs, events (such as pregnancy, drug addiction, incarceration) can occur that may ensnare them into a period of lengthier criminal involvement. Unfortunately, little is known about these snares, what they do to AL-path offenders, and the consequences of such snares.

Sixth, to what extent do risk factors for early onset have causal effects on offending? We know a good deal about between-individual differences, but what about within-individual differences? The taxonomy would predict that within-individual changes in the major risk factors for both LCPs and ALs would be followed by within-individual changes in offending. Among ALs, short-term situational factors such as peer delinquency should influence short-term within-individual variations in offending. Among LCPs, however, the initial causal process behind criminal and antisocial activity is set forth early in the life-course, and after the antisocial personality is constructed, short-term effects, such as situational factors, are relatively less relevant.

Seventh, little is known about risk factors, especially biological, peer, school, and neighborhood risk factors. The taxonomy would predict that biological and neighborhood risk factors would be particularly salient for LCPs and not ALs, while peer and school risk factors would matter for ALs and not LCPs. In a recent study, Piquero, Moffitt, and Lawton (2005) used data from the Baltimore site of the National Collaborative Perinatal Project to study race differences in the life-course-persistent pathway. Their analysis showed that several variables helped to explain differences between whites and blacks in the level of chronic offending measured to age 33. However, although black participants had higher mean levels of risk factors than whites, the developmental processes predicting chronic offending were the same across groups defined by race. Specifically, low birth weight in combination with adverse familial environments predicted chronic offending from adolescence to age 33 among white and African Americans alike, although the effect size reached statistical significance only among African Americans.

Relatedly, do the risk factors that cause onset also maintain offending (persistence)? In large part, the taxonomy would respond affirmatively. For ALs, the interaction between the maturity gap and the peer social context is expected to initiate and maintain delinquency, while among LCPs the interaction between neuropsychological risk and disadvantaged environment should also relate equally well to both initiation and persistence. What about risk factors for criminal career duration? Since ALs are not expected to exhibit lengthy careers, and LCPs are expected to exhibit lengthy criminal careers, we would expect that the risk factors that lead to initiation and persistence among LCPs, will also relate to career duration. This is so because the interaction between neuropsychological risk and disadvantaged environment is believed to be related to several similarly linked manifestations of LCP-type offending (Moffitt, 1994). A recent study by Piquero and his colleagues (2004) using data from a sample of parolees from the California Youth Authority indicated that poor cognitive test scores predicted lengthy criminal careers. Finally, what about protective factors? The taxonomy anticipates that LCPs will be exposed to few (if any) protective factors over the life-course. On the other hand, ALs, because of their non-injurious childhoods, good cognitive ability, and prosocial life skills, tend to be protected from continued criminal activity in adulthood. Thus, a defining distinction between the LCP versus AL groups of the taxonomy is the absence versus presence of protective factors in their lives.

Eighth, little is known about the types of life events that influence onset or continuation. The taxonomy does not anticipate that different risk factors will have different effects on antisocial activity at different ages for the two groups. In other words, the causes of criminal activity at age 15 for ALs should be similar to the causes of criminal activity at age 17 for ALs. The same should be the case for LCPs. The only type of life events that may be salient for continued criminal activity are the snares that may encapsulate ALs into continued criminal involvement. It is more rare for LCPs to be re-directed from their criminal paths, but among the small number of LCPs who show recovery, it remains unknown if life events were important (i.e., epiphanies, partner changes their ways, etc.).

Also, little is known about effects of the criminal justice system on persistence/desistance, and few developmental/life-course theories make expectations on this score. The taxonomy would predict that for both groups of offenders, criminal justice system contact is more negative than positive. In particular, among ALs, contact with the criminal justice system can ensnare individuals into a continued pathway of crime, while among LCPs, contact with the criminal justice system is likely to be viewed as routine hazard of their generally antisocial lives, and another factor contributing to the cumulative continuity of their antisocial lifestyle. Among both groups, the taxonomy would expect that criminal justice system contacts would operate in a labeling capacity knifing off other prosocial opportunities.

Ninth, the issue of intermittency is underdeveloped in most developmental/life-course theories. The fact that there may be gaps in offending has been well recognized, but researchers continue to know little about the factors that influence individuals for entering and exiting such gaps (Horney et al., 1995; Piquero et al., 2002; Piquero, 2004). Although the taxonomy is relatively silent about intermittency, we would expect that both AL-path and LCP-path offenders do not offend 24/7. Thus, looking over the criminal career of both groups of offenders, we would expect there to be several stops and starts. However, we would expect that intermittent periods grow longer and longer (and eventually show up as desistance) among ALs because of their early adulthood desistance. LCPs, however, are likely to continue to engage in all sorts of criminal and antisocial acts over their life-course such that intermittent periods will be marked more so by incarceration stints than by actual breaks from offending. Moffitt (2003) has recently reported intermittency characterized by a low-level chronic group in the Dunedin cohort. These men had been very aggressive as children, but evidenced no official delinquency and little self-reported delinquency as adolescents. However, they subsequently appeared in conviction registers as adults. Such individuals, who would be termed "adult onset" cases in a study relying on official crime record data, were revealed in the Dunedin study to have had serious and persistent conduct disorder from age 3 to 11 years. Thus, their antisocial behavior is more chronic than previously thought while being characterized by intermittency in adolescence.

Future empirical research should indicate how far these predictions are correct, incorrect, and/or in need of modification. We would also like to add that, in addition to age-differences in crime, a serious theory ought to address the race and sex difference as well. The taxonomy has already discussed this issue (Moffitt, 1994), and although a full discussion is beyond the remit of this chapter, information about how the taxonomy relates to race can be found in Piquero et al. (2005) and information about how the taxonomy relates to sex can be found in Moffitt et al. (2001).

Conclusion

The main aim of this chapter has been to (1) describe how Moffitt's developmental taxonomy fits into what we know about the development of offending over the life-course, (2) outline predictions regarding key empirical issues and answers to key theoretical and empirical questions, and (3) predict the outcomes of contentious developmental/life-course issues. Our review of the taxonomy and how it squares away with key facts about the development of offending over the life-course has led us to generate a number of important topics for future research.

First, it would be desirable to engage in empirical study of how Moffitt's developmental taxonomy explains life-course criminality compared to other developmental/life-course theories. This kind of research has provided important information (Paternoster et al., 1997; Paternoster and Brame, 1997; Simons et al., 1994, 1998), and following subjects well into adulthood should provide more concrete evidence.

Second, it would be of great interest to complete a detailed review of empirical evidence relevant to Moffitt's developmental taxonomy to assess particularly where the evidence might conflict with or challenge the taxonomy (Moffitt, 2003). It may also be useful to list more predictions from the theory that could be tested empirically in the future. These exercises may identify important places for revision and/or extension of the taxonomy.

Third, it is important to specify crucial tests, where predictions from Moffitt's taxonomy differ from predictions from other developmental/life-course theories. For example, both Sampson and Laub and Thornberry and Krohn suggest that early- and late-onset offenders differ more in degree than kind whereas Moffitt's taxonomy suggests that these two groups of offenders differ in kind, as well as in degree. This is a particularly important test because it strikes at the heart of the taxonomy.

Fourth, one of the central hypotheses of the taxonomy concerns the continuing of criminal activity among LCPs at least into mid-life. Given that this is a central expectation, future research should examine whether LCPs do in fact continue offending throughout the life-course or whether LCPs actually desist after a lengthy career (Sampson and Laub, 2003). The taxonomy should not be held to the "absolute stability" standard described earlier; instead, "individual-difference stability," that is, that throughout the life-course, LCPs should continue to manifest more antisocial activities than other men their age, should characterize LCP offenders.

Fifth, future tests of the taxonomy should not only continue to examine risk factors that distinguish ALs from LCPs, but also pay particular attention to protective factors, especially individual-level protective factors. It may be that some individuals react differently to major life events and that some individuals are protected from negative life events more so than other individuals (Caspi et al., 2002).

Sixth, future research with the taxonomy, as well as other developmental/life-course theories should compare development, risk factors, and life events for different ethnic/racial groups (Piquero et al., 2005) as well as for males and females (Moffitt et al., 2001). Unfortunately, there exists very little information regarding the patterning of criminal activity over the life-course across race and gender because most longitudinal studies only contain information for white males.

Finally, it would be important to compare predictions made both within and across developmental/life-course theories using both self-report and official records. Nagin and colleagues' (1995) analysis of data from the Cambridge Study uncovered that some offenders continued to offend via self-report records although they had appeared to desist via official records.

In the end, we hope that this chapter will provide readers with a detailed exposition of how Moffitt's taxonomy fits the conclusions of developmental/life-course criminology, how it answers the key theoretical and empirical issues described by Farrington in his Sutherland address, and what it would predict about several of the more "contentious" developmental/life-course issues. We will have succeeded in this task if researchers pick up on the several themes contained herein, attempt to seek answers to the future research directions described above, and most importantly, engage in the systematic comparison of developmental/life-course theories as they attempt to explain the patterning of criminal activity over the life-course.

Note

1.   We recognize that defining chronicity is somewhat arbitrary (Blumstein et al., 1986; Piquero, 2000; Wolfgang et al., 1972). Consider the following example using Wolfgang et al.'s 5+ cut-off for chronicity. Is someone who went sixteen years without committing an offense then commits five offenses at age seventeen a chronic offender? Or is someone who commits one offense per year for five years a chronic offender? Does each definition identify the same number of people? This is an important question that bears directly on key theoretical and empirical issues within the developmental/life-course criminology area. We believe that a new definition of chronicity is necessary, and that it should take into account both the number of offenses and the time period involved in offending.

References

Aguilar, Benjamin, Sroufe, L. Alan, Egeland, Byron, and Carlson, Elizabeth. (2000). Distinguishing the early-onset/persistent and adolescence-onset antisocial behavior types: From birth to 16 years. *Development and Psychopathology* 12: 109-132.

Arseneault, Louise, Tremblay, Richard E., Boulerice, B., and Saucier, J-F. (2002). Obstetric complications and adolescent violent behaviors: Testing two developmental pathways. *Child Development* 73: 496-508.

Bartusch, Dawn R. Jeglum, Lynam, Donald R., Moffitt, Terrie E., and Silva, Phil A. (1997). Is age important? Testing a general versus a developmental theory of antisocial behavior. *Criminology* 35: 13-48.

Blumstein, Alfred, Cohen, Jacqueline, Roth, Jeffrey A., and Visher, Christy A. (Eds.). (1986). *Criminal Careers and "Career Criminals."* Washington, DC: National Academy Press.

Britt, Chester L. (1992). Constancy and change in the U.S. age distribution of crime: A test of the "invariance hypothesis." *Journal of Quantitative Criminology* 8: 175-187.

Caspi, Avshalom, Lynam, Donald, Moffitt, Terrie E., and Silva, Phil A. (1993). Unraveling girls' delinquency: Biological, dispositional, and contextual contributions to adolescent misbehavior. *Developmental Psychology* 29: 19-30.

Caspi, Avshalom, McClay, Joseph, Moffitt, Terrie E., Mill, Jonathan, Martin, Judy, Craig, Ian W., Taylor, Alan, and Poulton, Ritchie. (2002). Role of genotype in the cycle of violence in maltreated children. *Science* 297: 851-854.

Farrington, David P. (2003). Developmental and life course criminology: Key theoretical and empirical issues. *Criminology,* 41: 221-255.

Farrington, David P., Jolliffe, Darrick, Hawkins, J. David, Catalano, Richard F., Hill, Karl G., and Kosterman, Rick (2003). Comparing delinquency careers in court records and self-reports. *Criminology,* 41: 933-958.

Gibson, Chris, Piquero, Alex R., and Tibbetts, Stephen G. (2001). The contribution of family adversity and verbal IQ relate to criminal behavior. *International Journal of Offender Therapy and Comparative Criminology* 45: 574-592.

Hirschi, Travis, and Gottfredson, Michael G. (1983). Age and the explanation of crime. *American Journal of Sociology* 89: 552-584.

Horney, Julie, Osgood, D. Wayne, and Marshall, Ineke Haen. (1995). Criminal careers in the short-term: Intra-individual variability in crime and its relation to local life circumstances. *American Sociological Review* 60: 655–73.

Kratzer, Lynn, and Hodgins, Sheilagh. (1999). A typology of offenders: A test of Moffitt's theory among males and females from childhood to age 30. *Criminal Behaviour and Mental Health* 9: 57-73.

Loeber, Rolf, and Snyder, Howard N. (1990). Rate of offending in juvenile careers: findings of constancy and change in Lambda. *Criminology* 28: 97–110.

Moffitt, Terrie E. (1993). "Life-course-persistent" and "adolescence-limited" antisocial behavior: A developmental taxonomy. *Psychological Review* 100: 674–701.

Moffitt, Terrie E. (1994). Natural histories of delinquency. In E. Weitekamp and H. Kerner (Eds.), *Cross-National Longitudinal Research on Human Development and Criminal Behaviour.* Amsterdam: Kluwer Academic Publishers.

Moffitt, Terrie E. (2003). Life-course-persistent and adolescence-limited antisocial behavior: A 10-year research review and a research agenda. In Benjamin B. Lahey, Moffitt, Terrie E., and Caspi, Avshalom (Eds.), *Causes of Conduct Disorder and Juvenile Delinquency.* New York: Guilford Press.

Moffitt, Terrie E., and Caspi, Avshalom. (2001). Childhood predictors differentiate life-course persistent and adolescence-limited pathways, among males and females. *Development and Psychopathology* 13: 355-375.

Moffitt, Terrie E., Lynam, Donald, and Silva, Phil A. (1994). Neuropsychological tests predict persistent male delinquency. *Criminology* 32: 277-300.

Moffitt, Terrie E., Caspi, Avshalom, Dickson, Nigel, Silva, Phil A., and Stanton, Warren. (1996). Childhood-onset versus adolescent-onset antisocial conduct in males: Natural history from age 3 to 18. *Development and Psychopathology* 8: 399-424.

Moffitt, Terrie E., Caspi, Avshalom, Rutter, Michael, and Silva, Phil A. (2001). *Sex Differences in Antisocial Behaviour: Conduct Disorder, Delinquency, and Violence in the Dunedin Longitudinal Study*. Cambridge: Cambridge University Press.

Nagin, Daniel S., Farrington, David P., and Moffitt, Terrie E. (1995). Life-course trajectories of different types of offenders. *Criminology* 33: 111-139.

Paternoster, Raymond, and Brame, Robert. (1997). Multiple routes to delinquency? A test of developmental and general theories of crime. *Criminology* 35: 49–84.

Paternoster, Raymond, Dean, Charles W., Piquero, Alex, Mazerolle, Paul, and Brame, Robert. (1997). Generality, continuity, and change in offending. *Journal of Quantitative Criminology* 13: 231-266.

Piquero, Alex R. (2000). Assessing the relationships between gender, chronicity, seriousness, and offense skewness in criminal offending. *Journal of Criminal Justice* 28: 103–16.

Piquero, Alex R. (2001). Testing Moffitt's neuropsychological variation hypothesis for the prediction of life-course persistent offending. *Psychology, Crime and Law* 7: 193-216.

Piquero, Alex R. (2004). The intermittency of criminal careers. In Shadd Maruna and Russ Immarigeon (Eds.), *Ex-Offender Reintegration: Pathways to Desistance from Crime*. London: Willan Publishing.

Piquero, Alex R., and Brezina, Timothy. (2001). Testing Moffitt's account of adolescence-limited delinquency. *Criminology* 39: 353-370.

Piquero, Alex R., and Tibbetts, Stephen G. (1999). The impact of pre/perinatal disturbances and disadvantaged environments in predicting violent crime. *Studies on Crime and Crime Prevention* 8: 52-70.

Piquero, Alex R., Paternoster, Raymond, Mazerolle, Paul, Brame, Robert, and Dean, Charles W. (1999). Onset age and offense specialization. *Journal of Research in Crime and Delinquency* 36: 275-99.

Piquero, Alex R., Brame, Robert, Mazerolle, Paul, and Haapanen, Rudy. (2002). Crime in emerging adulthood. *Criminology* 40: 137-70.

Piquero, Alex R., Farrington, David P., and Blumstein, Alfred. (2003). The criminal career paradigm: Background and recent developments. In Michael Tonry (Ed.), *Crime and Justice: A Review of Research, Volume 30*. Chicago: University of Chicago Press.

Piquero, Alex R., Moffitt, Terrie E., and Lawton, Brian. (2005). Race and crime: The contribution of individual, familial, and neighborhood level risk factors to life-course-persistent offending. In Darnell Hawkins and Kimberly Kempf-Leonard (Eds.), *Our Children, Their Children: Race, Crime, and the Juvenile Justice System*. Chicago: University of Chicago Press.

Piquero, Alex R., Brame, Robert, and Lynam, Donald. (2004). Studying criminal career length through early adulthood among serious offenders. *Crime & Delinquency* 50: 412-435.

Piquero, Alex R., Brezina, Timothy, and Turner, Michael G. (2005). Testing Moffitt's theory of abstention. *Journal of Research in Crime and Delinquency*, 42: 27-54.

Quetelet, Adolphe. (1831). *Research on the Propensity for Crime at Different Ages*. Cincinnati, OH: Anderson Publishing Company (1984 edition).

Sampson, Robert J., and Laub, John H. (1993). *Crime in the Making: Pathways and Turning Points through Life*. Cambridge, MA: Harvard University Press.

Sampson, Robert J., and Laub, John H. (2003). Life-course desistors? Trajectories of crime among delinquent boys followed to age 70. *Criminology*, 41: 555-592.

Shedler, J., and Block, J. (1990). Adolescent drug use and psychological health. *American Psychologist* 45: 612-630.

Simons, Ronald L., Wu, Chyi-In, Conger, Rand D., and Lorenz, Frederick O. (1994). Two routes to delinquency: Differences between early and late starters in the impact of parenting and deviant peers. *Criminology* 32: 247–76.

Simons, Ronald L., Johnson, Christine, Conger, Rand D., and Elder, Jr., Glen. (1998). A test of latent trait versus life-course perspectives on the stability of adolescent antisocial behavior. *Criminology* 36: 217-43.

Steffensmeier, Darrell J., Allan, Emilie Andersen, Harer, Miles D., and Streifel, Cathy. (1989). Age and the distribution of crime. *American Journal of Sociology* 94: 803-31.

Tibbetts, Stephen G., and Piquero, Alex R. (1999). The influence of gender, low birth weight, and disadvantaged environment in predicting early onset of offending: A test of Moffitt's interactional hypothesis. *Criminology* 37: 843-878.

Wolfgang, Marvin E., Figlio, Robert M., and Sellin, Thorsten. (1972). *Delinquency in a Birth Cohort*. Chicago: University of Chicago Press.

4

The Integrated Cognitive Antisocial
Potential (ICAP) Theory

David P. Farrington

In explaining individual criminal behavior, there are two rather different questions that need to be addressed:

1.   Why do people become offenders?
2.   Why do people commit offenses?

In the past, developmental criminologists have mainly focused on the first question, but it is also important to study the second. The first question is chiefly concerned with between-individual differences in the development of criminal potential (the potential to commit crimes). So a key question is: Why do some people have a relatively high potential to commit crimes in different situations, while others have a relatively low potential? The second question is mainly concerned with how the potential becomes the actuality of crimes in different situations. In other words, it is concerned with within-individual differences in the commission of crimes, or why crimes are more likely to be committed in some times and places than in others. Another key question is: Why is a person more likely to commit crimes in some situations than in others?

It follows that the commission of crimes depends partly on the individual, partly on the situation, and no doubt partly on the interaction between the individual and the situation, although less is known about this. The fundamental distinction between explaining the development of offenders and explaining the commission of offenses has not always been appreciated. Nor has the fundamental distinction between explaining between-individual differences in criminal potential and explaining within-individual differences in the commission of offenses. These fundamental distinctions are the starting point for my developmental/life-course (DLC) theory.

Between-Individual Differences vs. Within-Individual Change

Most research in criminology focuses on biological, individual, family, peer, school, community, and socioeconomic factors influencing offending, and on between-individual differences. Implications are then drawn from this research for the prevention or reduction of offending. For example, it is often found that offenders are more impulsive than nonoffenders, and so it is deduced that cognitive-behavioral skills training programs that reduce impulsivity should lead to a reduction in offending. As another example, it is often found that offenders received more inconsistent parental child-rearing methods than nonoffenders, and so it is deduced that parent training techniques that make child-rearing more consistent should lead to a reduction in offending.

The problem with these seemingly logical deductions is that they depend on within-individual change: if a person becomes less impulsive over time, that person will as a consequence decrease offending over time. And yet, knowledge about risk factors for offending is overwhelmingly based on between-individual research, showing for example that offenders are more impulsive than nonoffenders. Can we really draw valid conclusions about within-individual change from research on between-individual differences? This is a key question that needs to be addressed.

More research is needed on the relationship between within-individual changes in risk factors and within-individual changes in offending. For example, in the Cambridge Study in Delinquent Development, which is a prospective longitudinal survey of over 400 South London males from age 8 to age 48 (Farrington, 2003), the relationship between unemployment and crime was investigated by seeing whether each male committed more offenses during his periods of unemployment than during his periods of employment.

The results showed that the males did indeed commit more offenses while unemployed than while employed (Farrington et al., 1986). Furthermore, the difference was only found for offenses involving material gain, such as theft, burglary, robbery and fraud, which the males committed at a higher rate during periods of unemployment. They did not commit more offenses of other types (violence, vandalism, or drug use) during periods of unemployment than during periods of employment. These results suggested that the key link in the causal chain between unemployment and crime was a shortage of money: unemployment caused a shortage of money, which in turn caused offending to get money. It seemed very unlikely that unemployment caused boredom, which in turn caused offending to reduce boredom, such as violence, vandalism and drug use.

This type of within-individual research is more causally compelling than the corresponding between-individual research (Farrington, 1988). For example, in the Cambridge Study we also showed that unemployed males committed more offenses than employed males, or in other words that between-individual differences in unemployment predicted and correlated with between-individual differences in offending. This demonstrates that unemployment is a risk factor for offending but not, of course, that unemployment is a cause of offending. The problem is that unemployed males differ from employed males in many respects, and it is very difficult to disentangle the effects of unemployment from the effects of other explanatory variables.

For example, more antisocial males are more likely to be unsatisfactory employees and more likely to be fired (and hence unemployed) than less antisocial males. Lower-class males by definition have unskilled manual jobs. These jobs tend to be short term, so these males tend to have periods of unemployment between jobs, and hence are more likely to be unemployed than upper-class or middle-class males. Therefore, it is difficult to know whether unemployment causes offending, whether being antisocial causes unemployment, or whether lower-class males are both more likely to be unemployed and more likely to offend without there being any causal effect of unemployment on crime.

In within-individual research, long-term persisting individual characteristics such as antisociality or social class are held constant (and hence controlled) because the comparison is between an individual while unemployed and the same individual while employed. By carrying out quasi-experimental analyses addressing threats to internal validity (Cook and Campbell, 1979; Shadish et al., 2002), convincing conclusions about causes can be drawn from such research. It follows that more within-individual research is needed in criminology. This of course requires more prospective longitudinal studies.

Research is also needed that systematically compares results obtained in within-individual analyses and between-individual analyses. In the Pittsburgh Youth Study, which is a prospective longitudinal survey of over 1,500 Pittsburgh boys, Farrington et al. (2002) found that poor parental supervision predicted a boy's delinquency both between and within individuals, but peer delinquency predicted a boy's delinquency between individuals but not within individuals. In other words, variations in peer delinquency within individuals (from one assessment to the next) did not predict variations in a boy's delinquency over time. They suggested that peer delinquency might not be a cause of a boy's delinquency but might instead be measuring the same underlying construct (perhaps reflecting co-offending: see Reiss and Farrington, 1991). The message is that risk factors that predict offending between individuals may not predict offending within individuals, so that implications drawn from between-individual comparisons about interventions may not be valid.

The Integrated Cognitive Antisocial Potential (ICAP) Theory

Bernard and Snipes (1996) argued that there were too many theories and that competitive testing of theories was rarely appropriate. Instead, they recommended more of a "risk factor" approach focusing on the percentage of variance explained, the independent predictive power of different variables and the direction of causation. They argued that this approach facilitated theory-testing and was also policy-relevant.

For many years I did not attempt to formulate a wide-ranging developmental/life-course (DLC) theory of offending. In line with Bernard and Snipes (1996), I focused on identifying independently predictive risk factors, testing specific hypotheses (e.g., about the effects of unemployment on offending: see Farrington et al., 1986), and on investigating possible causal mechanisms intervening between risk factors and offending (e.g., why criminal parents tended to have delinquent sons: see West and Farrington, 1977, chap. 6). However, I was criticized for being "atheoretical," for focusing on empirical variables rather than underlying theoretical constructs. Therefore, encouraged by Joan McCord, I proposed a tentative theory in 1992 (Farrington, 1992). This chapter sets out the latest development of my DLC theory.

Figure 4.1 shows the key elements of this theory, which was primarily designed to explain offending by lower-class males, although it may apply to females as well. I have called it the "Integrated Cognitive Antisocial Potential" (ICAP) theory. It integrates ideas from many other theories, including strain, control, learning, labelling, and rational choice approaches; its key construct is antisocial potential (AP); and it assumes that the translation from antisocial potential to antisocial behavior depends on cognitive (thinking and decision-making) processes that take account of opportunities and victims. Figure 4.1 is deliberately simplified in order to show the key elements of the ICAP theory on one sheet of paper; for example, it does not show how the processes operate differently for onset compared with desistance or at different ages.

The key construct underlying offending is antisocial potential, which refers to the potential to commit antisocial acts. I prefer the term "potential" rather than "propensity," because propensity has more biological connotations. "Offending" refers to the most common crimes of theft, burglary, robbery, violence, vandalism, minor fraud, and drug use, and to behavior that in principle might lead to a conviction in Western industrialized societies such as the United States and the United Kingdom. Long-term persisting between-individual differences in AP are distinguished from short-term within-individual variations in AP. Long-term AP depends on impulsiveness, on strain, modelling and socialization processes, and on life events, while short-term variations in AP depend on motivating and situational factors.

Regarding long-term AP, people can be ordered on a continuum from low to high. The distribution of AP in the population at any age is highly skewed; relatively few people have relatively high levels of AP. People with high AP are more likely to commit many different types of antisocial acts including different types of offenses. Hence, offending and antisocial behavior are versatile not specialized. The relative ordering of people on AP (long-term between-individual variation) tends to be consistent over time, but absolute levels of AP vary with age, peaking in the teenage years, because of changes within individuals in the factors that influence long-term AP (e.g., from childhood to adolescence, the increasing importance of peers and decreasing importance of parents).

A key issue is whether the model should be the same for all types of crimes or whether different models are needed for different types of crimes. Because of their focus on the development of offenders, DLC researchers have concluded that, since offenders are versatile rather than specialized, it is not necessary to have different models for different types of crimes. For example, it is believed that the risk factors for violence are essentially the same as for property crime or substance abuse. However, researchers who have focused on situational influences (e.g., Clarke and Cornish, 1985) have argued that different models are needed for different types of crimes. It is suggested that situational influences on burglary may be very different from situational influences on violence.

One possible way to resolve these differing viewpoints would be to assume that long-term potential was very general (e.g., a long-term potential for antisocial behavior), whereas short-term potential was more specific (e.g., a short-term potential for violence). The top half of the model in Figure 4.1 could be the same for all types of crimes, whereas the bottom half could be different (with different situational influences) for different types of crimes.

In the interests of simplification, Figure 4.1 makes the DLC theory appear static rather than dynamic. For example, it does not explain changes in offending at different ages. Since it might be expected that different factors would be important at different ages or life stages, it seems likely that different models would be needed at different ages. Perhaps parents are more important in influencing children, peers are more important in influencing adolescents, and spouses and partners are more important in influencing adults.

Long-Term Risk Factors

A great deal is known about risk factors that predict long-term persisting between-individual differences in antisocial potential. For example, in the Cambridge Study, the most important childhood risk factors for later offending were hyperactivity-impulsivity-attention deficit, low intelligence or low school attainment, family criminality, family poverty, large family size, poor child-rearing, and disrupted families (Farrington, 2003). A risk factor, by definition, is a factor that predicts a relatively high probability of later offending.

I have not included measures of antisocial behavior (e.g., aggressiveness or dishonesty) as risk factors because of my concern with explanation, prevention, and treatment. These measures do not cause offending; they predict offending because of the underlying continuity over time in AP. Measures of

Figure 4.1
The Integrated Cognitive Antisocial Potential (ICAP) Theory

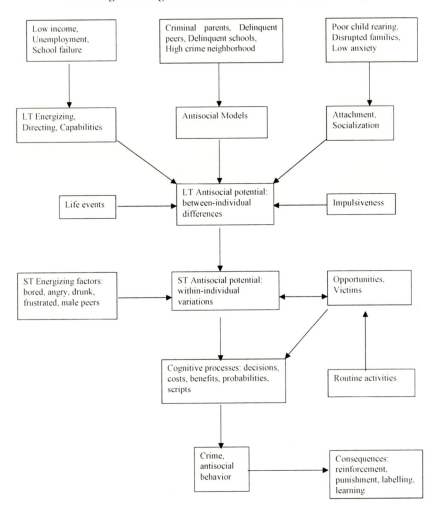

Note: LT = Long-Term; ST = Short-Term

antisocial behavior are useful in identifying risk groups but less useful in identifying causal factors to be targeted by interventions. Similarly, I have not
included variables that cannot be changed, such as gender or ethnicity. I assume that their relationships with offending are mediated by changeable risk
factors.

In the risk factor prevention paradigm (Farrington, 2000), the basic idea is
very simple: Identify the key risk factors for offending and implement preven-

tion methods designed to counteract them. Although the emphasis is on prevention, knowledge about risk factors can also be used to guide interventions after offending. Of course, a key question is whether the risk factors for offending (or for the onset of offending) are the same as or different from the risk factors for reoffending (or for the persistence of offending). Perhaps different models are needed in Figure 4.1 for onset, persistence, escalation, de-escalation, and desistance.

A major problem is to decide which risk factors are causes and which are merely markers or correlated with causes. Ideally, interventions should be targeted on risk factors that are causes. Interventions targeted on risk factors that are merely markers will not necessarily lead to any decrease in offending. Unfortunately, when risk factors are highly intercorrelated (as is usual), it is very difficult to establish which are causes in between-individual research. For example, the particular factors that appear to be independently important as predictors in any analysis may be greatly affected by measurement error and by essentially random variations between samples.

It is also important to establish how risk factors or causes have sequential or interactive effects on offending. Figure 4.1 shows how risk factors are hypothesized to influence long-term AP. Following strain theory, the main energizing factors that potentially lead to high long-term AP are desires for material goods, status among intimates, excitement and sexual satisfaction. However, these motivations only lead to high AP if antisocial methods of satisfying them are habitually chosen. Antisocial methods tend to be chosen by people who find it difficult to satisfy their needs legitimately, such as people with low income, unemployed people, and those who fail at school. However, the methods chosen also depend on physical capabilities and behavioral skills; for example, a 5-year-old would have difficulty in stealing a car. For simplicity, energizing and directing processes and capabilities are shown in one box in Figure 4.1. Ideally, I should develop an electronic map of my theory that allows people to click on different boxes to see more underlying detail, as with electronic street maps.

Long-term AP also depends on attachment and socialization processes. AP will be low if parents consistently and contingently reward good behavior and punish bad behavior. (Withdrawal of love may be a more effective method of socialization than hitting children.) Children with low anxiety will be less well socialized, because they care less about parental punishment. AP will be high if children are not attached to (prosocial) parents, for example if parents are cold and rejecting. Disrupted families (broken homes) may impair both attachment and socialization processes.

Long-term AP will also be high if people are exposed to and influenced by antisocial models, such as criminal parents, delinquent siblings, and delinquent peers, for example in high crime schools and neighborhoods. Long-term AP will also be high for impulsive people, because they tend to act without thinking about the consequences. Also, life events affect AP; it decreases (at least for males) after people get married or move out of high crime areas, and it increases after separation from a partner.

There may also be interaction effects between the influences on long-term AP. For example, people who experience strain or poor socialization may be disproportionally antisocial if they are also exposed to antisocial models. In the interests of simplicity, Figure 4.1 does not attempt to show such interactions.

Figure 4.1 shows some of the processes by which risk factors have effects on AP. It does not show biological factors but these could be incorporated in the theory at various points. For example, the children of criminal parents could have high AP partly because of genetic transmission, excitement-seeking could be driven by low cortical arousal, school failure could depend partly on low intelligence, and high impulsiveness and low anxiety could both reflect biological processes.

DLC researchers have particularly studied individual and family factors, and we know a great deal about these. Less is known about biological risk factors for offending, or about interactions between biological and psychosocial risk factors (Raine et al., 1997). Similarly, less is known about community or neighborhood risk factors, or about the development of offending in different neighborhood contexts.

Many researchers have measured only one risk factor (e.g., impulsivity) and have shown that it predicts or correlates with offending after controlling for a few other "confounding factors," often including social class. The message of Figure 4.1 is: Don't forget the big picture. The particular causal linkages shown in Figure 4.1 may not be correct, but it is important to measure and analyze all important risk factors in trying to draw conclusions about the causes of offending or the development of offenders.

Ideally, protective factors should be measured as well as risk factors. The risk factor prevention paradigm suggests that risk factors should be reduced while protective factors are enhanced. Often, programs focusing on protective factors (e.g., building on strengths, promoting healthy development) are more attractive to communities and consequently easier to implement than programs focussing on risk factors (which seem to emphasize undesirable features of communities and hence imply blame).

Unfortunately, both the definition and existence of protective factors are controversial. On one definition, a protective factor is merely the opposite end of the scale to a risk factor. Just as a risk factor predicts an increased probability of offending, a protective factor predicts a decreased probability. However, to the extent that explanatory variables are linearly related to offending, researchers may then object that risk and protective factors are merely different names for the same underlying construct.

Another possible definition of a protective factor is a variable that interacts with a risk factor to minimize the risk factor's effects (Rutter, 1985). Such interactive variables are often termed "moderators" (Baron and Kenny, 1986). If poor parental supervision predicted a high risk of offending only for males from low income families, and not for males from high income families, then high income might be regarded as a protective factor that counteracted the effects of the risk factor of poor parental supervision. Problems associated with the definition of protective factors may be alleviated by focusing on resilience or psychosocial skills and competencies.

From Risk Factors to Causal Mechanisms

The main problem with the risk factor prevention paradigm is that, while the most important risk factors are well established, there is a great deal of controversy about the intervening causal mechanisms that influence offending. Figure 4.1 is an over-simplification of the complex reality, as indeed all theories have to be. It is important to investigate links between risk factors and offending by testing alternative causal mechanisms or intervening processes between risk factors and offending. For example, large family size (a large number of children in the family) is a highly replicable predictor of offending (Farrington and Loeber, 1999), but it is not clear what is the key causal mechanism.

There are at least five possibilities. First, large family size could cause less supervision or attention per child, and this poorer child-rearing could cause long-term AP. Second, antisocial parents could have both large families and antisocial children, without there being any causal link between these. Third, large families could cause overcrowded households, which in turn could cause long-term AP because of more conflict, frustration, and competition for resources. Fourth, the larger the family, the more likely that children will be influenced by antisocial sibling models rather than by parents. Fifth, large families may be poorer than others, and poverty may cause long-term AP. While it is important not to lose sight of the big picture in Figure 4.1, it is also desirable to carry out smaller-scale studies to investigate causal mechanisms underlying one particular risk factor such as large family size.

As another example of investigating possible causal mechanisms, Juby and Farrington (2001) tested different explanations of the relationship between disrupted families and offending in the Cambridge Study. Most explanations fall within three theories. Trauma theories suggest that the loss of a parent has a damaging effect on a child, most commonly because of the effect on attachment to the parent. Life-course theories focus on separation as a sequence of stressful experiences, and on the effects of multiple stressors such as parental conflict, parental loss, reduced economic circumstances, changes in parent figures and poor child-rearing methods. Hence, what happens to the child after the separation is important. Selection theories argue that disrupted families produce delinquent children because of preexisting differences from other families in risk factors such as parental conflict, criminal or antisocial parents, low family income or poor child-rearing methods. These other variables are important in causing offending, not the family disruption.

Juby and Farrington (2001) concluded that the results favored life-course theories rather than trauma or selection theories. Contrary to trauma theories, the cause of the family disruption mattered: Families broken by disharmony produced higher delinquency rates than families broken by death. While boys from broken homes (permanently disrupted families) were more delinquent than boys from intact homes, they were not more delinquent than boys from intact high conflict families. Contrary to selection theories, the higher delinquency rates of boys from broken families held up after controlling for other predictors of delinquency, such as low family income, large family size, criminal parents, and poor parental supervision. In agreement with life-course theories, the most important factor was the post-disruption trajectory. Boys who remained with their mother after the separation had the same delinquency rate as boys from intact low conflict families. However, boys who remained with their father, with relatives or with others (e.g., foster parents) had high delinquency rates. The results were similar whether convictions or self-reported delinquency were studied.

Juby and Farrington (2001) concluded that some kinds of disrupted families were criminogenic (e.g., those where the boy did not remain with his mother), just as some kinds of intact families were criminogenic (e.g., those characterized by high parental conflict). Equally, some kinds of disrupted families (e.g., those where the boy remained with a lone mother) were no more criminogenic than intact harmonious families. This research again shows the need to investigate the causal mechanisms linking risk factors and offending.

In principle, a great deal can be learned about the causes of offending from the results of intervention experiments. For example, if an intervention that improves school success leads to a decrease in offending in a randomized experiment (e.g., Schweinhart et al., 1993), this might be good evidence that school failure is a cause of offending (assuming that alternative hypotheses can be eliminated). In practice, however, most intervention experiments in the past have been primarily designed to evaluate a technology rather than to test a causal hypothesis. Because of the previously widespread but erroneous belief that "nothing works," experimenters have been very concerned to maximize the likelihood that their intervention will lead to a reduction in offending.

This concern to demonstrate a desirable effect, together with the intercorrelations between long-term risk factors, has encouraged researchers to use multi-modal interventions. For example, in the Seattle Social Development Project, Hawkins et al. (1999) simultaneously used child skills training, parent training, and teacher training in classroom management in an intervention beginning in first grade (age 6). Their intervention was successful in reducing violence, alcohol abuse, and sexual promiscuity up to age 18. However, because this was a multi-modal program, it is difficult to know which was the active ingredient, and conversely difficult to conclude that any one of the targeted risk factors (e.g., childhood impulsivity, poor parental child-rearing, poor classroom management) was clearly a cause of offending.

Multi-modal interventions tend to be more effective than those using only a single modality (Wasserman and Miller, 1998). However, more intervention experiments should be designed so that conclusions can be drawn about which risk factors are causes (Robins, 1992).

Explaining the Commission of Crimes

According to the ICAP theory, the commission of offenses and other types of antisocial acts depends on the interaction between the individual (with his immediate level of AP) and the social environment (especially criminal opportunities and victims). Short-term AP varies within individuals according to short-term energizing factors such as being bored, angry, drunk, or frustrated, or being encouraged by male peers. Criminal opportunities and the availability of victims depend on routine activities. Encountering a tempting opportunity or victim may cause a short-term increase in AP, just as a short-term increase in AP may motivate a person to seek out criminal opportunities and victims.

Whether a person with a certain level of AP commits a crime in a given situation depends on cognitive processes, including considering the subjective benefits, costs, and probabilities of the different outcomes and stored behavioral repertoires or scripts (Clarke and Cornish, 1985; Huesmann and Eron, 1989). The subjective benefits and costs include immediate situational factors such as the material goods that can be stolen and the likelihood and consequences of being caught by the police. They also include social factors such as likely disapproval by parents or female partners, and encouragement or reinforcement from peers. In general, people tend to make decisions that seem rational to them, but those with low levels of AP will not commit offenses even when (on the basis of subjective expected utilities) it appears rational to do so. Equally, high short-term levels of AP (e.g., caused by anger or drunkenness) may induce people to commit offenses when it is not rational for them to do so.

The consequences of offending may, as a result of a learning process, lead to changes in long-term AP and in future cognitive decision-making processes. This is especially likely if the consequences are reinforcing (e.g., gaining material goods or peer approval) or punishing (e.g., receiving legal sanctions or parental disapproval). Also, if the consequences involve labelling or stigmatizing the offender, this may make it more difficult for him to achieve his aims legally, and hence may lead to an increase in AP. (It is difficult to show these feedback effects in Figure 4.1 without making it very complex.)

A further issue that needs to be addressed is how far types of offenders might be distinguished. Perhaps some people commit crimes primarily because of their high long-term AP (e.g., the life-course-persistent offenders of Moffitt,

1993) and others primarily because of situational influences and high short-term AP. Perhaps some people commit offenses primarily because of situational influences (e.g., getting drunk frequently) while others offend primarily because of the way they think and make decisions when faced with criminal opportunities. From the viewpoint of both explanation and prevention, research is needed to classify types of people according to their most influential risk factors and most important reasons for committing crimes.

It is desirable to link up studies of the development of offenders with studies of situational influences on offending by asking about influences on criminal events in prospective longitudinal studies. In the Cambridge Study, we asked about why people committed crimes. The most common reasons given for property offenses were utilitarian, rational, or economic ones: offenses were committed for material gain (West and Farrington, 1977). The next most common reasons might be termed hedonistic: offenses were committed for excitement, for enjoyment, or to relieve boredom. In general, utilitarian motives predominated for most types of property offenses such as burglary and theft, except that vandalism and motor vehicle theft were committed predominantly for hedonistic reasons, and shoplifting was partly utilitarian and partly hedonistic. Offenses at younger ages (under 17) were relatively more likely to be committed for hedonistic reasons, while offenses at older ages (17 or older) were relatively more likely to be committed for utilitarian reasons.

Reasons for aggressive acts (physical fights) were also investigated (Farrington et al., 1982). The key dimension was whether the male fought alone or in a group. In individual fights, the male was usually provoked, became angry, and hit out in order to hurt his opponent and to discharge his own internal feelings of tension. In group fights, the male often said that he became involved in order to help a friend or because he was attacked, and rarely said that he was angry. The group fights were more serious, occurring in bars or streets, and they were more likely to involve weapons, produce injuries, and lead to police intervention. Fights often occurred when minor incidents escalated, because both sides wanted to demonstrate their toughness and masculinity and were unwilling to react in a conciliatory way.

Psychologists tend to be doubtful about the value of asking people why they committed crimes (Farrington, 1993). It has been argued that people are lacking in introspective insight about the motives underlying their behavior, and/or that their memories are faulty or biased. Psychologists prefer to carry out experiments. More than twenty years ago, I carried out a series of experiments to investigate situational influences on offending using the lost letter technique (Farrington and Knight, 1979; Farrington and Knight, 1980). Stamped, addressed, apparently lost, unsealed letters, each containing a handwritten note and (except for control conditions) an amount of cash, were left on the streets of London, and picked up by members of the public (who were observed). The dependent variable was whether the cash was returned to the intended recipient. The amount of cash and the content of the note were varied.

Three experiments showed that people were more likely to steal when more cash was involved and that they were more likely to steal from a male victim than from a female victim. In general, men and women were equally likely to steal. The probability of stealing varied dramatically from 20 percent (when the victim was a female receiving a refund from a senior citizen's outing) to 78 percent (when the victim was a male enclosing money for *Yachting Monthly*). This suggested that, depending on the apparent victim, almost everyone would steal or almost no one would steal.

These types of real-life experiments on factors influencing the commission of crimes can be extremely informative. Most of our knowledge about offending is based on non-experimental studies using indirect and biased measures of offending such as official records or self-reports. Criminologists should carry out more research on situational influences on offending, preferably using experimental methods and systematic observation.

Answers to Key Questions

The key DLC empirical questions (see chapter 1) are answered as follows:

Q1:   Why do people start offending?
A1:   Because of: (a) increasing long-term AP, (b) increasing short-term AP, (c) changed decision-making processes:
(a)   is caused by increasing long-term motivation (e.g., desires for material goods, status, sex, and excitement), increasing physical capabilities and skills, and changes in socialization influences (decreasing importance of parents, increasing importance of peers).
(b)   is caused by increasing short-term motivation (e.g., more likely to be bored, angry, drunk, or frustrated) and increasing opportunities for offending because of changes in routine activities (e.g., going out more).
(c)   occurs because the subjective expected utility of offending increases (e.g., because of the greater importance of peer approval and lesser importance of parental disapproval).
Q2:   How are onset sequences explained?
A2:   Behavioral manifestations of the underlying AP vary over time because of changes in routine activities, opportunities, and victims, and in decision-making processes.
Q3:   Why is there continuity in offending?
A3:   There is continuity in offending because the relative ordering of people on long-term AP stays fairly consistent over time.
Q4:   Why do people stop offending?
A4:   Because of (a) decreasing long-term AP, (b) decreasing short-term AP, (c) changed decision-making processes:
(a)   is caused by decreasing long-term motivation, decreasing impulsiveness, a greater ability to satisfy needs legally, decreasing physical capabilities, changes in socialization influences (decreasing importance of peers, increasing importance of female partners and children), and life events such as getting married, having children, moving home, and getting a steady job.

(b)   is caused by decreases in short-term energizing factors (less bored, angry, drunk, frustrated), and decreasing opportunities for offending because of changes in routine activities (e.g., going out less with male peers).

(c)   occurs because the subjective expected utility of offending decreases (e.g., because of the lesser importance of peer approval and greater importance of female partner disapproval, because the subjective cost of being caught increases).

Q5:   Why does prevalence peak in the teenage years?

A5:   The prevalence of offending increases up to the teenage years because of the processes specified in A1 and decreases after the teenage years because of the processes specified in A4.

Q6:   Why does early onset predict a long criminal career?

A6:   Because early onset reflects a high level of long-term AP, and the relative ordering of people on long-term AP stays fairly consistent over time.

Q7:   Why is there versatility in offending and antisocial behavior?

A7:   Because all types of antisocial behavior, including offending, depend on the underlying AP as well as on situational factors and decision-making processes.

Q8:   Why does co-offending decrease from adolescence to adulthood?

A8:   Because boys offend mainly with male peers, and peer influence is more important in adolescence.

Q9:   Why are there between-individual differences in offending?

A9:   These reflect between-individual differences in long-term AP, which reflect strain, modelling, socialization, impulsiveness, and life events.

Q10:   What are the key risk factors for onset and desistance, and how can they be explained?

A10:   The key risk factors for onset are present in childhood and adolescence: coming from a low income family, school failure, impulsiveness, criminal parents, delinquent peers, delinquent schools, bad neighborhoods, erratic parental child-rearing, poor parental supervision, disrupted families, and low anxiety. In general, these childhood and adolescent risk factors will also predict persistence as opposed to desistance, because they predict a relatively high level of AP. However, later risk factors are also important for desistance. The key factors influencing desistance are present in adulthood: getting a steady job, getting married, having children, moving out of the city, decreasing physical capabilities (e.g., poor health), going out less, drinking less, spending less time with male peers.

Q11:   Why are there within-individual differences in offending?

Q11a: Long-term (over life):

A11a: This is explained in A1 and A4. Changes in risk factors and life events over time are assumed to cause changes in long-term AP within individuals.

Q11b: Short-term (over time and place):

A11b: People are more likely to offend at certain times and in certain places because of short-term variations in AP. In turn, short-term variations in AP are caused by short-term variations in energizing factors and in opportunities and victims as a consequence of routine activities.

Q12:   What are the main motives and reasons for offending?

A12:   The main motives change from adolescence to adulthood. In adolescence, the main motives are for excitement or enjoyment or to obtain material goods. After age 20, utilitarian motives become increasingly dominant.

Q13:   What are the effects of life events on offending?

A13:   Life events can affect long-term and short-term variations in AP:

A13a: Major life transitions such as getting a steady job, getting married and moving home affect long-term AP (e.g., because of changes in strain, socialization and models; arrows not shown in Figure 4.1).

A13b: Transitory life events such as an argument with a female partner can cause a short-term increase in anger and frustration that causes a short-term increase in AP.

A13c: The consequences of offending (getting convicted and legally punished, as opposed to getting away with crime) can affect the subjective expected utility of offending in the decision-making process.

The key DLC theoretical questions (see chapter 1) are answered as follows:

Q1:   What is the key construct underlying offending?

A1:   Antisocial potential (AP).

Q2:   What factors encourage offending?

A2:   (a) Long-term and (b) short-term factors.

A2a: Long-term factors include strain factors (low income, school failure), impulsiveness, and antisocial models.

A2b: Short-term factors include energizing factors (e.g., bored or angry), opportunities and victims, and a high subjective expected utility of offending.

Q3:   What factors inhibit offending?

A3:   To some extent these are the opposite of those specified in A2. However, there are more specific (a) long-term and (b) short-term inhibiting factors.

A3a: Attachment and socialization processes (based on loving parents who use consistent child-rearing methods) reduce long-term AP, as do life events such as getting married, moving out of the city, and getting a steady job.

A3b: A low level of short-term AP and a low subjective expected utility of offending (e.g., because of the fear of legal punishment) will reduce the likelihood of committing offenses.

Q4:   Is there a learning process?

A4:   There are at least two learning processes in the theory. The first describes the socialization processes of parents in child-rearing and the second describes the learning process that is contingent on the consequences of offending. In addition, the effects of antisocial models (e.g., delinquent peers) could involve learning as well as imitation.

Q5:   Is there a decision-making process?

A5:   Yes. Generally, people make decisions that seem rational to them, but other factors also influence whether crimes are committed (e.g., stored behavioral repertoires and the short-term level of AP).

Q6:   What is the structure of the theory?

A6:   This is shown in a simplified form in Figure 4.1. Separate figures could be shown for different age ranges or different processes (e.g., onset versus desistance).

Q7:   What are operational definitions of theoretical constructs?

A7:   AP could be inferred from measures of antisocial behavior. However, it might be objected that this is tautological, if AP is simultaneously measured by and used to explain antisocial behavior (Akers, 2000: 7; Vold et al., 2002: 192). Alternatively, antisocial attitude could be used as a measure of AP that is independent of antisocial behavior, or AP could be viewed as a latent or unobservable variable (Osgood and Rowe, 1994). Another possibility is to measure AP by using hypothetical questions about how people think they would behave in criminal opportunities (Farrington and Knight, 1980). Figure 4.1 shows both empirical variables (e.g., criminal parents) and theoretical constructs (e.g., antisocial models). Decision-making processes could be investigated using interviews, vignettes, or experiments.

Q8:   What does the theory explain?

A8:   The theory is designed generally to explain within-individual and between-individual variations in male offending throughout life, and more specifically to explain the findings listed in the section on "What do we know?"

Q9:   What does the theory not explain?

A9:   The theory is not designed to explain variations in crime rates (e.g., between countries, between areas of a country, over time). It includes peer influence and co-offending, but it is not designed to explain gang development or gang activities. The theory is not specifically designed to explain gender and race differences in offending, although it could be extended to do so. For example, it could be suggested that the basic structure of the theory was the same for males and females but that risk factors had different effects. Possibly, long-term and short-term energizing factors such as the desire for excitement and the influence of male peers may be less important for females, attachment and socialization processes may be more effective for females, impulsiveness may be lower for females, routine activities may be different for females, and females may be more affected by life events such as having a child.

Q10:   What findings might challenge the theory?

A10a: The theory does not propose types of offenders or trajectories (e.g., adolescent-limited versus life-course-persistent) but assumes that offending reflects an underlying continuum of AP.

A10b: The theory does not propose developmental pathways or sequences in which an early behavior acts as a stepping-stone towards a later behavior but assumes that there are different behavioral manifestations of AP over time.

A10c: The theory assumes that the consequences following a crime can change the future probability of offending, and hence that state dependence occurs. Hence, a pure persistent heterogeneity explanation would challenge the theory.

A10d: The theory does not focus on protective factors, although some influences could be interpreted as protective (e.g., the attachment and socializing effects of parents, or the effects of life events such as getting married and moving home).

A10e: The theory does not explain individual development in different neighborhoods (Loeber and Wikström, 1993).

A10f: The theory assumes that different factors influence onset and desistance. Hence, if the same factors influenced both (as Gottfredson and Hirschi, 1990, argued), this would challenge the theory.

Q11:   How much does the theory make different predictions from other DLC theories?

A11:   Chapter 10 summarizes major DLC theories and compares their assumptions with those of the ICAP theory.

Predictions About Contentious Issues

The ICAP theory makes the following predictions about the contentious issues listed in chapter 1. First, it predicts that the individual offending frequency and the seriousness of offending should increase to a peak in the teenage years and then decline, because both reflect AP. Second, the ICAP theory predicts that an early age of onset of offending predicts a high individual offending frequency and a high average seriousness of offending, again because both reflect AP. An early age of onset indicates a relatively high level of AP, and the ordering of people on AP tends to stay relatively consistent over time. Similarly, chronic offenders should have both a high frequency and a high seriousness of offending. Third, the ICAP theory predicts that onset sequences generally are age-appropriate behavioral manifestations of AP and hence that they reflect persistent heterogeneity. However, the ICAP theory also incorporates learning and labelling processes following offending, so this would predict some state dependence effects.

Fourth, the ICAP theory predicts that within-individual changes in the major risk factors would be followed by within-individual changes in AP and hence in offending. Fifth, the ICAP theory predicts that short-term energizing factors such as heavy drinking influence short-term within-individual variations in offending: why people commit offenses in some times and places but not others. Sixth, the ICAP theory predicts that different risk factors would influence early onset before age 20, continuation of offending after onset, later onset after age 20, and persistence or desistance of offending after age 20. This is because it assumes that risk factors have different effects on AP at different ages. Seventh, the ICAP theory predicts that the criminal justice system should have deterrent or labeling effects on future offending. Future research should indicate how far these predictions are correct or incorrect.

Conclusions

DLC researchers should study short-term influences on why people commit crimes as well as long-term influences on why people become offenders. They should aim to explain both between-individual differences in the development of antisocial potential and within-individual differences in the commission of crimes. They should carry out prospective longitudinal studies with frequent data collection in order to compare between-individual and within-individual relationships with offending. More quasi-experimental analysis of the effects of life events on offending should be carried out, based on within-individual data, to draw more convincing conclusions about causes.

Much is known about individual and family risk factors for offending. More research is needed on biological and community risk factors in particular. More research is also needed on protective factors, linked to intervention experiments targeting protective factors. DLC researchers should carry out experimental and quasi-experimental studies designed to establish which risk factors are causes, and study sequential and interactive effects of risk factors on offending. Also, they should conduct smaller-scale research to investigate intervening processes and causal mechanisms linking risk factors and offending.

DLC researchers should carry out more research on explaining why crimes are committed, and especially on situational influences and on cognitive, decision making and learning processes involved in offending. Research should also be conducted on interactions between individual and situational factors in explaining the commission of crimes. Research is also needed to classify types of people according to their most influential risk factors and most important reasons for committing crimes. Questions about situational influences on offending should be included in longitudinal studies of the development of offenders, and situational experiments should be carried out.

It is important to specify how DLC theories would explain well-established results and what predictions they would make about contentious issues. I have tried to do this here for the ICAP theory. However, it would be desirable to complete a more detailed review of empirical evidence relevant to this theory to assess particularly where the evidence might conflict with or challenge the theory. It would also be advantageous to list more predictions from the theory that could be tested empirically in the future. This would probably require a book-length manuscript.

More detailed electronic models of the theory should be developed, with more explicit specification of theoretical constructs and empirical variables. It would be better to make quantitative rather than qualitative predictions; criminological theories typically predict that X is related to Y or that X is greater than Y, but not the magnitude of relationships. It is particularly important to specify crucial tests, where predictions from the ICAP theory differ from predictions from another DLC theory.

It is not difficult to specify desirable research. In order to advance knowledge about DLC theories and DLC issues, prospective longitudinal studies are needed with repeated self-report and official record measures of offending. Many of the criminal career results of the 1980s were largely based on official records, and it is important to establish how far they are replicated (or not) in self-reports. Of course, self-reports reveal more offenses, but they often show similar results to official records in issues such as how the prevalence of offending varies with age, the fact that early onset predicts a long career and many offenses, continuity and versatility of offending, chronic offenders, and onset sequences.

It would also be desirable to derive implications for intervention from DLC theories, and to test these in randomized experiments. In principle, conclusions about causes can be drawn more convincingly in experimental research than in non-experimental longitudinal research (Robins, 1992). Future studies should compare within-individual changes in risk factors with within-individual changes in offending, and test hypotheses about causal processes intervening between risk factors and offending.

Future longitudinal studies should follow people up to later ages and focus on desistance processes. Past studies have generally focused on ages up to 30 and on onset. Future studies should compare risk factors for early onset, continuation after onset (compared with early desistance), frequency, seriousness, later onset, and persistence versus desistance. DLC theories should make explicit predictions about all these topics. Future studies should investigate sequences of onsets of antisocial behaviors and offending to test persistent heterogeneity versus state dependence hypotheses. Also, future studies should make more effort to investigate protective factors and biological, peer, school, and neighborhood risk factors. And future research should compare development, risk factors and life events for males versus females and for different ethnic and racial groups.

While I have laid out a daunting research agenda, I am happy to end on an optimistic note. Given the current state of DLC theories and DLC knowledge, there seems great scope for cumulative advancement of knowledge and for widespread agreement about key facts that need to be explained and key assumptions that need to be included in DLC theories.

References

Akers, R. L. (2000). *Criminological Theories: Introduction, Evaluation, and Application* (3rd ed.). Los Angeles: Roxbury.

Baron R. M. & Kenny, D. A. (1986). The moderator-mediator variable distinction in social psychological research: Conceptual, strategic and statistical considerations. *Journal of Personality and Social Psychology,* 51: 1173-1182.

Bernard, T. J. & Snipes, J. B. (1996). Theoretical integration in criminology. In M. Tonry (Ed.), *Crime and Justice,* Vol. 20 (pp. 301-348). Chicago: University of Chicago Press.

Clarke R. V. & Cornish, D. B. (1985). Modelling offenders' decisions: A framework for research and policy. In M. Tonry & N. Morris (Eds.), *Crime and Justice,* Vol. 6. (pp. 147-185) Chicago: University of Chicago Press.

Cook, T. D. & Campbell, D. T. (1979). *Quasi-Experimentation: Design and Analysis Issues for Field Settings.* Chicago: Rand McNally.

Farrington, D. P. (1988). Studying changes within individuals: The causes of offending. In M. Rutter (Ed.) *Studies of Psychosocial Risk: The Power of Longitudinal Data* (pp. 158-183). Cambridge: Cambridge University Press.

Farrington, D. P. (1992). Explaining the beginning, progress, and ending of antisocial behavior from birth to adulthood. In J. McCord (Ed.), *Facts, Frameworks and Forecasts.* Advances in Criminological Theory, Vol. 3 (pp. 253-286). New Brunswick, NJ: Transaction Publishers.

Farrington, D. P. (1993). Motivations for conduct disorder and delinquency. *Development and Psychopathology,* 5: 225-241.

Farrington, D. P. (2000). Explaining and preventing crime: The globalization of knowledge—The American Society of Criminology 1999 Presidential Address. *Criminology,* 38: 1-24.

Farrington, D. P. (2003). Key results from the first 40 years of the Cambridge Study in Delinquent Development. In T. P. Thornberry & M. D. Krohn (Eds.), *Taking Stock of Delinquency: An Overview of Findings from Contemporary Longitudinal Studies* (pp. 137-183). New York: Kluwer/Plenum.

Farrington, D. P., Berkowitz, L. & West, D. J. (1982). Differences between individual and group fights. *British Journal of Social Psychology,* 21:323-333.

Farrington, D. P., Gallagher, B., Morley, L., St. Ledger, R. J. & West, D. J. (1986). Unemployment, school leaving and crime. *British Journal of Criminology,* 26: 335-356.

Farrington, D. P. & Knight, B. J. (1979). Two non-reactive field experiments on stealing from a "lost" letter. *British Journal of Social and Clinical Psychology,* 18: 277-284.

Farrington, D. P. & Knight, B. J. (1980). Stealing from a "lost" letter: Effects of victim characteristics. *Criminal Justice and Behavior,* 7: 423-436.

Farrington, D. P. & Loeber, R. (1999). Transatlantic replicability of risk factors in the development of delinquency. In P. Cohen, C. Slomkowski & L. N. Robins (Eds.),

Historical and Geographical Influences on Psychopathology (pp. 299-329). Mahwah, NJ: Lawrence Erlbaum.

Farrington, D. P., Loeber, R., Yin, Y. & Anderson, S. J. (2002). Are within-individual causes of delinquency the same as between-individual causes? *Criminal Behavior and Mental Health,* 12: 53-68.

Gottfredson, M. R. & Hirschi, T. (1990). *A General Theory of Crime.* Stanford, CA: Stanford University Press.

Hawkins, J. D., Catalano, R. F., Kosterman, R., Abbott, R. & Hill, K. G. (1999). Preventing adolescent health risk behaviors by strengthening protection during childhood. *Archives of Pediatrics and Adolescent Medicine,* 153: 226-234.

Huesmann, L. R. & Eron, L. D. (1989). Individual differences and the trait of aggression. *European Journal of Personality,* 3: 95-106.

Juby, H. & Farrington, D. P. (2001). Disentangling the link between disrupted families and delinquency. *British Journal of Criminology,* 41: 22-40.

Loeber, R. & Wikström, P-O. H. (1993). Individual pathways to crime in different types of neighborhood. In D. P. Farrington, R. J. Sampson & P-O. H. Wikström (Eds.), *Integrating Individual and Ecological Aspects of Crime* (pp. 169-204). Stockholm, Sweden: National Council for Crime Prevention.

Moffitt, T. E. (1993). Adolescence-limited and life-course-persistent antisocial behavior: A developmental taxonomy. *Psychological Review,* 100, 674-701.

Osgood, D. W. & Rowe, D. C. (1994). Bridging criminal careers, theory, and policy through latent variable models of individual offending. *Criminology,* 32: 517-554.

Raine, A., Brennan, P. A. & Farrington, D. P. (1997). Biosocial bases of violence: Conceptual and theoretical issues. In A. Raine, P. A. Brennan, D. P. Farrington & S. A. Mednick (Eds.), *Biosocial Bases of Violence* (pp. 1-20). New York: Plenum.

Reiss, A. J. & Farrington, D. P. (1991). Advancing knowledge about co-offending: Results from a prospective longitudinal survey of London males. *Journal of Criminal Law and Criminology,* 82: 360-395.

Robins, L. N. (1992). The role of prevention experiments in discovering causes of children's antisocial behavior. In J. McCord & R. E. Tremblay (Eds.), *Preventing Antisocial Behavior: Interventions from Birth through Adolescence* (pp. 3-18). New York: Guilford.

Rutter. M. (1985). Resilience in the face of adversity: Protective factors and resistance to psychiatric disorder. *British Journal of Psychiatry,* 147: 598-611.

Schweinhart, L. J., Barnes, H. V. & Weikart, D. P. (1993). *Significant Benefits.* Ypsilanti, MI: High/Scope.

Shadish, W. R., Cook, T. D. & Campbell, D, T, (2002). *Experimental and Quasi-Experimental Designs for Generalized Causal Inference.* Boston: Houghton-Mifflin.

Vold, G. B., Bernard, T. J. & Snipes, J. B. (2002). *Theoretical Criminology* (5th ed.). Oxford, England: Oxford University Press.

Wasserman, G. A. & Miller, L. S. (1998). The prevention of serious and violent juvenile offending. In R. Loeber & D. P. Farrington (Eds.), *Serious and Violent Juvenile Offenders: Risk Factors and Successful Interventions* (pp. 197-247). Thousand Oaks, CA: Sage.

West, D. J. & Farrington, D. P. (1977). *The Delinquent Way of Life.* London: Heinemann.

5

Mediating the Effects of Poverty, Gender, Individual Characteristics, and External Constraints on Antisocial Behavior: A Test of the Social Development Model and Implications for Developmental Life-Course Theory*

Richard F. Catalano, Jisuk Park, Tracy W. Harachi,
Kevin P. Haggerty, Robert D. Abbott, and
J. David Hawkins

Introduction

This chapter has two parts. The first part is an exposition of the social development model (SDM) (Catalano & Hawkins, 1996) and a test of the degree to which the social development processes specified by the SDM mediate the effects of individual and environmental factors, specifically, low socioeconomic status, gender, individual characteristics, and external constraints, on antisocial behavior in early adolescence. The second part discusses how the SDM addresses key empirical and theoretical issues of developmental/life-course theory. It provides perspective on the similarities and differences between the SDM and other developmental life-course theories in this volume.

Social Developmental Processes as Mediators of Known Environmental and Individual Predictors of Antisocial Behavior

The development of antisocial behavior is influenced by multiple sources including factors located in the individual, the family, school experiences, in the peer group, and in the community (Farrington, 1989; Farrington & Loeber,

*Supported by grant number R01 DA08093 from the National Institute for Drug Abuse. The authors gratefully acknowledge the Edmonds School District #15 for its support and cooperation in the Raising Healthy Children Program.

1995; Hawkins, Arthur, & Catalano, 1995; Hawkins, Catalano, & Miller, 1992; Hawkins, Hill, Guo, & Battin-Pearson, 2002; Herrenkohl, Hawkins, Chung, Hill, & Battin-Pearson, 2000; Kandel, Simcha Fagan, & Davies, 1986; Rutter, 1990). Theory specifies the mechanisms through which these multiple predictors interact in the etiology of antisocial behavior (Bursik & Grasmick, 1996). The social development model (Catalano & Hawkins, 1996; Farrington & Hawkins, 1991; Hawkins & Weis, 1985) incorporates knowledge of empirical predictors into a theory of human behavior. It is consistent with efforts to develop integrated theory in criminology (e.g., Elliott, Huizinga, & Ageton, 1985; Flay & Petraitis, 1994; Hepburn, 1976; Messner, Krohn, & Liska, 1989). The social development model (SDM) has been found to predict various forms of antisocial behavior in childhood (Catalano, Kosterman, Hawkins, Newcomb, & Abbott, 1996), as well as substance use (Catalano et al., 1996), alcohol misuse (Lonczak et al., 2001), and violence (Huang, Kosterman, Catalano, Hawkins, & Abbott, 2001) at age 18. These tests have shown that the SDM fits empirical data well, and explains between 9 and 45 percent of the variance in the outcomes studied. Six other publications have used SDM constructs to organize analyses to predict a range of behavior outcomes including serious delinquency and substance use among aggressive boys (O'Donnell, Hawkins, & Abbott, 1995); alcohol use and dependence at age 21 (Guo, Hawkins, Hill, & Abbott, 2001); officially recorded crime to age 32 (Farrington & Hawkins, 1991); escalation and desistence from antisocial behavior at age 18 (Ayers et al., 1999; Williams, Van Dorn, Hawkins, Abbott, & Catalano, 2001); youth violence at age 18 (Herrenkohl et al., 2001); and alcohol abuse and dependence at age 21 (Guo et al., 2001).

While these tests in multiple data sets provide support for the social development processes hypothesized by the SDM, these studies have not tested whether the effects of known individual and environmental predictors of antisocial behavior, specifically sociodemographic factors, individual characteristics, and external constraints, are mediated by social development processes as hypothesized by the social development model (Catalano & Hawkins, 1996). In the SDM, these predictors are seen as exogenous to social developmental processes. They are categorized into three exogenous constructs: (1) position in the social structure including socioeconomic status and gender; (2) constitutional factors including poor concentration, shyness and early aggressiveness; and (3) external constraints including parent, school, and legal constraints on behavior. Each of these constructs has been shown to predict antisocial behavior (Dishion, Patterson, Stoolmiller, & Skinner, 1991; Gottfredson & Hirschi, 1990; Herrenkohl et al., 2000; Lipsey & Derzon, 1998; Loeber & Stouthamer Loeber, 1998; Moffitt, 1983; Patterson, 1982). Catalano and Hawkins (1996) hypothesized that the effects of these factors on antisocial behavior are fully mediated by the social development processes specified by the SDM.

A recent test of the SDM that included indicators of position in the social structure found that social development processes generalized across gender and class (Fleming, Catalano, Oxford, & Harachi, 2002). However, this analysis did not examine the degree to which social development processes mediated the effects of gender and class on antisocial behavior. This chapter examines the degree to which the effects of poverty, gender, individual characteristics, and external constraints on antisocial behavior are mediated by social development processes as hypothesized by the SDM using data spanning grades 3 through 8 from the Raising Healthy Children study.

The Social Development Model

The social development model integrates ideas drawn from three theoretical perspectives. Social control theory suggests that crime is a function of weak bonding with prosocial groups like family and school. Hirschi (1969) found that prosocial bonds of attachment, commitment, and belief provide protection against delinquency. Social learning theory argues that criminal behavior is learned through the reinforcement and punishment of such behavior (Akers, 1977; Bandura, 1973, 1977; Conger, 1976). The theory hypothesizes that criminal behavior is primarily learned in those groups or contexts that comprise the individual's major source of reinforcements. Key tenets of social learning theory have been supported in predicting antisocial behavior (Dishion et al., 1991; Fagan & Wexler, 1987). Differential association theory (Cressey, 1953; Matsueda, 1982, 1988; Sutherland, 1973) hypothesizes that antisocial behaviors are learned in interaction with other persons in a process of communication within intimate personal groups. A person is more likely to become delinquent if he or she is exposed to persons who are favorable to violations of the law relative to those who are not. Substantial evidence exists for the effects of delinquent peers on delinquent behavior during adolescence (Agnew, 1991; Benda & Whiteside, 1995; Reinarman & Fagan, 1988; Thornberry, Lizotte, Krohn, Farnworth, & Jang, 1994).

The social development model integrates key features of differential association, social learning, and social control theories to more fully describe causal and mediating processes hypothesized to predict behavior over the course of development (Catalano & Hawkins, 1996).

The general social development model is shown in Figure 5.1. The SDM hypothesizes that individuals learn patterns of behavior, whether prosocial or antisocial. The theory includes two socialization pathways, a prosocial path and an antisocial path, and hypothesizes that social development follows the same processes, whether it produces prosocial or antisocial behavior. Children are socialized through four social development processes: (1) perceived opportunities for involvement in activities and interactions with others, (2) the degree of involvement and interaction, (3) the skill to participate in these in-

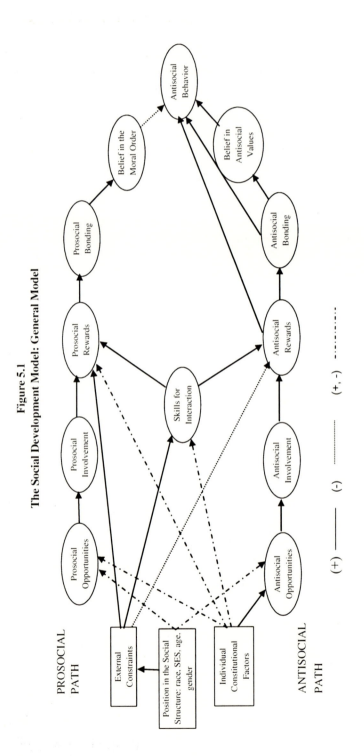

Figure 5.1
The Social Development Model: General Model

volvements and interactions, and (4) the reinforcement they perceive from these involvements and interactions. When opportunities and skills are commensurate and performance is rewarded, a social bond develops between those individuals and the socializing unit. The social bond consists of attachment or emotional connection, and commitment to, or investment in, the group or socializing unit. Once strongly established, this social bond has power to affect behavior independent of the above four processes. This social bond influences behaviors through the establishment of an individual's "stake" in conforming to the norms and values of the socializing unit. It is hypothesized that an individual's behavior will be prosocial or antisocial depending on the predominant behaviors, norms, and values held by those to whom the individual is bonded. The SDM departs from differential association theory which specifies that it is only exposure or involvement, not bonding, that is necessary to adopt the norms of the group, and departs from control theory, which asserts that bonding always inhibits deviance, by accounting for evidence that bonds with drug-involved and delinquent peers (Agnew, 1991; Cairns, Cairns, Neckerman, Gest, & Gariepy, 1988) and family members (Fleming, Brewer, Gainey, Haggerty, & Catalano, 1997; Foshee & Bauman, 1992) predict higher levels of drug use and delinquency in children. It extends differential association and social learning theory by asserting the importance of bonding in shaping behavior. It incorporates differential association theory in explicitly including both prosocial and antisocial paths. However, rather than the moderation effect of definitions favorable to law violations (normative beliefs) most often associated with differential association theory, the SDM follows Matsueda's (1988) and Sutherland's (1973) interpretation that there is "variation in the strength and content of both prosocial and antisocial motives, beliefs, and justifications. Variations in these applications, and not necessarily an oppositional normative system, give rise to normative conflict and constitute the crucial elements of definitions favorable to law violations" (p. 125). Thus, recognizing that many individuals experience both prosocial and antisocial influences, the SDM hypothesizes that one of the determinants of an individual's behavior is the degree of bonding to prosocial and antisocial individuals, and, in turn, the degree of adoption of associated beliefs, that is belief in the moral order or belief in antisocial values.

Direct paths to antisocial behavior from the prosocial path come from belief in the moral order, which is expected to inhibit problem behavior. In contrast, as indicated in Figure 5.1, the social development model hypothesizes three direct predictors of antisocial behavior from the antisocial path. The direct link from each predictor indicates a different etiological path to antisocial behavior. Antisocial behaviors are hypothesized to be directly caused by: (a) perceived rewards for antisocial interaction and involvement in problem behavior, (b) attachment and commitment to antisocial others or lines of action, and (c) belief in antisocial values. The first path to antisocial behavior hypothesizes that an individual can choose to engage in antisocial behavior simply for the rewards the individual perceives as forthcoming from the behavior. The personal calculation of reward is sufficient to produce antisocial behavior when low bonding to prosocial others results in low perceived costs of antisocial behavior (Hirschi, 1969) or when the perceptions of risks of detection, and thus, costs of antisocial behavior, are perceived as low. Attachment to those engaged in antisocial behavior and commitment to antisocial lines of action also are expected to directly increase antisocial behavior. Bonds of attachment and commitment may form to peers engaged in antisocial behavior and these attachments and commitments motivate involvement in antisocial behavior. These hypotheses are supported by Agnew's findings that "Delinquent Friends (Serious) has the greatest effect on delinquency when the adolescent is attached to these friends, spends much time with them, feels they approve of his or her delinquency and feels pressure from them to engage in delinquency" (1991: 64). Further, commitment to a deviant line of action is hypothesized to develop when deviant involvement and interaction consistently produce profit of rewards over costs, such that one decides to forego prosocial involvements for antisocial ones. This type of commitment does not imply value reversal; rather, it may imply rationalizations or acceptance of deviance when "preferred alternatives are out of reach" (Kornhauser, 1978: 243). Finally, antisocial behavior is hypothesized to be predicted by the internalization of norms or beliefs favorable to criminal involvement as illustrated by the reported belief structure of those engaged in organized crime (Bonanno, 1983).

The social development model identifies three constructs that research has shown predict crime and delinquency as exogenous, that is, distal predictors that affect the social development processes. These are: (1) position in the social structure, (2) external constraints, and (3) individual constitutional factors. The effects of these variables are hypothesized to be fully mediated by the social development processes described earlier. Position in the social structure includes socioeconomic status, age, gender, and race. The relationship between extreme poverty and antisocial behavior is well established (Elliott, Huizinga, & Menard, 1989; Hawkins, Catalano, Morrison et al., 1992). Extensive evidence exists for bivariate relationships between age, gender, and race with antisocial behavior (see for example, Elliott, 1994; Giordano & Cernkovich, 1997; Gottfredson & Hirschi, 1990). The SDM hypothesizes that these variables define the social structural context that affects the distribution of opportunities available to the individual. Thus, these social-structural characteristics are expected to affect behavior through their effects on prosocial and antisocial opportunity.

External constraints are formal and informal social controls on behavior that affect the degree of reinforcement one perceives for involvement in behavior. These include the explicit clarity of rules, laws, expectations for behavior, and monitoring of behavior (Conger, 1980; Oxford, Harachi, Catalano, & Abbott,

2001; Patterson, Reid, & Dishion, 1992; Peterson, Hawkins, Abbott, & Catalano, 1994).

Individual constitutional factors are stable personal characteristics of individuals that are associated with higher rates of antisocial behavior. These include characteristics such as difficult temperament, including frequent negative mood states, (Lerner & Vicary, 1984), early-onset depression (Burns et al., 2000; Mesman & Koot, 2000), aggressive behavior (Kellam, Rebok, Ialongo, & Mayer, 1994; Lewis, Robins, & Rice, 1985; Loeber, 1988; Tremblay & LeMarquand, 2000), and hyperactivity and attention-deficit disorders (Farrington, 1989; Hawkins et al., 2002; Herrenkohl et al., 2000; Rabiner & Coie 2000).

The SDM hypothesizes that the effects of position in the social structure, individual constitutional factors and external constraints on antisocial behavior are fully mediated by other social development processes experienced by individuals. This chapter tests this proposition.

Methods

Sample

The data used here are from the Raising Healthy Children project, a longitudinal study with an experiment nested within it (see Haggerty, Catalano, Harachi, & Abbott, 1998). The study population consisted of two grade cohorts, first- and second-grade students, in ten suburban public elementary schools in a Pacific Northwest school district. Schools were randomly assigned to intervention or control condition after being matched on variables known to be associated with antisocial behavior (low income status, ethnicity, single-parent families, low reading scores, high absenteeism, and mobility). Eligibility criteria for student participation in the study included: attending a mainstream classroom; remaining in the project school from baseline through the completion of the first student survey in May and June of 1994; and having a parent who spoke English, Spanish, Korean, or Vietnamese. The school principal and the principal investigator contacted eligible families by letter and then personal visits were made by project staff to explain the study and gain written voluntary consent. In the first two years of the project 1,040 students (76 percent of those eligible) were recruited into the study.

The sample consists of 82 percent European American, 7 percent Asian/Pacific Islander, 4 percent African American, 4 percent Hispanic, and 3 percent Native American students. Forty-six percent of the students are female. The mean age for children at grades 7 and 8 was 13.6 years. Twenty-eight percent were from low-income families based on parental report of receiving AFDC or TANF, food stamps, or eligibility for the free/reduced lunch program in third or fourth grade.

Parent, student, and teacher interviews were conducted annually. Telephone interviews with parents were conducted by trained interviewers. The child survey was group-administered by staff interviewers at school. As an incentive, parents received $15-20 and students received a small gift. Completion rates for parent survey were 91.7 percent at year three, 87.7 percent at year five, 87.5 percent at year six, and 89.5 percent at year seven; completion rates for student survey were 96.9 percent at year three, 91.2 percent at year five, 91.4 percent at year six, and 91.3 percent at year seven; completion rates for teacher report of students were 95.4 percent at year three, 88.2 percent at year five, 87.4 percent at year six, and 88.6 percent at year seven.

Measures

Multiple indicators of each latent construct were developed for use in confirmatory factor analysis and structural equation modeling. Multiple indicators were constructed for each latent variable specified by the model. Each social development indicator was the mean of Z-scored items that represented domains of community, school, family, and peer so that each indicator is a cross-domain composite. Where possible, indicators also included items from multiple reporters (Bandalos & Finney, 2001; MacCallum, Widaman, Zhang, & Hong, 1999). Items were coded so that higher scores reflect more of the indicated construct. Constructs exogenous to the social development processes were measured at grades 3 and 4, and social development mediating factors were measured at grades 5 and 6 and grades 6 and 7 depending on the cohort. Antisocial behavior was measured 1 year after the social development factors were measured, at grades 7 and 8.

Position in the Social Structure was represented by two measured dichotomous variables representing gender and whether the child lived in a low-income household. If a child received free or reduced price lunch in grade 3 or 4 or the parent received public assistance or food stamps, the child was designated low income. Each of these variables was a measured variable because each has hypothesized independent effects on social development processes. The SDM also identifies age and race as indicators of position in the social structure. However these indicators were not included in the present analyses because this sample did not vary greatly on them.

Individual Constitutional Factors (F1, V1-V4) was modeled as a latent variable with four indicators: depression, poor concentration, shyness/withdrawal, and early antisocial behavior. The depression indicator combined items measuring whether subjects feel like crying, are tired, and are upset much of the time. The poor concentration indicator combined items asking both students and teachers whether subjects have trouble paying attention in class and following directions. The shyness/withdrawal indicator combined items of teacher's assessment of the level of child's shyness and withdrawal. The early antisocial behavior indicator combined teacher's ratings of whether the child argues a lot, talks back to adults, and take others' property.

External Constraints (F2, V5-V7) consisted of parental monitoring, norms, and rules. The three indicators combined items asking youths' perceptions of parental knowledge of their whereabouts, friends, and activities the youth is involved in; parent's ratings of their expectation for the youth calling if he/she is going to be late; knowledge of whether the child came home on time; youth's perception of the likelihood of getting caught drinking; and parents' and youth's ratings regarding the clarity and existence of rules regarding issues such as homework, television, alcohol use, and bedtime.

Perceived Opportunities for Prosocial Involvement (F3, V8-V10) was modeled as a latent construct with three indicators which combined items asking whether students have opportunities to do things with their parents and participate in family decisions and activities; and whether students had opportunities at school to take part in class and get help from their teachers and other students.

Perceived Opportunities for Antisocial Involvement (F4, V11-V13): Indicators combined items asking whether lots of kids in their neighborhood got in trouble; the amount of crime and drug selling in their neighborhood; the accessibility to alcohol, cigarettes, and marijuana; the percentage of students at school who use alcohol and cigarettes; and whether they have parents who use alcohol, cigarettes, and drugs.

Involvement in Prosocial Activities (F5, V14-V16): Because the SDM hypothesizes that children will behave consistent with the norms and values of those they are bonded to, it is important to determine if those with whom they are involved should be viewed as prosocial or antisocial influences. Thus, we first created a variable that indicated whether parents were involved with high levels of alcohol use, drug use, or violence. Those who were not were identified as prosocial. Indicators of involvement in prosocial activities then were developed that combined items asking how often subjects interacted with prosocial parents. Other items included frequency of participating in extracurricular activities and time spent with friends approved of by parents.

Interaction with Those Involved in Antisocial Behaviors (F6, V17-V19): Indicators combined items asking how often subjects interacted with "problem involved" parents; involvement in family substance use (e.g., lighting a cigarette or pouring a drink for a family member); and involvement with friends who got in trouble.

Skills for Interaction (F7, V20-V22): Items for these indicators consisted of parent, child, and teacher report of the child's ability to make friends, share, listen to others, and understand others' feelings; the child's ability to control his/her temper; and the child's ability to solve problems and think before acting.

Perceived Rewards for Prosocial Involvement (F8, V23-V25): Indicators assessed whether parents and teachers complimented the subjects for doing well; the frequency of parents' praise or reward; and whether subjects are satisfied with school and its environment.

Perceived Rewards for Antisocial Involvement (F9, V26-V28): Items for these indicators asked whether subjects would be caught and punished for skipping school, whether their parents let them get away with misbehavior, and whether they thought drinking and fighting were cool.

Bonding (Attachment and Commitment) to Prosocial Others and Activities (F10, V29-V31): Indicators combined items asking whether subjects were close to, shared with, and wanted to emulate their "non-problem" parents; whether subjects liked their teacher, their school, and their classwork; and whether they were close to prosocial friends.

Bonding (Attachment and Commitment) to Antisocial Others and Activities (F11, V32-V34): These indicators combined questions about sharing with and the desire to be like "problem" parents; and whether respondents reported bonding to friends who drank alcohol, smoked cigarettes/marijuana, skipped school, and got into fights.

Belief in the Moral Order (F12, V35-V37): Items for these indicators assessed whether subjects believed in following the family rules, the importance of being honest with parents, and whether they helped other kids in need.

Belief in Antisocial Values (F13, V38-V40): These indicators assessed subjects' beliefs about doing things that they were not supposed to do; whether they thought it okay to cheat, lie, and take something without asking; and whether they would drink and smoke.

Antisocial Behavior (F14, V41-V44): The four indicators consisted of drug use, school problems, violence, and non-violent delinquency. The drug use indicator combined items measuring frequency of alcohol, cigarette, marijuana, and other illegal drug use in the past year. The school problem indicator combined items asking whether subjects received a school suspension/discipline slip, whether they have been expelled, and whether they have been removed from class in the past school year. The violence indicator combined items measuring frequency of fighting in the past year; hitting someone with the idea of hurting her/him, and throwing objects at cars or people. The non-violent delinquency indicator combined items asking whether subjects took other's property and broke things on purpose.

Analysis

Since some of the students in this sample are part of a prevention program, preliminary analyses were conducted to examine whether the program affected the structural relationships for experimental and control groups. The results indicated that the covariance structures were not different between experimental and control groups.[1] Based on these results, the subjects from the experimental and control groups were combined in the following analyses.

Analyses were carried out in Mplus 2.02 (Muthén & Muthén, 2001). Confirmatory factor analyses were run as a first step to determine the adequacy of factor loadings, model fit, and the pattern of intercorrelations among the latent factors. Selected error terms were allowed to covary to account for conceptual correspondence between variables. Next, a theoretical model was tested by including structural paths hypothesized by the social development model. The overall model fit was assessed by examining the Comparative Fit Index (CFI) (Bentler, 1990) which indicates an adequate fit with values around .90 or greater (Newcomb, 1994), and Root Mean Squared Error of Approximation (RMSEA), which indicates an adequate fit with values around .05 or less (Browne & Cudeck, 1993; MacCallum, Browne, & Sugawara, 1996).

Missing Data Analysis Strategies

Three outlier cases reporting extreme levels of antisocial behavior were excluded, and the nominal sample size of $N = 1,037$ was provided to Mplus to generate unbiased test statistics and standard errors. The present study used the full information maximum likelihood (FIML) missing data estimator available in Mplus 2.02 (Muthén & Muthén, 2001). This method provides unbiased parameter estimates and helps avoid potential bias associated with alternative procedures for handling missing data, such as list-wise or pair-wise deletion, or mean substitution (Little & Rubin, 1987; Schafer & Graham, 2002).

Results

Measurement Model

A confirmatory factor analysis (CFA) was run on the social development model constructs shown in Figure 5.1. In this analysis, all factor loadings (except for one indicator per factor fixed to 1.00) and all factor variances were estimated freely. All factor intercorrelations were freed, and for one construct, belief in the moral order, one pair of indicator error terms was allowed to correlate freely in order to account for the stronger relationship within the construct.

All factor loadings were significant and in the expected direction (see Table 5.1). The CFA model also fit the data reasonably well, $c^2_{(870)} = 2232.62$; CFI = .93, and RMSEA = .04. Factor intercorrelations were in the expected direction with positive correlations among prosocial constructs, among antisocial constructs, and negative correlations between prosocial and antisocial constructs. Correlations, means, and standard deviations for all indicators are available from the first author.

The significant correlations between antisocial behavior and external constraints, individual constitutional factors, gender, and free lunch eligibility

Table 5.1
Factor Loadings and Robust Z-Statistics for the Measurement Models

Measures			Standardized Factor Loading	Robust Z-Statistic
F1	Individual	V1 (depression)	.33	
	Constitutional Factors	V2 (low concentration)	.64	8.95
		V3 (withdrawal)	.24	5.57
		V4 (antisocial behavior)	.62	8.91
F2	External	V5	.62	
	Constraints	V6	.72	14.12
		V7	.67	13.92
F3	Prosocial	V8	.73	
	Opportunities	V9	.69	17.81
		V10	.48	12.74
F4	Antisocial	V11	.51	
	Opportunities	V12	.81	13.63
		V13	.75	13.49
F5	Prosocial	V14	.79	
	Involvement	V15	.45	9.05
		V16	.35	7.57
F6	Antisocial	V17	.81	
	Involvement	V18	.83	20.81
		V19	.51	14.52
F7	Skills for	V20	.94	
	Interaction	V21	.92	49.11
		V22	.90	46.51

Table 5.1 (cont.)

Measures			Standardized Factor Loading	Robust Z-Statistic
F8	Prosocial	V23	.86	
	Rewards	V24	.79	28.53
		V25	.87	32.16
F9	Antisocial	V26	.87	
	Rewards	V27	.66	19.66
		V28	.79	22.53
F10	Prosocial	V29	.86	
	Bonding	V30	.94	39.13
		V31	.90	36.82
F11	Antisocial	V32	.64	
	Bonding	V33	.76	16.09
		V34	.69	15.56
F12	Prosocial	V35	.60	
	Belief	V36	.51	15.86
		V37	.72	15.87
F13	Antisocial	V38	.68	
	Belief	V39	.84	21.04
		V40	.77	20.00
F14	Antisocial	V41 (drug use)	.61	
	Behavior	V42 (school problem)	.77	18.28
		V43 (violence)	.83	19.15
		V44 (non-violent delinquency)	.82	19.03

Note. All factor loadings are significant at $p < .001$.

reflect the total correlation of these factors and antisocial behavior.

Structural Model

To examine the extent to which social development processes of the SDM mediate the relationships between antisocial behavior and external constraints, individual constitutional factors, gender, and low income, two competing models were compared. First, the SDM model in Figure 5.1 was fit without direct paths from external constraints, individual constitutional factors, gender, or low income to antisocial behavior. Second, the SDM model in Figure 5.1 with the addition of direct paths from external constraints, individual constitutional factors, gender, and low income to antisocial behavior was fit.

Figure 5.2 presents the estimated path coefficients for the structural relationships hypothesized by the social development model in Figure 5.1. The variances of all error and disturbance terms were freed, and the variances of the three exogenous variables (individual constitutional factors, gender, and low income) were fixed at 1.00. The same pair of error terms as described for the CFA was allowed to correlate freely.

The overall model fit the data well, $c^2_{(956)} = 3412.68$; CFI = .87, and RMSEA = .05. As shown in Figure 5.2, most paths were significant and in the expected direction.

To test whether external constraints, individual constitutional factors, and two indicators of position in the social structure (i.e., gender and low income) had a direct effect on antisocial behavior, a direct path from each of these variables to antisocial behavior was added to the full model, and the difference in chi-square was compared. The direct paths from gender (path = .10, $p < .001$), income (path = .07, $p < .001$), and individual constitutional factors (path = -.36, $p < .001$) to antisocial behavior were significant. The direct path from external constraints to antisocial behavior was not significant (path = .01, ns).

To examine the extent to which social development processes of the SDM mediate the relationship between external constraints, individual constitutional factors, position in the social structure, and antisocial behavior, a direct path from each of these variables to antisocial behavior was added to the full model, but constrained to the zero-order covariance value. This allowed comparison of the magnitude of the structural path coefficient with the zero-order covariance value. Reductions of the correlations from the CFA between each of these variables and antisocial behavior were found: from -.11 to .01 for external constraints, from .51 to .36 for individual constitutional factors, from .27 to .10 for gender, and from .12 to .07 for low-income status. The effect of external constraints on antisocial behavior was fully mediated by social development processes. The effects of individual constitutional factors, gender, and low income on antisocial behavior were partially mediated by social development processes as measured here.

Figure 5.2

Structural Equation Model Predicting Antisocial Behavior Using the Social Development Model

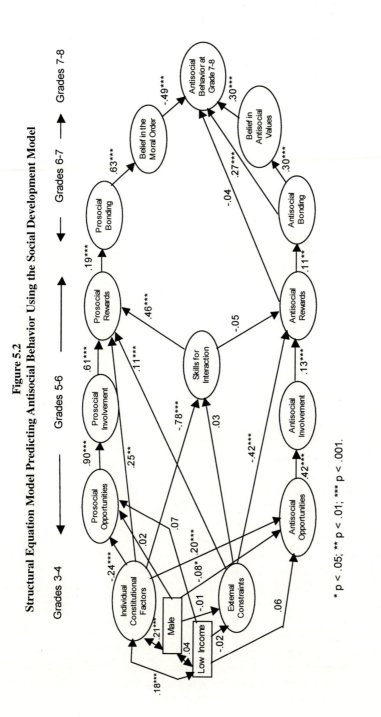

Grades 3-4 ———— Grades 5-6 ———— Grades 6-7 ——→ Grades 7-8

* p < .05; ** p < .01; *** p < .001.

$X^2 = 3412.68$, df = 956, CFI = .87, RMSEA = .05, $R^2 = 49\%$

The paths among the social development factors shown in Figure 5.2 support the hypothesized relationships among the factors. Prosocial constructs are positively influencing each other and negatively associated with antisocial behavior. Antisocial constructs are positively influencing each other and positively associated with antisocial behavior. Mediation on the prosocial paths and on the antisocial paths is consistent with theoretical predictions.

Discussion

This section of the chapter has reported a test of the SDM's hypotheses that position in the social structure, constitutional factors, and external constraints are mediated by social development processes in predicting antisocial behavior in early adolescence. As in prior tests, the hypothesized social development pathways of the model were empirically supported, with two exceptions: skills for interaction did not predict perceived rewards for antisocial involvement, and perceived rewards for antisocial involvement did not directly predict antisocial behavior. The overall model fit the data well and explained about 49 percent of the variance in antisocial behavior assessed when panel students were in grades 7 and 8.

Three of the four hypothesized relationships between individual constitutional factors and social development processes were significant and in the expected direction. Early indicators of depression, poor concentration, shyness/withdrawal, and antisocial behavior increased opportunities for antisocial involvement and reduced opportunities for prosocial involvement as well as skills for interaction. As hypothesized, external constraints increased perceived rewards for prosocial involvement and decreased perceived rewards for antisocial involvement. The effect of external constraints was fully mediated by the social development processes as hypothesized.

The effect of individual constitutional factors was only partially mediated by social development processes. About a third of the total effects of individual factors on antisocial behavior were mediated by social development processes.

The effects of gender and income also were only partially mediated. About two-thirds of the effect of gender on antisocial behavior was mediated and about half of the effect of coming from a low-income family on antisocial behavior was mediated by social development processes.

It is surprising that the two indicators of position in the social structure measured here were not related to the indicators of opportunity for prosocial or opportunity for antisocial involvement. Gender was expected to be related to the types of opportunities available to participants. However, neither the structural model nor the CFA correlations supported this hypothesis. It may be that there are not gender differences in opportunities available in mid-childhood in this suburban community. Alternatively, our measures may not be sensitive to differences in prosocial and antisocial opportunities available to girls and boys.

Boys spend more leisure time than girls away from supervising guardians (Osgood, Wilson, O' Malley, Bachman, & Johnston, 1996). Thus, activities that appear to be prosocial, like involvement in sports, may offer greater opportunities for boys than for girls to interact with antisocial peers or to engage in antisocial activities.

Coming from a low-income family as measured by free lunch eligibility was not related to opportunities in the structural model. In the CFA, low income had a small but significant relationship to antisocial opportunities, but no relationship to prosocial opportunities. It is possible that in this suburban community, schools and neighborhoods are providing prosocial opportunities equally regardless of family income, at least through eighth grade. Alternatively, it is possible that this suburban sample did not contain a sufficient income range to allow observation of the hypothesized relationship between coming from a low-income family and opportunities. The effects of both indicators of position in the social structure measured here were partially mediated through correlations with individual constitutional factors.

Although the total correlation of external constraints and skills was significant (correlation = .17, P <.001) when the mediating paths were taken into account, the direct effect of external constraints on skills was not significant. Through its correlation with individual constitutional factors, the model mediates the effects of external constraints on skills. This mediation was sufficient to reduce the significant total effect to the non-significant direct effect. Theory provides a basis to design approaches to prevent and reduce antisocial behavior. Theory contributes to our ability to design effective strategies to prevent antisocial behavior. When the etiological pathways to antisocial behavior are specified, it is possible to identify intervention points to interrupt the causal process. Interventions to prevent or reduce antisocial behavior seek to interrupt the causal processes that lead to antisocial outcomes and strengthen the processes that lead to prosocial outcomes. Preventive strategies that target the hypothesized constructs and processes have an increased likelihood of effectiveness. This study provides support of the SDM as a theory to explain the development of antisocial behavior. Given that 49 percent of the variance in middle school antisocial behavior was explained by the theory, it can be a useful guide for designing preventive interventions. Preventive interventions that seek to strengthen prosocial development processes specified in the SDM in elementary school are likely to reduce antisocial behavior in middle school. Further, given that a significant amount of the total effect of individual and environmental variables is mediated by the social development processes, it is likely that these preventive programs targeting social development processes in elementary school can significantly reduce the effects of individual and environmental disadvantage. That significant direct effects of position in the social structure and individual constitutional factors remain, suggests that additional targeting on these characteristics may also be warranted.

This study has several limitations. First, the effect of ethnicity, an indicator of position in the social structure, was not examined. Second, the suburban sample might not have had sufficient variation in income to fully examine the effect of this component of position in the social structure. Third, these results apply only to predicting antisocial behavior in early adolescence from predictors measured in childhood and early adolescence.

While these limitations should be noted, the present study indicates that social development processes specified by the SDM partially mediate the effects of position in the social structure and individual characteristics and fully mediate the effects of external constraints in predicting antisocial behavior in early adolescence.

The Social Development Model and Widely Accepted Conclusions in Criminology

We turn now to discussion of how the Social Development Model (SDM) explains widely accepted conclusions in criminology. (SDM constructs are in italics or parentheses.)

1. Different types of offenses tend to be first committed at distinctly different ages. Offenses arise out of an interaction between the person (with a certain degree of criminal potential) and the environment (including opportunities and victims). The peak age of onset of offending is between 8 and 14. The prevalence of offending peaks in the late teenage years—15-19.

The SDM asserts that different environmental and socializing forces influence behavior at different developmental stages and that positive and antisocial behaviors have different expression over development. For example, positive behaviors among young children include compliance, sharing, and expressions of love for caretakers. Early antisocial behaviors include defiance, oppositional behavior, and physical aggression. Actual behavioral manifestations change over time as young children develop the physical and mental capacity (constitutional factors) and *opportunity* to express positive and antisocial behavior in different ways. Offending becomes possible at ages 8 to 14 as physical capacity and social definitions of behaviors change. During this developmental time, for example, aggressive behaviors defined as troublesome earlier in development are redefined as offending because of their capacity to cause harm. Thus, the definition of offending itself is an interaction between the environment and the individual. Offending peaks during the late teen years because *antisocial opportunities* peak during this period due to decreased supervision, large aggregations of adolescents in high schools allowing those with delinquent propensities to associate with others who are similarly inclined, the availability of drugs, and low *perceived costs for antisocial behavior* associated with low likelihood of detection for such behavior.

2. Offending is versatile rather than specialized. The types of acts defined as offenses are elements of a larger syndrome of antisocial behavior, including heavy drinking, reckless driving, sexual promiscuity, bullying, and truancy. An early age of onset predicts a relatively long criminal career duration and commission of relatively many offenses. There is marked continuity in offending and antisocial behavior from childhood to the teenage years and to adulthood.

Offending is versatile over development in part because of the changing potential for developmental expression of positive and antisocial behavior. Offending also is versatile because it is opportunistic. Different offenses are, in part, differential manifestations of the same processes of weak prosocial bonding and antisocial development beginning with opportunities for antisocial involvement. Different antisocial opportunities are presented in different social contexts and peer groups and the prevalence of antisocial behaviors decreases with increased social disapproval in the society. Thus, in the SDM, the antisocial development pathway is expressed as theft when an opportunity to steal (antisocial opportunity) presents itself to an individual who has the *skills* to steal the object and who also *perceives more reward than cost* will come from the theft. An individual who perceives rewards over costs for antisocial involvement may take advantage of another antisocial opportunity with a similar cost benefit calculation, for example he or she may engage in truancy, sexual promiscuity or drug use. Individuals, who discover how to perceive *antisocial opportunities* early, develop the *skills* to successfully take advantage of the opportunity and those who *perceive more rewards than costs* for involvement are likely to continue *antisocial involvement* over time because their involvement is reinforced or brings social, emotional, or monetary rewards. The SDM postulates that children who do not have early developmental experiences with caregivers that promote *attachment and commitment* to family are more likely to engage in early antisocial behavior. In turn, this early onset of antisocial behavior, such as aggression in the primary grades, causes these early onsetters to encounter fewer *prosocial opportunities*, due to individual differences, they are hypothesized to be less *skilled* in taking advantage of prosocial opportunities that they do encounter, and some may *perceive fewer rewards* for prosocial involvement due to low basal arousal levels. These individuals do not have developmental experiences that build *commitment or attachment to prosocial individuals or activities* to protect them from antisocial involvements as similar peers begin to appear in the school context due to the aggregation and mixing of larger numbers of children in a single social unit, the middle school. During adolescence, the patterns of antisocial involvement are strengthened by *antisocial peer involvements* during this period, and, continuity for early starters is enhanced. Without a change in opportunity or reward structure, the SDM predicts continuity across development, with frequent versatile offending among early starters.

3. A small fraction of the population commits a large fraction of all crimes.

The SDM assumes a normative consensus on the rules of behavior in society (Catalano & Hawkins, 1996). Given this normative consensus, the SDM predicts that few people encounter reinforcement for antisocial behavior and simultaneously experience no reinforcement for prosocial behavior. In fact, the more deviant the definition of a behavior, the less frequent it is in the population. However, even those who experience a combination of influences manifested in offending at one point in time are likely to encounter future opportunities for prosocial involvement through normal social development processes, for example through attending school. The SDM predicts that few individuals experience absence of *prosocial opportunities, skills, reinforcement, and bonding* and multiple sustained *antisocial opportunities*. Those few who do, offend early and often.

4. Most offenses up to the late teenage years are committed with others, whereas most offenses from age 20 onwards are committed alone. The reasons given for offending up to the late teenage years are quite variable, including utilitarian, excitement or enjoyment, or because of anger. From age 20 onwards, utilitarian motives become increasingly dominant.

The developmental expression of antisocial behavior peaks in adolescence. Antisocial behavior is more normative during adolescence both in a statistical sense, and in the sense that greater social tolerance is given to a wide range of behaviors during this period that are, by law, illegal. As people mature into the 20s, smaller proportions commit offenses because approval of offending decreases. In SDM terms, the *rewards for antisocial involvement* in the teenage years from social approval are greater than in young adulthood. The need to hide offending from others increases in early adulthood because some forms of *antisocial behavior* earlier accepted, are redefined as unacceptable and therefore more likely to produce *perceived costs than rewards*. To summarize, during the teen years, antisocial behavior is more normatively acceptable, that is the *perceived rewards for antisocial involvement* during the teen years come from multiple sources, peer approval, shared excitement, as well as utilitarian rewards. As the normative environment becomes less approving of antisocial behavior, social rewards for offending diminish. Only utilitarian rewards may remain.

SDM Predictions about Contentious DLC Issues

1. It is not clear how the individual offending frequency varies with age. It is not clear whether the seriousness of offending escalates up to a certain age and then de-escalates, or whether it does not change with age.

Frequency of offending depends on the *antisocial opportunity* structure to which an offender is exposed and the offender's *ability to perceive the opportunity structure*. The SDM encourages consideration of the moderating effect that the *antisocial opportunity* structure and the individual's ability to *perceive these opportunities* have on frequency of offending. For example, an individual with high individual potential to be an offender who encounters an enriched *antisocial opportunity* structure is likely to be a high-rate offender. The same individual placed in an environment that has few *antisocial opportunities* is likely to offend less frequently though the individual has high potential for offending.

2. It is not clear whether onset sequences of offending are merely age-appropriate behavioral manifestations of some underlying theoretical construct or if the onset of one type of behavior facilitates or acts as a stepping-stone towards the onset of another. Little is also known about onset sequences in which childhood antisocial behavior has some kind of influence on later offending.

The SDM would predict that onset sequences are age-appropriate behavioral manifestation of the underlying construct of *antisocial behavior*. In addition, the SDM predicts that gaining *skill* in earlier behavioral manifestations of *antisocial behavior* enhances the *perceived rewards* from such involvement leading to stronger *commitment to antisocial lines of behavior*. As such, the SDM also predicts that successful engagement in an earlier *antisocial behavior* can act as a stepping-stone to later behavior, the mechanism being *skill* mastery and earning *reinforcement over costs* for the prior behavior.

3. To what extent known risk factors have causal effects on offending is not known. Few DLC theories include specific postulates about the effects of interventions.

The SDM was built incorporating empirical knowledge regarding risk and protective factors and makes causal predictions about how they affect offending. Differentiating cause from longitudinal prediction requires evidence of individual change in risk after manipulation of the risk factor and a corresponding change in offending. Experimental and quasi-experimental designs provide the best basis for establishing cause. Interventions that are theory driven and explicitly attempt to address theoretical constructs are the most likely to provide this type of evidence. We have used the SDM to guide family, school, individual, and community intervention to change SDM constructs (Catalano et al., 2003; Hawkins, Catalano, Kosterman, Abbott, & Hill, 1999). SDM intervention models specify how intervention is likely to change specific SDM constructs. We have demonstrated that these interventions have impacted both SDM constructs and positive and antisocial behaviors including violence.

4. Less is known about life events that influence onset or continuation after onset.

The SDM does not make predictions about life events per se; rather, it tries to understand the impact of a life event on model processes. For example, divorce has been shown to have mixed effects on delinquency. The SDM would hypothesize that if the divorce *reduced costs for family involvement* (due perhaps to high levels of spousal conflict), or removed an *antisocial influence* (criminally or drug involved parent), the divorce might have a positive impact in reducing antisocial behavior or offending of the child.

5. The effect of the criminal justice system on desistance is highly controversial.

Using the SDM to analyze the effect of the criminal justice system would entail translating this experience into model terms. For instance, incarceration increases the *opportunity for involvement with antisocial others*, the ability to learn *skills useful for antisocial involvement*. This is balanced by the *perceived cost of incarceration* and the potential for *prosocial involvement* in learning *skills* that might be applied for benefit once an inmate returns to the community.

Key Empirical Issues That Need to be Addressed by DLC Theory

1. Why do people start offending?

The SDM asserts that prosocial development and antisocial development processes can operate simultaneously in any individual's life. If an individual perceives *prosocial opportunities*, becomes *involved in prosocial activities and interactions*, comports him or herself *skillfully* and experiences *rewards* over costs for involvement, the individual will over time develop *bonds* of commitment and attachment to prosocial activities and people. As these *bonds* are strengthened by similar experiences, the individual will develop *prosocial beliefs* consistent with these prosocial interactions and involvements. *Prosocial bonding* and *beliefs* protect an individual from antisocial influences due to the stake in conformity built up by successful prosocial development processes. According to the SDM, three conditions are sufficient for the initiation of offending: (1) when individuals encounter more antisocial developmental influences than prosocial developmental influences, (2), when people presented with *antisocial opportunities* calculate that the *rewards for antisocial involvement* will be greater than the *costs* of that involvement, (3) when people develop *bonds to antisocial others* that encourage them to participate in antisocial behavior to maintain these bonds.

2. How are onset sequences explained?

Onset sequences are viewed as developmental expressions of antisocial behaviors that change as young children develop the physical and mental capacity (*constitutional factors*) and *opportunity* to express positive and negative behavior in different ways. Offending begins to be developmentally possible during the ages of 8-14. At this time, for example, aggression can begin to be more intentional, and due to size, cause more harm, and thus be sanctioned by society to become offending rather than troublesome behavior. Offending variety peaks during the late teen years due to the developmental/environmental peaks in *antisocial opportunities* due to unsupervised time, socialization at school with older students, and the availability of drugs. During this time, earlier criminal potential due to exposure to risk and lack of protection is joined with an increase in *antisocial opportunity,* lack of supervision, and low likelihood of *perceived costs of antisocial behavior* due to low probability of detection, to produce the greatest increase in frequency of offending.

As suggested above, the SDM views onset sequences as a developmental behavioral manifestation of the underlying construct of negative or *antisocial behavior.* In addition, the SDM predicts that gaining *skill* in earlier behavioral manifestations of *antisocial behavior* enhances the *perceived rewards* from such involvement leading to stronger *commitment to antisocial lines of behavior.* As such, the SDM also predicts that successful engagement in an earlier *antisocial behavior* can act as a stepping-stone to later behavior, the mechanism being *skill* mastery and earning *reinforcement over costs* for the prior behavior.

3. Why is there continuity in offending from adolescence to adulthood?

The SDM predicts that continuity in offending is produced by socialization forces that reinforce antisocial behavior over prosocial behavior. When *perceived antisocial opportunities* predominate over *perceived prosocial opportunities,* when *skill* is developed to engage successfully in antisocial activities or interactions and when the *rewards* forthcoming from skillful antisocial involvement predominate over costs and are more rewarding than *prosocial involvements,* individuals will engage in antisocial behavior. As long as these conditions remain there will be continuity.

4. Why do people stop offending?

From a social development perspective, people stop offending when the opportunity and/or reward structure change from one that is rich in *antisocial opportunities* and *rewards* to one rich in *prosocial opportunities* and *rewards.* When this occurs for an extended period of time a shift in the relative importance of the bonding and belief structure occurs, from one where *antisocial bonds* and *beliefs* are more valued to one where *prosocial bonds* and *beliefs* are valued. This shift can occur when environments are changed physically or socially. For example, this may occur when one moves to a better neighborhood with more *prosocial opportunities* and more *reinforcement* for prosocial behavior, or when one makes role transitions such as marriage that shift one's social network and responsibilities towards where *rewards* come from more *prosocial interactions and involvements.*

5. Why does prevalence peak in the teenage years?

Offending peaks during the late teen years due to the developmental-environmental peaks in *antisocial opportunities* due to unsupervised time, socialization at school with older students, and the availability of drugs. During this time, earlier criminal potential due to exposure to risk and lack of protection is joined with an increase in *antisocial opportunity* due in part to lack of *external constraints* from supervision and low likelihood of *perceived costs of antisocial behavior* due to low probability of detection. In addition, there is an increase in *perceived rewards from antisocial involvement* from social approval, in addition to utilitarian or emotional rewards. This developmental confluence of forces produces the greatest prevalence of offending.

6. Why does an early onset predict a long criminal career?

Individuals who discover how to perceive *antisocial opportunities* early, develop the *skills* to successfully take advantage of the opportunity and those who *perceive more rewards than costs* for involvement are likely to continue *antisocial involvement* over time because their involvement is reinforced or brings social, emotional or monetary profit. Those with early onset also have fewer *prosocial opportunities*, are less *skilled* in taking advantage of prosocial opportunities, and may *perceive fewer rewards* for prosocial involvement. Individuals with early onset are less likely to have later prosocial development experiences that build *commitment or attachment to prosocial individuals or activities* and that could protect them from antisocial involvement in the future. Without a change in opportunity or reward structure, the SDM predicts continuity across development, with frequent versatile offending.

7. Why is there versatility in offending and antisocial behavior?

See answer 2 to widely accepted conclusions section.

8. Why does co-offending decrease from adolescence to adulthood?

The developmental expression of antisocial behavior peaks in adolescence. That is, antisocial behavior is more normative during adolescence. As children mature into the 20s there are fewer offenders and the approval of offending decreases. In SDM terms, the *rewards for antisocial involvement* from social approval in the teenage years are greater than in young adulthood. The need to hide offending from others increases because *antisocial involvement* is more likely to produce *perceived costs than rewards* due to reduced social approval.

9. Why are there between-individual differences in offending?

These come from individual differences in prosocial and antisocial socialization experiences including differences in environmental *opportunities*, differences in *skills* to master prosocial and antisocial involvements, differences in *reinforcement* experiences and differences in resulting *bonding* and *beliefs*. In addition, individual constitutional factors and position in the social structure are expected to influence differences in opportunities and skills.

10. What are the key risk factors for onset and desistance, and how can they be explained?

The key risk factors for onset are *antisocial opportunities, skills for antisocial involvement*, and *perceived rewards for antisocial involvement*. The key risk factors for desistance once offending has occurred are increases in *prosocial opportunities*, development of *skills for prosocial involvement, reinforcement for prosocial involvement, bonding to prosocial others* and development of *beliefs in prosocial action*. These are often coincident with decreases in *antiso-

cial opportunities, reduction in *skills for antisocial involvement* (e.g., it is harder to fight younger men as one ages) and *reinforcement for antisocial behavior*.

11. Why are there within-individual differences in offending?

a. Over life (long term)

This is explained in 2 above. The SDM is a life-course theory that recognizes that the nature of interactions between an individual and his or her environment change over development, as does his or her antisocial behaviors.

b. Over time and place (short term)

Individuals engage in different offending behaviors due to different *antisocial opportunities* over the short run. Offending is versatile because the *antisocial opportunities* of today (an open car door) are different than the *antisocial opportunities* (a six pack of beer offered by a friend) presented tomorrow.

12. What are the main motives and reasons for offending?

The SDM hypothesizes that the calculation of *rewards and costs of offending*, the *bonds to antisocial others* and the *belief in antisocial values* directly affect the decision to offend. Included in the calculation of rewards and cost of offending are the strength of the offender's *belief in the moral order* and the threat to his/her *bonds to prosocial others* represented by the particular offense.

13. What are the effects of life events on offending?

According to the SDM, life events have impact on offending through their impact on model variables. For example, marriage to a non-offender increases *prosocial opportunities and involvements* and is likely to increase *rewards for prosocial involvement* and increase *costs for involvement in offending*. The death of a co-offender is likely to *decrease antisocial opportunities and involvements* and increase *perceived costs of crime*. The SDM focuses on understanding the impact of each life event as it affects prosocial and antisocial opportunities in order to understand its potential impact on offending.

Key Theoretical Issues That Need to be Addressed by DLC Theory

1. What are the key constructs underlying offending?

The key constructs underlying offending are the balance of prosocial and antisocial development experiences. The key constructs underlying continuity of offending are the balance of prosocial and antisocial bonding and beliefs.

2. What factors encourage offending?

Antisocial development, antisocial bonding, and antisocial beliefs.

3. What factors inhibit offending?

Prosocial development, prosocial bonding, and prosocial beliefs.

4. Is there a learning process?

The SDM is a synthesis of control, social learning, and differential association theories. Social learning theory provides the learning process in the SDM. Social learning theory suggests that behavior will tend to be repeated if it is *reinforced*, that is, has a surplus of rewards over costs. Behavior is likely to be reinforced if one has the ability or *skill* to perform well. This applies equally to prosocial and antisocial behavior.

5. Is there a decision-making process?

The decision making process in the SDM is the individual calculation of relative strength and importance of prosocial versus antisocial socialization, *bonding,* and *beliefs.*

6. What is the structure of the theory?

The structure of the theory is shown in Figure 5.1 for the middle school development period. There are models for preschool, elementary school, high school, and young adulthood as well. Each model recognizes that different environmental and socializing forces are at work in each developmental period and that prosocial and antisocial behaviors are expressed differently during different periods.

7. What are the operational definitions of theoretical constructs?

The operational definitions of theoretical constructs change with development. These have been articulated in existing theoretical and empirical work (see Catalano & Hawkins, 1996; Catalano et al., 1996; Catalano, Oxford, Harachi, Abbott, & Haggerty, 1999; Farrington & Hawkins, 1991; Hawkins & Weis, 1985; Huang et al., 2001; Lonczak et al., 2001).

8. What does the theory explain?

The theory explains prosocial and antisocial behavior within and between individuals.

9. What does the theory not explain?

Seriousness of offending.

10. What findings challenge the theory? (Can the theory be tested?)

The theory has been tested in a number of studies. This chapter describes the most recent results, some of which challenge the theory. See the discussion of results for these challenges. The impact of *skills* directly on antisocial behavior is a finding that has been replicated in more than one empirical investigation, and challenges the theoretical proposition that the impact of *skills* on antisocial behavior is fully mediated by its effects on *prosocial and antisocial rewards.*

Conclusion

This chapter first assessed the degree to which social development processes mediate the effects of low socioeconomic status, gender, individual characteristics, and external constraints on antisocial behavior in early adolescence. Structural equation modeling analyses used longitudinal data from the Raising Healthy Children panel from grade three through grade eight. The effects of external constraints on antisocial behavior were fully mediated by social development processes as hypothesized by the SDM. Low income status and gender were partially, but not wholly, mediated by social development processes in predicting antisocial behavior. Individual factors including depression, poor concentration, shyness/withdrawal, and early antisocial behavior were partially mediated by social development processes. The findings suggest that interventions that strengthen social development processes may eliminate or weaken the connections between known environmental and individual predictors and antisocial behavior.

The second part of the chapter discussed how the SDM addresses key empirical and theoretical issues of developmental life-course theory.

Note

1.   Structural Equation Modeling analyses were run with experimental (N = 560) and control (N = 477) groups to examine whether the structural relationships differed for children in the two different conditions. The structural path coefficients were compared in a multi-group analysis. The structural path coefficients among SDM constructs between the two groups were similar and in the same direction. The change in chi-square between the unconstrained and constrained regression models was examined (Kline, 1998), and the result showed that the structural path coefficients between two groups were not statistically different ($\Delta\chi^2$ = 23.79, df = 30, p > .10).

References

Agnew, R. (1991). The interactive effects of peer variables on delinquency. *Criminology*, 29: 47-72.

Akers, R. L. (1977). *Deviant Behavior: A Social Learning Approach* (2nd ed.). Belmont, CA: Wadsworth Publishing Company.

Ayers, C. D., Williams, J. H., Hawkins, J. D., Peterson, P. L., Catalano, R. F., & Abbott, R. D. (1999). Assessing correlates of onset, escalation, deescalation, and desistance of delinquent behavior. *Journal of Quantitative Criminology*, 15: 277-306.

Bandalos, D. L., & Finney, S. J. (2001). Item parceling issues in structural equation modeling. In G. A. Marcoulides & R. E. Schumacker (Eds.), *New Developments and Techniques in Structural Equation Modeling* (pp. 269-296). Mahwah, NJ: Lawrence Erlbaum Associates, Inc.

Bandura, A. (1973). *Aggression: A Social Learning Analysis*. Englewood Cliffs, NJ: Prentice Hall.

Bandura, A. (1977). *Social Learning Theory*. Englewood Cliffs, NJ: Prentice Hall.

Benda, B. B., & Whiteside, L. (1995). Testing an integrated model of delinquency using LISREL. *Journal of Social Service Research*, 21: 1-32.

Bentler, P. M. (1990). Comparative fit indexes in structural models. *Psychological Bulletin*, 107: 238-246.

Bonanno, J. (1983). *A Man of Honor*. New York: Simon & Schuster.

Browne, M. W., & Cudeck, R. (1993). Alternative ways of assessing model fit. In K. A. Bollen & J. S. Long (Eds.), *Testing Structural Equation Models* (pp. 136-162). Newbury Park, CA: Sage.

Burns, B. J., Landsverk, J., Kelleher, K., Faw, L., Hazen, A., & Keeler, G. (2000). Mental health, education, child welfare, and juvenile justice service use. In R. Loeber & D. P. Farrington (Eds.), *Child Delinquents: Development, Intervention, and Service Needs* (pp. 273-303). Thousand Oaks, CA: Sage.

Bursik, R. J., Jr., & Grasmick, H. G. (1996). The use of contextual analysis in models of criminal behavior. In J. D. Hawkins (Ed.), *Delinquency and Crime: Current Theories* (pp. 236-267). New York: Cambridge University Press.

Cairns, R. B., Cairns, B. D., Neckerman, H. J., Gest, S. D., & Gariepy, J. L. (1988). Social networks and aggressive behavior: Peer support or peer rejection? *Developmental Psychology*, 24: 815-823.

Catalano, R. F., & Hawkins, J. D. (1996). The social development model: A theory of antisocial behavior. In J. D. Hawkins (Ed.), *Delinquency and Crime: Current Theories* (pp. 149-197). New York: Cambridge University Press.

Catalano, R. F., Kosterman, R., Hawkins, J. D., Newcomb, M. D., & Abbott, R. D. (1996). Modeling the etiology of adolescent substance use: A test of the social development model. *Journal of Drug Issues*, 26: 429-455.

Catalano, R. F., Mazza, J. J., Harachi, T. W., Abbott, R. D., Haggerty, K. P., & Fleming, C. B. (2003). Raising healthy children through enhancing social development in elementary school: Results after 1.5 years. *Journal of School Psychology*, 41: 143-164.

Catalano, R. F., Oxford, M. L., Harachi, T. W., Abbott, R. D., & Haggerty, K. P. (1999). A test of the social development model to predict problem behaviour during the elementary school period. *Criminal Behaviour and Mental Health*, 9: 39-56.

Conger, R. D. (1976). Social control and social learning models of delinquent behavior. *Criminology: An Interdisciplinary Journal*, 14: 17-40.

Conger, R. D. (1980). Juvenile delinquency: Behavior restraint for behavior facilitation. In T. Hirschi & M. Gottfredson (Eds.), *Understanding Crime* (pp. 131-142). Beverly Hills, CA: Sage.

Cressey, D. R. (1953). *Other People's Money, a Study of the Social Psychology of Embezzlement*. New York: The Free Press.

Dishion, T. J., Patterson, G. R., Stoolmiller, M., & Skinner, M. L. (1991). Family, school, and behavioral antecedents to early adolescent involvement with antisocial peers. *Developmental Psychology*, 27: 172-180.

Elliott, D. S. (1994). Serious violent offenders: Onset, developmental course, and termination. The American Society of Criminology 1993 Presidential Address. *Criminology*, 32: 1-22.

Elliott, D. S., Huizinga, D., & Ageton, S. S. (1985). *Explaining Delinquency and Drug Use*. Beverly Hills, CA: Sage.

Elliott, D. S., Huizinga, D., & Menard, S. (1989). *Multiple Problem Youth: Delinquency, Substance Use, and Mental Health Problems*. New York: Springer-Verlag.

Fagan, J., & Wexler, S. (1987). Crime at home and in the streets: the relationship between family and stranger violence. *Violence and Victims*, 2: 5-23.

Farrington, D. P. (1989). Early predictors of adolescent aggression and adult violence. *Violence and Victims*, 4: 79-100.

Farrington, D. P., & Hawkins, J. D. (1991). Predicting participation, early onset and later persistence in officially recorded offending. *Criminal Behaviour and Mental Health*, 1: 1-33.

Farrington, D. P., & Loeber, R. (1995, October). Transatlantic replicability of risk factors in the development of delinquency. Paper presented at the Society for Life History Research in Psychopathology, Chatham, MA.

Flay, B. R., & Petraitis, J. (1994). The theory of triadic influence: A new theory of health behavior with implications for preventive interventions. *Advances in Medical Sociology*, 4: 19-44.

Fleming, C. B., Brewer, D. D., Gainey, R. R., Haggerty, K. P., & Catalano, R. F. (1997). Parent drug use and bonding to parents as predictors of substance use in children of substance abusers. *Journal of Child and Adolescent Substance Abuse*, 6: 75-86.

Fleming, C. B., Catalano, R. F., Oxford, M. L., & Harachi, T. W. (2002). A test of generalizability of the social development model across gender and income groups with longitudinal data from the elementary school developmental period. *Journal of Quantitative Criminology*, 18: 423-439.

Foshee, V., & Bauman, K. E. (1992). Parental and peer characteristics as modifiers of the bond-behavior relationship: An elaboration of control theory. *The Journal of Health and Social Behavior*, 33: 66-76.

Giordano, P. C., & Cernkovich, S. A. (1997). Gender and antisocial behavior. In D. M. Stoff, J. Breiling, & J. D. Maser (Eds.), *Handbook of Antisocial Behavior* (pp. 496-510). New York: Wiley.

Gottfredson, M. R., & Hirschi, T. (1990). *A General Theory of Crime*. Stanford, CA: Stanford University Press.

Guo, J., Hawkins, J. D., Hill, K. G., & Abbott, R. D. (2001). Childhood and adolescent predictors of alcohol abuse and dependence in young adulthood. *Journal of Studies on Alcohol*, 62: 754-762.

Haggerty, K. P., Catalano, R. F., Harachi, T. W., & Abbott, R. D. (1998). Description de l'implementation d'un programme de prévention des problèmes de comportement à l'adolescence. (Preventing adolescent problem behaviors: A comprehensive intervention description). *Criminologie*, 31: 25-47.

Hawkins, J. D., Arthur, M. W., & Catalano, R. F. (1995). Preventing substance abuse. In M. Tonry & D. Farrington (Eds.), *Crime and Justice*, Vol. 19. *Building a Safer Society: Strategic Approaches to Crime Prevention* (pp. 343-427). Chicago: University of Chicago Press.

Hawkins, J. D., Catalano, R. F., Kosterman, R., Abbott, R., & Hill, K. G. (1999). Preventing adolescent health-risk behaviors by strengthening protection during childhood. *Archives of Pediatrics and Adolescent Medicine*, 153: 226-234.

Hawkins, J. D., Catalano, R. F., & Miller, J. Y. (1992). Risk and protective factors for alcohol and other drug problems in adolescence and early adulthood—Implications for substance-abuse prevention. *Psychological Bulletin*, 112: 64-105.

Hawkins, J. D., Catalano, R. F., Morrison, D. M., O'Donnell, J., Abbott, R. D., & Day, L. E. (1992). The Seattle Social Development Project: Effects of the first four years on protective factors and problem behaviors. In J. McCord & R. E. Tremblay (Eds.), *Preventing Antisocial Behavior: Interventions from Birth through Adolescence* (pp. 139-161). New York: Guilford Press.

Hawkins, J. D., Hill, K. G., Guo, J., & Battin-Pearson, S. R. (2002). Substance use norms and transitions in substance use: Implications for the gateway hypothesis. In D. B. Kandel (Ed.) *Stages and Pathways of Drug Involvement. Examining the Gateway Hypothesis* (pp. 42-64). New York: Cambridge University Press.

Hawkins, J. D., & Weis, J. G. (1985). The social development model: An integrated approach to delinquency prevention. *Journal of Primary Prevention*, 6: 73-97.

Hepburn, J. R. (1976). Listing alternative models of delinquency causation. *Journal of Crime Law and Criminology*, 67: 4-17.

Herrenkohl, T. I., Hawkins, J. D., Chung, I.-J., Hill, K. G., & Battin-Pearson, S. R. (2000). School and community risk factors and interventions. In R. Loeber & D. P. Farrington (Eds.), *Child Delinquents: Development, Intervention, and Service Needs* (pp. 211-246). Thousand Oaks, CA: Sage.

Herrenkohl, T. I., Huang, B., Kosterman, R., Hawkins, J. D., Catalano, R. F., & Smith, B. H. (2001). A comparison of social development processes leading to violent behavior in late adolescence for childhood initiators and adolescent initiators of violence. *Journal of Research in Crime and Delinquency*, 38: 45-63.

Hirschi, T. (1969). *Causes of Delinquency*. Berkeley: University of California Press.

Huang, B., Kosterman, R., Catalano, R. F., Hawkins, J. D., & Abbott, R. D. (2001).

Modeling mediation in the etiology of violent behavior and adolescence: A test of the social development model. *Criminology*, 39: 75-107.

Kandel, D. B., Simcha Fagan, O., & Davies, M. (1986). Risk factors for delinquency and illicit drug use from adolescence to young adulthood. *Journal of Drug Issues*, 16: 67-90.

Kellam, S. G., Rebok, G. W., Ialongo, N. S., & Mayer, L. S. (1994). The course and malleability of aggressive behavior from early first grade into middle school: Results of a developmental epidemiology-based preventive trial. *Journal of Child Psychology and Psychiatry and Allied Disciplines*, 35: 259-281.

Kline, R. B. (1998). *Principles and Practice of Structural Equation Modeling*. New York: The Guilford Press.

Kornhauser, R. R. (1978). *Social Sources of Delinquency: An Appraisal of Analytic Models*. Chicago: University of Chicago Press.

Lerner, J. V., & Vicary, J. R. (1984). Difficult temperament and drug use: Analyses from the New York Longitudinal Study. *Journal of Drug Education*, 14: 1-8.

Lewis, C. E., Robins, L. N., & Rice, J. (1985). Association of alcoholism with antisocial personality in urban men. *Journal of Nervous and Mental Disease*, 173: 166-174.

Lipsey, M. W., & Derzon, J. H. (1998). Predictors of violent or serious delinquency in adolescence and early adulthood: A synthesis of longitudinal research. In R. Loeber & D. P. Farrington (Eds.), *Serious and Violent Juvenile Offenders: Risk Factors and Successful Interventions* (pp. 86-105). Thousand Oaks, CA: Sage.

Little, R. J. A., & Rubin, D. B. (1987). *Statistical Analysis with Missing Data*. New York: John Wiley and Sons.

Loeber, R. (1988). Natural histories of conduct problems, delinquency, and associated substance use: Evidence for developmental progressions. In B. B. Lahey & A. E. Kazdin (Eds.), *Advances in Clinical Child Psychology*, Vol. 11 (pp. 73-124). New York: Plenum.

Loeber, R., & Stouthamer-Loeber, M. (1998). Development of juvenile aggression and violence: Some common misconceptions and controversies. *American Psychologist*, 53: 242-259.

Lonczak, H. S., Huang, B., Catalano, R. F., Hawkins, J. D., Hill, K. G., Abbott, R. D., et al. (2001). The social predictors of adolescent alcohol misuse: A test of the social development model. *Journal of Studies on Alcohol*, 62: 179-189.

MacCallum, R. C., Browne, M. W., & Sugawara, H. M. (1996). Power analysis and determination of sample size for covariance structure modeling. *Psychological Methods*, 1: 130-149.

MacCallum, R. C., Widaman, K. F., Zhang, S., & Hong, S. (1999). Sample size in factor analysis. *Psychological Methods*, 4: 84-99.

Matsueda, R. L. (1982). Testing control theory and differential association: A causal modeling approach. *American Sociological Review*, 47: 489-504.

Matsueda, R. L. (1988). The current state of differential association theory. *Crime and Delinquency*, 34: 277-306.

Mesman, J., & Koot, H. M. (2000). Child-reported depression and anxiety in preadolescence: I. Associations with parent-and teacher-reported problems. *Journal of the American Academy of Child and Adolescent Psychiatry*, 39: 1371-1378.

Messner, S. F., Krohn, M. D., & Liska, A. E. (1989). *Theoretical integration in the study of deviance and crime: Problems and prospects*. Albany: State University of New York Press.

Moffitt, T. E. (1983). The learning theory model of punishment: Implications for delinquency deterrence. *Criminal Justice and Behavior*, 10: 131-158.

Muthén, L. K., & Muthén, B. O. (2001). *Mplus* (Version 2). Los Angeles: Muthén & Muthén.

Newcomb, M. D. (1994). Drug use and intimate relationships among women and men: Separating specific from general effects in prospective data using structural equation models. *Journal of Consulting and Clinical Psychology*, 62: 463-476.

O'Donnell, J., Hawkins, J. D., & Abbott, R. D. (1995). Predicting serious delinquency and substance use among aggressive boys. *Journal of Consulting and Clinical Psychology*, 63: 529-537.

Osgood, D. W., Wilson, J. K., O' Malley, P. M., Bachman, J. G., & Johnston, L. D. (1996). Routine activities and individual deviant behavior. *American Sociological Review*, 61: 635-655.

Oxford, M. L., Harachi, T. W., Catalano, R. F., & Abbott, R. D. (2001). Preadolescent predictors of substance initiation: A test of both the direct and mediated effect of family social control factors on deviant peer associations and substance initiation. *American Journal of Drug and Alcohol Abuse*, 27: 599-616.

Patterson, G. R. (1982). *A Social Learning Approach, Vol. 3. Coercive Family Process.* Eugene, OR: Castalia.

Patterson, G. R., Reid, J. B., & Dishion, T. J. (1992). *A Social Interactional Approach, Vol. 4. Antisocial Boys.* Eugene, OR: Castalia.

Peterson, P. L., Hawkins, J. D., Abbott, R. D., & Catalano, R. F. (1994). Disentangling the effects of parental drinking, family management, and parental alcohol norms on current drinking by black and white adolescents. *Journal of Research on Adolescence*, 4: 203-227.

Rabiner, D., Coie, J. D. Conduct Problems Prevention Research Group. (2000). Early attention problems and children's reading achievement: A longitudinal investigation. *Journal of the American Academy of Child and Adolescent Psychiatry*, 39: 859-867.

Reinarman, C., & Fagan, J. (1988). Social organization and differential association: A research note from a longitudinal study of violent juvenile offenders. *Crime and Delinquency*, 34: 307-327.

Rutter, M. (1990). Psychosocial resilience and protective mechanisms. In J. E. Rolf, A. S. Masten, D. Cicchette, K. Neuchterlein, & S. Weintraub (Eds.), *Risk and Protective Factors in the Development of Psychopathology* (pp. 181-214). New York: Cambridge University Press.

Schafer, J. L., & Graham, J. W. (2002). Missing data: Our view of the state of the art. *Psychological Methods*, 7: 147-177.

Sutherland, E. H. (1973). Development of the theory [Private paper published posthumously]. In K. Schuessler (Ed.), *Edwin Sutherland on Analyzing Crime* (pp. 13-29). Chicago: University of Chicago Press.

Thornberry, T. P., Lizotte, A. J., Krohn, M. D., Farnworth, M., & Jang, S. J. (1994). Delinquent peers, beliefs, and delinquent behavior: A longitudinal test of interactional theory. *Criminology*, 32: 47-83.

Tremblay, R. E., & LeMarquand, D. (2000). Individual risk and protective factors. In R. Loeber & D. P. Farrington (Eds.), *Child Delinquents: Development, Intervention, and Service Needs* (pp. 137-164). Thousand Oaks, CA: Sage.

Williams, J. H., Van Dorn, R. A., Hawkins, J. D., Abbott, R. D., & Catalano, R. F. (2001). Correlates contributing to involvement in violent behaviors among young adults. *Violence and Victims*, 16: 371-388.

6

An Integrative Personal Control Theory of Deviant Behavior: Answers to Contemporary Empirical and Theoretical Developmental Criminology Issues[1, 2]

Marc Le Blanc

Developmental criminology is concerned with the description and explanation of within-individual changes in deviant behavior along the life course. There are numerous theoretical and empirical publications on the development of general deviance, as sociologists label it, or problem behavior as it is called by psychologists. The analytical tools for the description of the developmental course of general deviance are well established. We have reviewed them with a particular attention to offending (Loeber & Le Blanc, 1990; Le Blanc & Loeber, 1998). Whatever the point of view on the development of deviant behavior, criminology is only considering solely the dependent variable.

Criminology also needs to allow for the impact of independent variables and, in this case, it also has to account for the independent development of the explanatory variables. There are very few theoretical writings on the mechanisms that are producing the course of deviant behavior. Existing criminological theories are structural rather than developmental. They identify the relevant concepts, for example, social disorganization, strain, control, cultural deviance, criminal personality, differential association, social learning, labeling, deterrence, and so on. These theories also specify the interactions between their component concepts, for example, bonding theory defines the interactions between involvement, attachment, commitment, and beliefs. However, virtually all criminological theories do not specify how these explanatory phenomena are built over time; they do not describe the mechanisms by which these phenomena are created, developed, maintained, and transformed along the life course. One exception is differential association and social learning theories that specify how a favorable definition toward delinquency is acquired and maintained, but these theories are concerned only with the beginning of the course of deviant behavior and they do not indicate what are the mechanisms of desistance. On the contrary, developmental psychology offers statements of the principles and processes of the psychological development in general (see Lerner's, 1986, synthesis) without a concrete description of how they affect the course of deviant behavior. In this chapter, we will apply this knowledge to control concepts that explain the particular characteristics of the life span course of deviant behavior.

Over the last fifty years, criminology has not witnessed any major theoretical innovations. Numerous theories were available, such as social disorganization, strain, control, cultural deviance, criminal personality, differential association, social learning, labeling, deterrence, and so on (see Shoemaker review, 1996). In addition, these theories were elaborations of ideas of nineteen-century theorists such as Quételet, Durkheim, Marx, Tarde, and others. However, over the last five decades, criminology witnessed enormous theoretical activities that took the form of theoretical elaboration, formalization, integration, modeling, and testing of these theories. This situation is particularly true of Hirschi's bonding theory, a theory formulated in 1969. It is also becoming increasingly true of self-control theory that was proposed by Gottfredson and Hirschi in 1990.

Bonding and self-control theories are elaborations of the well-known control perspective. Such theorists as Durkheim (1902-1903), Thrasher (1927), Freud (1963), Reiss (1951), Nye (1958), and Reckless (1961), to name earlier proponents of this perspective, formulated a control theory. While these theorists used different constructs, they accept the same basic assumptions concerning human nature (see Empey's, 1978, and Kornhauser's, 1978, discussions and Shoemaker's, 1996, summary). Over the last few decades, bonding theory has become and remains the most prominent empirically based criminological theory for the explanation of juvenile deviant behavior (see Kempf, 1993, for a review of empirical studies). Self-control theory is now regularly referred to and it is increasingly empirically tested (see Platt and Cullen, 2000, meta-analysis). Existing control theories and models are structural and static in nature (see Shoemaker's, 1996, review). They identify the major causes of deviant behavior, such as bonds, self-control, constraints, and opportunities, and they state some of the interactions between these constructs. However, they do not indicate how controls develop during the life course. They are not concerned with questions such as what is the course and what are the processes that are responsible for continuity and change in controls, and, in turn, the course of deviant behavior. Adopting the control perspective, this chapter proposes an integrative personal control theory that shows how continuity and change in controls explains the course of general deviance along the life course (Le Blanc, 1997a; Le Blanc & Janosz, 1998). In this chapter, we use this theory to respond to the list of what do we know, contentious questions and key issues outlined by

David Farrington's chapter.

1. The Life Span Course of Deviant Behavior

In this section, we will propose a theory of the growth and decline of general deviance, illustrated with offending, that will address David Farrington's list of known facts and contentious issues about offending, the what questions. In addition, we will describe the developmental process characterizing deviant behavior using the chaos-order paradigm. This is a response to the how question that is generally ignored in criminology. Our theory of the development of deviant behavior and particularly offending goes beyond the basic facts about its diversity, onset, offset, versatility, and continuity.

1.1 What is the Key Concept Underlying Deviant Behavior?

The key phenomenon to be explained by criminology is the course of *conformity to conventional standards of behavior*. This notion is represented by the construct of general deviance that we delimit with four subconstructs: covert, overt, authority conflict, and reckless behaviors. These subconstructs are composed of twelve forms of deviant behavior (Figure 6.1; see Le Blanc & Bouthillier, 2003, for a test of such model for onset and frequency). Of these twelve forms of deviant behavior, five are relative to offending: vandalism, violent behavior, theft, sex crimes, and fraud. Our notion of conformity to conventional standards is the classical sociological position in criminology; it is delimited by population behavioral norms for a particular society at a specific historical period. A law defines many of these behavioral norms, for example, crime is delimited by the criminal code, school attendance is specified in a law, and so on for many other deviant behaviors. All the behaviors of the general deviance syndrome can be measured through a self-reported questionnaire or an interview and many can be measured with official records.

The deviant behavior syndrome manifests itself in different ways along the life span. It is a heterotypic phenomenon and, in consequence, there is continuity and change in the nature of deviant behaviors that compose the syndrome through the life span. Figure 6.2 illustrates this phenomenon; the ages of onset and offset are based on self-reported data at age 40 for our sample of adjudicated males. During infancy, it takes the form of authority conflict behaviors such as stubbornness, disobedience, and defiance behaviors and physical aggressions (see Loeber & Hay, 1997). During childhood, these behaviors change in seriousness and diversity and, in addition, the authority conflict manifests itself at school and covert behaviors (minor thefts and lying) are added to the syndrome according to Loeber & Hay (1997). With adolescence, the syndrome is diversified in terms of covert, overt, and authority conflict behaviors and reckless behaviors are added (see Le Blanc & Bouthillier, 2003, data on onset

Figure 6.1
A Comprehensive Hierarchical Model of General Deviance

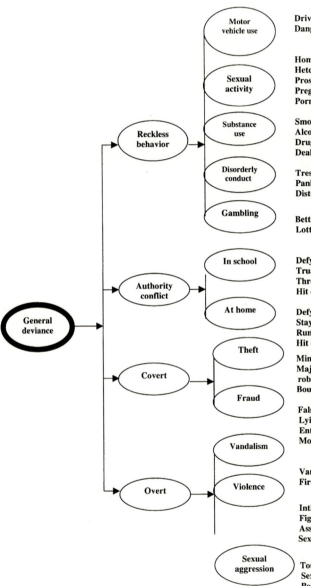

for a large array of deviant behaviors). Later on, during adulthood, some criminal behaviors gradually stop (for example, serious theft) and new forms of offending are introduced (tax evasion and family violence, for example) and school authority conflict is replaced by problems at work and there are new forms of reckless behavior. This description of the nature of deviant behavior and offending is compatible with the facts outlined in David Farrington's chapter, particularly the continuity in deviant behavior and the syndrome characteristic of all deviant behaviors along the life course.

1.2 What is the Course of Deviant Behavior?

Our developmental theory stated that *the course of deviant behavior takes the form of a reverse U-shape for every individual during his/her life course.* Individuals vary in the timing and the height of their reverse U-shape trajectory of deviant behavior. The first task of criminology has to do with the identification of the mechanisms that create the form of this trajectory, the mechanisms that perform quantitative and qualitative changes on that trajectory along the life course. The second task of criminology is to explain theses changes with biological, psychological, interpersonal, and social changes in the life of the individual.

In our developmental criminology paradigmatic papers (Loeber & Le Blanc, 1990; Le Blanc & Loeber, 1998) and in our analysis of offending (Le Blanc & Fréchette, 1989), we specified the analytical tools necessary to characterize the course of deviant behavior. This was done, particularly, for the quantitative and qualitative changes, a distinction fundamental for developmentalists. Table 6.1, adapted from Loeber & Le Blanc (1990), summarizes these changes.

The *quantitative* changes are defined in terms of growth and decline in deviant behavior. First, quantitative changes are manifested by the degree of change on various forms of deviant behavior: changes in participation. Second, quantitative changes correspond to the direction of change; they manifest themselves in the form of progression or regression in frequency. Third, quantitative changes refer to the rate of change, or the velocity, primarily in the form of the degree of change over time. In addition, the growth can be inferred from the relation between the onset of deviant behavior and its frequency (acceleration), variety (diversification), and duration (stabilization: a known fact in David Farrington's chapter). Finally, there is a gradual desistance from deviant behavior. This process is observable through deceleration (decrease of the frequency), specialization (decrease of the variety), and reaching a ceiling (stabilizing the seriousness). David Farrington did not identify these growth and decline mechanisms or state that they are contentious facts. We agree with him that the replications of these mechanisms in studies are not yet sufficient. However, there were good indications that they should survive future tests (see Le Blanc & Loeber, 1998, review).

Figure 6.2
Course of General Deviance, Adjudicated Youths

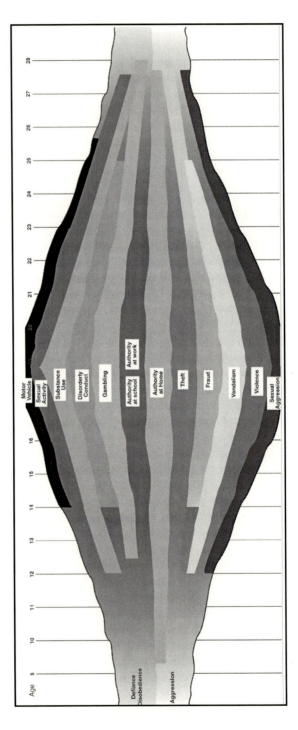

Table 6.1
The Course of Deviant Behavior: Quantitative and Qualitative Changes

Quantitative changes	Qualitative changes
Degree: percent of individuals who are stable or change.	**Developmental sequence in deviant behavior** - **stages:** sequence in behaviors - **escalation:** tendency to move to more serious behaviors
Direction: percent of individuals who progress or regress.	- **de-escalation**: reducing seriousness
Velocity: degree of change to time **Growth:** - **growth rate**: according to time - **acceleration**: frequency to onset - **diversification**: variety to onset - **stabilization**: duration to onset	**Conservation:** stability - **innovation:** introducing a new behavior - **retention:** an existing behavior persists **Synchrony between types of deviant behavior** - **adjacency:** behaviors of two types are temporally adjacent (transition probabilities)
Decline: - **shrinking rate**: according to time - **deceleration**: frequency to offset - **reaching ceiling**: seriousness to offset - **specialization**: variety to offset	- **simultaneity:** same level of seriousness on two types of deviant behavior **Paths:** percent of individuals who go through the full developmental sequence or parts of it

Qualitative changes are a more difficult phenomenon. They refer to something new, something that is different from what went on before, and something that is more complex according to the ontogenetic principle. These changes in nature are habitually subdivided into a developmental sequence that comprises a certain number of hierarchical stages. Le Blanc and Fréchette (1989) showed that there was a developmental sequence in crime and reviews (Loeber & Le Blanc, 1990; Le Blanc & Loeber, 1998) indicate that there is clearly a developmental sequence for some other types of deviant behavior, such as violence (Loeber & Hay, 1997) and drug use (Kandel, 2002). The qualitative changes can be analyzed in terms of escalation/de-escalation on a developmental sequence (moving across the stages of seriousness of a particular type of deviant behavior), conservation of the behaviors that are part of the person repertory (innovation, the introduction of a new behavior in the repertory; retention, maintaining a less serious type of behavior while moving to more serious behaviors), synchrony of development of different types of deviant behavior (simultaneity, attaining the same level of seriousness on two or more types of problem behavior; adjacency, the embedding of deviant behavior of different types), and paths (going through parts or the whole sequence). David Farrington classifies these phenomena as contentious issues or does not list them. We agree with him that replications are needed for all of these types of qualitative changes and for all types of deviant behavior. However, the developmental sequence is well demonstrated for drug use and there are many facts to support the offending and violence developmental sequence. The escalation hypothesis is a strong fact rather then a contentious issue, which is not the case for the de-escalation hypothesis (see Le Blanc, 2002, review).

The quantitative and qualitative changes form an individual trajectory or the individual life span course of deviant behavior. These individual trajectories vary in timing (onset and offset) and degree (frequency, seriousness,...) and nature (content, synchrony, conservation,...). In consequence, each individual displays a particular reverse U-shape course. If we take offending as an example, the individual trajectories of offending form an average trajectory and three meta-trajectories (common, transitory, and persistent deviant behavior: Fréchette & Le Blanc, 1987; and some sub-trajectories for each of the meta-trajectories: Le Blanc & Fréchette, 1989). There are some preliminary indications that the same phenomenon applies to other forms of deviant behavior, particularly drug use. This descriptive theory of the course of offending accounts for the portraits of the characteristics of offending that are replicated by studies conducted at different times (see the synthesis of Blumstein, Cohen, Roth, & Visher, 1986; Le Blanc & Loeber, 1998; Piquero, Farrington, & Blumstein, 2003). This descriptive theory helps in reorganizing David Farrington's lists of known and contentious facts in the form of three trajectories (Figure 6.3).

The *persistent* (Le Blanc & Fréchette, 1989) or life-course (Moffitt, 1993) offending trajectory is well known. The individuals that follow this trajectory represent a small fraction of the population that commits a large fraction of all crimes, 50 percent of the self-reported behaviors (Elliott, Huizinga, & Menard, 1989); these chronic delinquents represent around 5 percent of the population and 45 percent of the wards of the juvenile court that are placed in institutions or on probation and commit two-fifths of the crimes known to police and two-thirds of the violent crimes according to Wolfgang, Figlio, & Sellin, (1972). According to our data, they start offending during childhood, around 8; the growth is rapid and important during the first half of adolescence; their offending peaks toward the end of adolescence; they maintain a high level of offending until the middle of the twenties; their offending declines and ends on the average around the middle of the thirties. This trajectory is characterized by high versatility, frequency, and seriousness. The growth rate and velocity are rapid during early adolescence and this trajectory is characterized by acceleration, diversification, and stabilization. During that growth, their offending escalates from the less to the more serious crimes on the developmental sequence of crimes and it displays high levels of innovation, retention, and simultaneity.

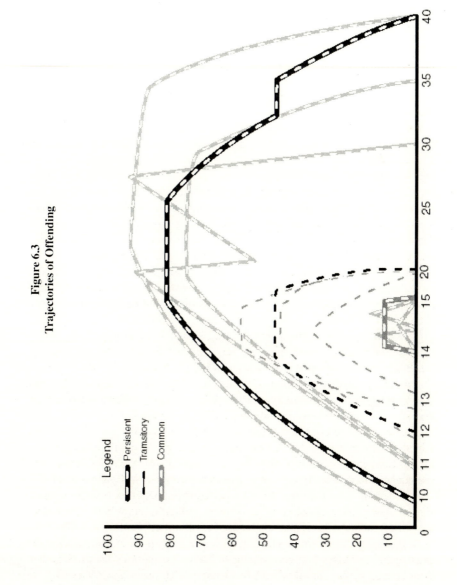

Figure 6.3
Trajectories of Offending

Legend
Persistent
Transitory
Common

During the decline, the shrinking rate accelerates and the frequency decelerates, the seriousness reaches a ceiling, and specialization increases. There are
some indications that this trajectory exists for other forms of deviant behavior,
particularly drug use. In addition, the persistent offender tends to adopt a similar trajectory for other forms of deviant behavior either simultaneously or at
other phases of the life course.

The *transitory* or temporary (Le Blanc & Fréchette, 1989) or adolescence-
limited (Moffitt, 1993) offending trajectory is also well known. The individuals that follow this trajectory represent an important percentage of the population, 45 percent, and they commit 40 percent the self-reported crimes (Elliott et
al., 1989) and 25 percent of the crimes reported to police (Le Blanc, 1995a).
They start offending during adolescence; the growth is rapid and significant
during the middle of adolescence; their offending peaks around 16; their offending decline is also rapid at the end of adolescence; they may display an
episode of relatively minor offending in their early twenties. This trajectory is
characterized by versatility, frequency, and some serious crimes against property. The growth rate and velocity are rapid as mid-adolescence approaches and
this trajectory is then characterized by acceleration, diversification, and a short
stabilization. During that growth their offending escalates from the less to the
more serious crimes without violence on the developmental sequence of crimes
and it displays innovation, retention, and simultaneity. During the decline, the
shrinking rate accelerates and the frequency decelerates quickly, the seriousness reaches a ceiling, and specialization increases. Some indications show
that this trajectory also exists for other forms of deviant behavior, particularly
drug use. This trajectory is also observable during adulthood for a late onset
group of offenders (Le Blanc & Morizot, 2002). In addition, the temporary
offender tends to adopt a similar trajectory for a few forms of deviant behavior
either simultaneously or at other phases of the life course.

The last trajectory, *common* offending (Le Blanc & Fréchette, 1989), has
also been described by some researchers (see Le Blanc, 1995a). Offenders are
occasional in an otherwise law-abiding existence for around 45 percent of the
population. Their crimes occur mainly around mid-adolescence and are manifested in acts of vandalism, shoplifting, minor theft or public mischief. The
annual frequency for each of these types of crime is less than one. If common
delinquency represents 16 percent of arrests according to Wolfgang et al. (1972)
data, it accounts for 9 percent of the reported delinquent acts by a representative sample of the population of adolescents (Elliott et al., 1989). This trajectory of offending is an epiphenomenon of adolescence (Le Blanc, 1983).

If these trajectories are average in a reverse U-shape overall trajectory, the
phenomenon of offending corresponds to David Farrington's list of facts: late
adolescence as the period when prevalence peaks, onset and offset vary by
types of offenses and they peak, respectively, between 8 and 14 and 20 and 29.
Then the contentious issues may be resolved within some trajectories and us-

ing adjudicated samples rather than population samples. For example from our data on adjudicated males (Le Blanc & Fréchette, 1989), there is a relationship between age and frequency, a sequence of offenses, escalation in seriousness, continuity in offending, de-escalation, and so on. These observations are more characteristic of the persistent trajectory.

1.3. How are These Changes Accomplished?

Descriptions of the continuity and change of deviant behavior can be accomplished easily with the tools of the developmental paradigm presented in Table 6.1. However, these measures of quantitative and qualitative changes do not describe the processes that characterize the course of deviant behavior. In an unpublished paper (Le Blanc & Janosz), we show how the chaos-order paradigm can help our understanding of these processes. To illustrate the construction of the course of offending, we used the Briggs & Peat (1989) phase space map. The phase space map exposes the hidden complexities of the system's change. Figures 6.4 and 6.5 are such general maps for the development of offending, particularly theft, during the whole life course. Phase maps have two principal tools: attractors and bifurcations.

An *attractor* is a sort of magnetic point that structures a phenomenon, in our case deviant behavior. The magnetic nature of an attractor would be represented by the tendency of behaviors, once initiated, to repeat themselves. Minor deviant behaviors are normative since only 5 percent of the adolescents are abstinent regarding a large array of problem behavior (Dunford & Elliott, 1984; Fréchette & Le Blanc, 1987). Most adolescents have the opportunity to try soft drugs, get drunk, pet, have sex, vandalize, fight, shoplift, and so on. These experimentations of an occasional nature are not enduring (Le Blanc, 1983; Steinberg, 1996); they are part of the common offending trajectory. In such a case, the value of an attractor is low for the majority of adolescents. Fewer adolescents have the occasion to try hard drugs, force someone to have sex, steal a car, commit a robbery, and so on. A few do and most do not. However, neither the minor nor the serious deviant behaviors are operating as attractors at the same age for each individual nor necessarily in the same sequence, as we know for the analysis of their course (see Loeber & Le Blanc, 1990; Le Blanc & Loeber, 1998). The pull of each problem behavior is dependent on changes in the behavioral system parameters (characteristics of particular behavior: nature, quantity, frequency) and degrees of freedom (the number of ways a system has the ability to move—trajectories, for example), but particularly on modifications of the parameters of the control system, the independent variables.

Some deviant behaviors may also be *repellors* (Abraham, 1995). For example, the opportunity to use a hard drug or to administer a drug with a syringe may be a repellor for most adolescents. The repellant value of hard drug is high for most adolescents and even most drug users. A syringe may be a repellor for

Figure 6.4
The Development of Theft from a Chaos Point of View: Escalation

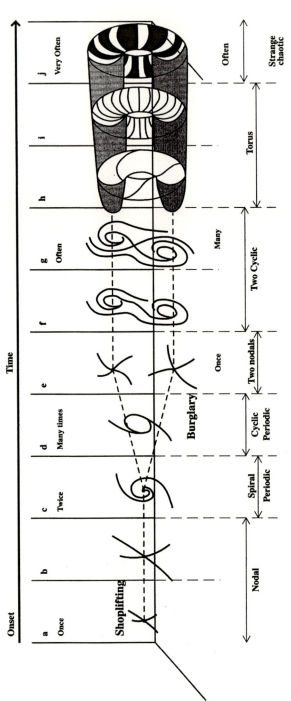

Adapted from Abraham 1992

Figure 6.5

The Development of Theft from a Chaos Point of View: Deescalation

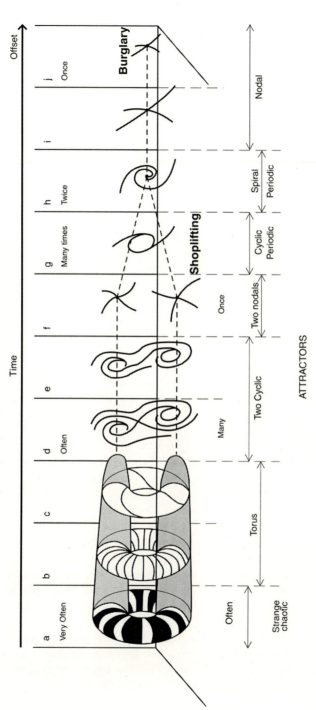

Adapted from Abraham 1992

most drug users. Figure 6.5 illustrates the de-escalation process; in this case, shoplifting becomes a repellor.

In addition, we must note that to become an attractor a deviant behavior has to be supported by a particular state of control, an appropriate level of bond, allocentrism, constraint, and model. In consequence, to continue to be a magnet a behavior has to be amplified by a particular state of control. Conversely, a behavior becomes a repellor in relation to a particular state of personal control. In a social learning perspective, attractors and repellors are producing positive and negative reinforcements.

Many *types of attractors* generate change. The three main types are the nodal, the periodic, and the strange attractors (Abraham, 1995). Figure 6.4 illustrates how these attractors operate. A nodal attractor is a magnetic point in the phase space map. It is the onset of a particular problem behavior. Shoplifting is a nodal attractor, a behavior that may be repeated if the controls favor it, for example if that adolescent has friends that are shoplifting (section a of Figure 6.4). If shoplifting increases in frequency, the pull of the attractor is amplified (section b of Figure 6.4). Shoplifting occasionally, the nodal attractor, then becomes a periodic attractor with the increased frequency of shoplifting. A periodic attractor consists of a series of repeated states. A periodic attractor can represent shoplifting if shoplifting happens many times. In the first cases, shoplifting is pictured as a spiral attractor (section c of Figure 6.4), while in the second case, shoplifting can be illustrated by a cyclic attractor (section d of Figure 6.4); the frequency of the repetition is higher.

A periodic attractor is a way of showing the self-regulation aspect of a system, the positive and negative feedbacks. According to Briggs & Peat (1989), positive feedbacks amplify the system's initial condition (shoplifting the first time), while negative feedbacks regulate the system's initial condition (diminishing and stopping shoplifting). Positive feedbacks can come from the behavioral system itself, for example, the thrill of shoplifting, one of the parameters of shoplifting, introducing the adolescent to a good feeling, or from the control system, parental attitude toward shoplifting and offending in general as a model for the adolescent. It is the same for negative feedbacks; they can originate from the behavioral system, the idea of shoplifting produces a fear of arrest, or from the control system, friends disapprove of shoplifting. A repellor can also produce positive and negative feedbacks. For example, shoplifting can become a repellor if the adolescent has negative feedbacks, such as having been intercepted by the store manager, even if shoplifting was not a repellor initially.

As age increases and opportunities and controls are modified, occasional burglary is added to shoplifting. Shoplifting is now a cyclic attractor, while burglary becomes a nodal point attractor (section e of Figure 6.4). We have two cyclic attractors (section f and g of Figure 6.4) if shoplifting is increased or maintained at a relatively high level and if the person burglarizes more often.

The difference in the quantity of the cycles between sections f and g represents the increasing frequency of shoplifting and burglary.

Later, the system will go through different phases of uncertainty. This situation is represented by the torus attractor situation in sections h and i of Figure 6.4. Shoplifting and burglary have become cyclic attractors and, in addition, they *interact*. The interactions between shoplifting and burglary form a torus attractor or a high turbulence exists in the theft behavioral system. The couple motion of the interactions between the shoplifting and burglary systems wraps itself around the surface of a torus. There is then an increased unpredictability in the theft system. In addition, the interactions with other behavioral systems, covert and overt behaviors, authority conflicts, and reckless behaviors, and the regulatory system of controls, social status, biological capacity, bonds, allocentrism, constraints and models in Le Blanc's (1997a) control theory, will cause perturbations in the initial condition; the result will then be an amplification of the key parameters. Because of this evolution, a high level of unpredictability can result and we have then a strange attractor. Section j of Figure 6.4 represents this type of attractor. This situation of chaos could happen when a person offends (thefts, frauds, violent crimes) frequently and regularly. Then the offending behavioral system loses its ability to regulate itself toward conventional behavior and this comorbid extreme situation is called the persistent offending trajectory. As we showed in our reviews (Loeber & Le Blanc, 1990; Le Blanc & Loeber, 1998), there are quantitative and qualitative changes in the course of offending, growth, and escalation. Nevertheless, there is also decline and de-escalation. Figure 6.5 illustrates the processes by which high levels of shoplifting and burglary are replaced by non-offending. Studies support the idea of increased complexity and increased uncertainty in offending and deviant behavior (see Le Blanc & Loeber, 1998, review), but very few studies describe the de-escalation process.

The growth and decline of offending is qualitatively characterized by a sequence of escalation and de-escalation stages as indicated in Table 6.1. In turn, the consequence of the presence of these stages is the apparition of critical periods at the intersections of these stages, periods when the system of deviant behavior is in a state of desequilibrium. Classical developmentalists call these periods transitions (see Lerner's review, 1986). Some criminologists refer to turning points to indicate these periods (Sampson & Laub, 1993); others use the notions of drift (Matza, 1957) or strain (Cohen, 1955). Behaviorists define these transitions as learning that represents a change in the behavioral repertoire of an organism (see Lerner, 1986). These transitions are called bifurcation by chaos theorists (Glieck, 1987; Briggs & Peat, 1989). For all these authors, a varying level of turbulence and chaos characterizes these critical periods. The course of development, because of the difficulty or ease of the transitions, can manifest sleeper effects (Kagan & Moss, 1962), abrupt changes (Flavell, 1971), ceiling effects (Le Blanc & Fréchette, 1989), or there may be other non-conceptualized effects.

A *bifurcation* is a forking or a splitting due to a change in one or more parameter that regulates an attractor. It happens when a system changes in a major way (Abraham, 1995). In section e of Figure 6.4, the splitting of a system is represented by the onset of burglary, the introduction of a new problem behavior in the theft subsystem. The same type of bifurcation is represented in section f of Figure 6.5 when shoplifting is stopped. Shoplifting has increased and the exploration of a new type of theft becomes a possibility. We are here referring to changes in internal parameters of the theft subsystem. The forking, the onset of burglary, is necessarily reinforced by changes in the external control system parameters. An example of a change in external parameters of the theft system is that friends are inviting the person to take part in a burglary. Figure 6.4 also illustrates the fractal nature of systems. When there is a bifurcation in a system, the attractor basin is increased as well as the degrees of freedoms and parameters. In consequence, the uncertainty level and turbulence are also increased. Abraham (1995) proposes many types of bifurcation for a phase space map (see Le Blanc & Janosz, unpublished, which applies the many types of bifurcations to drug use).

Self-organization is a characteristic of systems, as well as all living and human beings. It is a basic principle of developmental theories (see Lerner, 1986). Developmentalists recognize the importance of the self-regulating process when they state that the individual is active in his development. The individual gives form to his experience by activating or deactivating environments. In the theft subsystem, this principle implies that individuals can modify the parameters of shoplifting by altering the quantity, the nature of the theft, and so on. Individuals are not obliged to try burglary even if they shoplift, a possible bifurcation in their theft subsystem. Individuals can learn from their experience; they can stop aggravated theft after a particularly bad experience. Whatever the relative importance of this self-organization process over the influence of the external control system, a behavior system, such as a theft system, has a tendency to become more complex as illustrated by sections a to j in Figure 6.4. This complexity can take the form of chaos or a strange attractor. There are at least two major types of chaos according to Briggs & Peat (1989): the far-from-equilibrium chaos, a spontaneous emergence of order (reversible system in which offending will dissipate the transitory offending trajectory), and the equilibrium-thermal chaos, a conservative system in which offending is irreversible for a long period of time (persistent offending trajectory) (see Le Blanc & Janosz, unpublished).

Until now, we have considered each type of deviant behavior as a closed subsystem and the developmental processes, escalation, and de-escalation in each of them could be represented by Figures 6.4 and 6.5, respectively. For each deviant behavior subsystem, we would change the shoplifting and burglary examples by other behaviors. As we all know, in the case that each deviant behavior subsystem is subject to interactions with other deviant behavior subsystems, they are *interdependent*. In the chaos-order paradigm, interactions are feedback loops represented in Figure 6.4. These feedback loops are governed by the autopoetic paradox according to Briggs and Peat (1989). This paradox says that the degree of autonomy of a system is a function of the number of feedback loops that maintain the system. However, the number of feedback loops thus increases opportunities for other systems to enter in the movement. In our theft example, we could say that the frequency of shoplifting preserves that habit. In this case, each additional shoplift is a supplementary positive feedback loop. These feedback loops will open avenues for burglary, and so on for the theft sequence of behaviors.

Figure 6.7 represents the overall dynamics of the general deviance system. This figure integrates the mechanisms of the developmental course of controls and the developmental processes for general deviance and their interactions. We will come back to this figure later on.

In this section, we characterized the course of deviant behavior, the *what* question, and we illustrated the developmental processes of the construction of general deviance and offending in particular, the *how* question. We are in a position to approach the second task of criminology: the explanation theses changes with biological, psychological, interpersonal, and social changes in the life of the individual.

2. The Personal Regulation of the Course and Development of Deviant Behavior

Le Blanc (1997a) proposed an integrative multilayered control theory to explain the development of deviant behavior, the occurrence of deviant behavior events, and community rates of deviant behavior. The key concepts are conformity to conventional standards of behavior (the dependent variable), controls (the independent variables), and contexts (the contextual variables). The concept of control refers to Gibbs's (1989: 23) definition: "...control is *overt* behavior by human in belief that (1) the behavior increases the probability of some subsequent condition and (2) the increase or decrease is desirable." The concept of context refers to environments to favor or inhibit control. In our generic theory, there are four control mechanism: bonding, unfolding, modeling, and constraining. Two types of context modulate these mechanisms, the environment and the setting. Each category of control mechanism and each type of context represent numerous risk and protective factors that have a potential impact on deviant behavior. In this chapter, we will limit ourselves to the personal control theory, leaving aside the interaction of personal control with community control and event control.

2.1. What are the Constructs of the Theory?

Durkheim, in his 1902-1903 course at the Sorbonne, proposed the first formulation of control theory with the introduction of two constructs, attachment and constraints, and the discussion of their relationships. Reiss's (1951) statement of control theory proposed the distinction between social and personal control. However, Hirschi's formulation of control theory (1969) did not include psychological variables. Gottfredson & Hirschi (1990) overcome this deficiency with the elaboration of the notion of self-control. Our initial elaboration of control theory involved social and self-control constructs (Le Blanc & Biron, 1980). After a formalization of Hirschi's control theory using the Gibbs's procedure (Le Blanc & Caplan, 1993), we proposed the following discursive statement of control theory (Le Blanc, 1997a). Figure 6.6 abstracts the integrative personal control theory.

> At the level of the individual, conformity to conventional standards of behavior occurs and persists, on one hand, if an appropriate level of allocentrism exists and the bond to society is firm and, on the other hand, if constraints are appropriate and models of behavior pro-social. This personal and social regulation of conformity is conditional to the biological capacities of the person and his position in the social structure.
>
> Alternatively, deviant behavior emerges and continues when egocentrism persists, when the social bond is tenuous, when constraints are insufficient and deviant models abundant. These causes of deviant behavior will be more efficient when the individual has some biological deficiencies and when he comes from a lower social class. (pp. 228-229)

This discursive statement introduces four control mechanisms, fundamental personal processes responsible for an action, deviant behavior. Bonding refers to the various ways by which individuals are held together. Unfolding is the natural growth and development toward a desirable state of greater quality, the psychological development of the person according to expectations of allocentrism. Modeling is the existence of patterns than can shape conformity, opportunities that are available to individuals. Constraining is the regulation of conformity through various direct and indirect restraints; these restraints are limits imposed by the social network of the person and his beliefs. The functioning of these mechanisms is dependent of the context, the position of the individual in the social structure, and his biological capacity and environment. These mechanisms are simultaneously and causally interacting to produce conformity as illustrated in Figure 6.6. They also have their own life or ontogeneticity. This theory is systemic in the sense that it defines a structure, a sequence between the components, as well as reciprocal (in Figure 6.6, the arrows between the mechanisms of control at the same point in time) and directional relationships between the components (in Figure 6.6, the arrows between the mechanisms of control at different point in time going from left to right), including feedback (in Figure 6.6, the arrows between the mechanisms of control at different points in time going from right to left). It is also a dynamic theory because over time there is continuity and change within the mechanisms as well as because of their mutual interdependence. Let us now briefly define the component of this integrative control theory (see Le Blanc, 1997a, for more justifications of the importance of these components).

The position of the individual in the social structure is the first contextual set of conditions that affect the biological capacity of the individual and the organization of the four means of controls—bonds, allocentrism, constraints, and models.

Arnold and Brungardt (1983) were the first to introduce the construct of *biological capacity* in a control theory of delinquency. More and more studies document that biological deficiencies and a difficult temperament are conditions that limit the possibilities for the improvement of controls, such as personality and bonds.

Following Hirschi (1969), the numerous replications of his theory (Kempf, 1993), and its formalization (Le Blanc & Caplan, 1993), we can state that an individual's *bond to society* manifests itself towards several institutions constituting the different spheres of the person's world. Three institutions receive particular emphasis for the adolescent: family, school, and peers. The person relates to these institutions through three avenues: involvement in conventional activities, attachment to persons, and commitment to social institutions

The criminological literature documents the importance of individual differences in the emergence and development of individual deviant behavior (see Miller & Lynam's meta-analysis, 2001). As shown by Empey (1978), the psychodynamic perspective is compatible with control theory. In addition, bonding theorists are now considering the psychological dimensions more explicitly. Gottfredson and Hirschi (1990) propose the construct of low self-control. However, in our view, this construct is a highly limited selection of the possible psychological traits of an individual that are associated with deviant behavior (Le Blanc, 1992, 1997b). In consequence, we propose the unfolding construct of allocentrism, which is the movement away from the natural egocentrism of the individual. It manifests itself by a genuine consideration of what surrounds a person; it is the disposition to think about others and to behave in relation to them. This egocentrism-allocentrism axis of the development of humans serves to synthesize the personality dimensions that associate with deviant behavior (see Lerner, 1986).

Following Durkheim's (1895, 1934) classic distinction between norms, defined as rules of law, and moral values, and discipline, characterized as monitoring and punishment, we propose that there are two major sources of restraint when an individual envisages a deviant act, *internal and external constraints* (see the full elaboration of the constraint component in Le Blanc, 1995b). Labeling theorists fully elaborate the formal external constraint perspective, which is the impact of the imposition of a formal label by society, school, and other social institutions. While bonding theorists develop the informal social reaction point of view, for example, parental constraints in the forms of rules, monitoring, and discipline. In addition, bonding theorists elaborate the notion of internal constraint under the concept of beliefs and under the concept of

Figure 6.6
The Structure of the Personal Control Theory

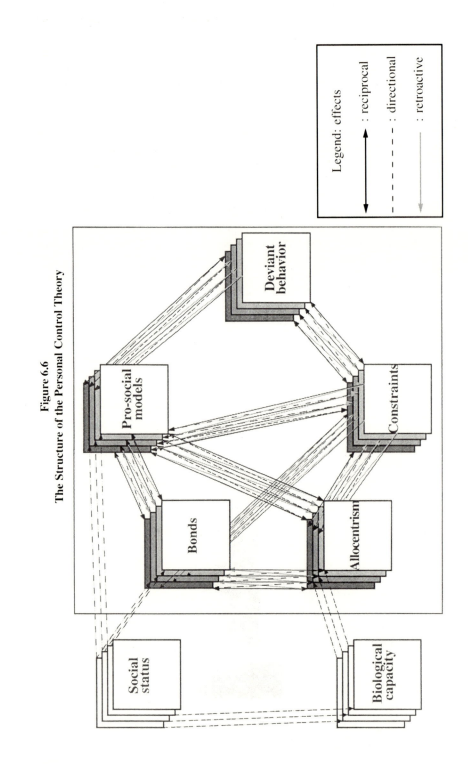

perceived certainty and severity of sanctions, a notion borrowed from deterrence theorists.

Tarde (1924) introduced a *modeling* explanation of delinquency, which was developed by Sutherland (Sutherland and Cressey, 1960) and elaborated on particularly by Akers (1997). Modeling, particularly antisocial, is an important cause of adolescent delinquency according to numerous studies. Bonding theory accepts that delinquent companions have a direct or causal impact on the commission of crimes (see Hirschi, 1969, analysis; and Le Blanc and Caplan, 1993, formalization). In addition, Gottfredson and Hirschi (1990) suggest that low self-control leads to street life and to membership in a deviant group. These factors, in turn, lead to more frequent deviant behavior.

2.2. What is the Structure of the Theory?

The structure of the theory indicates the direct and indirect impacts of the various mechanisms of control relative to deviant behavior in Figure 6.6. The relative position of the mechanisms of control depends on the principle of prerequisites and on the distinction between continuity and change. The theory states that there are exogenous factors that do not have a direct impact on deviant behavior; they are the position in the social structure and the biological capacity (in Figure 6.6, the arrows going from their box to the control mechanisms indicate only directional relationships). The mechanisms of control mediate their impact. Two of these mechanisms of control, bonding and psychological unfolding (allocentrism), are prerequisites or remote sets of factors that impact indirectly on deviant behavior. They are the foundations of the control mechanism. Without bonds, models cannot be significant and constraints cannot be operate. In consequence, an unbounded individual cannot be sensitive to direct controls or influenced by the available pro-social models. In addition, since the psychological unfolding mechanism refers to a desirable state, the definition of what ought to be, in terms of psychological maturation, necessarily precede the influence of available models and constraints, what is available as direct controls. In addition, the bonding and the allocentrism mechanisms modulate deviant behavior through the mechanisms of modeling and constraining.

These mechanisms are proximal causes of the criminal phenomenon. Models and constraints are more specific to the space-time dimension. They change frequently. They are not the more permanent dimensions of control such as bonding and modeling. The bonding and the allocentrism mechanisms are also in a situation of reciprocal causation at a specific moment. The modeling and the constraining mechanisms are in the same situation; a causal order cannot be established theoretically or empirically at a specific time. In sum, the bonding and psychological unfolding mechanisms are the foundations and the continuity component of control, while the modeling and constraining mechanisms are catalysts of conformity; they are the changeable dimensions of control. Even in that context, we postulate that the four mechanisms of control are in a synergetic relation. They interact to produce an overall level of control of deviant behavior. This synergy is the result of three types of relationships between them. First, there are the reciprocal relations, at a specific point in time, between the bonding, the allocentrism, the modeling, and the constraining mechanisms. Second, the directional relations between these mechanisms, that is from time one to time two; for example, tenuous bonds at time one favor the association with deviant peers at time two. Third, the retroactive effects between the mechanisms, that is, for example, school sanctions at time one will reduce the commitment toward education at time two.

We performed empirical tests of the general structure of the model of personal control for representative samples of males and females in the 1970s and the 1980s (Le Blanc & Biron, 1980; Le Blanc, Ouimet, & Tremblay, 1988) and an adjudicated sample of males in the 1990s (Le Blanc, 1997b). The path analysis with canonical correlations supported the hypothesize structure of the theory. We also obtained similar structures for middle range models of the family functioning (Le Blanc, 1992) and the school experience (Le Blanc, Vallières & McDuff, 1992).

In consequence, we can state that the position of the individual in the social structure is an indirect cause of general deviance, as shown in Figure 6.6. In addition, biological deficiencies will restrict the development of allocentrism in the person and, in particular, it should affect his cognitive development, as well as the affective and relational maturation. Such factors are also indirect causes of conformity and deviant behavior as shown in Figure 6.6. In turn, the building of the bond to society may be more difficult when the person lives in adverse socioeconomic conditions and when the person is highly egocentric and less able cognitively. In order to install a solid bond, the involvement in conventional activities is a requirement for the attachment to persons and they both support the commitment to social institutions. The theory also states that a solid bond counters the impact of deviant models and favors the acceptance of existing internal and external constraints. Figure 6.6 also indicates that an appropriate level of allocentrism favors the establishment of a solid bond to society, receptivity to social constraints, and preference for pro-social influences, and, in turn, conformity to conventional standards of behavior. However, the levels of allocentrism and cognition are dependent on the individual's biological capacity and his position in the social structure. Figure 6.6 also represents the idea that the individual's receptivity to social constraints depends on the quality of the person's bond to society, the level of development of his allocentrism, and on the presence of strong pro-social influences. It is one of the last protections against deviant behavior. When constraints are inappropriate to the age of the person, erratic or absent, they are direct and proximal causes of deviant behavior as shown in numerous studies (see Le Blanc review,

1995b). Finally, Figure 6.6 states that the person's receptivity to criminal influences depends on the quality of his bond to society, the development of his allocentrism, and the tightness and appropriateness of the constraints imposed by him or others. Thus, the receptivity to deviant influences is a direct and proximal cause of general deviance as shown by numerous criminological studies (see Akers review, 1997).

The development of conformity, control, and contexts manifests itself in terms of course, processes, and trajectories. Their course is observable through quantitative and qualitative changes over time. The tools of the chaos-order paradigm can be applied to characterize the development of conformity and control. In addition, there are a limited number of developmental social and psychological trajectories for individuals.

2.3. What is the Course of Personal Control?

Developmental control theory can be traced back to Quetelet's (1842: 95) statement that

> This fatal propensity appears to be developed in proportion to the intensity of the physical power and passions of man.... The intellectual and moral development...subsequently weakens the propensity to crime...

The course of personal control can take the forms of quantitative and qualitative changes. *Quantitative* changes can be conceived in terms of growth, however, there are fewer studies on the course of controls than on the course of deviant behavior. For example, quantitative changes in personal control refer to variations, for example, in height (biological capacity), social class (position in the social structure), attachment (bonds), neuroticism (allocentrism), adhesion to norms (constraints), and participation in a delinquent gang (models). The growths in these areas are viewed as governed by the aging-stability law (Glenn, 1980). According to that law, personal controls would tend to stabilize and become less likely to change as a person grows older. In most domains, the changes would be more important during adolescence and youth. In addition, they are in the direction of greater conformity, according to some studies (Jessor & Jessor, 1977; Jessor, Donovan & Costa, 1991; Le Blanc, Charland, Côté & Pronovost, 1980; Le Blanc, 1992: Le Blanc, 1994). We are of the opinion that we can easily apply the measures of degree, direction, and velocity of change (see Table 6.1) to any of the mechanisms of personal control and their components.

In the personality domain (the allocentrism mechanism of regulation), there are numerous growth curves for the cognitive, emotional, and relational components of allocentrism. Following Costa and McRae, we can expect the personality structure to be invariant, at least from adolescence through adulthood (Costa & McRae, 1997), an improvement on the personality measures through various tests, and a point of full maturity after which there are little changes, around 30 years of age (Costa & McRae, 1997) (see our data on the development of allocentrism from 15 to 40, Morizot & Le Blanc, 2003a; and the trajectories, Morizot & Le Blanc, 2003b, 2005). If the direction of change is well established, that is maturation, there are also indications about the degree of change, its velocity, and the nature of the changes in existing studies. However, the backwardness of the males of the adjudicated sample remained similar in adolescence and at the beginning of the 30s and 40s (Morizot & Le Blanc, 2003a).

There are very rare studies in each domain of social controls. We do not know of any growth curves for bonds, that is, the attachment to parents and other adult figures, and the commitment to education. However, a recent meta-analysis by Laursen, Coy, and Collins (1998) concludes that parent-child frequency of conflict decreases from early adolescence to mid-adolescence and from mid-adolescence to late adolescence, while the conflict affect increases during puberty and with age during adolescence. In sum, disagreements are less frequent as the adolescent advances toward the end of adolescence. However, when there are such conflicts, they are more intense emotionally.

Turning to the modeling constructs of the integrative control theory, there are also some striking age trends in many activities of everyday life, which our control theory calls involvement in conventional activities or routine activities (Larson & Richards, 1989; Larson & Verma, 1999; Le Blanc et al. (1989) showed that, for their representative and adjudicated samples, involvement in leisure activities and participation in activities with family members are increasing. In addition, Le Blanc et al. (1980) find a decrease in loitering, a trend particularly important in the adjudicated sample. The same tendency can be observed for criminogenic routine activities (unstructured socializing, activities outside the home, and at-home activities) (Osgood, Wilson, O'Malley, Bachman, & Johnston, 1996).

Peers are also part of the modeling construct of our personal control theory. Le Blanc et al. (1980) find a decrease in attachment to delinquent peers. In addition, Elliott and Menard (1996) observed an increased percentage of youths in less delinquent groups and a declining percentage of individuals in more delinquent groups during late adolescence. However, there is a considerable stability in the type of group adolescents affiliate with from one year to the next and, when change occurs, it is a gradual transition from one peer group type to a type not too dissimilar. Finally, these authors observe an increase in the status of isolation as adolescents approach adulthood and enter into monogamous relationships. In addition, there are some data on the changes in the relevance of peers during adolescence. In particular, changes are observable concerning the importance of peers, time spent in their company, and loyalty to peers. There are also changes in the exposure to delinquent peers. All these variables are operationalizing the bond and the modeling constructs of the control theory. The relevance of peers is rising (confirmed by Stoolmiller, 1994, from late childhood and early adolescence) and falling during a relatively brief period around mid-adolescence according to Warr (2002).

Finally, for the components of the constraint construct, there are very few indications for external constraints and not much more for internal constraints. Jessor and Jessor (1977) note a decrease in perceived parental control during adolescence. Internal controls also vary during adolescence. The tolerance to deviance increases during adolescence (Jessor & Jessor, 1977), but decreases during youth (Jessor et al. 1991). Le Blanc et al. (1980), for their representative sample of adolescents, confirm the first tendency, while the second tendency happens during the second half of adolescence in the adjudicated sample. In addition, Zhang, Loeber and Stouthamer-Loeber (1997) demonstrated that delinquent attitudes progress during adolescence, particularly toward serious violence and minor and serious theft. They tend to decrease before 11, remain stable until 14, and increase sharply thereafter. Whatever the level of the changes, the stability of the beliefs is impressive in the Thornberry, Lizotte, Krohn, and Farnworth (1994) and Elliott and Menard (1996) studies for example.

In addition to the few growth curves reported in the literature, some studies use cross-lagged analysis with two or more waves of data during adolescence and variables that could operationalize some of the construct of our integrative control theory. For example, the Rochester group has produced a number of interesting publications with four to six variables and two to five data waves (for example Thornberry et al., 1991, and 1994; Krohn et al., 1996; see Thornberry, 1996, for a review). In all of these models, the effect of a particular variable on itself at a subsequent point in time is higher than its impact on other control variables or deviant behavior at the same point in time or another moment. These data are confirming the existence of the self-organization principle put forth by the developmentalists and the principles of the sensitivity to the initial condition proposed by the chaos-order paradigm (in criminology we would say state dependent).

In sum, there are some good indications about continuity and change in the nature of social and personal control during the life of an individual. Bonding, modeling, allocentrism, and constraining, as well as the biological capacity and environment and the position of the individual in the social structure, are evolving according to the maturational hypothesis.

We do not know that much about quantitative changes, but we know much less about qualitative changes. Concerning the allocentrism construct of the theory, numerous theories, case studies, and empirical studies show that stages exist and that they are related to age. For example, there are psychosexual (Freud), cognitive (Piaget), moral (Kohlberg), psychosocial (Erickson), ego development (Lovinger), and interpersonal (Sullivan, Grant and Grant) developmental sequences of stages to name a few domains and the principal theorist, thus leaving aside the empirical studies. For the types of social control, there is virtually no evidence that a developmental sequence exist. The statements about the existence of a normative developmental sequence can be found only for peer relations (Oden, 1988), external control (Durkheim, 1934), and play (Berk, 1989).

What are the Developmental Processes of Personal Control?

We are of the opinion that the tools of the chaos-order paradigm, described in section 1.3 and illustrated in Figures 6.4 and 6.5, apply to the understanding of the development of personal control. Since it would be repetitive to talk at length about the six categories of control, we will limit ourselves to some examples. This option is reasonable because all systems are self-similar; they repeat themselves in descending scales as explained earlier.

Concerning the bond control system, there are at least three subsystems: involvement in conventional activities, attachment to persons, and commitment to institutions (see our formalization of Hirschi's bonding theory, Le Blanc, 1993, and our discursive statement of our integrative control theory, Le Blanc, 1997a). These subsystems are attractors in the bonding system, but we can easily think of attractors in each of these subsystems. As an example, we can list some of the attractors in the attachment subsystem: mother, father, siblings, teacher, coach, neighbor, intimate friend, girlfriend, and so on. Some of these figures can be minor nodal attractors, for example, a neighbor of the same age that a child plays with once in a while; some would be cyclic, for example, a friend that is kept for many years. Some other figures could be chaotic, for example if the attachment to the mother is very insecure the child will have difficulties in relating to other figures of the attachment subsystem or the delinquent peers are particularly unstable as we know. In the constraints domain, there are external and internal subsystems; external constraints could be formal attractors (for example, the sanctions from the school or the justice system) or informal attractors (for example, the reactions of parents, peers, teachers, and others to attitudes and behaviors) (see Le Blanc, 1995b, 1997a, b). Finally, in the models system of control, there are two majors subsystems, routine activities favoring deviance and the availability of persons or groups involved in deviance, that are composed of many attractors or repellors (see Le Blanc, 1997a, b).

The six categories of controls are then attractors; they are magnetic points that structure and organize personal control. For example, in terms of bonds, all individuals have the opportunity to attach to a mother, a father, a friend, a teacher, and so on. They have the occasion to invest and commit themselves to school, work, sport, and so on. All individuals will encounter various types of prosocial and antisocial models and will participate in various routine activities and, in addition, they will be submitted to many types of internal and external constraints. The pull of these attractors is dependent on changes in the control system parameters and degrees of freedom, but particularly on modifications of the parameters and degree of freedom regarding bonds, allocentrism, constraints, and models.

In the control system, the parameters are characteristic of the particular components. For example, if we think about bonds, the parameters of attachment to the mother as an attractor could be the nature (secure, avoidant, disorganized, and so on), the degree, the duration, and so on. The degrees of freedom are the number of ways a system has the ability to move. For example, in the attachment system there are numerous possible trajectories, for example a secure attachment with the mother, a disoriented attachment with the father, an avoidant attachment with teachers, and so on. The existence of the numerous figures of attachment could be represented in Figures 6.1 and 6.2 if we change the labels of the behaviors by labels of figures of attachment. Then, these attractors create some turbulence in the system as in Figures 6.4 and 6.5. We can imagine the same situation with the commitment (school, work, sport, hobby, and so on) and the involvement components of the bonding system. The same could also be said for the constraint (internal and external) and the models (routine activities and affiliation with peers and adults), components of the personal control system.

If we come back to the attachment example, some attachment figures may be repellors. For example, some of the following figures could play that role: the mother, the father, a sibling, a teacher, a coach, a gay friend could be a repellor for some adolescents. In sum, all systems and subsystems of control, as well as general deviance, have their own attractors and repellors. The attractors or repellors in the personal control system and subsystems can produce desequilibrium or chaos in their own systems. In addition, as we have seen, many types of attractor generate change. The behavior labels in Figures 6.4 and 6.5 could be changed to labels referring to any of the components of the personal control system. A nodal attractor is a magnetic point in the phase space map. It is the initial phase of the attachment to the mother, for example. A secure attachment is a nodal attractor, an experience that could be reinforced if the other controls are favoring it, for example if the mother invests in her child (section a of Figure 6.4). If attachment increases, the pull of the attractor is amplified (section b of Figure 6.4). A periodic attractor consists of a series of repeated states. A periodic attractor can represent the attachment if the level of security is increased. It could be pictured as a spiral attractor (section c of Figure 6.4) or a cyclic attractor (section d of Figure 6.4), depending on the degree of attachment. A periodic attractor shows the self-regulation aspect of a system, the positive and negative feedbacks. Positive feedbacks can come from the bonding system itself, for example, the security of the attachment, one of the parameters of attachment, introduce the child to a good experience, or other components of the control system, for example, appropriate parental management techniques. It is the same for negative feedbacks; they can originate from the bonding system and other components of the control system.

As age increases, opportunities and controls are modified, attachment to a teacher is added to attachment to the mother. Attachments to the mother and to the teacher are then two attractors (section e of Figure 6.4). If the attachment to the mother is tenuous and if the attachment to the teacher becomes weak, we have then two cyclic attractors (sections f and g of Figure 6.4). The difference in the quantity of the cycles between sections f and g represents the increasing degree of poor attachment. Later, the system will go through different phases of uncertainty. The system is the torus attractor situation in sections h and i of Figure 6.4. Poor attachment to various figures become cyclic attractors and, in addition, they interact. Their interactions form a torus attractor. There is then an increased unpredictability. Because of this trajectory, a high level of unpredictability can result and we have then a strange attractor. The dark portion of Figure 6.4 section j represents this type of attractor. This situation of chaos could be when a person has a disorganized attachment. Then the bonding system loses its ability to regulate itself toward a normative situation, a secure attachment.

Qualitative changes imply a developmental sequence of stages as indicated in Table 6.1. In turn, the consequence of the existence of these stages is the presence of critical periods at the intersections of these stages, periods when the system of behavior and the system control are in a state of desequilibrium. A bifurcation is a forking or a splitting due to a change in one or more parameters that regulate an attractor. The opportunities for attachment represented by the various figures that the individual encounters during the life course involve such bifurcations.

In this section, we tried to show how the tools of the chaos-order paradigm could be used to map the changes in the personal control system. Particularly, we argued that a phase space map could be draw for each subsystem of the control system, bonds, allocentrism, constraints, models, biological capacity, and social status.

2.5. How Does the Course of Controls Interact with the Course of Deviant Behavior?

At the beginning of this section on the course and development of personal control, we announced that we were in a position to approach the second task of criminology, that is the explanation of the changes in deviant behavior with biological, psychological, interpersonal, and social changes in the life of the individual. Until now, we illustrated how the tools of developmental criminology were helpful to describe the course of personal control and how the tools of the chaos-order paradigm were useful for the mapping of the developmental processes of the personal control.

Figure 6.7 represents the overall dynamics of the control system of general deviance. This figure integrates the mechanisms of the developmental course of controls and the developmental course for general deviance and their interactions. The beginnings of the behavior and control systems represent the initial condition, while the rest of the course is state dependent. The independent systems are there to indicate that each is a self-organizing phenomenon. In addition, in each system there are probabilistic quantitative and qualitative changes. Figure 6.7 shows the combined action of continuity and change in each subsystem, coevolution, and the interworking on each other, interaction. The changes in each subsystem are described in sections 1.3 and 2.4 of this chapter. In Figure 6.7, coevolution is represented by the changes on each side of the horizontal line dividing the plans of the figure, the changes in deviant behavior and the changes in personal controls.

Figure 6.7 also illustrates that the personal controls are progressively constructed (sections a and b of Figure 6.7). Criminologists associate that period of the course of personal control as the creation of a criminal propensity that is called low self-control by Gottfredson and Hirschi (1990). At some point, a bifurcation is encountered, an offense is committed (section c of Figure 6.7). This offense, according to our understanding of the processes, is probably precipitated by antisocial models (exposure to deviant friends or particular routine activities) (in our multilayered control theory we would then refer to the criminal event level of explanation and its particular constructs: see Le Blanc, 1997a). The interdependence of the course of personal control and the course of offending is synergistic. This synergy is manifested by the relationships between the two attractors, the personal control system and the offending or deviant behavior system; these interactions are illustrated in sections d to j in Figure 6.7. This synergy is the result of three underlining phenomena. First, there are the reciprocal relationships between these two systems; at a specific point in time the level of bonding influences the level of deviant behavior and reciprocally. Second, there are directional relationships between the two systems; changes in the personal control system will subsequently introduce changes in the deviant behavior system. Third, there are retroactive effects between the two systems; changes in the deviant behavior system will subsequently produce new adaptations in the personal control system. In fact, these interactions, synergy, exist all along the time dimension, the life span.

3. Explaining Key Empirical Issues

In section 2, we formulated our theory of the course and development of personal control. We will now apply the theory to some key empirical issues formulated in David Farrington's chapter. They will be addressed for each offending trajectory. We do so because the general discursive statement of the theory talks about levels of control, degree that are not necessarily synchronized between the bonding, allocentrism, constraining, and modeling mechanisms.

3.1. Why Do People Start Offending?

Figure 6.7
The Interactional Development of General Deviance and Controls from a Chaos Point of View: Escalation

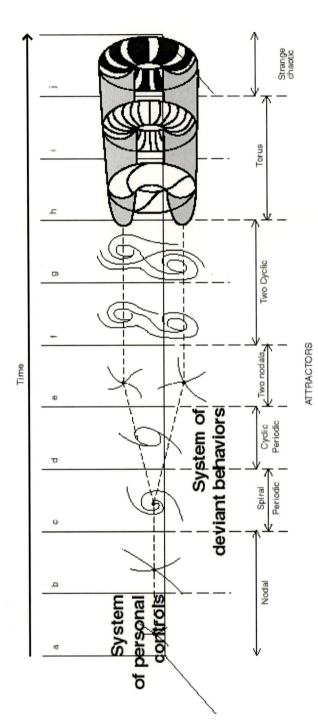

Adapted from Abraham 1992

Offending starts because the push of the control system is significantly increased by changes in its system parameters and degrees of freedom.

Persistent offending is primarily a question of propensity rather then opportunities. Offending starts early because the level of control has always been low. The individual is egocentric, has weak bonds, is influenced by antisocial models, and experiences little constraints from socialization agents. These conditions are maintained by adverse socioeconomic conditions and biological deficiencies.

Transitory offending is the result of a weak propensity and opportunities and it is generated through three processes. First, offending starts because of tenuous bonding, psychological unfolding, inappropriate constraints, and antisocial models. Second, offending rests on tenuous controls but is triggered by particular adverse life events. Third, offending starts when strong antisocial models are operant and bonds are tenuous in the family or school domains.

Common offending is the result of opportunities. The control mechanisms are of good quality, but some opportunities unfold at random in the routine activities of the individual or are pursued in an exploratory manner.

3.2. Why Do People Continue Offending?

Offending continues because the push of the control system remains stable in terms of its system parameters and degrees of freedom. There is continuity in offending because of the relative ordering of people on personal controls stays fairly consistent over time. People continue offending for two reasons. First, they maintain their offending and escalate because of socialization or learning that is the relatively permanent change in behavioral potentiality that occurs as a result of reinforced practice. Second, they maintain their offending because there is synchrony between their trajectory of offending and their nonconventional trajectory of personal controls (bonds, allocentrism, models and constraints).

Persistent offending perseveres when the level of control remains low, the individual remains egocentric, with weak bonds, with antisocial models, and with little constraints. The development on the mechanisms of control is halted and the context, position in the social structure and the biological environment, involves a high risk of problem behaviors.

Transitory offending is maintained by opportunities. It will continue until the transition to young adult activities (work or study) and the peer group loses its importance to more intimate relationships.

3.3. Why Do People Stop Offending?

Offending stops when two conditions are synchronized: offenses become repellors and the control system becomes more prosocial. Committing an offense is no longer possible or in the interest of the individual. In addition, the prosocial pull of the control system is significantly increased by changes in its system parameters and degrees of freedom.

Persistent delinquents will stop late without modifying their propensity of offending; they seek new opportunities for their level of personal control that remains low. The individual is egocentric, has weak bonds, is influenced by antisocial models, and experiences little constraints from socialization agents. These conditions are maintained by adverse socioeconomic conditions and biological deficiencies (drug abuse, for example). The push of these mechanisms of personal controls becomes insignificant, mainly after 30. They move from predatory crimes to criminal markets activities and marginal social status (welfare recipients, black market).

Transitory delinquents will stop offending when their level of prosocial controls increases. The individual becomes more allocentric, develops new bonds, is influenced by prosocial models, and solidifies his/her internal constraints. The development on these mechanisms of personal control shows a very significant increase, mainly between 18 and 30.

3.4. Why Does the Prevalence of Offending Peak during the Second Half of Adolescence?

Offending peaks during the second half of adolescence as the result of a combination of three phenomena: the period of escalation in offending by persistent delinquents, the moment of exploration by common offenders, and the main period of activity of the transitory delinquents. This peak can be explained by the replacement of external controls by internal controls. The adolescent seeks more autonomy and parents grant it. As a result, a disequilibrium is created in the control mechanism. This momentary disorganization of controls favors the commission of crimes.

3.5. Why are There Between-Individual Differences in Offending?

Individuals are unique at birth and they remain unique throughout the life span. As a consequence, the level of control is different for each individual and they do not experience the same set of situations (see our criminal event control theory, Le Blanc, 1997a). As we have stated, these differences seem to remain stable between individuals and groups of individuals such as adjudicated adolescents (this is at least the case for personality traits, Morizot and Le Blanc, 2003). There is continuity in offending because the relative ordering of people on personal controls stays fairly consistent over time.

3.6. Why are There Within-Individual Differences in Offending?

There are long-term within-individual differences in offending because of maturation, the natural growth and differentiation that characterize every system or individual over time. In addition, there are short-term (over time and place) within-individual differences in offending because of adaptation, the way an organism adapts through the integration of new external elements or through structural change to fit with the environment.

3.7. What are the Effects of Life Events on Offending?

Life events can appear at any time of the life span. They are attractors. They are contextual conditions that have only indirect effects on deviant behavior. They alter controls positively or negatively and their fluctuations, in turn, increase or decease offending. They modify the general level of personal control or in particular some control mechanisms (bonds, allocentrism, models or constraints).

3.8. What is the Scope of the Theory?

The theory is designed to explain within-individual and between-individual variations in deviance throughout life. The theory applies to males and females, specifically to Western industrialized countries, but the same concepts may have to be operationalized differently in other countries. It has been adapted to explain gender difference (Lanctôt & Le Blanc 2002). Our personal control theory of course and development of offending does not explain criminal events and crime rates. However, there is a formulation of the theory for these levels of explanation and the interaction of these levels is modeled (Le Blanc, 1997a).

3.9. Can the Theory be Operationalized and Tested?

There are several tests of the personal control model with population samples (Le Blanc & Biron, 1980; Le Blanc, Ouimet & Tremblay, 1988) and an adjudicated sample (Le Blanc, 1997b). In addition, we performed some tests of components of the theory (Le Blanc, 1995b; Morizot & le Blanc, 2003) or middle range theories (Le Blanc, 1992; Le Blanc et al., 1992) and they are concordant with known facts (see the review of Kempf, 1993, for bonds).

General deviance can be measured in a variety of ways, by self-reports and official records, and carefully designed interviews and questionnaires; in addition, informants (parents, teachers, peers...) can be used. We constructed interviews and questionnaires to measure the main constructs and each main construct was composed of subconstructs (for example, bonds are assessed through attachment [parents, peers, adults...] and commitment [school, work, sport...]). Each subconstruct was composed of measures, for example, attachment to parents was assessed through reciprocal communication with parents, affective identification, acceptation-rejection, and so on (see Le Blanc, 1996).

Conclusion

In this chapter, we tried to illustrate how the tools of developmental criminology and of the chaos-order paradigm could help us to map the development of the general deviance syndrome and its personal control explanation. Developmental criminology, with its paradigm and its large body of data on the continuity and change of general deviance, offers significant tools to describe the course of problem behavior along the life course. However, we have argued that it does not help us to gain a genuine understanding of the processes that support continuity and change. The processes are identified by developmental criminologists, such as escalation or desistance, but the way in which these processes come about is not described. With the tools of the chaos-order paradigm, we tried to show how these processes happen, for example, escalation in offending and the course of attachment. Moving from the analysis of the course of general deviance and personal controls to the examination of its underlying processes is the next challenge for developmental criminology.

This question is also the next challenge of the twenty-first century for criminologists because the development and the explanation of general deviance are characterized by complexity. Every scientist now accepts that the syndrome of general deviance is the result of multiple influences: biological, psychological, social, cultural, and so on. However, our ability to understand and describe how these influences interact is limited. There is a large gap between our perception of the complexities of these interactions, our discursive statements of these phenomena, our operational models describing them, and the results of the empirical tests of these models. The discursive statements and models of the social and behavioral disciplines are characterized by oversimplification.

The reasons explaining that gap between these levels of apprehension of reality are numerous. We can name the state of empirical knowledge about general deviance and its possible explanatory factors, our cognitive capacities to consider simultaneously many factors from different levels of explanation in continuous interactions, our abilities to communicate our perceptions of these interactions, the availability of an appropriate technology to model them, and our difficulty of communicating intelligibly the complexity of the interactions between explanatory factors. In this chapter, we were trying to fill partly the gap between our perceptions and our models with the geometrical tools of the chaos-order paradigm. We were trying to consider and manage more complexity rather then simplify the reality.

Until recently, most of the discursive theoretical statements and the quantitative models, in the behavioral and social sciences and in criminology in particular, have been dominated by linear thinking. Let us mention, as one example among all possible others, bonding (Hirschi, 1969) and low self-control theories (Gottfredson and Hirschi, 1990), and some of our integrative models (Le Blanc et al., 1988; Le Blanc, 1997a). Everyone will recognize that everything in life is not linear. Everything does not happen as expected; there are many detours and unpredictable outcomes. Human development, as stressed by developmentalists, is only partially the result of a linear process; linearity is only part of the puzzle. Case studies of adolescent delinquents have showed us repeatedly that our theories and models are reductionist. One blunt example of such simplification is that integrative models rarely attain 50 percent of explained variance. It is the case in our studies (Le Blanc et al. 1988; Le Blanc, 1997b) as in many other cases. Why?

We can state at least three categories of reasons for our inefficiency: our explanatory models are incomplete; our constructs are badly operationalized; our measures are deficient, and the strategies and methods of analysis are inadequate. Independently of these reasons, we think that we are inefficient because our theories and models are linear, even if they are sometimes interactional and recursive (see, for example, Thornberry, 1987; 1996) or if they consider multiple levels of explanations (Le Blanc, 1997a). Even these models do not take completely into account numerous and complex interactions and the random component that is part of development, this independently of the limits of our usual statistical tools. These theories and models still suffer from two difficulties: considering the maximum possible number of interactions that we can perceive and integrating a random component in the development of general deviance and controls.

In this chapter, we were exploring a new way of overcoming these difficulties. We are convinced that this new perspective has helped us to model known empirical and contentious facts in criminology. Before judging the heuristic utility of the integration of developmental criminology and the chaos-order paradigm for the understanding of the development of general deviance, we had to apply their tools. We believe that the obtained description of the developmental processes of general deviance was compatible with existing knowledge in the social and behavioral sciences. In particular, we showed that notions such as continuity-discontinuity, equilibrium-disequilibrium, probabilistic determinism, and self-organization are compatible with developmental theories in psychology, sociology, and criminology and with empirical facts about offending.

Notes

1.   Our empirical and theoretical work has been supported by the Social Sciences and Humanities Research Council of Canada and the Fond pour la Formation des Chercheurs et l'Aide à la Recherche du Québec over the last thirty years.

2.   We thank Marcel Fréchette, Rolf Loeber, and Michel Janosz for their contribution to our work. Some of the tools of the developmental criminology paradigm were initially operationalized with Marcel Fréchette and this paradigm was conceptualized and formulated with Rolf Loeber. The application of the chaos-order paradigm for the understanding of the development of offending and controls was done through long discussion with Michel Janosz. Without these colleagues the formulation of our developmental theory of deviant behavior would not have attain its actual maturity.

References

Abraham, F. D. (1992). *Visual Introduction to Dynamical Systems Theory for Psychology*. Santa Cruz: Aerial Press.

Abraham, F. D. (1995). Introduction to dynamics: A basic language; A basic metamodeling strategy. In F. D. Abraham, A. R. Gilgen (Eds.), *Chaos Theory in Psychology*. Westport, CT, Greenwood Press.

Akers, R. L. (1997). *Social Learning and Social Structure: A General Theory of Crime and Deviance*. Boston: Northeastern University Press.

Arnold, W. R., & Brungardt, T. (1983). *Juvenile Misconduct and Delinquency*. Boston: Houghton Mifflin.

Berk, L. (1989). *Child Development*. Boston: Allyn and Bacon.

Blumstein, A., Cohen, J., Roth, J. A., & Visher, C. A. (1986). *Criminal Careers and "Career Criminals."* Washington, DC: National Academy Press.

Briggs, J., & Peat, F. D. (1989). *Turbulent Mirror*. New York: Harper and Row.

Cohen, A. K. (1955). *Delinquent Boys: The Culture of the Gang*. New York: Free Press.

Costa, P. T., & McCrae, R. R. (1997). Longitudinal stability of adult personality. In R. Hogan, J. Johnson & S. Briggs (Eds.), *Handbook of Personality Psychology* (pp. 269-290). San Diego, CA: Academic Press

Dunford, F. W., & Elliott, D. S. (1984). Identifying career offenders using self-reported data. *Journal of Research in Crime and Delinquency*, 21, 1: 57-86.

Durkheim, E. (1895). Les règles de la méthode sociologique. Paris: Alcan (1960, nouvelle edition, Presses Universi-taires de France).

Durkheim, E. (1934). De l'éducation morale. Paris: Alcan (1963, nouvelle édition, Presses Universitaires de France).

Empey, L. T. (1978). *American Delinquency*. Homewood: Dorsey Press.

Elliott, D. S., Huizinga, D., & Menard, S. (1989). *Multiple Problem Youth: Delinquency, Substance Abuse, and Mental Health Problems*. New York: Springer-Verlag.

Elliott, D. S., & Menard, S. (1996). Delinquent friends and delinquent behavior: Temporal and developmental patterns. In J. D. Hawkins (Ed.), *Delinquency and Crime, Current Theories*. New York: Cambridge University Press.

Flavell, J. H. (1971). Stage related properties of cognitive development. *Cognitive Psychology*, 2: 421-453.

Gibbs, J. P. (1989). *Control Sociology's Central Notion*. Chicago: University of Illinois Press.

Gleick, J. (1987). *Chaos, Making of a New Science*. New York: Viking Penguin.

Glenn, N. D. (1980). Values, attitudes, and beliefs. In O.G. Brim & J. Kagan (Eds.), *Constancy and Change in Human Development*. Cambridge, MA: Harvard University Press.

Gottfredson, M. R., & Hirschi, T. (1990). *A General Theory of Crime*. Stanford, CA: Stanford University Press.

Hirschi, T. (1969). *Causes of Delinquency*. Berkeley: University of California Press.

Jessor, R., Donovan, J. E., & Costa, F. M. (1991). *Beyond Adolescence, Problem Behavior and Young Adult Development*. New York: Cambridge University Press.

Jessor, R., & Jessor, S. L. (1977). *Problem Behavior and Psychological Development, A Longitudinal Study*. New York: Academic Press.

Kandel, D. (2002). *Stages and Pathways of Drug Involvement*. Cambridge: Cambridge University Press.

Kagan, J., & Moss, H. (1962). *Birth to Maturity*. New York: Wiley.

Kempf, K. (1993). Hirschi's theory of social control: Is it fecund but not yet fertile? *Advances in Theoretical Criminology*, 4: 143-186.

Kornhauser, R. R. (1978). *Social Sources of Delinquency: An Appraisal of Analytic Models*. Chicago: University of Chicago Press.

Krohn, M. D., Lizotte, A. J., Thornberry, T. P., Smith, C. & McDowall, D. (1996). Reciprocal causal relationships among drug use, peers, and belief: A five waves panel model. *Journal of Drug Issues*, 2: 405-26.

Lanctôt, N., & Le Blanc, M. (2002). Explaining adolescent females' involvement in general deviance: Towards integration of theoretical perspectives. *Crime and Justice*, 26: 113-202.

Larson, R.W., & Richards, M.H. (1989). Introduction: The changing life space of early adolescence. *Journal of Youth and Adolescence*, 18: 501-509.

Larson, R. W., & Verma, S. (1999). How children and adolescents spend time across the world: Work, play, and developmental opportunities. *Psychological Bulletin*. 125: 701-736.

Laursen, B., Coy, K. C., & Collins, W. A. (1998). Reconsidering changes in parent-child conflict across adolescence. A meta-analysis. *Child Development*, 69: 817-832.

Le Blanc, M. (1983). Delinquency as an epiphenomenon of adolescence. In R. Corrado, M. Le Blanc, & J. Trépanier (Eds.), *Current Issues in Juvenile Justice* (pp. 31-48). Toronto: Butterworths.

Le Blanc, M. (1992). Family dynamics, adolescent delinquency and adult criminality. *Psychiatry*, 55, 4: 336-353.

Le Blanc, M. (1994). Measures of escalation and their personal and social predictors. In H. J. Kerner, & E. Weitekamp (Eds.), *Longitudinal Research on Human Development and Criminal Behaviour* (pp. 149-176). Amsterdam: Kluwer Academic Publishers.

Le Blanc, M. (1995a). Common, temporary, and chronic delinquencies: Prevention strategies during compulsory school. In P-O Wikström, J. McCord, & R. W. Clarke (Eds.), *Integrating Crime Prevention Strategies: Motivation and Opportunity* (pp.169-205). Stockholm: The National Council for Crime Prevention.

Le Blanc, M. (1995b). The relative importance of internal and external constraints in the explanation of late adolescence delinquency and adult criminality. In J. McCord (Ed.), *Coercion and Punishment in Long-Term Perspectives* (pp. 272-288). New York: Cambridge University Press.

Le Blanc, M. (1996). *MASPAQ: Mesures de l'adaptation sociale et personnelle pour les adolescents québécois*. Manuel et guide d'utilisation 3ᵉ édition. Montréal, École de psychoéducation, Groupe de recherche sur les adolescents en difficulté, Université de Montréal.

Le Blanc, M. (1997a). A generic control theory of the criminal phenomenon, the structural and the dynamical statements of an integrative multilayered control theory. In T. P. Thornberry (Ed.). *Developmental Theories of Crime and Delinquency*. Advances in Criminological Theory, Vol. 7 (pp. 215-286). New Brunswick, NJ: Transaction Publishers.

Le Blanc, M. (1997b). Socialization or propensity: A test of an integrative control theory with adjudicated boys. *Studies in Crime and Crime Prevention*, 6, 2: 200-224.

Le Blanc, M. (2002). The offending cycle, escalation and de-escalation in delinquent behavior, A challenge for criminology. *International Journal of Comparative and Applied Criminal Justice*, 26, 1: 53-84.

Le Blanc, M., & Biron, L. (l980). *Vers une théorie intégrative de la régulation de la conduite délinquante des garçons*. Montréal, Groupe de recherche sur l'inadaptation juvénile, Université de Montréal.

Le Blanc, M., & Bouthillier, C. (2003). A developmental test of the general deviance syndrome with adjudicated girls and boys using hierarchical confirmatory factor analysis. *Criminal Behavior and Mental Health*, 13 : 81-105.

Le Blanc, M., & Caplan, M. (1993). Theoretical formalization, a necessity: The example of Hirschi's social control theory. Advances in Criminological Theory, Vol. 4 (pp. 329-431). New Brunswick, NJ: Transaction Publishers.

Le Blanc, M., Charland, R., Cote, G., & Pronovost, L. (1980). *Développement psycho-social et évolution de la délinquance au cours de l'adolescence.* Montréal, Groupe de recherche sur l'inadaptation juvénile, Université de Montréal.

Le Blanc, M., & Fréchette, M. (1989). *Male Criminal Activity from Childhood through Youth: Multilevel and Developmental Perspectives.* New York: Springer-Verlag.

Le Blanc, M., & Janosz, M. (1998). The development of problem behavior, course and processes. Paper given at Life History Research Society, May 6-9.

Le Blanc, M., & Janosz, M. (unpublished). The development of control and general deviance, course and processes. The contribution of the developmental and the chaos-order paradigms.

Le Blanc, M., & Loeber, R. (1998). Developmental criminology updated. In M. Tonry (Ed.), *Crime and Justice*, Vol. 23 (pp.115-198). Chicago: University of Chicago Press.

Le Blanc, M., & Morizot, J. (2002). Adjudicated males self-reported criminality trajectories from adolescence to midlife. Paper given at American Society of Criminology, Annual Meeting, 13-16 November, Chicago.

Le Blanc, M., Ouimet, M., & Tremblay, R. E. (1988). An integrative control theory of delinquent behavior: A validation 1976-1985. *Psychiatry*, 51:164-176.

Le Blanc, M., Vallières, E., & McDuff, P. (1992). Adolescents' school experience and self-reported offending, A longitudinal test of a social control theory. *International Journal of Adolescence and Youth*, 3: 197-247.

Lerner, R. M. (1986). *Concepts and Theories of Human Development.* New York: Random House.

Loeber, R., & Hay, D. (1997). Key issues in the development of aggression and violence from childhood to early adulthood. *Annual Review of Psychology*, 48: 371-410.

Loeber, R., & Le Blanc, M. (1990). Toward a developmental criminology. In M. Tonry, & N. Morris (Eds.), *Crime and Justice: An Annual Review*. 13: 1-98. Chicago: University of Chicago Press.

Matza, D. (1957). *Delinquency and Drift.* New York: Wiley.

Miller, J. D., & Lynam, D. (2001). Structural models of personality and their relation to antisocial behavior: A meta-analytic review. *Criminology*, 39: 765-798.

Moffitt, T. E. (1993). "Life-course-persistent" and "adolescent-limited" antisocial behavior: A developmental taxonomy. *Psychological Review*, 100: 674-701.

Morizot, J., & Le Blanc, M. (2003a). Continuity and change in personality from mid-adolescence to mid-life: A 25-year longitudinal study comparing conventional and adjudicated men. *Journal of Personality*, 71: 705-755.

Morizot, J., & Le Blanc, M. (2003b). Searching for a developmental typology of personality in an adjudicated men's sample and its relations to antisocial behaviors from adolescence to midlife: A 25-year longitudinal study. *Criminal Behavior and Mental Health*, 13: 241-277.

Morizot, J., & Le Blanc, M. (2005). Searching for developmental types of personality and their relation to antisocial behaviors: A 25-year longitudinal study comparing conventional and adjudicated men from adolescence to midlife. *Journal of Personality*, 73: 1-43.

Nye, F.I. (1958). *Family Relationships and Delinquent Behavior.* New York: Wiley.

Oden, S. (1988). Alternative perspectives on children's peer relationships. In T. D. Yawkey & J. E Johnson (Eds.), *Integrative Process and Socialization: Early to Middle Childhood.* Hillsdale: Erlbaum.

Osgood, D. W., Wilson, J. K., O'Malley, P. M., Bachman, J. G., & Johnston, L. D. (1996). Routine activities and individual deviant behavior. *American Sociological Review*, 61: 635-655.

Piquero, A. R., Farrington, D. P., & Blumstein, A. (2003). The criminal career paradigm. *Crime and Justice*, 30: 359-506.

Platt, T. C., & Cullen, F. C. (2000). The empirical status of Gottfredson and Hirschi's general theory of crime: Meta-analysis. *Criminology*, 38: 932-964.

Quetelet, A. (1835). *Sur l'homme et le développement de ses facultés, ou essai de physique sociale*. Paris: Bachelier.

Reckless, W. C. (1961). A new theory of delinquency and crime. *Federal Probation*, 25 (December): 42-46.

Reiss, A. J. (1951) Delinquency as the failure of personal and social controls. *American Sociological Review*, 16, 2: 196-207.

Sampson, R. J., & Laub, J. H. (1993). *Crime in the Making: Pathways and Turning Points through Life*. Cambridge, MA: Harvard University Press.

Shoemaker, D. J. (1996). *Theories of Delinquency: An Examination of Explanations of Delinquent Behavior*. New York: Oxford University Press.

Steinberg, L. (1991). *Adolescence*. Toronto: McGraw Hill.

Stoolmiller, M. (1994). Antisocial behavior, delinquent peer association, and unsupervised wandering for boys: Growth and change from childhood to early adolescence. *Multivariate Behavioral Research*, 29: 263-288.

Sutherland, E. H., & Cressey, D. R. (1960). *Principles of Criminology* (6th ed.). Philadelphia: Lippincott.

Tarde, G. (1924). *La criminalité comparée*. Paris: Alcan.

Thornberry, T. P. (1987). Toward an interactional theory of delinquency. *Criminology*, 25, 4: 963-892.

Thornberry, T. P. (1996). Empirical support for interactional theory: A review of the literature. In J. D. Hawkins (Ed.), *Delinquency and Crime: Current Theories*. New York: Cambridge University Press.

Thornberry, T. P., Lizotte, A. J., Korhn, M. V., Farnworth, M., & Jang, S. J. (1991). Testing interactional theory: An examination of reciprocal causal relationship among family, school and delinquency. *Journal of Criminal Law and Criminology*, 82: 3-33.

Thornberry, T. P., Lizotte, A. J., Krohn, M. D., & Farnworth, M. (1994). Delinquent peers, beliefs, and delinquent behavior: A longitudinal test of interactional theory. *Criminology*, 32, 1: 47-84.

Warr, M. (2002). *Companions in Crime: The Social Aspect of the Criminal Conduct*. Cambridge: Cambridge University Press.

Wolfgang, M. E., Figlio, R. M., & Sellin, T. (1972). *Delinquency in a Birth Cohort*. Chicago: University of Chicago Press.

Zhang, Q., Loeber, R., & Stouthamer-Loeber, M. (1997). Developmental trends of delinquency attitudes and delinquency: Replication and synthesis across time and samples. *Journal of Quantitative Criminology*, 13: 181-216.

7

A General Age-Graded Theory of Crime: Lessons Learned and the Future of Life-Course Criminology

Robert J. Sampson and John H. Laub

The intellectual move we take in this chapter is to elucidate the life-course implications of a general age-graded theory of crime. In doing so we depart from the modus operandi of most developmental criminological theory by looking at changes in criminal behavior through a common theoretical lens that we have built through a longstanding inquiry (Sampson & Laub, 1993; Laub & Sampson, 2003). The growing tendency in developmental criminology is for greater specificity, not generality, manifested most noticeably in moves to subdivide the offender population and characteristics of the so-called criminal career, apportioning bits and pieces to different theoretical positions and different causal influences. Hirschi (1979) once called this the end–to-end or side-by-side strategy of theoretical integration.

Considering that the pieces of the developmental criminological pie are large, this temptation is understandable. Farrington (2003), for example, notes key results developmental criminology ought to explain, such as the onset of delinquency, versatility, escalation, co-offending, persistence, and desistance, to name a few. With all the complexity implied, it follows that one might need to posit a theory for onset and another for continuation, or one theory for violent crime and another for property crime, and so on and so forth. The list is endless and indeed many have argued for just such an approach. Or even more likely and increasingly attractive to many, one might divide up the offender population into different types, asserting that some factors uniquely explain persistent offenders whereas another set of causal factors explain desistance. Interdisciplinary theory is also all the rage, with "multilevel" attempts to integrate biological, psychological, and sociological theories seemingly everywhere.

In this chapter we take a different route to explanation by tracing out the implications of a general age-graded theory of informal social control, focusing especially on the largely unchartered territory of persistence and desistance across the *adult* life course. Although at first it may seem counterintuitive, our fundamental argument is that persistent offending and desistance can be meaningfully understood within the same theoretical framework. In its strong form, our argument is that persistence in crime is explained by a lack of social controls, few structured routine activities, and purposeful human agency. Simultaneously, desistance from crime is explained by a confluence of social controls, structured routine activities, and purposeful human agency. In this version of our argument the fundamental causes of offending are the same for all persons, although for some there may be a single pathway to crime or desistance, whereas for others there are multiple pathways. Regardless of the number of pathways, however, we hypothesize that the same class of causal mechanisms account for trajectories (pathways) of criminal behavior over the life course. Moreover, the specific manifestations of violence may be different than the specific manifestations of property crime, but both can nevertheless be explained by the same general processes, namely, informal social control, routine activities, and human agency. Expanding on this notion, the dynamics of persistence in crime may be different than the dynamics of desistance from crime, but both can still logically be explained by general processes of social control, routine activities, and human agency.

In short, our approach stands in opposition to the subdivision of offenders and offenses. We seek instead to explicate the implications for developmental criminology of a general approach to the adult life course by drawing out the lessons learned in an earlier study, *Crime in the Making: Pathways and Turning Points Through Life* (Sampson & Laub, 1993), and the more recent *Shared Beginnings, Divergent Lives: Delinquent Boys to Age 70* (Laub & Sampson, 2003).

Crime in the Making and the Origins of Life-Course Criminology

We begin with a brief historical perspective. The story began for us in 1986 when we stumbled across the dusty archives of a classic but largely forgotten study of delinquency housed in the basement of the Harvard Law School. The study was *Unraveling Juvenile Delinquency* and subsequent follow-ups conducted by Sheldon and Eleanor Glueck of the Harvard Law School. This study is considered to be one of the most influential in the history of criminological research. The Gluecks' data were derived from a three wave prospective study of juvenile and adult criminal behavior. The research design involved a sample of 500 male delinquents ages 10-17 and 500 male nondelinquents ages 10-17 matched case-by-case on age, race/ethnicity, IQ, and low-income residence in Boston. Extensive data were collected on the 1,000 boys at three points in time—ages 14, 25, and 32 (see Glueck & Glueck, 1950, 1968). Over a period of six years (1987-1993), we reconstructed, augmented, and analyzed the full longitudinal data set, now housed in the Murray Research Center archive at the Radcliffe Institute for Advanced Study at Harvard University. These data are immensely rich, and will likely never be repeated given modern IRB restrictions (e.g., wide-ranging interviews with teachers, neighbors, and employers; detailed psychiatric assessments; pictures; searches of multiple agency records).

Crime in the Making was driven by the following challenge: could we develop and test a theoretical model that accounts for crime and deviance in childhood, adolescence, *and* adulthood? To answer this question we synthesized and integrated the criminological literature on childhood antisocial behavior, adolescent delinquency, and adult crime with theory and research on the life course. This strategy led us to develop a theory of age-graded informal social control to explain childhood antisocial behavior, adolescent delinquency, and crime in early adulthood. The general organizing principle was that crime is more likely to occur when an individual's bond to society is attenuated, a move that contrasted both to the Gluecks' emphasis on "psychodynamic" individual factors and to the focus on poverty and legal sanctions in much of traditional criminology.

Our theoretical framework was organized around three major themes. The first is that structural context is mediated in fundamental respects by informal family and school social controls, which in turn explain delinquency in childhood and adolescence. The second theme is that there is strong continuity in antisocial behavior running from childhood through adulthood across a variety of life domains. The third theme is that informal social control in adulthood explains changes in criminal behavior over the life span, independent of prior individual differences in criminal propensity. In our view, childhood pathways to crime and conformity over the life course are significantly influenced by adult social bonds.

Our theory explicitly links delinquency and adult crime to childhood and adolescent characteristics as well as socializing influences in adulthood. Early delinquency predicts weak adult social bonds, and weak adult social bonds predict concurrent and later adult crime and deviance. The process is thus one in which childhood antisocial behavior and adolescent delinquency are linked to adult crime and deviance in part through weak social bonds.

We also believe, however, that salient life events and socialization experiences in adulthood can counteract, at least to some extent, the influence of early life experiences. For instance, late onset of criminal behavior can be accounted for by weak social bonds in adulthood, despite a background of nondelinquent behavior. Conversely, desistance from criminal behavior in adulthood can be explained by strong social bonds in adulthood, despite a background of delinquent behavior. In short, our theory provides a social explanation of stability *and* change in crime and deviance over the life course with an explicit focus on within-individual changes in offending and deviance.

What are the major findings from *Crime in the Making* with regard to key theoretical and empirical issues facing life-course criminology?

Causes of Delinquency

We found that the strongest and most consistent effects on both official and unofficial delinquency in adolescence flow from processes of social control connected to family, school, and peers. Three family factors stood out as strongly predictive of delinquency: low levels of parental supervision; the combination of erratic, threatening, and harsh discipline; and weak parental attachment. In addition, school attachment had large negative associations with delinquency independent of family processes. Both family and school factors behaved much as would be predicted from Hirschi's *Causes of Delinquency* (1969), including the fact that they were more closely associated with delinquency than the more distal and structural predictors of family background (e.g., size, class).

Attachment to delinquent peers had a significant positive effect on delinquency regardless of family and school process, but we were unable to separate effectively the fact of delinquency itself from the delinquency of peers. In the Glueck data the only satisfactory way to address this dilemma was to compare the influence of attachment to delinquent siblings with attachment to delinquent peers, on the argument that sibling influences are less contaminated by selection than peer influences. The results showed that sibling influences were insignificant yet peer delinquency remained a strong correlate of the delinquency of the boy, an indication that the latter two measures were tapping the same construct. Based on this analysis we concluded that family and school processes were more important factors in the causal chain than peers.

Perhaps more important, we found that structural background factors (e.g., family poverty) had little direct effect on delinquency, but instead were mediated by intervening sources of informal social control. Moreover, whereas difficult children who display early antisocial tendencies (e.g., violent temperament) do sort themselves into later stages of delinquency, the processes of informal social control explained the largest share of variance in adolescent delinquency. Individual predisposition, in other words, cannot explain away the relationship between social control and delinquency.

Stability and Change in Criminal Behavior over the Life Course

Whereas our analysis of delinquency shared much in common with classical control theory, the reality of later life-course milestones required us to develop a new theoretical perspective. After all, the transition to young adulthood brings with it new social control institutions and turning points that go well beyond adolescence. We thus developed an age-graded theory that focused on informal social controls that were manifested in shifting and possibly transformative ways as individuals age. This theoretical perspective was applied to both continuity and change in adult crime.

For example, independent of age, IQ, neighborhood SES, and ethnicity, the original delinquents and nondelinquents in the Gluecks' study displayed behavioral consistency—both homotypic and heterotypic—well into adulthood. Indeed, delinquency and other forms of antisocial conduct in childhood were strongly related to troublesome adult behavior across a variety of life's domains (e.g., crime, military offenses, economic dependence, and marital discord). But why? One of the mechanisms of continuity that we emphasized was "cumulative disadvantage," whereby delinquency undermined later bonds of social control, which in turn enhanced the chances of continued offending.

Consistent with an emphasis on adult developmental change and informal social control, however, we found that job stability and marital attachment in adulthood were significantly related to changes in adult crime—the stronger the adult ties to work and family, the less crime and deviance among both the delinquent and control groups. We even found that strong marital attachment inhibits crime and deviance regardless of that spouse's own deviant behavior, and that job instability fosters crime regardless of heavy drinking. Moreover, social bonds to employment were directly influenced by state sanctions—incarceration as a juvenile and as an adult had negative effects on later job stability, which in turn was negatively related to continued involvement in crime over the life course. Although we found little direct effect of incarceration on subsequent criminality, the indirect "criminogenic" effects appear substantively important.

Despite differences in early childhood experiences, adult social bonds to work and family thus had similar consequences for the life trajectories of the 500 delinquents and 500 nondelinquent controls. These results were consistent for a wide variety of crime outcome measures, control variables (e.g., childhood antisocial behavior and individual-difference constructs) and analytical techniques, including methods that accounted for persistent unobserved heterogeneity in criminal propensity.

In *Crime in the Making* we also explored a new way of portraying life histories of persons in context. Our strategy was to challenge the quantitative findings with a systematic and intensive examination of qualitative data drawn from the Gluecks' original case files. Integrating divergent sources of information on life histories, the qualitative analysis supported the central idea of our theoretical model that there is stability and change in behavior over the life course and that these changes are systematically linked to the institutions of work and family relations in adulthood. Through an analysis of the narrative data found in the Glueck case files, we found evidence supporting the notion that poor job stability and weak marital attachment to one's spouse increased the likelihood of criminal activity and deviant behavior. Conversely, the case records supported the idea that strong job stability and attachment to one's spouse reduce the likelihood of involvement in criminal and deviant behavior.

Taken as a whole, then, our qualitative and quantitative findings suggest that social ties embedded in adult transitions (e.g., marital attachment, job stability) help explain variations in crime unaccounted for by childhood propensities. This empirical regularity supports our dual concern with continuity and change in the life course. A fundamental thesis of our age-graded theory of informal social control and crime was that whereas individual traits and childhood experiences are important for understanding behavioral stability, experiences in adolescence and adulthood can redirect criminal trajectories in either a more positive or more negative manner. In particular, we found that job stability and marital attachment in adulthood were significantly related to changes in adult crime—the stronger the adult ties to work and family, the less crime and deviance among both delinquents and nondelinquent controls. We concluded that adult "turning points" were crucial for understanding processes of change.

The Legacy of *Crime in the Making*

Crime in the Making raised many questions, and in its concluding chapter we highlighted possible directions for future research and theoretical development that appeared fruitful. Two of these directions seemed especially relevant for developmental/life-course theories of crime; namely, the merging of quantitative and qualitative data and further understanding of age and crime (see Sampson & Laub, 1993: 251-253). After the publication of *Crime in the Making* we thus began to contemplate its limitations and considered where these directions might lead. For example, what about crime in middle age? Older age? Is there really such a thing as a life-long career criminal—or what have been dubbed "life-course persisters?" How far does our age-graded theory reach? In short, what about crime across the full life course?

We also became interested in how qualitative narratives might allow for a more person-based exploration of the life course. In our view, life-history narratives combined with quantitative approaches can be used to develop a richer and more comprehensive picture of why some men persist in offending and why others stop. Narratives help us unpack mechanisms that connect salient life events across the life course, especially personal choice and situational context. Life histories can provide the human voices to counterbalance the wide range of statistical data and the social sciences at large (see also Bennett, 1981; Clausen, 1993; Hagan & McCarthy, 1997). We made a start on narrative inquiry in *Crime in the Making* but were forced to rely on the Gluecks' original records rather than our own life-history interviews.

These motivations led us to follow up the Glueck men to the present. Our study involved three sources of new data collection—criminal record checks (local and national), death record checks (local and national) and personal interviews with a sample of fifty-two of the original Glueck men, stratified to ensure variability in patterns of persistence and desistance in crime (for details, see Laub & Sampson, 2003: chap. 4). These combined data represent a roughly fifty-year window on "criminal careers," allowing us to update the Glueck men's lives at the close of the twentieth century and connect them to life experiences all the way back to early childhood. We believe these data represent the longest longitudinal study to date in criminology of the same men, and thus can provide important lessons for future life course/developmental theories of crime. Before we turn to these lessons, we provide a brief summary of our key findings.

Shared Beginnings, Divergent Lives: An Overview

Although counterintuitive at first, we came to the conclusion that the data supported the notion that explanations of desistance from crime and persistent offending in crime are two sides of the same coin. Consider the phenomenon of desistance. From our analysis of offender narratives and life histories it appears that offenders desist as a result of individual actions (choice) in conjunction with situational contexts and structural influences linked to key institutions that help sustain desistance. As such we argued that desistance is a process rather than an event, and that it must be continually renewed. This fundamental theme underscores the need to examine individual motivation and the social context in which individuals are embedded. The processes of desistance operate simultaneously at different levels (individual, situational, and community) and across different contextual environments (especially family, work, and military service). The process of desistance is more than mere aging and more than individual predisposition.

It appears that successful cessation from crime occurs when the proximate causes of crime are disrupted. A central element in the desistance process is the "knifing off" of individual offenders from their immediate environment and offering them a new script for the future (see also Moffitt, 1993). Institutions like the military and reform school have this knifing-off potential, as does marriage, although the knifing-off effect of marriage may not be as dramatic. Another component in the desistance process is the "structured role stability" that emerges across various life domains (for example, marriage, work, community). The men who desisted from crime shared a daily routine that provided both structure and meaningful activity.

Overall, then, while there are multiple pathways to desistance, we found what appear to be important general processes or mechanisms at work that are consistent with the idea of informal social control. The major self-described turning points that we found implicated in the desistance process included marriage/spouses, the military, reform school, work, and neighborhood change. What appears to be important about these institutional or structural turning points is that they all involve, to varying degrees: (1) *New situations that knife off the past from the present*; (2) *New situations that provide both supervision and monitoring as well as new opportunities of social support and growth*; (3) *New situations that change and structure routine activities*; (4) *New situations that provide the opportunity for identity transformation.* While some offenders may seek to "make good" or engage in "up-front work" to better their lives (Maruna, 2001; Giordano et al., 2002), we believe that most offenders choose to desist in response to structurally induced turning points that serve as the catalyst for sustaining long-term behavioral change. In a way, then, we propose that crime is analogous to addiction. The addiction is not physiological but rather more profound—crime, and the action that is entailed in committing it, is seductive, alluring, and hard to give up despite its clear costs.

Persistent Offenders

Is there something unique about "persistent" offenders that distinguishes them from other offenders? Space limitations do not allow us to reflect in detail on our narrative understanding, but the take away is that the same general factors that explain desistance are relevant for persistence as well. From our data, more than being identified by a single trait like poor verbal intelligence or low self-control, or even a series of static traits, the persistent offender, to the extent the term has meaning, seems devoid of linking structures at each phase of the life course, especially involving relationships that can provide nurturing, social support, and informal social control. Generally, the persistent offenders we interviewed experienced considerable residential instability, marital instability, job instability, failure in the school and the military, and relatively long periods of incarceration. Except when in prison or jail, they were "social nomads," to use Michel Foucault's (1995) term. Without permanent addresses, steady jobs, spouses, children, and other rooted forms of life, crime and deviance are an unsurprising result. As a consequence of chaotic and unstructured routines, the Glueck men had increased contact with those individuals who were similarly situated—in this case, similarly unattached and free from nurturing and informal social control. Interestingly, however, even persistent offenders eventually gave up crime and exhibited the classic pattern of declining crime with age. Thus, age itself plays a key role, with the same mechanisms discussed earlier taking time to kick in and playing a more tenuous role. In the case of adult persistent offenders, the eventual sustaining of desistance seemed almost a daily struggle, even at older ages.

Having briefly summarized our theory and findings, we turn to the lessons we have learned that we believe bear on future thinking about life-course/developmental criminology. We view these not so much as specific hypotheses such as those discussed above (e.g., that delinquency is more likely to result when informal social controls are diminished). Rather, we highlight broad-based implications of our findings that can serve as an orienting framework for organizing research and the testing of causal theories of crime across the full life course.

Theoretical Lesson 1: The Importance of the Adult Life Course

Our analyses have shown that the aggregate age-crime curve is not the same as individual trajectories, lending support to one of the main claims of the criminal career model. One striking characteristic of our data is the heterogeneity in criminal behavior over the adult life course (see also Rutter, Giller, & Hagell, 1998). On the other hand, we find that crime declines with age even for active offenders and that trajectories of desistance cannot be prospectively identified based on typological accounts rooted in childhood and individual differences. While childhood prognoses are reasonably accurate in terms of predicting levels of crime between individuals up to their 20s, they do not yield distinct groupings that are valid prospectively over the life course.

That all offenses eventually decline by the middle adult years for all groups of offenders identified according to extant theory and a multitude of childhood and adolescent risk factors suggests to us that general desistance processes are at work across the life course and that these processes can only be explained by examining the full interplay of childhood, adolescent, and adult experiences. Certainly the data are clear that adult trajectories of offending among former delinquents cannot be reduced to the past. Moreover, our analysis of within-individual change demonstrates the impact of time-varying life events, especially marriage, even as the men were in their 50s and 60s. Overall, our data show that the question of predicting adult criminal trajectories among troubled boys is not an easy one if one limits the causal matrix to childhood endowments. What, then, accounts for child-focused models and the emphasis in criminology on "early" prediction? We believe the disconnect stems in part from a dominant bias in our culture that assigns divergent adult outcomes to the realm of varying childhood experiences. In *Three Seductive Ideas* (1998), Jerome Kagan wrote on why notions of childhood determinism have such appeal, and David Bordua wrote back in 1961 on the false seductions of prediction in criminology. Whatever the source, it is almost as if a "psychiatric impulse" has gripped developmental criminology anew, with cultural beliefs about the childhood-adult connection distorted by methodological approaches that look back over the life course of adult offenders, where the simple "bad boys-bad men" connection seems to fit quite well. However, if we begin with children and follow their paths to adulthood, we find considerable heterogeneity in adult outcomes. It follows that the adult life course matters and that childhood causation models are woefully inadequate.

Theoretical Lesson 2: Group-Based Theories are Not Supported

The "group" question might be said to be the question of the day in developmental criminology. From proponents of the criminal career approach, the idea has proliferated that chronic offenders are a distinct group that, as the adjective implies, do not desist from crime. A variation on this theme is Moffitt's (1993) notion that there is a causally distinct group—"life-course persisters"—that continues offending at a high rate as they age. Nagin (2005) has also developed a group-based methodology that rests on the assumption that there are distinct offender groups, which in turn implies that each group has distinct causal mechanisms.

Unfortunately, criminal careers are typically studied over circumscribed portions of the life course, and trajectories of crime are usually identified retrospectively, based on the outcome, rather than prospectively, based on the causal factors presumed to differentiate groups of offenders. Post-hoc typologies of offenders are thus ubiquitous, whereas prospective categorization of risk typologies and valid criminal trajectories over the long run that would support or invalidate them, are not.

One of the major strengths of our study, by contrast, is its ability to examine within-individual variability over nearly the entire life course. Moreover, the original design in *Unraveling Juvenile Delinquency* targeted serious, persistent delinquents in adolescence, providing an important opportunity to assess patterns of continuity and change in crime for a population of high interest and concern to policy efforts that target "high risk" children.

Our findings can be succinctly summarized. The age-crime curve is essentially replicated for offender groups that are prospectively defined. That is, offenses eventually decline for all groups of offenders identified according to extant theory and a multitude of childhood and adolescent risk factors. Whether low IQ, aggressive temperament, or early onset of antisocial behavior, desistance processes are at work even for the highest-risk and predicted life-course persistent offenders. While childhood prognoses are modestly accurate in predicting level differences, they simply do not yield distinct groupings that are valid prospectively for troubled kids. Not only is prediction clearly poor at the individual level, our data reveal the tenuous basis for the sorts of distinct groupings that dominate theoretical discussion (e.g., "super predator"; "life-course persistent offender"). These groupings wither when placed under the microscope of long-term observation (Laub & Sampson, 2003: chap. 5; Sampson & Laub, 2003).

Our data thus undermine what might be termed the causal theory of groups and the idea that offender groupings are meaningful in the sense of social ontology. The widely noted "life-course persister" group, for example, may be useful in terms of a *heuristic* device, but in terms of theoretical validity as a distinctive and replicable group that has decisive implications for etiological theory, we believe the evidence is thin. It is interesting to note that group-based research has by now firmly rejected the notion that there are only two groups of offenders, with the apparent result that life-course persisters have become subdivided into multiple chronic-offender groups (see also Eggleston et al., 2004). We question the wisdom of this move. An additional interesting dilemma, of course, is that group-based methodologies *begin* with the methodological assumption that groups exist. It is then easy for one to conclude that groups exist because they are discovered, even though a model cannot be said to discover what it assumes!

So lesson 2, we would assert, is that childhood typologies are disconfirmed at the prospective level. Put differently, we do not find good evidence that there are causally distinct groups with causally distinct trajectories. Even when we selected a small subgroup of men with criminal activity in each decade of life (less than 10 percent), the age-crime curve was obtained. We believe these findings, if replicated in future research, have important implications for developmental criminology, similar to those put forth by Gottfredson and Hirschi (1990). Namely, our theory implies that offender subdivision is not warranted and that general mechanisms should in the first instance be sought for explaining crime at each age. We disagree with Gottfredson and Hirschi's (1990) specific causal focus on low self-control, however, which brings us to our next lesson.

Theoretical Lesson 3: The Causal Importance of Institutional Turning Points

The fact remaining to be explained is that there are important variations in adult criminal trajectories that cannot be predicted from childhood, contra the policy world and much yearning among criminologists. The question we are thus left with is what *does* account for these important patterns of offending? Many of the original Glueck delinquents did in fact persist, at least for a while, whereas other delinquents desisted soon after adolescence. To examine this issue, our recent analysis of adult crime uncovered some common features of explanation.

The lesson we would draw is that institutions matter for understanding crime over the life course. More precisely, involvement in institutions such as marriage, work, and the military reorders short-term situational inducements to crime and, over time, redirects long-term commitments to conformity. In making the case for the importance of the adult life course we have referred to involvement in these institutions as turning points because they can change trajectories over time (see Sampson & Laub, 1993, and Laub & Sampson, 1993). A potential objection, however, is that turning points are a result of selection bias, or put differently, the unobserved characteristics of the person.

To shed further light on the causal nature of life events we exploited the rich nature of the longitudinal data set that we collected. Specifically, we have

statistical power to examine within-individual change where the unit of variation is across time, not persons. As such stable characteristics of the person are
held constant and we can examine changes in social location, such as marriage,
in terms of deviations from the person's expected trajectory. Holding age constant and allowing individual heterogeneity we found that *when* in a state of
marriage, propensity to crime is lower for the same person than when not in
marriage. Similar results were found for military service and steady employment. Quantitative models of within-individual change thus give strong statistical evidence of the probabilistic enhancement of desistance associated with
life-course events like marriage, military service, and employment (Laub &
Sampson, 2003: chap. 9). *More generally, our theory predicts that controlling
for all stable characteristics of the person, time-varying indicators of informal
social control will be negatively associated with crime at each stage of life.*

Another insight with respect to the role of institutions and their influence on
criminal behavior was what might be characterized as the "drift" hypothesis of
desistance, or what we came to call "desistance by default." The idea is that
commitments were not necessarily made with great forethought, but rather were
"by default"—the result of "side bets." The men made a commitment (or choice)
to go straight without much realizing it. Before they knew it, they had invested
so much in a marriage or a job that they did not want to risk losing their
investment—hence desistance by default.

Theoretical Lesson 4: The Importance of Agency and Choice

But institutions are not the entire story, and in no way does our theory view
human beings as merely passive. Indeed, another factor that we discovered as
notable in the desistance process was personal agency—the purposeful execu-
tion of choice and individual will (Matza, 1964). For example, a vital feature
that emerged from our qualitative narratives is that personal conceptions about
the past and future are often transformed as men maneuver through the transition from adolescence to adulthood. Many men engaged in what can be called
"transformative action." Although informed by the past, such action-oriented
agency is oriented toward the future (and hence a future self). Projective actions
in the transition from adolescence to adulthood that we uncovered were the
advancement of a new sense of self and identity as a desister from crime or,
perhaps more aptly, as a family man, hard worker, and good provider. As a result
the men we studied were active participants in the choice to give up crime.

We also believe that human agency is vitally important for understanding
persistent offending. Some men simply insist on a criminal lifestyle, not out of
impulsivity or lack of knowledge of future consequences, but rather because of
the rewards of crime itself (Katz, 1988) or a willful resistance to perceived
domination (Sherman, 1993)–all at the expense of the future self. As revealed in
many of our life history narratives, calculated and articulated resistance to

authority is a recurrent theme in lives of persistent offenders. The men's defiance seemed to have been fueled by a perceived sense of injustice resulting from corrosive contacts with officials of the criminal justice system, coupled with a general sense of working-class alienation from elite society. Many persistent offenders see "the system" (criminal justice and work alike) as unfair and corrupt (see also Willis, 1977).

In crucial ways then, criminal persistence is more than a weakening of social bonds, and desistance is more than the presence of a social bond, as one might be led to conclude (mistakenly) from *Crime in the Making*. At a meta-theoretical level, our long-term follow-up data direct us to insist that a focus purely on institutional, or structural, turning points and opportunities is incomplete, for such opportunities are mediated by perceptions and human decision-making. Even if below the surface of active consciousness, as in the concept of desistance by default, actions to desist are in a fundamental sense willed by the offender, bringing a richer meaning to the notion of commitment. Further support for this idea is that the men who desisted from crime, but even those who persisted, accepted responsibility for their actions and freely admitted getting into trouble. They did not, for the most part, offer excuses. Tough times due to the Great Depression, uncaring parents, poor schools, discrimination based on ethnicity and class, and the like, were not invoked to explain their criminal pasts. One man captured this opinion the best when he said, *"Not because of my mother and father. Because of me. I'm the one that made it shitty."*

In short, our findings imply that agency induces a seeming instability or random component into life-course turning points, making neat prediction—even from adult factors—inherently a difficult if not impossible endeavor. As we conclude below, turning points and structural supports may be necessary conditions in our theory but they are not sufficient. Human beings make choices to participate in crime or not, and theories of the life course have been remiss to have left agency—which is essentially human social action—largely out of the theoretical picture. Our effort can be seen as one to reposition human agency as a central element in understanding crime and deviance over the life course (Laub & Sampson, 2003: chaps. 6-8; see also Wikström, 2004). To be sure, *Shared Beginnings* is not a complete response, for we did not develop an explicit theory of human agency replete with testable causal hypotheses. Our theoretical claim herein is simply that the data make clear that agency is a crucial ingredient in causation and thus will be a first-order challenge for future work in life-course criminology.

Summary Implications for Developmental Criminology

Development (svillupo in Italian, dessarrollo in Spanish, Entwicklung in German) is literally an unfolding or unrolling of something that is *already present and in some way preformed.*

—Richard Lewontin

If one defines development as life-history change, then developmental criminology should focus on changes in the development of crime and antisocial
behavior over time. Researchers such as David Farrington, David Hawkins,
Marc Le Blanc, Rolf Loeber, Joan McCord, Terrie Moffitt, Daniel Nagin, Gerry
Patterson, Lee Robins, Terry Thornberry, and Richard Tremblay have been in
the forefront of this important movement in criminology. Relying on a central
insight from Shakespeare—that the child is father to the man (see Caspi, 2000)—
these researchers have addressed how developmental processes are linked to
the onset, continuation, and cessation of criminal and antisocial behavior. Much
has been learned and developmental criminology is now ascendant.

In our view, however, a key misunderstood issue concerns the very meaning
of development in developmental criminology. Lewontin has stated that "...the
term *development* is a metaphor that carries with it a prior commitment to the
nature of the process" (2000: 5, emphasis in the original). Using the analogy of
a photographic image, Lewontin argues that the way the term development is
used is a process that makes the latent image apparent. This seems to be what
developmental criminological theory is all about. For example, in Moffitt's
theory of crime, the environment offers a "set of enabling conditions" that
allow individual traits to express themselves. Although reciprocal interactions
with the environment are allowed, life-course persistent offenders and adolescent-limited offenders follow a pre-programmed line of development in a crucial respect—an unwinding, an unfolding, or an unrolling of what is fundamentally "already there." The view of development as a predetermined unfolding is
linked to a typological understanding of the world—different internal programs will have different outcomes for individuals of a different type. As
Lewontin writes, "If the development of an individual is the unfolding of a
genetic program immanent in the fertilized egg, then variations in the outcome
of development must be consequences of variations in that program" (2000:
17).

Debates about development in the social sciences are not new (see, for example, the exchange between Dannefer, 1984, and Baltes and Nesselroade,
1984). Some developmentalists recognize social interactions, but in the end
most embrace a between-individual focus that emphasizes the primacy of early
childhood attributes that are presumed to be stable. In our theory of crime,
development is better conceived as the constant interaction between individuals and their environment, coupled with purposeful human agency and "random developmental noise" (Lewontin, 2000: 35-36). Recognizing developmental noise implies that "The organism is determined neither by its genes nor
by its environment nor even by interaction between them, but bears a significant mark of random processes" (2000: 38). The challenge is that random processes and human agency are ever-present realities, making prediction once
again problematic. It further follows that long-term patterns of offending among
high-risk populations cannot be divined by individual differences (for example,

low verbal IQ), childhood characteristics (for example, early onset of misbehavior), or even adolescent characteristics (for example, chronic juvenile offending).

A key difference between our perspective and most developmental criminology concerns what would happen in an imagined world of perfect measurement. Even if *all* risk factors (even social controls!) were measured without error, our framework posits the continuous influence of randomizing events and human agency, leading again to heterogeneity, emergent processes, and lack of causal prediction. The logic of prediction that drives the search for early risk factors takes more nearly the opposite view. Indeed, one gets the sense from early interveners that it is just a matter of time before risk factors are measured well enough that the false positive problem will become ancient history. From the perspective of our theory this is wishful thinking and we instead predict enormous heterogeneity in criminal offending over the life course no matter what the childhood classification scheme of the future. Some "destined" offenders will always start late or refrain from crime altogether, whereas some "innocents" will always start early and continue for long periods of time. And a sizable portion of the offending population will always display a zigzag pattern of offending over long time periods.

Concluding Thoughts

We view our work as offering a dual critique of social science theory and current policy about crime over the life course. Developmentalists tend to believe that childhood and adolescent risk characteristics are what really matter—hence the rise of the "early risk-factor" paradigm. Our work shows otherwise. Another strand of developmental theory focuses, yet again in the history of criminology, on typologies and the idea of causally distinct groups. But these, too, fail to materialize over the long run. Simply put, there is no such thing as a foretold life-course persister or career criminal, the organizing focus of the "prediction" paradigm in criminal justice and selective incapacitation policies. Moreover, we see strong evidence that persistent offending and desistance from crime can be understood through a common theoretical lens, namely, a revised age-graded general theory of informal social control that emphasizes social ties, routine activities, and human agency (Laub & Sampson, 2003).

Not to be overlooked and equally important, our work critiques structuralist approaches in sociological criminology contending that location in the social structure, namely poverty and social class, are what really matter. Pure deprivation or materialist theories are not just antediluvian but wrong by offenders' own accounts. Our recent work even questions the idea that some inferred from *Crime in the Making*—that institutional turning points are purely exogenous events that act on individuals. The men we studied in *Shared Beginnings, Divergent Lives* were not blank slates any more than they were rational actors in an unconstrained market of life chances. They were active participants in constructing interdependent lives—including turning points themselves.

From our perspective, then, it is especially important to reconcile the idea of choice or will with a structuralist notion of turning points. As Abbott has written, "A major turning point has the potential to open a system the way a key has the potential to open a lock...action is necessary to complete the turning" (1997: 102). In this instance, individual action needs to align with the social structure in order to produce behavioral change and to maintain change (or stability) over the life course. Choice alone without structural support, or the offering of support alone absent a decision to desist, however inchoate, seems destined to fail. What this means is that neither agency nor structure alone are capable of explaining the life course of crime (Wikström, 2004). Studying them simultaneously, as we have done, allows the possibility of discovering common themes in the ways that turning points across the adult life course align with individual decisions. To more process-oriented, non-reductionist, and generalized accounts of within-individual change, the field of life-course criminology might therefore profitably turn.

References

Abbott, Andrew. (1997). On the concept of turning point. *Comparative Social Research*, 16: 85-105.

Baltes, Paul, & Nesselroade, John. (1984). Paradigm lost and paradigm regained: Critique of Dannefer's portrayal of life-span developmental psychology. *American Sociological Review*, 49: 841-847.

Bennett, James. (1981). *Oral History and Delinquency: The Rhetoric of Criminology.* Chicago: University of Chicago Press.

Bordua, David J. (1961). *Prediction and Selection of Delinquents*. Washington, DC: U.S. Department of Health, Education, and Welfare.

Caspi, Avshalom. (2000). The child is father of the man: Personality continuities from childhood to adulthood. *Journal of Personality and Social Psychology*, 78: 158-172.

Clausen, John A. (1993). *American Lives: Looking Back at the Children of the Great Depression*. New York: Free Press.

Dannefer, Dale. (1984). Adult development and social theory: A paradigmatic reappraisal. *American Sociological Review*, 49: 100-116.

Eggleston, Elaine P., Laub, John H., & Sampson, Robert J. (2004). Methodological sensitivities to latent class analysis of long-term criminal trajectories. *Journal of Quantitative Criminology*, 20: 1-26.

Farrington, David P. (2003). Developmental and life course criminology: Key theoretical and empirical issues. *Criminology*, 41: 221-255.

Foucault, Michel. (1995) [1975]. *Discipline and Punish: The Birth of the Prison*. 2nd Vintage Books ed. New York: Vintage Books.

Giordano, Peggy C., Cernkovich, Stephen A., & Rudolph, Jennifer L. (2002). Gender, crime, and desistance: Toward a theory of cognitive transformation. *American Journal of Sociology*, 107: 990-1064.

Glueck, Sheldon, & Glueck, Eleanor. (1950). *Unraveling Juvenile Delinquency*. New York: The Commonwealth Fund.

_____. (1968). *Delinquents and Nondelinquents in Perspective*. Cambridge, MA: Harvard University Press.

Gottfredson, Michael R., & Hirschi, Travis. (1990). *A General Theory of Crime*. Stanford, CA: Stanford University Press.

Hagan, John, & McCarthy, Bill. (1997). *Mean Streets: Youth Crime and Homelessness*. Cambridge: Cambridge University Press.

Hirschi, Travis. (1969. *Causes of Delinquency*. Berkeley: University of California Press.

_____. (1979). Separate and unequal is better. *Journal of Research in Crime and Delinquency*, 16: 34-38.

Kagan, Jerome. (1998). *Three Seductive Ideas*. Cambridge, MA: Harvard University Press.

Katz, Jack. (1988). *Seductions of Crime*. New York: Basic Books.

Laub, John H., & Sampson, Robert J. (1993). Turning points in the life course: Why change matters to the study of crime. *Criminology*, 31: 301-325.

_____. (2003). *Shared Beginnings, Divergent Lives: Delinquent Boys to Age 70*. Cambridge, MA: Harvard University Press.

Lewontin, Richard. 2000. *The Triple Helix: Gene, Organism, and Environment*. Cambridge, MA: Harvard University Press.

Maruna, Shadd. (2001). *Making Good: How Ex-Convicts Reform and Rebuild Their Lives*. Washington, DC: American Psychological Association Books.

Matza, David. (1964). *Delinquency and Drift*. New York: Wiley.

Moffitt, Terrie E. (1993). Adolescence-limited and life-course-persistent antisocial behavior: A developmental taxonomy. *Psychological Review*, 100: 674-701.

Nagin, Daniel S. (2005). *Group-Based Modeling of Development*. Cambridge, MA: Harvard University Press.

Rutter, Michael, Giller, Henri, & Hagell, Ann. (1998). *Antisocial Behavior by Young People*. Cambridge: Cambridge University Press.

Sampson, Robert J., & Laub, John H. (1993). *Crime in the Making: Pathways and Turning Points Through Life*. Cambridge, MA: Harvard University Press.

Sampson. Robert J., & Laub, John H. (2003). Life-course desisters? Trajectories of crime among delinquent boys followed to age 70. *Criminology*, 41: 301-339.

Sherman, Lawrence W. (1993). Defiance, deterrence, and irrelevance: A theory of the criminal sanction. *Journal of Research in Crime and Delinquency*, 30: 445-473.

Wikström, Per-Olof. (2004). Crime as alternative: Towards a cross-level situational action theory of crime causation. In Joan McCord (Ed.), *Beyond Empiricism: Institutions and Intentions in the Study of Crime*. New Brunswick, NJ: Transaction Publishers.

Willis, Paul E. (1977). *Learning to Labour: How Working Class Kids Get Working Class Jobs*. Farnborough, England: Saxon House.

8

Applying Interactional Theory to the Explanation of Continuity and Change in Antisocial Behavior *

Terence P. Thornberry and Marvin D. Krohn

Prior research has demonstrated a substantial level of continuity in antisocial behavior over the life course. Robins has suggested that, "...adult antisocial behavior virtually requires childhood antisocial behavior..." (1978: 611). At the same time, however, there is a substantial degree of change evident in delinquent behavior; many offenders, even those with an early onset of antisocial behavior, do not persist in their offending. This leads to the second part of what has come to be called Robins' paradox: "...yet most antisocial children do not become antisocial adults" (1978: 611). How can we account for this twin observation—that childhood antisocial behavior is almost a prerequisite for later antisocial behavior, yet most children who are antisocial outgrow that behavior and avoid later involvement in delinquency and crime? In this chapter, we offer an explanation of both continuity and change in antisocial behavior that is rooted in interactional theory, first proposed by Thornberry (1987) and later extended by Thornberry and Krohn (2001).

In preparing this chapter, we were guided first by the basic premises of interactional theory and, secondly, by the developmental questions and issues raised by Farrington (2003) in his Sutherland Address. Many of those issues—for example, explanations for onset, desistance, and the relationship between ear-

*Support for this work was provided by the National Institute of Mental Health (5 R01 MH56486), the U.S. Department of Justice's Office of Juvenile Justice and Delinquency Prevention (96-MU-FX-0014), the National Institute on Drug Abuse (5 R01 DA05512-07), and the National Science Foundation (SES-8912274), and was aided by grants to the Center for Social and Demographic Analysis at the University at Albany from NICHD (P30 HD32041) and NSF (SBR-9512290). Points of view or opinions in this document are those of the authors and do not necessarily represent the official position or policies of the funding agencies.

lier onset and longer careers—are at the heart of interactional theory and are discussed at length in the pages that follow.

Continuity and Change in Antisocial Behavior

We adopt a broad definition of antisocial behavior as "…a spectrum of behavior usually marked by aggression but representing transgressions against societal norms. In many cases, such behavior represents illegal acts, but not always. Antisocial behavior can range from relatively innocuous but obnoxious behavior such as tantrums and oppositional behavior to the most socially and criminally offensive acts" (Tolan, Guerra, & Kendall, 1995: 515). This conception of antisocial behavior is quite similar to the definition of problem behaviors offered by Jessor, Donovan, & Costa (1991).[1]

In the criminological literature, the concepts of continuity and change are often discussed solely in terms of antisocial behavior. That is, continuity is primarily portrayed as the continuation of antisocial behavior across the life course. As suggested by Robins' quote, the central question is: Why are children who begin offending early likely to continue offending? Similarly, change is primarily portrayed as the termination of offending. Here the central issue concerns what Rutter has called "escape from the risk process" (1988: 3). While identifying the causal processes associated both with the continuity and with the termination of offending is of fundamental importance, a full understanding of continuity and change involves more than an examination of early onset offenders and why some of them continue offending while others stop. At a minimum, it also requires an understanding of behavioral continuity and change that is initiated with prosocial behaviors. Why do some prosocial children continue to avoid antisocial behavior throughout their lives while others eventually change, initiating antisocial behavior at later ages? From this perspective, there are two patterns of continuity—continuity in antisocial behavior and in prosocial behavior—and two patterns of change—desistance (offending to non-offending) and late bloomers (non-offending to offending)—that need to be taken into account. We begin our explanation of these varying patterns of continuity and change with a discussion of the role of the age of onset of antisocial behavior.

Age of Onset and the Duration of Antisocial Careers

Stemming from Robins' initial observation, age of onset has played a critical role in explanations for continuity and change in delinquent behavior. Indeed, two of the more prominent developmental theories are hinged on the expectation that early onset offending is strongly associated with the duration of careers. Patterson and colleagues (Patterson, Capaldi, & Bank, 1991; Patterson, Reid, & Dishion, 1992) and Moffitt (1993, 1997) have presented theories that argue that the delinquent population consists of two fundamentally different types of offenders with different etiologies. In both theories, age of onset is the key defining attribute for the types. For Moffitt, the types are called life-course-persistent and adolescence-limited offenders; for Patterson and associates they are called early starters and late starters. Life-course-persistent offenders or early starters begin offending in early childhood and are expected to continue offending throughout large portions of the life course. Adolescence-limited offenders or late starters wait until adolescence to begin their offending careers, and they are expected to desist relatively quickly. In other words, these models posit a tight relationship between early onset and continuity in offending, on the one hand, and between late onset and change in offending (desistance), on the other.

Empirically, there is a substantial literature that demonstrates the general correlation between early onset and longer, more persistent careers. For example, Elliott reports that of the serious violent offenders in the National Youth Survey who initiated offending prior to age 11, 45 percent continued offending into their 20s. Of those who started at ages 11-12, only about 25 percent continued offending and "the probability was lower and relatively constant for those who initiated at ages 13-17" (1994: 14).

While virtually all developmental theories agree that there is an inverse correlation between onset and continuity, there is less agreement about the strength of the correlation and its implications for theory. Typological perspectives (e.g., Moffitt, 1993, 1997; Patterson et al., 1991, 1992) postulate that age of onset is essential in differentiating the two types of delinquents. Interactional theory takes a fundamentally different view.

First, we do not view the offending population as being divided into different types of delinquents with different etiologies defined by age of onset. While some offenders do start early and some do start late, longitudinal data suggest that onset is better conceived of as *earlier* or *later*, continuously distributed over childhood, adolescence, and even into the early adult years (Eggleston & Laub, 2002; Thornberry & Krohn, 2001). Second, we view the relationship between early onset and later persistence as moderate, at best. "While there is a clear correlation between early onset and length of careers, it is also clear that these two dimensions of antisocial careers are to a substantial degree independent" (Thornberry & Krohn, 2001: 302). In other words, we hypothesize that among earlier starters some offenders will persist, but many others will desist, a hypothesis that is consistent with Robins' original observation. Similarly, we hypothesize that among later starters some offenders will desist relatively quickly, but others will persist in their offending.

Recent results from studies using group-based modeling techniques, such as the approach developed by Nagin and Land (1993), are consistent with interactional theory's hypotheses. To illustrate, Figure 8.1 presents offending trajectories for the subjects of the Rochester Youth Development Study from age 13 to age 22.5.[2] Several observations about continuity and change can be made from

these descriptive data. First, the delinquent population is not divided into two dominant groups of early starters and late starters. There is substantially more diversity in offending careers than implied by the typological theories.[3] Second, the onset patterns displayed in Figure 8.1 are consistent with the notion that onset is continuously distributed from earlier to later ages. Some people, those labeled high-level chronic offenders and intermittent offenders, start quite early. In fact, the average age of onset is 9.7 and 11.1, respectively. For other groups, in particular the bell-shaped desistors and the slow-uptake chronic offenders, offending emerges in early adolescence. One group, the late bloomers, has an unusually late upswing, with offending beginning to increase from a near-zero level only in mid-to-late adolescence. There are two other groups with very low levels of offending throughout the observation period; they are essentially non-offenders and sporadic experimenters.

Third, and perhaps most importantly, these curves demonstrate the modesty of the relationship between onset and persistence. Consider the two groups that have the earliest ages of onset. The high-level chronic offenders are quite persistent over time, exhibiting the highest offending rates for most of the observation period. The intermittent offenders also start offending quite early but then change, exhibiting a near-zero level of offending for most of the observation period. The bell-shaped desistors and the slow-uptake chronic offenders offer another interesting contrast. They are nearly identical in terms of onset and early careers, but one group desists while the other persists in offending through their early 20s. Finally, the two groups of low-level offenders and the late starters have similar onsets and virtually identical careers to age 17 but then diverge dramatically. Overall, onset is not destiny. Some early onset offenders persist, others do not. Some who begin offending during early adolescence desist rather rapidly, while others persist and are among the highest rate offenders during their early 20s. The challenge before theoretical criminology is to account for these varying patterns of continuity and change in delinquent behavior and the complexity of the relationship between onset and persistence. With respect to continuity, the most central questions are:

1.   Why do some individuals persist in offending over long portions of the life course, especially if they initiated offending at very early ages?

2.   Why are some people persistently prosocial, avoiding involvement in crime entirely or becoming involved at only the most trivial levels?

With respect to change, the most central questions are:

3.   Why do some offenders, even some with a very early age of onset, change and at some point forego further involvement in crime? And why is this pattern somewhat more evident for those with a later onset?

4.   Finally, why do some people on a generally prosocial trajectory change and initiate offending at unusually late ages?

Figure 8.1

Predicted Offending Trajectories: Rochester Youth Development Study

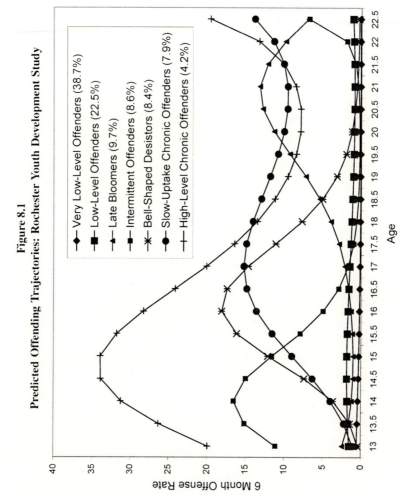

Legend:
- Very Low-Level Offenders (38.7%)
- Low-Level Offenders (22.5%)
- Late Bloomers (9.7%)
- Intermittent Offenders (8.6%)
- Bell-Shaped Desistors (8.4%)
- Slow-Uptake Chronic Offenders (7.9%)
- High-Level Chronic Offenders (4.2%)

Y-axis: 6 Month Offense Rate

X-axis: Age

Source: Bushway et al., 2003.

In the remainder of this chapter, we address these and related questions from the perspective of interactional theory. We begin with a brief overview of the theory's principles.

Interactional Theory

There are three fundamental premises to an interactional theory of delinquency that, in combination, can be used to explain continuity and change in delinquent behavior. They are: a developmental or life-course perspective, bidirectional causality, and the proportionality of cause and effect.

Life-Course Influences

Elder and colleagues define the life course as the "sequence of culturally defined age-graded roles and social transitions that are enacted over time" (Caspi, Elder, & Herbener, 1990: 15; Elder, 1997). These sequences are described in terms of trajectories—long-term patterns of development—and transitions—events or short-term changes in these trajectories.

Delinquency itself can be considered a behavioral trajectory that unfolds over time; for most people it has an onset, duration, and, for most offenders, a termination. Movement along this behavioral trajectory can be explained, at least in part, by movement along other life-course trajectories that are related to major social institutions, such as family and work (Thornberry, 1997).

The causes of delinquency vary systematically with stages of the life course. As a result, the mix of causes that generate delinquency during childhood differs, to some extent, from the mix of causes that generate delinquency during other stages. Also, antisocial behavior is, in part, brought about by the success or failure with which previous developmental stages have been traversed. As a sociogenetic model, interactional theory takes into account the opportunities that are opened (and closed) to individuals by the effect that their behavior has on others and on their life chances. Prior states and behaviors, including antisocial behavior, have important developmental consequences and, in fact, are causally related to later states and behaviors. This leads to the second fundamental premise of interactional theory.

Bidirectional Causality

Delinquent behavior and many of its causes become involved in mutually reinforcing causal loops as delinquent careers unfold. For example, while association with delinquent peers may increase delinquency, delinquency is likely to further isolate the person in delinquent social networks. Similarly, while unemployment is likely to increase involvement in crime, crime is likely to foreclose future employment opportunities. More generally, behavior patterns emerge from interactions between the person and his or her environment and not simply from the environment acting upon the individual. Prosocial behavior patterns are also brought about in this manner, that is, by interactions between the person and the environment. These interactional processes are embedded in the social structure. To understand how they develop, it is necessary to understand how they are produced by, and related to, structural factors such as social class, race, and neighborhood.

Proportionality of Cause and Effect

Delinquency and crime are not brought about by a single cause. Consistent with the developmental premise of equifinality (Cicchetti & Rogosch, 1996), there are multiple causes for this outcome, and not all causal factors need to be activated to produce the outcome. A useful heuristic concept to summarize their influence is the notion of the magnitude of the causal force needed for a particular outcome. The causal force varies considerably across people in terms of the strength or extremity of any particular causal variable; the number of causal factors in one's environment; the accumulation of causes, weighted by the strength or level of each of the individual causal factors; and the presence or absence of offsetting assets. The magnitude of the causal force for antisocial behavior is maximized when there are multiple causal variables, many of which have extreme values and few, if any, offsetting assets.[4]

In turn, the concept of the proportionality of cause and effect states that as the magnitude of the causal force increases, so, too, does (a) the likelihood of the effect and (b) the magnitude of the effect. Applied to crime, this means that as the magnitude of the causal force increases, the person's involvement in crime (a) becomes more likely and (b) increases in severity. The severity of criminal involvement has several dimensions, including early onset, frequency, seriousness, and persistence.

These basic building blocks of interactional theory can be used to respond to the four basic questions posed earlier about continuity and change in delinquent behavior over time. We begin with an explanation for varying ages of onset.

Explaining the Onset of Delinquent Careers

Delinquent behavior can emerge at virtually any age, from toddlerhood and the preschool years (Shaw, Keenan, & Vondra, 1994) to adulthood (Eggleston & Laub, 2002). Here we discuss the initiation of offending in four broad developmental stages: the preschool years, childhood, adolescence, and late adolescence/early adulthood. We do not view these stages as having sharp boundaries; rather, we view them as areas or regions of the more gradual, continuous process of human development.

Only a small portion of the population initiates antisocial behavior during toddlerhood and the preschool years (Krohn, Thornberry, Rivera, & Le Blanc, 2001). These children are more likely than others to persist in delinquency, especially serious delinquency, over long portions of the life course.

Their very early onset can be explained by the combination and interaction of individual characteristics, ineffective parenting, and position in the social structure. Children who exhibit very early manifestations of antisocial behavior are likely to have a variety of negative temperamental qualities and neuropsychological deficits; by ages 2-3, such toddlers show higher rates of negative emotionality, impulsivity, poorer emotion regulation skills, and demonstrate greater fearlessness to noxious stimuli (Bates, Maslin, & Frankel, 1985; Gilliom, Shaw, Beck, Schonberg, & Lukon, 2002; Grolnick, Bridges, & Connell, 1996; Kopp, 1989; Shaw, Owens, Vondra, Keenan, & Winslow, 1996). At the same time, they are likely to have parents who exhibit a variety of parenting deficits that reflect the parent's inability to monitor and reward prosocial behaviors, to provide guidance in the development of problem-solving skills, and to monitor and effectively punish antisocial behavior. Parenting deficits include low affective ties and involvement with the child, explosive physical disciplinary styles, frequent irritable exchanges, poor teaching and problem-solving strategies, and inconsistent standard setting.

Importantly, the child's individual characteristics and the parent's inept parenting style are likely to become causally interwoven. Bidirectional influences between the child's temperamental qualities and the parent's child management style can be observed as early as toddlerhood. Young children with negative temperamental qualities are more subject to parental hostility, criticism, irritability, and coercive responses (Lee & Bates, 1985; Rutter & Quinton, 1984; Zahn-Waxler, Iannotti, Cummings, & Denham, 1990). In turn, ineffective parenting creates maladaptive, coercive, and uncontrolled responses in the child (Belsky, Woodworth & Crnic, 1996; Moffitt, 1993; Shaw & Bell, 1993). This combination of negative child characteristics and an adverse family context increases the odds that parent and child will develop a coercive style of interaction (Patterson et al., 1992) and that the child will develop persistent patterns of oppositional and aggressive behavior (Shaw, Gilliom, Ingoldsby, & Nagin, 2003).

Onset of antisocial behavior during the preschool years is not caused entirely by individual and familial influences, however. These influences exist in a broader social context and, to a substantial degree, are brought about by that context. These children are likely to be born to families experiencing severe structural adversity, which we define as a position in the social structure that leads to accumulated disadvantage for the individual and his or her family. Important components of adversity are chronic poverty, unemployment, welfare dependence, residence in areas of concentrated poverty, and, especially, the co-occurrence of these attributes. The impact of structural adversity may be particularly salient for minority youth who face additional barriers to successful development because of societal discrimination and stigmatization (Jones, 1989; McLoyd, 1990; Spencer & Dornbusch, 1990).

Structural adversity has several negative consequences at this developmental stage. It increases parental stress and reduces their social capital, which, in turn, increases poor family management skills and ineffective parenting (Belsky et al., 1996; Conger, Ge, Elder, Lorenz, & Simons, 1994; Patterson et al., 1992). Structural adversity also accompanies elevated rates of negative temperamental qualities (Moffitt, 1996, 1997; Prior, Sanson, Carroll, & Oberklaid, 1989; Simons, Beaman, Conger, & Chao, 1993; Stott, 1978) and Tibbetts and Piquero (1999) show that neuropsychological risk and disadvantaged environments interact to predict early onset offending.

Overall, the early onset of antisocial behavior is brought about by the intense coupling of structural, individual, and parental influences, that is, when the causal force associated with childhood antisocial behavior is near a maximum. Extreme social adversity contributes to both parenting deficits and negative temperamental qualities in the child; in turn, both of these attributes, and especially their interaction, greatly increase the likelihood of early onset offending.

For a sizable portion of the population, involvement in antisocial behavior and delinquency begins during the elementary school years, from about ages 6 through 12. Onset is less common at the lower end of this age range and becomes more common as the individual approaches adolescence. Thus, after a period of avoiding antisocial behavior during the preschool years, the behavior of these children changes and they begin some period of involvement in antisocial behavior and delinquency. What triggers this change in behavior?

It is unlikely that their antisocial behavior is caused by the intense coupling of difficult temperament, ineffective parenting, and structural adversity that characterizes those who initiate antisocial behavior as toddlers and preschoolers. If those attributes are indeed intensely coupled, there would be little to inhibit the onset of antisocial behavior until the school-age years.

If these attributes are uncoupled, however, the overall causal force weakens and the onset of antisocial behavior is likely to be delayed. For example, not all children with negative temperamental qualities are born into distressed families living in disorganized neighborhoods. The resources available to more advantaged families reduce the behavioral consequences of the child's difficult temperament, at least until they start school and expand their peer relationships. Once the child reaches school and broadened social networks, however, the consequences of difficult temperament, for example, attention problems in school and rejection by peers, are more likely to emerge and to increase the chances of antisocial behavior.

Given the biological and neuropsychological underpinnings of temperament and the likelihood that temperamental qualities will be expressed at very young ages, however, individual temperamental qualities are less likely to be a major cause of antisocial behavior that starts during childhood. Instead, interactional theory looks to the social environment as the more likely point of origin.

We hypothesize that childhood onset of delinquency, especially at the younger end of this developmental stage, is strongly associated with growing up in families and neighborhoods characterized by poverty and disorganization. Structural adversity increases stressors such as parental depression, negative life events, and financial worries, all of which impede effective parenting and increase poor family management styles. In turn, ineffective parenting styles have a strong impact on antisocial behavior (Conger et al., 1994; Jang & Smith, 1997; Patterson et al., 1992). Family effects are particularly strong at these ages as the child, lacking autonomy, is more tightly enmeshed in the family environment.

As the children age and move toward the upper end of this developmental stage, the mix of causal influences expands to include school and peer effects. Preparation for and success in school become increasingly important for warding off delinquent careers. But, both structural adversity and ineffective parenting reduce the child's ability to succeed in school, leading to weakened bonds of commitment to school and attachment to teachers. Structural adversity—especially residence in areas of concentrated poverty—and ineffective parenting also increase access to deviant opportunity structures. Gangs, drug markets, and what Hagan (1992) has labeled "deviance service centers" are embedded in the social fabric of many impoverished communities. These deviant opportunities generate delinquent behavior and involvement in deviant social networks. They become increasingly important for explaining the onset of offending as the child ages and gains more independence from his or her parents.

In general, ineffective parenting, weak social bonds, and abundant deviant opportunities are likely to produce the initiation of antisocial behavior during the childhood years. We also predict a negative association between the strength and number of these deficits and age of onset. As the strength of these deficits increases, delinquent behavior is likely to emerge at younger ages. As the strength of these deficits diminishes, however, that is, as bonding increases and deviant opportunities decrease, age of onset will increase and move toward the modal age of onset that occurs during early adolescence.

Up to this point, we have discussed the origins of early onset offending; while the age of onset varied from toddlerhood through childhood, it was always, to some extent, precocious. We now turn to the period of age-appropriate or normative onset. For the population as a whole, the modal age of onset occurs in early to mid-adolescence, from about age 12 to age 16 (Stouthamer-Loeber, Loeber, Huizinga, & Porter, 1997; Wolfgang, Thornberry, & Figlio, 1987).

We hypothesize that the youngsters in this proportionately large onset group are unlikely to have been exposed to the more extreme and interwoven causal forces described up to this point. They are less likely to be drawn from positions in the social structure characterized by structural adversity, they are more likely to have adequate prosocial bonds, and they are less likely to have easy access to deviant opportunity structures. They are also likely to have compensating mechanisms in their backgrounds to offset the consequences of exposure to any major risk factors that do exist. For example, some youngsters growing up under conditions of structural adversity avoid delinquency, in part because of strong parental relationships and controls that buffer them from the effects of limited prosocial opportunities. What generates their break from conformity to involvement in antisocial behavior?

As was true at younger ages, the characteristics and behavior of children, the style of parenting, and environmental influences interact to produce the causal forces that result in the onset of delinquency during the teenage years. However, these causal forces are not only substantially less strong, but their source is developmentally specific. Prior to adolescence, the behavior of these children is largely controlled by parents and teachers, they are embedded in conventional networks, and they are largely dependent on those networks for resources. By the end of adolescence, however, they are expected to be independent of their parents and prepared to enter and succeed in the adult world. Thus, one of the major developmental tasks of adolescence is establishing age-appropriate autonomy (Conger, 1991; Cooper, Grotevant, & Condon, 1983). Adolescents are expected to make more of their own decisions and to be more responsible for those decisions. With this added responsibility, comes the expectation of more adult-like behavior. Conger suggests that the successful development of such autonomy relies on the processes of both separation and continued connectedness. Whereas adolescents must have sufficient freedom from parental authority to make decisions about their lives, they still need guidance and support from their parents. Balancing the need for adolescent autonomy with the concern for parental monitoring of attitudes, behaviors, and decisions creates a tension between parents and children that is often evident during adolescence. While adolescence may not be the period of "storm and stress" it was once characterized to be, it is still a stressful period for many parents and adolescents (Gecas & Seff, 1990; Steinberg & Morris, 2001).

In the process of establishing age-appropriate autonomy, young adolescents seek distance from parents, teachers, and, more generally, adult authority. Their emerging physical, sexual, and social maturity provide the human capital needed for increased independence. Benson, Williams, and Johnson (1987: 36) report that "the importance of making one's own decisions, grows more dramatically than any other value area" during the adolescent years. The attainment of autonomy does not increase at the same rate, however, creating the tension between parents and their children. For adolescents, it is often manifested in feelings of anger toward parents, who continue to exert control over their lives (Benson et al., 1987). Parents are concerned about their loss of control and, as a result, they worry over the safety and welfare of their child (Gecas & Seff, 1990). Ambert suggests that, just as parents adapt parenting practices to their children's behaviors during their childhood years, there is "every reason to believe that parents also adapt to their adolescents' personalities and demand for independence" (1997: 46). Thus, while the extreme parenting deficits that were influential for early onset are unlikely to be present for those who onset in adolescence, parents may still adapt to their child's assertion of independence in a dysfunctional manner (Silverberg & Steinberg, 1990), increasing the probability of the onset of delinquency. In this way, "it can be said that adolescents co-produce the parental child-rearing practices of which they are the beneficiaries or the victims" (Ambert, 1997: 46). Conflict and alienation from parents reduce the impact of parental bonds and parental control on the behavior of their adolescent children. Similar processes unfold with teachers and other adult authority figures. Although these young adolescents are never entirely alienated from parents and teachers, distance is created in these relationships.

Cut free from the strict bounds of parental and adult supervision, adolescents gravitate toward each other—toward adolescent peer groups—as their dominant social networks. In large part, peers replace parents, or at least are added to parents, as major sources of rewards and approval of behavior (Gecas & Seff, 1990). But, since age-graded peers are going through the same process of searching for autonomy at roughly the same time, adolescent peer groups are closed to adult authority while valuing behaviors that demonstrate rebellion from adult authority (Cohen, 1955; Stinchecomb, 1964).

One consequence is that the peer culture encourages and reinforces deviant behaviors—deviant life-styles, experimentation with alcohol and drug use, and involvement in minor forms of delinquency. Much of this behavior involves precocious behavior typically reserved for adults, e.g., smoking, drinking, and sexual relations, and much of it is, in Albert Cohen's felicitous phrase, "non-utilitarian, malicious, and negativistic" (1955: 25). While clearly delinquent, this behavior typically involves less serious forms of delinquency, and involvement in the most serious forms—e.g., armed robbery, burglary, heroin use—is not very common.

Youngsters who were buffered at earlier ages from the negative consequences of structural adversity by strong prosocial bonds are in a particularly precarious position during this stage of their lives. In part, this is because their parents do not have the resources to provide alternative activities that could keep their children away from problematic influences. For example, Ambert asserts that, "disadvantaged parents are less able to counteract negative peer pressures than middle-class parents" (1997: 101), an effect that may be particularly acute for adolescents who live in single-parent families. More generally, for youngsters from impoverished backgrounds, the realization of limitations on their conventional opportunities is more salient and access to deviant opportunities more abundant. Increased responsibility for decisions about short-term behavior often leads to choosing the increasingly attractive alternative of deviant behavior.

Finally, we discuss the onset of antisocial behavior that occurs during late adolescence and into the early adult years (Bushway et al., 2003; Eggleston & Laub, 2002). We refer to individuals who begin at this stage as late starters or late bloomers but caution that we use these terms differently from the way they have been used in typological theories (e.g., Patterson et al., 1991; Moffitt, 1993). In those theories, anyone who is not an early starter is a late starter. This results in a residual concept that actually includes the large group of age-normative starters that we just discussed and a small group of truly late starters. We reserve the terms late starter and late bloomer for those who begin frequent offending at ages beyond the modal onset years of adolescence. (See Figure 8.1 for an illustration.) Thus, early and late starters are both characterized by being "off-time" (Elder, 1997), bracketing the larger group that initiates involvement in crime in early adolescence.

Eggleston and Laub (2002) found that, averaged across eighteen studies, 17.2 percent of non-delinquents begin offending in adulthood. Approximately half of the adult offender population is comprised of these late bloomers, and they are serious offenders who continue offending into their adult years (e.g., Farrington, 1983; Glueck & Glueck, 1968; Nagin, Farrington, & Moffitt, 1995; Sampson & Laub, 1993; Wolfgang et al., 1987). These individuals present an intriguing pattern of offending. Why, after successfully traversing most of the adolescent years when offending is quite common, do they initiate and then continue serious offending? The difficulty in accounting for this pattern is exacerbated by the fact that little research has been done on late bloomers (Eggleston & Laub, 2002).

We hypothesize that although these individuals have a number of deficits that eventually cause offending, other aspects of their lives prior to late adolescence serve to buffer them from the effects of these deficits. As a result, the causal force during childhood and adolescence is relatively weak, thus delaying the onset of offending until late adolescence or emerging adulthood (Arnett, 2000).

In particular, we hypothesize that late bloomers have reduced human capital, especially lower intelligence and lower academic competence, and thus are less successful in building social capital than other adolescents. At early ages, however, they are buffered from the effects of these deficits by a supportive family and school environment. We expect the family to provide a strong, supportive environment, in part brought about by their more advantageous structural position, thus enabling youth to cope with academic deficits. These individuals adapt to their academic deficiencies and, perhaps, even find the social control and support services offered at school as providing needed structure. During emerging adulthood, however, individuals begin to leave the protective environments of the family and school to seek employment and independence. According to Arnett, the stage of emerging adulthood, roughly ages 18 to 25, is characterized by "relative independence from social roles and from normative expectations" (2000: 469). Given the freedom and instability of this developmental stage, deficits in human capital now become a serious disadvantage for acquiring meaningful employment and, in turn, establishing a quality relationship with a partner. In addition, losing the protection of the family and the controlling environment of school may make those with human capital deficiencies more vulnerable to the influence of deviant friends.

This explanation is consistent with the few studies that have explicitly examined late bloomers. Nagin et al. (1995) found that late bloomers had low IQs (at ages 8-11) and did poorly in school during early adolescence. Mannheim (1967) observed that the family served to protect late bloomers from offending but after this protection was outgrown, onset occurred. Sampson and Laub (1993), using the control group from the Glueck study, examined those who began offending at later ages and found that job stability and, to a lesser extent, marital attachment measured between the ages of 17 and 25 are related to offending between ages 25 and 32.

In addition to the causal forces outlined above, involvement in other problem behaviors, especially alcohol and drug use, which typically escalate during the late teenage years, may also contribute to both the onset of antisocial behavior and its relatively serious nature. The loss of buffering factors, coupled with the accumulation of life stressors due to unsatisfactory work and interpersonal adjustment (Rutter, Giller, & Hagell, 1998) and the increasing influence of deviant peers, leads to excessive alcohol use. Alcohol use and difficulties in making the transition to adult statuses continue to interact to increase the probability of continuing criminal offending. Sampson and Laub's (1993) finding that late bloomers are likely to be excessive alcohol users is consistent with this explanation.

Explaining Continuity and Change in Delinquent Careers

Up to this point, we have focused entirely on issues related to the onset of antisocial behavior. Life-course theories also need to account for continuity and change in delinquent behavior and the relationships between onset, on the one hand, and both continuity and change, on the other. Some offenders exhibit high levels of continuity in antisocial behavior over the life course and, as noted earlier, people who start earlier are somewhat more likely to persist than those who start later (Elliott, 1994; Krohn et al., 2001). Nevertheless, there is also a substantial amount of change in offending over time. Many early onset offenders stop offending (e.g., the intermittent offenders in Figure 8.1) and many later onset offenders appear to be persistent (e.g., the late bloomers in

Figure 8.1). What accounts for these varying patterns of continuity and change in antisocial behavior?

In the previous discussion we hypothesized that early onset is associated with the strength of the causal force associated with delinquency. Individuals with the earliest onset of antisocial behavior are likely to have multiple, interwoven causal factors—especially structural adversity, ineffective parenting, and negative temperamental characteristics—and few offsetting assets. In addition, we hypothesized that as the magnitude of the causal force diminished, that is, as the causal factors became uncoupled and less extreme and as offsetting assets increased, the age of onset of offending would increase. These characteristics also offer an explanation for patterns of continuity and change.

Continuity in Offending

Two developmental processes help to account for the higher level of continuity for offenders with earlier ages of onset. The first stems from the stability of the causal factors themselves across the life course. If, as argued above, early onset offending is caused by exposure to multiple deficits and more extreme levels of those deficits, it is reasonable to assume that the stronger the deficits are, the more stable they are likely to be over time. For example, families experiencing extreme levels of structural adversity do not easily or often escape that adversity, and the development of children raised in those families is constantly compromised. Similarly, there is continuity in ineffective parenting styles, in part caused by the constancy of the social environment in which these families often find themselves (Patterson et al., 1992). Finally, there is evidence of continuity in negative temperamental traits and neuropsychological deficits from childhood through the adult years (Caspi, Bem, & Elder, 1989; Moffitt, Lynam, & Silva, 1994).

The stability of these attributes helps to explain the negative relationship between age of onset and continuity of offending. Since more extreme deficits are needed to bring about early onset offending and since more extreme deficits are themselves more likely to be stable, these deficits will remain in place to continue causing antisocial behavior over time. And, since the strongest deficits are associated with the earliest ages of onset, this source of continuity is likely to be greatest for offenders with earlier rather than later onsets.

The second process that accounts for continuity concerns the developmental consequences of behavior, including early manifestations of antisocial behavior. Prolonged involvement in antisocial behavior, especially the more serious forms of antisocial behavior, can have severe negative consequences for many aspects of a child's development. Persistent antisocial behavior will continue to elicit coercive responses from the parent as the child ages (Lee & Bates, 1985). In addition, children who have learned coercive behavioral styles in the family are apt to extend them to external settings such as peer relationships and school behavior. "There is now substantial evidence that aggressive children are likely to be rejected by their peers" (Coie & Dodge, 1998: 828; see also Coie, Dodge, & Kupersmidt, 1990) and that rejected children lose the positive influence of prosocial peers in acquiring social and behavioral competencies (Coie, Lochman, Terry, & Hyman, 1992; Ladd, 1990). Aggressive children are also at risk for school failure (Patterson et al., 1992). The coercive training they received in the family and the rejection by peers increase the chances of early academic adjustment problems, even controlling for prior academic competence (Ladd, 1990). There is substantial evidence that isolation in deviant peer networks, coercive behavioral styles, and academic failure, all influenced in part by earlier antisocial behavior, lead to continuing involvement in delinquency during adolescence.

As these youths age, they are ill prepared to meet the developmental challenges of adolescence and to prepare themselves for adult life. In a series of papers, we and our colleagues have shown that delinquent behavior reduces social bonds (Jang & Smith, 1997; Krohn, Thornberry, Collins-Hall, & Lizotte, 1995; Thornberry, Lizotte, Krohn, Farnworth, & Jang, 1991), increases affiliation with deviant peers and fosters deviant belief systems (Krohn, Lizotte, Thornberry, Smith, & McDowall, 1996; Thornberry, Lizotte, Krohn, Farnworth, & Jang, 1994), and disrupts orderly and timely transitions to adult roles (Krohn, Lizotte, & Perez, 1997; Thornberry, Smith, & Howard, 1997).

In brief, we hypothesize that individuals who initiate antisocial behavior at very young ages are more likely than average to persist because the causal factors are likely to remain in place and because early involvement in antisocial behavior generates cumulative and cascading consequences in the person's life course. All of this reduces the formation of social bonds and social capital and increases embeddedness in deviant networks and belief systems, foreclosing conventional lifestyles and entrapping the individual in deviant lifestyles. These processes are most likely to be evident for youngsters with a precocious onset, hence the general correlation between childhood onset and more persistent careers. However, as the age of onset moves towards adolescence, the processes that account for persistence become somewhat less likely precisely because the strength of the causal force that brought delinquency about in the first place was weaker.

For individuals who initiate offending during early to mid-adolescence—the larger, more age-normative group—there is an even stronger tendency towards shorter careers. For reasons discussed in the next section, this is likely to be the modal response. But, even for these offenders, there are noticeable levels of persistence, as shown earlier in Figure 8.1. Some of these age-normative-onset individuals continue to commit crimes well into their early adult years. Indeed, Moffitt (2002) has recently observed that many of her adolescence-limited offenders continued to commit crimes at age 26. Why, if they do not have multiple and extreme deficits, would they continue to offend into their early adult years?

Adolescence is a stage in the life course when children are in the process of asserting their independence, and the way parents respond to that challenge to their authority explains, in part, the onset of delinquent behavior. However, the tension between parents and their adolescent children is unlikely to account for continuity in offending. The problem that emerges between these adolescents and their parents is typically a temporary one brought on by the transitional nature of adolescence, and there is evidence that as these conflicts are resolved parent-child relationships improve (Steinberg & Morris, 2001).

We hypothesize that continuity for later onset offenders is overwhelmingly due to the reciprocal consequences of their behaviors and their association with deviant peers. For some youth, delinquent behavior can have adverse consequences that serve as obstacles in making a successful transition to adulthood. This may be particularly true if youths are also involved in heavy alcohol or drug use (Jessor et al., 1991; Krohn et al., 1997; Newcomb & Bentler, 1988). These behaviors jeopardize their performance in conventional arenas such as school, the workplace, and establishing a quality relationship with a significant other. Failure to make successful transitions in these arenas increases the probability of continued offending.

An additional consequence of offending is solidifying ties with deviant others (Krohn et al., 1996; Thornberry et al., 1994). For those later onset offenders who become enmeshed in deviant social networks, especially street gangs, offending is likely to continue beyond the teenage years (Thornberry, Krohn, Lizotte, Smith, & Tobin, 2003). Relatedly, Warr (1998) found that one of the reasons successful partnering reduces offending is that it changes the associational patterns of youth away from those who participate in delinquent behavior.

Up to this point, we have argued that the level of continuity in offending is likely to be highest for those who start earliest and to gradually diminish for those who start later, especially those who start in adolescence. However, for late bloomers, whose antisocial careers emerge in late adolescence or early adulthood, we hypothesize that this general relationship is reversed and that the level of continuity in offending increases. In other words, there is a U-shaped distribution between age of onset and the level of continuity in offending, as shown in Figure 8.2.

Late bloomers are hypothesized to have serious deficits in human capital that had been camouflaged by strong protective factors of family and school during adolescence. Once removed from the protective cocoon of those arenas, however, these deficits in human capital create difficulties in making successful transitions to adult roles. Problems in acquiring stable, meaningful work and quality relationships with significant others are likely to increase, thus making continuity in offending a more likely outcome. These problems are

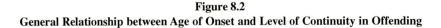

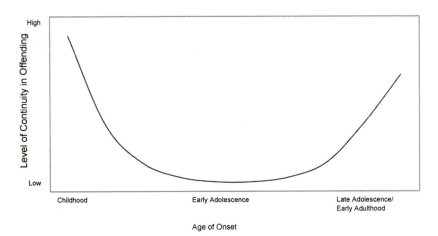

Figure 8.2
General Relationship between Age of Onset and Level of Continuity in Offending

exacerbated by the use of alcohol and drugs. Consistent with our view, Guo, Hill, Hawkins, Catalano, and Abbott (2002) recently showed that late-onset substance use, in particular late-onset binge drinking and marijuana use, had strong effects on early adult risky sexual behaviors.

To summarize our views about continuity, we hypothesize that earlier onset offenders will be most likely to continue offending because of the stability in the strength of the causal forces that led to their early onset and the negative consequences of that behavior. Later age-normative-onset offenders are less likely to have serious deficits in childhood and therefore are less likely to experience continuity in offending. If they do continue to offend, it is most likely due to the consequences of their offending behaviors, especially becoming enmeshed in deviant social networks. Late bloomers, on the other hand, are more likely to continue offending because their deficits in human capital increase the difficulty of making successful transitions to adult roles. Continuing economic and relationship problems, combined with the use of alcohol and drugs, are likely to lead to offending well into the adult years for the late bloomers.

Change in Offending

As noted earlier, there are two patterns of behavioral change. The first, movement from some sustained period of non-offending to involvement in offending, has already been discussed in our explanations for offending that emerges later in the life course, especially from early adolescence onward. In this section we concentrate on the second pattern of change, from some sustained period of offending to non-offending.

Although some offending careers are marked by high levels of continuity, there is also a substantial degree of change in levels of offending. Indeed, that is the whole point of Robins' paradox: "most antisocial children do *not* become antisocial adults" (1978: 611, emphasis added). This form of change is represented both by de-escalation—substantial reductions in the rate of offending—and by desistance (Bushway et al., 2003; Loeber & Le Blanc, 1990). Three developmental processes can be used to account for this type of change.

First, we hypothesize that as the age of onset increases, the strength of the causal force diminishes. That is, the causal factors are less numerous, less extreme, and less intertwined. Because of that, they are also less likely to be highly stable over time. Families do experience upward mobility and move to new neighborhoods and better schools; parental stressors such as family conflict, depression, and drug use can be ameliorated; and bonds between parents and children can improve. These attributes are more apt to change if they have not reached an extraordinary level. For example, poverty generated by marginal job skills and sporadic employment is easier to escape than chronic, grinding poverty that has existed over several generations in a family. As a sociogenetic model, interactional theory hypothesizes that as the person's social environment changes, so, too, will the person's behavior, regardless of age or age of onset. Thus, changes in causal factors potentially provide turning points in the person's life-course trajectories and in their antisocial behavior. These changes are more likely if the causal factors themselves are less extreme and, therefore, they are more likely to occur for later age-normative-onset offenders. Indeed, this developmental process is particularly salient in accounting for the high rates of desistance observed for those who initiate offending during the age-normative period of early to mid-adolescence. A large part of the impetus for their offending was generated by a specific developmental challenge of adolescence—the search for identity and autonomy. As that search unfolds, tension between parent and child and involvement in deviant peer groups often follow, increasing the likelihood of delinquency. As the challenges of adolescence are successfully met, and identity and autonomy are gained, the motivation for rebellion and deviance subsides. To be sure, this transition does not happen for all, but it is the modal outcome in most societies. We view the dissipation of a developmentally specific motivating factor as a special case of the instability of causal factors.

The second process associated with the movement away from active offending occurs when the causal factors that give rise to the initial antisocial behavior are not intensely coupled. There are many youth with deficits in some areas, say a distressed family, who have compensating assets in other areas, say intelligence and school performance. The deficits they do experience put them at risk for delinquency, but the offsetting assets reduce the chances that they will have long, persistent antisocial careers. More generally, these youngsters have a richer set of protective factors, in part brought about by the somewhat less tenuous social position of their families (see Rutter, 1987; Smith & Carlson, 1997; Smith, Lizotte, Thornberry, & Krohn, 1995; Werner & Smith, 1992). Again, consistent with our explanation for onset, the presence of offsetting assets is more likely as the age of onset increases.

Third, given the presence of protective assets, these youth are less likely to experience the negative consequences brought about by feedback effects from delinquent behavior. Although the negative consequences of delinquency will find fertile soil in areas in which deficits already exist (the distressed family in our example), they will also find resistance in areas of resilience (school performance in our example). Thus, it is less likely that the various life-course trajectories will become interwoven to create an amplifying loop towards increasing involvement in antisocial careers. As with the other processes, this is less likely to happen for the earlier onset offenders, because of the strength and coupling of causal factors in their case. Even there, however, some earlier onset offenders can be expected to have protective factors (e.g., high IQ) that may have been camouflaged by deficits in other domains. Those protective factors may enable even early onset offenders the opportunity to change the course of their lives.

When these developmental processes are evident, youth are more likely to successfully complete the developmental challenges of adolescence and are better prepared to make on-time, successful transitions to adulthood, especially in the areas of family formation and stable employment. Attachment to partner and children and commitment to work and conventional activities create new social bonds and social capital to control behavior. They also alter social networks away from antisocial and toward prosocial venues (see Warr, 1998). The reciprocal relationships between prosocial trajectories in family and work and trajectories of antisocial behavior now serve to maintain low or zero levels of offending.

Prosocial Careers

Just as there is a small portion of the population that persists in offending across the life course, there is a small portion that manages to avoid involvement in delinquency entirely. To establish a persistent pattern of prosocial behavior, conditions in childhood must either prevent the development of predispositions to antisocial behavior or be able to compensate for those predispositions so that they do not lead to antisocial behavior. Social and economic circumstances at levels well above those characterized as indicative of structural adversity play a key role in generating conforming behavior early in the life course. Although having the economic means to provide for one's family does not preclude the possibility of having children with antisocial behavior, it does reduce the risk. A secure financial position reduces parental levels of stress and antisocial behavior, thereby increasing the probability that they will exhibit more appropriate parenting behaviors. They are also likely to have the human and social capital to ameliorate or correct the developmental consequences of early temperamental difficulties such as oppositional behavior.

The strong bond to the family and the absence or control of negative temperamental qualities set the stage for continuity of prosocial behavior. Serious antisocial behavior is not part of the behavioral repertoire of these children and, therefore, such behavior cannot generate adverse effects on family life, peer relationships, and school success. Indeed, the prosocial behavior exhibited by these children serves to increase the strength of the child's ties to conventionality. Parents respond to the good behavior of their children by rewarding them, exhibiting more affection and greater involvement (Gecas & Seff, 1990). Teachers favor children who are attentive and interested in their schoolwork. Children tend to establish friendship ties with peers who behave in similar ways (Kandel, 1978), thus establishing a social network that constrains behavior toward conformity (Krohn, 1986).

The pattern of relationships established in the early years not only increases ties to conventionality, but as these children enter adolescence they are unlikely to have access to deviant social networks and learning environments. The boundaries of social groupings that are formed in adolescence are often hard to penetrate (Schwendinger & Schwendinger, 1985). Thus, prosocial youth are encapsulated in a prosocial cocoon facilitating their continued conformity. The increased demand for autonomy that characterizes adolescence results in decisions between alternative prosocial activities rather than between prosocial and antisocial behavior.

These youth are also more likely to have developed the necessary human and social capital to successfully meet the challenges of the transition to adulthood. Not burdened with severe structural adversities, poor school records, or deviant labels that beset the youth who are involved in antisocial behavior, prosocial adolescents are more likely to experience smooth, on-time transitions to adulthood and to avoid the late onset of antisocial behavior.

Developmental Puzzles

In his invitation to contribute to this volume and in his Sutherland Address (2003), David Farrington posed a number of questions that developmental theories should address. The full set is too numerous to respond to within the confines of a single chapter. In closing, though, we would like to suggest that these questions can be divided into two categories.

The first category contains general questions that formed the basis of the theoretical model just presented here and in previous versions of interactional theory (Thornberry, 1987; Thornberry & Krohn, 2001). We were particularly interested in offering an explanation for the onset of offending, continuity and change in offending, and the link between onset and continuity. In the course of addressing these issues, we discuss a number of others such as the high prevalence of delinquency in mid-adolescence, the small proportion of chronic offenders, and why they commit more serious crimes.

The second category of questions focuses on specific observations that may be unique to specific populations, methodologies, or theories. These questions are not very central to an interactional theory perspective and are therefore not addressed in this chapter. For example, we did not focus on why the onset of offending peaks at ages 8 to 14. We view onset as continuously distributed from toddlerhood onward, and to us the more pertinent theoretical question is to account for the full distribution, not just parts of it.

The issue of desistance can be used as an illustration. One question posed was to account for the peak ages of desistance between 20 and 29. This empirical observation is based on the age-crime curve observed for the entire population. In the Rochester data, however, the clearest pattern of desistance is observed for the bell-shaped desistors (see Figure 8.1). Their offending begins to decline at about age 17, reaches a near-zero level by age 20, and remains there (although it can obviously increase at later ages.) This suggests that focusing solely on the population average may miss important patterns of desistance that only emerge when the overall curve is subdivided into different patterns or trajectories of offending (Bushway et al., 2003). If true, then recognizing this diversity and using it in generating theoretical explanations is an important theoretical issue in its own right. For example, in the case of the bell-shaped desistors, the explanations for desistance that are typically offered—marriage and work—are not very appropriate given the ages at which the desistance process unfolds, 17 to 20. Interestingly, though, these two factors—marriage and work—emerge as expected explanations precisely because of the population average.

Our more general point is that many of these empirical observations about crime are themselves theory-laden. Explaining any given observation may be more central to some theories than others. From our vantage point, both onset and desistance are continuously distributed, and we need to describe patterns of each and variability around those patterns using life-course data. Hopefully, the theory offered above moves us in that direction.

Notes

1. We use the terms antisocial behavior, delinquency, and criminal offending interchangeably in this chapter but with concern for the developmental or age-appropriateness of these various manifestations of antisocial behavior.

2. The estimation of these trajectories is described in detail in Bushway, Thornberry, & Krohn (2003). Briefly, the trajectory method divides the population into some number of subgroups, the members of which have similar offending careers in terms of onset, level, and duration. As Nagin has noted, the groups are probabilistically determined and reflect areas under a continuous distribution rather than actual, discrete groups (1999).

3.   Interestingly, Moffitt (2002) has recently re-analyzed her data and discovered more diverse patterns of offending than her theory originally proposed and her earlier research found.

4.   Jessor et al. (1991) refer to a similar process as the person's overall psychosocial proneness and Catalano and Hawkins (1986) refer to this as the balance of prosocial and antisocial influences

References

Ambert, A.-M. (1997). *Parents, Children, and Adolescents: Interactive Relationships and Development in Context.* New York: The Haworth Press.

Arnett, J. J. (2000). Emerging adulthood: A theory of development from the late teens through the twenties. *American Psychologist,* 55: 469-480.

Bates, J. E., Maslin, C., & Frankel, K. (1985). Attachment security, mother-child interaction, and temperament as predictors of behavior problem ratings at 3 years. In I. Bretherton & E. Waters (Eds.), *Growing Points of Attachment Theory and Research* (pp. 167-193). Monographs of the Society for Research in Child Development 50.

Belsky, J., Woodworth, S., & Crnic, K. (1996). Troubled family interaction during toddlerhood. *Development and Psychopathology,* 8: 477-495.

Benson, P., Williams, D., & Johnson, A. (1987). *The Quicksilver Years: The Hopes and Fears of Early Adolescence.* San Francisco: Harper and Row Publishers.

Bushway, S. D., Thornberry, T. P., & Krohn, M. D. (2003). Desistance as a developmental process: A comparison of static and dynamic approaches. *Journal of Quantitative Criminology,* 19: 129-153.

Caspi, A., Bem, D. J., & Elder, Jr., G. H. (1989). Continuities and consequences of interactional styles across the life course. *Journal of Personality,* 57: 75-406.

Caspi, A., Elder, Jr., G. H., & Herbener, E. S. (1990). Childhood personality and the prediction of life-course patterns. In L. Robins & M. Rutter (Eds.), *Straight and Devious Pathways from Childhood to Adulthood* (pp. 13-35). New York: Cambridge University Press.

Catalano, R. F., & Hawkins, J. D. (1986). The social development model: A theory of antisocial behavior. Paper presented at the Safeco Lectureship on Crime and Delinquency, School of Social Work, University of Washington, Seattle.

Cicchetti, D. & Rogosch, F. A. (1996). Equifinality and multifinality in developmental psychopathology. *Development and Psychopathology,* 8: 597-600.

Cohen, A. K. (1955). *Delinquent Boys.* New York: Free Press.

Coie, J. D. & Dodge, K. A. (1998). Aggression and antisocial behavior. In W. Damon (Ed.), *Handbook of Child Psychology, Vol. 3* (pp. 779-862). New York: Wiley.

Coie, J. D., Dodge, K. A. & Kupersmidt, J. (1990). Peer group behavior and social status. In S. R. Asher & J. D. Coie (Eds.), *Peer Rejection in Childhood* (pp. 17-59). New York: Cambridge University Press.

Coie, J. D., Lochman, J. E., Terry, R. & Hyman, C. (1992). Predicting early adolescent disorder from childhood aggression and peer rejection. *Journal of Consulting and Clinical Psychology,* 60: 783-792.

Conger, J. J. (1991). *Adolescence and Youth: Psychological Development in a Changing World,* 4th ed. New York: HarperCollins Publishers.

Conger, R. D., Ge, X., Elder, Jr., G. H., Lorenz, F. O. & Simons, R. L. (1994). Economic stress, coercive family process and developmental problems of adolescents. *Child Development,* 65: 541-561.

Cooper, C., Grotevant, H., & Condon, S. (1983). Individuality and connectedness in the family as a context for the development of adolescent identity formation and role-taking skill. In H. Grotevant & C. Cooper (Eds.), *Adolescent Development in the Family* (pp. 43-59). San Francisco: Jossey-Bass.

Eggleston, E. P. & Laub, J. H. (2002). The onset of adult offending: A neglected dimension of the criminal career. *Journal of Criminal Justice*, 30: 603-622.

Elder, G. H., Jr. (1997). The life course and human development. In R.M. Lerner (Ed.), *Handbook of Child Psychology, Volume 1: Theoretical Models of Human Development* (pp. 939-991) New York: Wiley.

Elliott, D. S. (1994). Serious violent offenders: Onset, developmental course, and termination. *Criminology*, 32: 1-21.

Farrington, D. P. (1983). Offending from 10 to 25 years of age. In K. T. van Dusen & S. A. Mednick (Eds.), *Prospective Studies of Crime and Delinquency* (pp. 17-37). Boston: Kluwer-Nijhoff Publishing.

Farrington, D. P. (2003). Developmental and life-course criminology: Key theoretical and empirical issues—The American Society of Criminology 2002 Sutherland Award Address. *Criminology*, 41: 221-255.

Gecas, V. & Seff, M. A. (1990). Social class and self-esteem: Psychological centrality, compensation, and the relative effects of work and home. *Social Psychology Quarterly*, 53: 165-173.

Gilliom, M., Shaw, D. S., Beck, J. E., Schonberg, M. A. & Lukon, J. L. (2002). Anger regulation in disadvantaged preschool boys: Strategies, antecedents, and the development of self-control. *Developmental Psychology*, 38: 222-235.

Glueck, S. & Glueck, E. (1968). *Delinquents and Nondelinquents in Perspective*. Cambridge, MA: Harvard University Press.

Grolnick, W. S., Bridges, L. S. & Connell, J. P. (1996). Emotion regulation in two-year-olds: Strategies and emotional expression in four contexts. *Child Development*, 67:928-941.

Guo, J., Hill, K., Hawkins, J. D., Catalano, R. F. & Abbott, R. D.. (2002). A developmental analysis of sociodemographic, family, and peer effects on adolescent illicit drug initiation. *Journal of the American Academy of Child and Adolescent Psychiatry*, 41: 838-845.

Hagan, J. (1992). The poverty of a classless criminology—The American Society of Criminology 1991 Presidential Address. *Criminology*, 30: 1-19.

Jang, S. J. & Smith, C. A. (1997). A test of reciprocal causal relationships among parental supervision, affective ties, and delinquency. *Journal of Research in Crime and Delinquency*, 34: 307-336.

Jessor, R., Donovan, J. E. & Costa, F. M. (1991). *Beyond Adolescence: Problem Behavior and Young Adult Development.* Cambridge: Cambridge University Press.

Jones, R. L. (Ed.). (1989). *Black Adolescents*. Berkeley, CA: Cobb and Henry.

Kandel, D. B. (1978). Similarity in real life adolescent friendship pairs. *Journal of Personality and Social Psychology*, 36: 306-312.

Kopp, C. B. (1989). Regulation of distress and negative emotions: A developmental view. *Developmental Psychology*, 25: 343-354.

Krohn, M. D. (1986). The web of conformity: A network approach to the explanation of delinquent behavior. *Social Problems*, 33: 581-593.

Krohn, M. D., Lizotte, A. J. & Perez, C. M. (1997). The interrelationship between substance use and precocious transitions to adult statuses. *Journal of Health and Social Behavior*, 38: 87-103.

Krohn, M. D., Lizotte, A. J., Thornberry, T. P., Smith, C. A. & McDowall, D. (1996). Reciprocal causal relationships among drug use, peers, and beliefs: A five-wave panel model. *Journal of Drug Issues*, 26: 405-428.

Krohn, M. D., Thornberry, T. P., Collins-Hall, L. & Lizotte, A. J. (1995). School dropout, delinquent behavior, and drug use: An examination of the causes and consequences of dropping out of school. In H. B. Kaplan (Ed.), *Drugs, Crime, and Other Deviant Adaptations: Longitudinal Studies* (pp. 163-183). New York: Plenum Press.

Krohn, M. D., Thornberry, T. P., Rivera, C. & Le Blanc, M. (2001). Later delinquency careers. In R. Loeber and D. P. Farrington (Eds.), *Child Delinquents: Development, Intervention, and Service Needs* (pp. 67-93). Thousand Oaks, CA: Sage.

Ladd, G. W. (1990). Having friends, keeping friends, making friends, and being liked by peers in the classroom: Predictors of children's early school adjustment. *Child Development*, 61: 312-331.

Lee, C. L. & Bates, J. E. (1985). Mother-child interaction at two years and perceived difficult temperament. *Child Development*, 56: 1314-1325.

Loeber, R. & Le Blanc, M. (1990). Toward a developmental criminology. In M. Tonry & N. Morris (Eds.), *Crime and Justice: An Annual Review of Research, Volume 11* (pp. 375-473). Chicago: University of Chicago Press.

Mannheim, H. (1967). *Comparative Criminology*. Boston: Houghton Mifflin Company.

McLoyd, V. (1990). The impact of economic hardship on black families and children: Psychological distress, parenting, and socioemotional development. *Child Development* 61:311-346.

Moffitt, T. E. (1993). "Life-course-persistent" and "adolescence-limited" antisocial behavior: A developmental taxonomy. *Psychological Review*, 100: 674-701.

Moffitt, T. E. (1996). The neuropsychology of conduct disorder. In P. Cordella & L. J. Siegel (Eds.), *Readings in Contemporary Criminological Theory* (pp. 85-106). Boston: Northeastern University Press.

Moffitt, T. E. (1997). Adolescence-limited and life-course-persistent offending: A complementary pair of developmental theories. In T. P. Thornberry (Ed.), *Developmental Theories of Crime and Delinquency.* Advances in Criminological Theory, Vol. 7 (pp. 11-54). New Brunswick, NJ: Transaction Publishers.

Moffitt, T. E. (2002). Males on the life-course-persistent and adolescence-limited antisocial pathways: Follow-up at 26 years. *Development and Psychopathology*, 14: 179-207.

Moffitt, T. E., Lynam, D. R. & Silva, P. A. (1994). Neuropsychological tests predict persistent male delinquency. *Criminology*, 32: 101-124.

Nagin, D. S. (1999). Analyzing developmental trajectories: A semiparametric, group-based approach. *Psychological Methods*, 4: 139-157.

Nagin, D. S., Farrington, D. P. & Moffitt, T. E. (1995). Life-course trajectores of different types of offenders. *Criminology*, 33: 111-139.

Nagin, D. & Land, K. C. (1993). Age, criminal careers, and population heterogeneity: Specification and estimation of a nonparametric, mixed Poisson model. *Criminology*, 31: 327-362.

Newcomb, M. D. & Bentler, P. M. (1988). *Consequences of Adolescent Drug Use: Impact on the Lives of Young Adults.* Newbury Park, CA: Sage Publications.

Patterson, G. R., Capaldi, D. & Bank, L. (1991) An early starter model for predicting delinquency. In D. J. Pepler & K. H. Rubin (Eds.), *The Development and Treatment of Childhood Aggression* (pp. 139-168). Hillsdale, NJ: Erlbaum.

Patterson, G. R., Reid, J. B. & Dishion, T. J. (1992). *Antisocial Boys*. Eugene, OR: Castalia.

Prior, M., Sanson, A., Carroll, R. & Oberklaid, F. (1989). Social class differences in temperament ratings by mothers of preschool children. *Merrill-Palmer Quarterly*, 35: 239-248.

Robins, L. N. (1978). Sturdy childhood predictors of adult antisocial behavior: Replications from longitudinal studies. *Psychological Medicine*, 8: 611-622.

Rutter, M. (1987). Psychological resilience and protective mechanisms. *American Journal of Orthopsychiatry*, 47: 316-331.

Rutter, M. (1988). Longitudinal data in the study of causal processes: Some uses and some pitfalls. In M. Rutter (Ed.), *Studies of Psychosocial Risk: The Power of Longitudinal Data* (pp. 1-28). Cambridge: Cambridge University Press.

Rutter, M., Giller, H. & Hagell, A. (1998). *Antisocial Behavior by Young People*. Cambridge: Cambridge University Press.

Rutter, M. & Quinton, D. (1984). Parental psychiatric disorder: Effects on children. *Psychological Medicine*, 14: 853-880.

Sampson, R. J. & Laub, J. (1993). *Crime in the Making: Pathways and Turning Points Through Life*. Cambridge, MA: Harvard University Press.

Schwendinger, H. & Schwendinger, J. S. (1985). *Adolescent Subcultures and Delinquency*. Westport, CT: Praeger Publishers.

Shaw, D. S. & Bell, R. Q. (1993). Developmental theories of parental contributors to antisocial behavior. *Journal of Abnormal Child Psychology*, 21: 35-49.

Shaw, D. S., Gilliom, M., Ingoldsby, E. M. & Nagin, D. S. (2003). Trajectories leading to school-age conduct problems. *Developmental Psychology*, 39: 189-200.

Shaw, D. S., Keenan, K. & Vondra, J. I. (1994). Developmental precursors of antisocial behaviors ages 1 to 3. *Developmental Psychology*, 30: 355-364.

Shaw, D. S., Owens, E. B., Vondra, J. I., Keenan, K. & Winslow, E. B. (1996). Early risk factors and pathways in the development of early disruptive behavior problems. *Development and Psychopathology*, 8: 679-699.

Silverberg, S. B. & Steinberg, L. (1990). Psychological well-being of parents with early adolescent children. *Developmental Psychology*, 26: 658-666.

Simons, R. L., Beaman, J., Conger, R. D. & Chao, W. (1993). Childhood experience, conceptions of parenting, and attitudes of spouse as determinants of parental behavior. *Journal of Marriage and the Family*, 55: 91-106.

Smith, C. A. & Carlson, B. (1997). Stress, coping, and resilience in children and youth. *Social Service Review*, 71: 231-256.

Smith, C. A., Lizotte, A. J., Thornberry, T. P. & Krohn, M. D. (1995). Resilient youth: Identifying factors that prevent high-risk youth from engaging in delinquency and drug use. In J. Hagan (Ed.), *Delinquency and Disrepute in the Life Course* (pp. 217-247). Greenwich, CT: JAI Press.

Spencer, M. B. & Dornbusch, S. M. (1990). Challenges in studying minority youth. In S. S. Feldman & G. R. Elliott (Eds.), *At the Threshold: The Developing Adolescent*. (pp. 123-146). Cambridge, MA: Harvard University Press.

Steinberg, L. & Morris, A. S. (2001). Adolescent development. *Annual Review of Psychology*, 52: 83-110.

Stinchcomb, A. L. (1964). *Rebellion in a High School*. Chicago: Quadrangle Press.

Stott, D. H. (1978). Epidemiological indicators of the origins of behavior disturbance as measured by the Bristol Social Adjustment Guides. *Genetic Psychology Monographs*, 97: 127-159.

Stouthamer-Loeber, M., Loeber, R., Huizinga, D. & Porter, P. (1997). The early onset of persistent serious offending. Unpublished report to the Office of Juvenile Justice and Delinquency Prevention, Washington, DC.

Thornberry, T. P. (1987). Toward an interactional theory of delinquency. *Criminology*, 25: 863-891.

Thornberry, T. P. (Ed.). (1997). Introduction: Some advantages of developmental and life-course perspectives for the study of crime and delinquency. In *Developmental Theories of Crime and Delinquency*. Advances in Criminological Theory, Vol. 7 (pp. 1-10). New Brunswick, NJ: Transaction Publishers.

Thornberry, T. P. & Krohn, M. D. (2001). The development of delinquency: An interactional perspective. In S. O. White (Ed.), *Handbook of Youth and Justice* (pp. 289-305). New York: Plenum.

Thornberry, T. P., Krohn, M. D., Lizotte, A. J., Smith, C. A. & Tobin, K. (2003). *Gangs and Delinquency in Developmental Perspective.* New York: Cambridge University Press.

Thornberry, T. P., Lizotte, A. J., Krohn, M. D., Farnworth, M. & Jang, S. J. (1991). Testing interactional theory: An examination of reciprocal causal relationships among family, school, and delinquency. *Journal of Criminal Law and Criminology*, 82: 3-35.

Thornberry, T. P., Lizotte, A. J., Krohn, M. D., Farnworth, M. & Jang, S. J. (1994). Delinquent peers, beliefs, and delinquent behavior: A longitudinal test of interactional theory. *Criminology*, 32: 47-83.

Thornberry, T. P., Smith, C. A. & Howard, G. J. (1997). Risk factors for teenage fatherhood. *Journal of Marriage and the Family*, 59: 505-522.

Tibbetts, S. G. & Piquero, A. R. (1999). The influence of gender, low birth weight, and disadvantaged environment in predicting early onset of offending: A test of Moffitt's interactional hypothesis. *Criminology*, 37: 843-878.

Tolan, P. H., Guerra, N. G. & Kendall, P. C. (1995). Introduction to special section: Prediction and prevention of antisocial behavior in children and adolescents. *Journal of Consulting and Clinical Psychology,* 63: 515-517.

Warr, M. (1998). Life-course transitions and desistance from crime. *Criminology*, 36: 183-216.

Werner, E. E. & Smith, R. S. (1992). *Overcoming the Odds: High Risk Children from Birth to Adulthood.* Ithaca, NY: Cornell University Press.

Wolfgang, M. E., Thornberry, T. P. & Figlio, R. M. (1987). *From Boy to Man, From Delinquency to Crime.* Chicago: University of Chicago Press.

Zahn-Waxler, C., Iannotti, R. J., Cummings, E. M., & Denham, S. (1990). Antecedents of problem behaviors in children of depressed mothers. *Development and Psychopathology*, 2: 271-291.

9

The Social Origins of Pathways in Crime: Towards a Developmental Ecological Action Theory of Crime Involvement and Its Changes

Per-Olof H. Wikström[*]

A fruitful analysis of human action requires us to avoid the atomization implicit in the theoretical extremes of under- and oversocialized conceptions. Actors do not behave or decide as atoms outside a social context, nor do they adhere slavishly to a script written for them by the particular intersection of social categories that they happen to occupy. Their attempts at purposive *action are instead embedded in concrete, ongoing systems of social relations.*

—M. Granovetter

Criminological research has documented a range of important non-random patterns in individual offending, its development and their correlates (see e.g., Thornberry & Krohn, 2003; Piquero, Farrington & Blumstein, 2003). However, what is less well understood are the origins of these patterns, or, in other words, the mechanisms (processes) that generate these patterns.[1] The task of this chapter is to discuss potential generative mechanisms of patterns of development and change in individual offending from the perspective of a *Developmental Ecological Action Theory of Crime Involvement.*

The proposed outline for a Developmental Ecological Action Theory of Crime Involvement attempts to break away from the common but, in my opinion, unfruitful division into individually or ecologically oriented explanations of crime involvement.[2] It explicitly addresses (1) the simultaneous importance of both the individual and the setting in crime causation, and (2) the

[*]The foundational work for this chapter was carried out while the author was a fellow of the Center for Advanced Study in the Behavioral Sciences, Stanford. I gratefully acknowledge the financial support provided by the William and Flora Hewlett Foundation, Grant No. 2000-5633.

211

importance of the link between individuals' development and change, and the stability and change in the settings in which they participate, in explaining individual development and change in crime involvement.

This chapter complements and builds on an earlier paper proposing a *Situational Action Theory* of crime causation (see Wikström, 2004). In that paper the focus was primarily on the role of the *context of action* for crime causation (the mechanisms linking individual, setting and action). In this chapter I take that discussion forward by addressing the role of the *context of development and change* for crime involvement (mechanisms of stability and change in individuals' characteristics and experiences and in the settings in which they take part, and, linked to that, stability and change in their actions). This will introduce a dynamic element (development and change) to the previous discussions of crime causation.

The key argument put forward in this chapter is that *stability or change in an individual's involvement in (and nature of) crime is primarily a result of stability or change in the individual's context of action.* I submit that criminal career patterns (e.g., onset, duration, escalation and desistance) can be explained with reference to patterns of development and change in individuals' context of action. The context of action is the individual's configuration of *intersections* with settings.

Central Problems in Criminological Theory

Two central problems of criminological theory concern identifying causal mechanisms and integrating levels of explanation (see Wikström & Sampson, 2003: 119-120). The former refers to the problem of *causes and correlates* (e.g., Farrington, 2000: 7; Rutter, 2003), the latter to the problem of connecting *individual and ecological levels of explanation* (e.g., Reiss, 1986; Jensen & Akers, 2003: 13). A third central problem is how to deal with *development and change* in the context of addressing causal mechanisms and linking levels of explanation. To address the first two problems, we need a situational action theory of crime causation (as I have previously argued in Wikström, 2004), to address the third problem we need a developmental ecological action theory (as I will argue in this chapter). A fourth central problem is how to deal with *the concept of crime.* That is, what should theories of the causes of crime explain?

The Concept of Crime

There is little question that *the concept of crime has to do with morals*, i.e., crime is a breaking of (formal) prescriptions for what is right or wrong to do.[3] Therefore explaining crime has to do with explaining moral behavior (why people follow or break rules about what is right or wrong to do). With the exception of (the probably less common) cases in which an individual is unaware of the existence (or application) of a law, the breaking of a law is done intentionally (i.e., the individual knows he or she is breaking a law).[4] Explaining crime is therefore ultimately about explaining why people knowingly break a rule of law (a moral prescription).[5] It is not primarily the particular act (e.g., hitting, destroying, deceiving or having sex) that should be explained, but the fact that the individual performs the particular act knowing that it is illegal (the rule-breaking). For example, it is not principally about why some people smoke, hit their children, drive their car at 100 mph, engage in public sexual acts, etc., but why they do this if and when they know such acts are defined as illegal.[6] The main implication of this is that theories aimed at explaining acts of crime should focus on the individual and environmental factors (and processes) that influence whether the individual acts in compliance (or non-compliance) with the rules of law (moral rules).

Crimes are acts, not propensities. To explain crime is to explain the act (of moral rule breaking) not the propensity (to break moral rules). Propensity may be part of the explanation of why an individual may commit a crime (he or she may have a propensity to break moral rules) but it is not the same as an act of crime.[7] I believe it is analytically helpful to clearly distinguish between individual characteristics and experiences, crime propensity and acts of crime. I have suggested (Wikström, 2004) that *crime propensity* may be conceptualized as the individual tendency to see crime (the breaking of a moral rule) as an alternative and to choose that option. Propensity is thus not individual characteristics and experiences (which causes propensity), and it is not action (which is the outcome), but the process that links the two (the *tendency* to see and choose in particular ways).

Situational Action

Crime is an act of moral rule breaking, committed by an individual, in a particular setting. *Motivation* to commit acts of crime arises as an outcome of the *interaction* of individual (crime propensity) and setting (criminogenic features).[8]

From individual-level studies in criminology we have learned much about the relationship between individual characteristics and individual involvement in crime (for an overview, see Farrington, 2002). However, most theory in the individual tradition (individual propensity theory) fails to specify in any detail the *situational mechanisms* by which individual characteristics and experiences transform into action (acts of crime). That is, what it is about an individual's *intersection* with a setting that *moves* him or her to action (acts of crime). At best, general reference is made to the importance of choice, typically alluding to self-interest, cost-benefits, pleasure and pain or similar grounds for action, and the role of opportunity (often without making fully clear the relationship between "action," "choice," and "opportunity" and the key proposed "risk factors").

Similar problems apply to socioecological-oriented theories on individual crime involvement (e.g., Kornhauser, 1978; Bursik & Grasmick, 1993; Sampson, Raudenbush & Earls, 1997). These theories have contributed significantly to our understanding of the link between local social context (e.g., neighborhood social cohesion and informal social control) and individual crime involvement. However, it is difficult to find more direct discussions about the *social mechanisms* through which, for example, community context (structural and organizational features) create settings that encourage (or discourage) individuals to commit acts of crime (but cf., Wikström & Sampson, 2003: 126-130).

The theoretical approach in criminology that has most strongly advocated the importance in crime causation of the *intersection of individual and setting* is the routine activity approach, which is an ecology-based theory (e.g., Cohen & Felson, 1979; Felson, 1994). However, I think it is fair to say that the main focus of this approach initially was, and largely remains, the setting (good targets and poor control[9]), not the individual's intersection with settings.[10] It is predominantly about how types of settings influence the occurrence of crime events, rather than about how *types of individuals'* intersections with types of settings create specific action (acts of crime).

Routine activity theory, and related theory (e.g., Brantingham & Brantingham, 1993), has done a lot to advance our understanding of the role of settings in crime causation (e.g., the role of opportunity and surveillance) and their link to wider societal organizational features (routine activities). It has also helped to advance knowledge about the role of changes in collective routine activities for changes in the types of settings that confront members of a society. However, the routine activity approach has so far largely failed to take the role of individual differences seriously. Neither has the routine activity approach succeeded very well in providing ideas about the mechanisms through which the intersection of individual and setting *move* individuals to commit acts of crime. The attempts to link routine activity theory (ecological theory) and self-control theory (individual propensity theory) to rational choice theory (action theory) are steps in the right direction (e.g., Clarke & Felson, 1993; Felson, 1994; Hirschi, 1986; Hirschi & Gottfredson, 1988; Gottfredson & Hirschi, 1989; Gottfredson & Hirschi, 1990: 22-25; Gottfredson & Hirschi, 2003).[11] However, this has so far mostly been a question of saying it is a good idea and possible to link these types of theory, or that they are complementary, rather than actually suggesting that they should (and how they can) be integrated.[12]

I submit that to advance knowledge about the causes of crime we need a situational theory of action that specifies the *mechanisms* that link individual *and* setting to action (acts of crime). I also submit that without a theory of situational action as its basis it is difficult to develop compelling explanations of the role of individual and environmental change for individual change in crime involvement (action).

Development and Action

If crime is an act of moral rule breaking, committed by an individual, in a particular setting, *changes* in the individual (how he or she reacts to particular settings) or the settings in which the individual takes part (the settings the individual reacts to) may cause *changes* in the individual's crime involvement.[13] However, our current knowledge about the processes that link individual and ecological *change* (particularly ecological change) to *changes* in individual action (acts of crime) is very limited.

The study of "criminal careers"(Blumstein et al., 1986), or "developmental criminology" (Loeber & Le Blanc, 1990; Le Blanc & Loeber, 1998) or, as it has recently been labelled by Farrington (2003), "development and life-course criminology," focuses on how individual involvement in crime develops and changes over time (within-individual variation).[14] The key concepts refer to individuals' involvement in crime (e.g., participation and frequency), stability and change in crime involvement (e.g., onset, persistence and desistance), the nature of involvement in crime (e.g., crime seriousness, specialization and versatility), and changes in the nature of crime involvement (e.g., escalation and de-escalation).

This research has contributed greatly to our knowledge about non-random patterns in the development and change of individual crime involvement (e.g., Wolfgang, Figlio & Sellin, 1972; Farrington, 1986; Wolfgang, Thornberry & Figlio, 1987; Wikström, 1987; 1990; Le Blanc & Frechette, 1989; Farrington & Wikström, 1994; Loeber et al., 2003). It has provided useful conceptualizations of the dimensions and trajectories of individual development and change (pathways) in crime involvement (e.g., Loeber, 1996; Moffitt, 1993; Nagin, Farrington & Moffitt, 1995; Le Blanc & Loeber, 1998; Brody et al., 2003).

However, by and large, "developmental and life-course criminology" does not say much about *how* individuals change, and (particularly) *how* changes in the settings in which the individual takes part cause changes in individual involvement in acts of crime. In other words, it does not say much about the *mechanisms of development and change*[15] that cause change in individual involvement in *acts of crime*. Our understanding of *what* processes link individual change, and change in the settings in which the individual takes part, to changes in individual action (acts of crime) is generally quite poor.[16]

The predominant paradigm of explanation in "developmental and life-course criminology" appears to be that of risk and protective factors (e.g., Loeber, 1990; Loeber & Farrington, 1999; 2001; Farrington, 2003).[17] It has, for example, been suggested that risk factors vary by age, that risk factors may be cumulative, and that risk factors may be different as regards explaining, for example, why people start, continue, and stop their involvement in acts of crime. However, as has been pointed out in a recent research review by Piquero, Farrington & Blumstein (2003: 462), "the evidence thus far on correlates of different criminal career dimensions suggests that in most studies, some variables are associated with two or more dimensions and some are uniquely associated with one dimension. Thus, no clear pattern has yet emerged."

A major shortcoming of the risk factor approach, as has been repeatedly stressed by Farrington (e.g., 2000: 7; 2003: 206), is that it is difficult to know which risk factors (correlates) are causes and which are merely correlates.[18] To address this problem Farrington et al. (2002) have argued that, "the concept of cause fundamentally refers to the concept of change within individual units" (p. 54) and advocated the analytic strategy of focusing on "comparing within-individual changes in risk factors over time with within-individual changes in delinquency over time"(p. 54).

Although focusing on within-individual change (rather than between-individual variation) takes us much further in *empirically* establishing causes, we also need *theoretically* to identify a credible mechanism that specifies how the risk factor in question transforms into action (acts of crime) to justify its status as a probable cause.[19] In other words, if changes in an individual's risk factors are followed by changes in the same individual's crime involvement this is an indication that the former *may* be a cause (or part cause) of the latter, but we *also* need to specify how this happens. The same argument is easily transferable to the problem of establishing the causal effects of, so-called, *life events* (e.g., marriage).[20]

I believe that a focus on establishing key causal mechanisms (processes)[21] that link individual change, and changes in the settings in which the individual takes part, to individual change in action (acts of crime) may help advance theory on the causes of individual patterns of development and change in crime involvement. However, as Farrington has recently observed, "Little is known about the causal processes that intervene between risk factors and offending" (2003: 207).

Developmental and life-course criminology has largely neglected the role of individuals' activity fields and its changes.[22] An individual's *activity field*[23] is the configuration of settings in which the individual develops *and* acts. The *settings* are the persons, objects, and events in specific locations to which the individual is directly exposed and reacts. A change in the individual's environment is a change in the individual's activity field.

If one likes to take seriously the role of the individual-environment interaction and its changes in crime causation, future longitudinal studies need to incorporate measures of individuals' activity fields and its changes. In short, developmental and life-course criminology needs a stronger ecological dimension.

I submit that to advance knowledge about individual development and change in crime involvement we need a developmental ecological action theory that specifies the mechanisms of change in individual contexts of action.

The Context of Action

The *context of action* refers to an individual's (with his or her current characteristics and experiences) intersection with a particular type of setting (with its particular characteristics: other persons, objects, and events). The key point here is that the context of action is neither the setting, nor the individual, but the *intersection* of the two. Action (including acts of crime) is seen as an outcome of the *interaction* between individual and setting. What links the individual and the setting to *action* is the individual's *perception of alternatives* and *process of choice*, which I will refer to as the situation/the situational mechanism[24] (Figure 9.1). Sometimes the individual, and sometimes the setting, has the greater impact on the course of action taken, but there is always an interaction between the two that influences what alternatives the individual perceives and what choices he or she makes.

I have previously argued (Wikström, 2004) that one can conceptualize the key individual differences of relevance to individual engagement in acts of crime (causes of individual propensity), as *morals* (moral values and emotions[25]) and *executive functions*[26] (Figure 9.2). The key mechanisms linking an individual to action (acts of crime) might be conceptualized as *moral judgment*[27] (the application of individual morals to a setting) and *self-control* (the executive function-based capability to exercise moral management of the temptations and provocations the individual encounters in a setting). I suggested that an individual's moral judgments predominantly influence what alternatives for action the individual perceives (whether an act of crime is seen as an alternative), and that the individual's self-control predominantly influences (is part of) the individual's process of choice (whether or not to act upon a perceived alternative that constitutes an act of crime)

No individual action takes place in a vacuum and therefore it is equally important to consider the setting in which an individual act occurs when explaining acts of crime. In the proposed Situational Action Theory (Wikström, 2004) the key suggested characteristics of the setting, influencing whether an individual perceives crime as an action alternative and whether he/she chooses to act upon it, is conceptualized as *opportunity* and *friction* (promoting) and *monitoring* (inhibiting).

Figure 9.1
The Context of Action. Key Elements

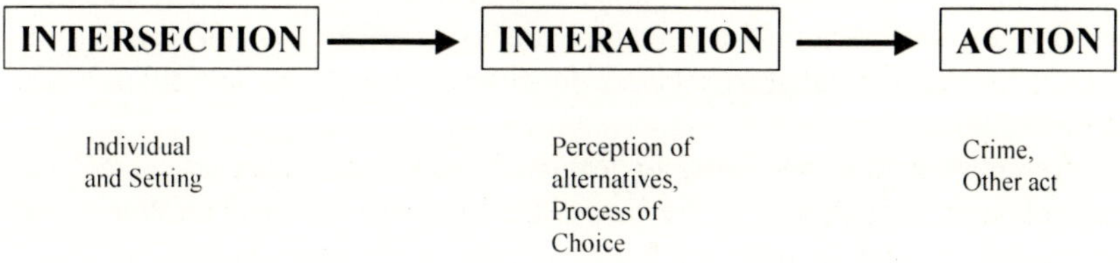

INTERSECTION ➝	**INTERACTION** ➝	**ACTION**
Individual and Setting	Perception of alternatives, Process of Choice	Crime, Other act

Figure 9.2
An Overview of Key Factors and Mechanisms of the Situational Action Theory of Crime Causation

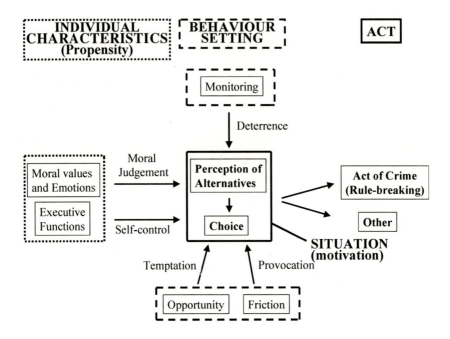

I argued that the key promoting mechanisms linking the characteristics of the setting (opportunity and friction) and individual action (acts of crime) are *temptation*, defined as a perceived option to satisfy a particular desire (need, want) in an unlawful way, and *provocation*, defined as a perceived attack on the person's (or his or her significant others) property, security or self-respect encouraging an unlawful response. Temptation occurs in response to opportunity, while provocation occurs in response to frictions. An individual's morals influence (through the moral judgments made) what opportunities he or she finds tempting, and what frictions he or she finds provoking. The key suggested inhibiting mechanism is conceptualized as *deterrence*, defined as the perceived risk of intervention, and associated risk of sanction if acting unlawfully in pursuing a temptation or responding to a provocation. Deterrence occurs in response to monitoring. The potentially deterrent effect of monitoring is influenced by the individual's executive functions, through the self-control exercised (Figure 9.2).

Temptations and provocations influence what action alternatives an individual perceives (whether or not an act of crime is seen as an alternative), while deterrence predominantly is relevant for the individual's process of choice (whether or not to act upon a perceived alternative that constitutes an act of crime).

The Context of Action and Its Changes

Increasing knowledge about the relationship between individual change, and change in the settings in which the individual takes part, is of paramount importance for advancing the understanding and explanation of "criminal careers." I submit that changes in individual offending patterns (e.g., escalation or desistance) are brought about because there is a change in the individual's context of action (i.e., changes in the individual's intersections with settings).

There are two major sources of change to an individual's context of action: (1) *individual development and change* (causing change in how the individual reacts to particular settings), and (2) *changes in the individual's activity field* (causing change in the settings to which the individual reacts).[28] Changes in one may be followed by (or cause) changes in the other. *Change* in the individual's context of action is likely to result in changes in the individual's actions. *Stability* in the individual's context of action is likely to generate stability in the individual's actions.

Based upon the argument regarding the key factors/mechanisms in crime causation put forward in the Situational Action Theory, I propose that *stability or change in an individual's crime involvement* is predominantly caused by stability or change in the individual's morals and executive functions, and the characteristics (opportunity, friction, and monitoring) of the settings in which the individual routinely takes part (Figure 9.3).

An individual's *life course* can be conceptualized as the individual's *path of individual-setting intersections throughout life,* at each point in time with specific implications for his or her course of actions. The key point is that neither individual change, nor environmental change *alone* is enough to explain individual development and change in crime involvement *over the life span*[29] (Figure 9.3).

Changes in an individual's morals and executive functions may cause change in the individual's crime involvement because it changes how the individual reacts to the settings in which he or she takes part (whether he or she perceives crime as an alternative, and whether he or she is likely to choose action alternatives that constitute acts of crime). Changes in the individual's activity field (particularly as regards exposure to opportunity and friction, and levels of monitoring) may cause changes in the individual's crime involvement because it involves changes in the types of settings to which the individual is exposed and reacts (influencing whether he or she perceives crime as an alternative, and whether he or she is likely to choose action alternatives that constitute acts of crime).

Figure 9.3

Development and Changes in Conditions for Situational Action

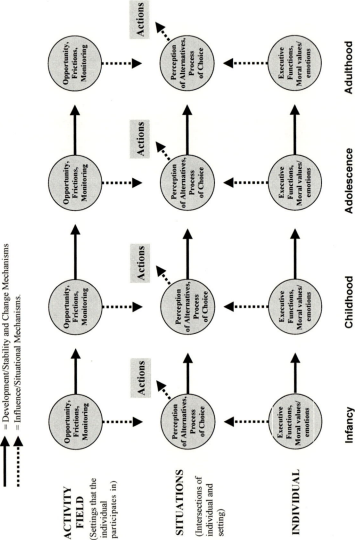

➔ = Development/Stability and Change Mechanisms

┅➤ = Influence/Situational Mechanisms.

Individual Development and Change: Crime Propensity

Individual development and change is *one* source of change in an individual's contexts of action (i.e., changes in how the individual reacts to particular settings affecting the outcome of the individual's intersection with the particular settings). Bronfenbrenner (1979: 3) has defined *individual development* as, "a lasting change in the way a person perceives and deals with his environment." Bronfenbrenner's view on individual development and change fits quite well with the suggested conception in the proposed Situational Action Theory (Wikström, 2004) of individual and setting as linked to action through individual perception of alternatives (perceives environment) and process of choice (deals with environment).

The idea that individual development and change fundamentally is about changes in how people perceive and deal with the environment provides *the key mechanism* that links individual development and change to changes in individual actions. Changes in individual characteristics and experiences will influence changes in individual action through changes in how the individual perceives alternatives and makes choices in particular settings.

An individual develops and changes in response to his/her interactions with the settings in which he/she takes part (his/her activity field).[30] An individual's role in his/her development (from embryo to adulthood) can be described as going from *total dependency* (the prenatal state) to *increasing agency* (through childhood and adolescence).[31] Increasing agency means that an individual becomes a greater active force in influencing his/her development as a result of increased human and social capital.[32] Increasing agency also means that the *independent* role of an individual's environment as an influence on development will decrease because the individual will become a greater force in his/her development and, related to that, in the creation of his/her activity field. In other words, while the environment always has an important influence on development and change, its influence will increasingly be a result of its *interaction* with the individual. The extent to which an individual can influence his/her activity field (through his/her agency) is also the degree to which the individual can actively influence the environmental factors that shape and form his/her development and change.[33]

Morals

Individuals acquire norms and values through the process of socialization (e.g., Durkheim, 1961; Aronfreed, 1968; Settersten Jr. & Owen, 2002). The *socialization practices* an individual encounters in his/her day-to-day life (the settings in which he or she routinely takes part) are likely to be important for the development and change (or stability) in his or her morals. The *key mechanisms* of socialization practices may be conceptualized as *teaching* (learning) and *monitoring*[34] (and associated reactions and sanctions).[35] For example, individuals are taught what is right and wrong by instruction and through observation. Individuals' potential to feel shame and guilt develops and changes in response to the reactions (and sanctions) of others in response to specific moral rule breaking,[36] or through direct observation of, or indirect reporting (e.g., stories or media reporting) of the reaction to (and sanctions of) the moral rule breaking of others.

The influence on individual morals by specific teaching (of morals) and particular monitoring (of moral rule breaking) is likely to vary depending on the individual's *attachments* to the particular sources of teaching or monitoring (e.g., parents, neighbors, and police officers).

Attachments can be seen as a *foundation for effective moral socialization* (a ground for responsiveness to moral teaching and monitoring of moral rule breaking). Those persons to whom the individual has a strong attachment are the most potent agents of moral socialization. They will have the greatest influence on the individual's formation and internalization of moral values and emotions. Individuals that have strong attachments will create stronger morals than those having weak attachments.[37]

I suggest that the main *mechanism* creating attachment can be conceptualized as *caring*. Individuals will tend to create attachments to people who provide for their physical and emotional well-being (typically parents in early life, and typically among friends, teachers, and spouses in later life[38]).

The degree of *consistency* in the teaching of morals and monitoring of moral rule breaking among the persons to which the individual has strong attachments, and the *correspondence* between the moral values (and emotions) they transfer (through teaching and monitoring) and what is stated in the law,[39] will influence the extent to which the individual sees crime as an alternative.

An individual's early formation of and later changes in moral values and emotions (and attachments) occur in interactions with the settings in which he or she take part (his/her activity field). As individuals become a greater force in their development they will increase their ability to reflect over, evaluate, and modify their morals[40] and influence the selection of the settings in which they take part (influencing what moral teaching and monitoring they encounter).[41] Individual development and change (or stability) in morals is most likely the result of the continuous interaction between the morals individuals hold (have internalized) and the external teaching and monitoring of morals they experience. In this process any encounters with *conflicting* moral teachings and monitoring will constitute potential external incitements to change or modification of internalized morals (for example, moving from one place to another may trigger such a process of change, a somewhat extreme example being the change of country of residence). This may be particularly so if the emergence of conflicting teaching is related to changes in attachments to other persons. Individuals are likely to change (and develop new) attachments over the life-course partly as a consequence of their expanding and changing activity field. For example, starting school or entering the work force may be important events that trigger changes in individual patterns of attachments to others.

Executive Functions

Individuals not only react differently to their environment (see different action alternatives), they also differ in their *capacity to regulate their reactions* (emotions and behavior) depending on their *executive functions* (e.g., Shonkoff & Phillips, 2000: 93-123; Barkley, 1977: 51-58; Ishikawa & Raine, 2003). This self-regulating capacity (of relevance for the *process* of choice) develops most rapidly through childhood into late adolescence and probably stays fairly stable after that.[42]

The level and content of *nurturing* (external promotion of cognitive skill development) an individual encounters in their day-to-day life is likely to be important for his or her development and change in executive functions, particularly the nurturing the individual experience in childhood and into late adolescence. A particularly intriguing question in this context is the potential importance of *time windows*, that is, the idea that there are certain critical periods of development of neurobehavioral capabilities. Lack of adequate nurturing during critical periods may have effects that are difficult (or impossible) to retract later (e.g., Earls & Carlson, 1995). I suggest that nurturing may be considered a *key mechanism* in development and change in executive functions.[43]

Individual Crime Propensity: Key Mechanisms of Development and Change

The key individual factors causing individual *propensity* to engage in acts of crime has been conceptualized as individual morals and executive function. I propose that individual development and change that involves changes in morals (affecting perception of moral rule breaking as an alternative) or executive functions (affecting the process of choice) *may* cause changes in an individual's involvement in acts of crime by affecting the individual's contexts of action through changes in how the individual reacts to particular settings.

The main suggested mechanisms of development and change relevant to development and change of morals and executive function are summarized in Table 9.1. Individual change in morals and executive function is most likely *gradual* rather than instant.[44] For example, *a life-event* (starting school, getting married, etc.) can be viewed as an event that (potentially) *triggers changes* in *the processes* of moral teaching and monitoring, and caring and nurturing, that the individual experiences.

A life-event may fundamentally be viewed as a change in the individual's activity field.

Table 9.1
Main Suggested Developmental Mechanisms Relevant to
Individual Development and Change in Morals,
Attachments and Executive Functions

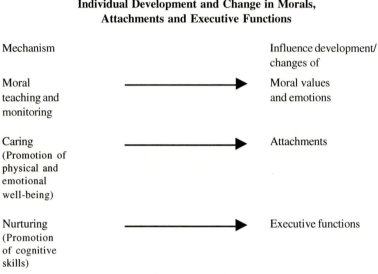

Mechanism	Influence development/ changes of
Moral teaching and monitoring	Moral values and emotions
Caring (Promotion of physical and emotional well-being)	Attachments
Nurturing (Promotion of cognitive skills)	Executive functions

The Role of the Activity Field in Individual Development and Change

Individuals are *born into an environment not of their choosing*. They are born into a specific historical time period, a specific society (nation), a specific segment of that society, and a specific family (caregivers). The individual's social location, within the broader patterns of inequality and segregation, and the social norms, that apply to the society into which he/she is born, will *set the stage* for his/her activity field and its initial development.

At the start of their lives, individuals will have practically *no agency* and therefore no real influence on the settings (and their characteristics) in which their early development takes place.[45] They will be dependent on their caregivers (within the constraints set by the wider environment in which they operate) to provide the settings in which they develop. For example, caregivers may make decisions about where they live and whether to move, what kindergarten they attend, and what other children they meet and socialize with and where.

However, as individuals age and develop they *acquire a greater potential to influence their activity field* (a stronger agency) within the constraints set by the wider environment in which they operate. This is partly a consequence of organismic change (e.g., biological maturation) and partly a consequence of increased experiences and (culturally age-defined) increases in social independence. For example, while a one-year-old may have little influence over his/her activity field, a twenty-year-old may have a significant influence over his/hers.

Individual *early growth* normally involves an *expanding activity field*. As the individual ages (from infancy into childhood) the environment outside the home becomes of increasing importance as a source of supply of potential settings. The location of the individual's home (*the neighborhood effect*) is therefore *one* important factor influencing the early scope and content of an individual's activity field. For example, some reside in highly advantaged and others in highly disadvantaged residential areas (i.e., areas with configurations of settings characterized by advantage or disadvantage). Another important source of influence is the caregivers' *management* (or lack of management) of the neighborhood settings (and out-of-neighborhood settings) to which the individual is exposed (*the caregiver effect*). The individual's early life activity field is largely dependent on the *interaction* between neighborhood conditions (supply of local settings) and the caregiver's management strategies (managing exposure to local and non-local settings).[46]

As the individual ages and his/her activity field expands, the activity field normally also becomes more *diversified* (i.e., the types and characteristics of the settings to which the individual is exposed become more varied). This, in turn, results in a more diversified environmental influence on an individual's development, for example, an increased exposure to conflicting morals, which may have some impact on his/her development of and change in morals.

As individuals age they are likely to develop stronger *preferences* for certain types of settings. For example, some may have a strong preference for settings that contain criminogenic characteristics (i.e., settings that provide great opportunity, or cause strong friction, and entail poor monitoring).[47] The individual's current setting preferences are likely to be a result of his or her previous *developmental history* (the characteristics and experiences he/she has acquired in interaction with past activity fields, and related to that, his/her emergent desires and wants). It is plausible that the individual will actively seek out, or aspire to take part in, settings that he or she believes may fulfill his/her current desires and wants. The individual's current potential to realize his/her setting preferences is dependent on his/her agency (which will vary between individuals) and what is on offer in the environment in which he or she operates or can access (which will vary between individuals).

It is conceivable that individual development and change often occurs in a *sequential* fashion in which, at each stage, the interaction between the individual's agency and setting preferences, and the characteristics of his/her current activity field, have an important role in influencing his/her future development and change. In other words, an individual's current characteristics and experiences, and his/her current activity field, are likely to play major roles as forces enabling or constraining different *paths of future development and change*.

I suggest that preference and agency are the *key individual mechanisms* that influence the development and change of an individual's activity field.

Figure 9.4
Individual Development and Change. The Continuous Interaction between
Individual Change and Changes in the Individual's Activity Field

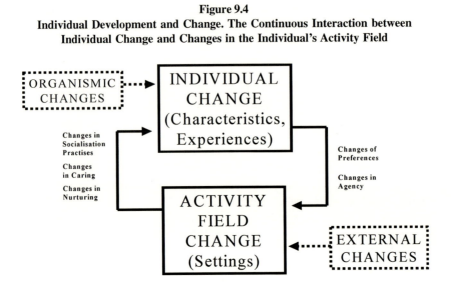

The role of the activity field in individual development and change can be summarized as follows; the individual develops and changes in continuous interaction with his or her activity field and its changes (Figure 9.4). Changes in (1) individual agency and preferences, or (2) external changes (over which the individual has little or no control[48]) may cause changes in their activity field. Changes in individual characteristics and experiences (affecting agency and preferences) may be caused by (1) changes in the individual's activity field, for example, by initiating change in the socialization practices, the caring and nurturing, the individual experience, or (2) by organismic change (e.g., biological maturation). These interactive processes all take place within the constraints set by the wider social context and its changes.

Individual's Activity Field and Its Changes: Exposure to Criminogenic Settings

The basic idea of a differential crime propensity is that *different individuals* encountering the *same setting* react differently to the characteristics of that setting. Some individuals are more likely to perceive crime as an alternative (depending on their morals), and of those that perceive crime as an alternative, some are more likely to act upon it (depending on their executive functions). As discussed above, crime propensity (based on individual morals and executive function) is likely to develop and change as a result of the process of interaction between the individual and his or her activity field. However, *the development and change in individual crime propensity is just part of the story when explaining the development and change in individual crime involvement.*

An individual's crime propensity is *always applied in a setting* (the making of moral judgments and the exercise of self-control) and therefore the other main component of an individual's context of action (relevant to engagement in crime) is the *criminogenic characteristics* (opportunities, frictions, and levels of monitoring) of the settings that constitute the individual's activity field.

Direct Environmental Influences on the Motivation for and Nature of Individuals' Engagement in Acts of Crime

The idea of a *direct environmental effect* on individuals' motivation to engage in acts of crime is the idea that the *same individual* reacts differently to *different settings*. Individuals are more likely to see acts of crime as alternatives, and to choose to act upon such alternatives, in some settings. In other words, some settings are more *criminogenic* than others.[49]

However, the question whether "the setting" has any motivational qualities (contributes to crime motivation)[50] or whether the setting merely influences the expression of individual crime propensity (the nature of crime) is a contentious issue. For example, for Gottfredson & Hirschi (2003) the role of settings appears to be restricted to influencing the *expression of propensity*. They talk about, "the interaction of varying individual predispositions for delinquency and *logically possible* opportunities" (p. 11, my emphasis), and give the following example of the role of opportunity, "the 12-year-old who cannot steal a car may well steal a bicycle; the 30-year-old who cannot be truant from school may well be truant from work and family obligation" (p. 10). On the other hand, Felson (1994) appears to assign a significant motivational role to the setting. He claims, for example, that, "temptation helps to produce criminal acts *that might not otherwise occur*" (p. 17, my emphasis) and he goes on to state that the saying, " 'Opportunity makes the thief' reflects this insight" (p. 17).[51]

I shall take the view that settings both influence the *nature* of individuals' criminality (e.g., versatility and seriousness) and their *motivation* to engage in acts of crime (participation and frequency). The view that settings have to play a role in crime motivation is based on the position (as previously argued) that motivation arises out of the *interaction* between individual and setting. It appears implausible that circumstance does not at all affect motivation (the readiness to act based on perception of alternatives and process of choice).

Combining the idea that an individual's crime motivation is partly dependent on his/her crime propensity (morals, executive function) and partly on the criminogenic features of the settings (opportunity, friction, and monitoring) in which he or she operates, suggests that the degree to which a particular setting contributes to an individual's motivation to engage in acts of crime will vary depending on the individual's crime propensity.

I propose that for individuals with a low crime propensity the setting (opportunity, friction, and levels of monitoring) will play a greater role in influencing their crime motivation than for those with a high crime propensity. In other words, individuals with a low crime propensity may (potentially) only be motivated to offend in settings with strong criminogenic characteristics (because their temptation and provocation *thresholds* are much higher, and their *sensitivity* to deterrence much stronger, than for those with a high crime propensity).

The Role of the Activity Field in Individual Development and Change in Crime Involvement

Change in an individual's activity field is *one* source of change in the individual's context of action (i.e., changes in the settings to which the individual reacts). *Changes* in an individual's activity field (*independently* of his or her current crime propensity[52]) might cause *changes* in the individual's *involvement* in acts of crime if the changes involve an increase (or decrease) in the individual's exposure to criminogenic settings (e.g., increased exposure to settings involving vast opportunity or extensive friction and poor monitoring).

Changes in an individual's activity field may *also* be a particularly pertinent cause of *changes* in *the nature* of the individual's criminality because it may influence the expression of crime propensity (e.g., cause changes in patterns of versatility and seriousness).

A particularly intriguing question for "developmental and life-course criminology" is *to what extent* individual "criminal careers" are shaped and formed by development and change in individual crime propensity or changes in the criminogenic features of the activity field in which they operate. I suspect that the characteristics of and changes in the criminogenic features of the individual's activity field play a far more important role in the shape and form of "criminal careers" than that for which it is generally credited in "developmental and life-course criminology."

Explaining Individual Trajectories in Crime Involvement and the Nature of Crime

The proposed Developmental Ecological Action Theory of Crime Involvement emphasizes the important role played by an individual's activity field and its changes for the individual's crime involvement, and the nature of his or her crimes. The individual's activity field and its changes are important because individuals develop and change, and act, in settings:

1.   individuals are born into a preexisting activity field that sets the stage for their early development,

2.   it is in interaction with the activity field and its changes that individual crime propensity develops and changes,

3.   an individual's activity field has a direct impact on (contributes to) the individual's motivation to engage in acts of crime and the nature of their crime involvement.

The proposed theory stipulates that, at each stage of life, the likelihood of an individual engaging in acts of crime (and the nature of the crimes) may be viewed as an outcome of his/her current temptation and provocation thresholds, and sensitivity to deterrence, based on his/her current morals and executive functions, as applied (through the perception of alternatives and process of choice) to the opportunities, frictions and levels of monitoring that characterize his/her current activity field (see Figure 9.3).

In the proposed theory, an individual's *life-course trajectory* in crime involvement (and its nature) is explained as an outcome of the sequential and intertwined processes of (a) individual early life development, and later life stability and changes, in executive functions and morals, as caused by organismic change, and stability and change in processes of caring, nurturing, and moral teaching and monitoring, and (b) stability and changes in the individual's activity field, as caused by stability and change in individual agency and setting preferences and external changes (Figure 9.5).

Changes in the individual's activity field may trigger changes in processes of caring, nurturing, moral teaching, and monitoring that, in turn, may produce changes in crime propensity (as based on changes in executive functions and morals).

Changes in the activity field may also (separately or concurrently with processes affecting crime propensity) produce changes in the criminogenic features (opportunities, frictions, and levels of monitoring) of the individual's activity field.

Figure 9.5
Processes Causing Change in Individual Crime Involvement and Its Nature

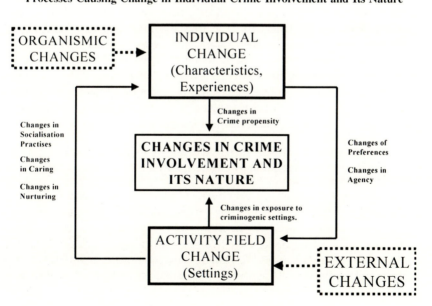

Changes in an individual's morals and executive functions may cause changes in the individual's preferences for participation in settings that are criminogenic and hence cause changes in the criminogenic features of his/her activity field.

Having outlined the basic proposed processes that cause individual involvement in crime, and that shape and form individuals' trajectories in crime involvement (and its nature), I shall conclude by (1) specifying the scope of the proposed theory, (2) summarizing how the theory explains between-individual differences and within-individual variation in crime involvement (and its nature), and (3) giving a somewhat more detailed account of how the theory *predicts* how the sequential and intertwined processes of development and change in crime propensity and the individual's activity field may work in producing differential pathways of crime involvement at various stages over the life-course.

Scope of Theory

The proposed theory, in the first instance, is about explaining acts of crime, and, in the second instance, is a broader theory about moral rule breaking. I suggest that the concept of "moral rule breaking" is better than the commonly used "antisocial behavior" because the former emphasizes the fact that we are talking about acts conflicting with moral rules (that can change over time and vary by place). The theory does not explain why we have the particular laws and moral rules we have, just why people break them.

The theory concerns only acts of crime (moral rule breaking) where the perpetrator knows that the act constitutes a crime (moral rule breaking),[53] regardless of whether the perpetrator is of an age of criminal responsibility (which varies between countries). The theory does not, however, explain "acts of crime" ("moral rule breaking") committed by infants or very young children who have not as yet developed any clear conception of "right and wrong." The exact age when children (normally) have developed a capability to make "informed" moral judgments may be difficult to pinpoint, but this concern is not immediately important for the argument put forward here.

Between-Individual Differences and Within-Individual Variation in Crime Involvement

In the theory proposed, *between-individual differences* in crime involvement (and its nature) are explained by between-individual differences in contexts of action. Individuals vary in crime propensity and in the criminogenic features of their activity field, the outcome of which are differences in crime involvement (and its nature). To explain between-individual differences in crime involvement (and its nature) it is therefore not enough to consider between-individual differences in morals and executive functions, one also needs to consider between-individual differences in the levels of opportunity, frictions, and monitoring that characterize individuals' activity fields. For example, the question of whether variation in crime involvement (and its nature) by gender, social class, or ethnic group is due primarily to group differences in crime propensity or to group differences in the criminogenic features of their activity fields is an intriguing question, but not one we know a lot about.

Within-individual variations in offending (i.e., individual change over time in crime involvement and its nature) are explained by the theory as being caused by changes and variation over time in an individual's context of action. For example, the variation of an individual's involvement in crime over the course of a day, month, year and the life-course is viewed as reflecting the individual's temporally varying and changing contexts of action.

Short-term variations in crime involvement (e.g., by hour and day, even by weeks and months) are likely to reflect short-term variation in the (propensity dependent[54]) strength of *environmentally induced motivation* (as caused by variation in levels of opportunity, friction, and monitoring). Short-term variation in the nature of crime committed is likely to reflect short-term variation in the types of settings (and their features) in which the individual takes part (the home, the school, the shopping mall, the pub, etc.)

Long-term changes in individual crime involvement (and its nature) may be caused by (gradual) changes in individual *crime propensity* (as based on development and changes in executive functions and morals) and (instant or gradual) changes in the *criminogenic features of the activity field* in which the individual operates. The main driving force of change in crime involvement (and its nature) may vary between periods of an individual's life. In some periods, changes in crime involvement (and its nature) may primarily reflect development and change in crime propensity, during other periods it may reflect mainly changes in the criminogenic features of his/her activity field. Combinations of (often-linked) changes in an individual's crime propensity and the criminogenic features of his/her activity field may generate many different trajectories in crime involvement (and its nature) over the life course. An intriguing question in this context is to what extent there are individuals for whom extensive periods of crime involvement are predominantly driven by environmental inducements (i.e., activity fields with strong criminogenic features).

Some Specific Developmental Predictions from the Proposed Theory

Early Onset

The theory assumes that the *foundation* for an individual's morals and (particularly) executive functions is laid during the individual's early development (infancy and childhood).[55]

Individuals who are born into and grow up in an activity field that is characterized by poor caring and nurturing, and "defective" moral teaching[56] and poor monitoring of moral rule breaking, are likely to early develop a strong crime propensity (i.e., to early develop a tendency to see and choose crime as an action alternative). They are therefore also more likely to have an *early age of onset* (childhood onset) of acts of crime, particularly if the high crime propensity is "supported" by an activity field with strong criminogenic features. The latter may also *instigate* an early "criminal career."

However, the theory does not stipulate that an individual's crime propensity *necessarily* has to remain stable throughout the life course (particularly not as regards the individual's morals). Later changes in an individual's activity field may instigate processes of change in caring and moral teaching and monitoring of moral rule breaking that may cause changes in the individual's morals, and hence affect his/her crime propensity. It is also important to bear in mind that persistent crime involvement over the life course is dependent both on stability in crime propensity and stability in the criminogenic features of the individual's activity field. In principle, an individual may have stable high crime propensity over the life course yet have periods of low crime involvement due to the varying or changing characteristics of his/her activity field (an extreme example of change in activity field being periods of imprisonment).

Adolescent Crime Involvement

The theory predicts that depending on their early development of morals and executive functions, individuals will vary as they enter *adolescence* in their *vulnerability to environmental inducements* to crime. They will vary from those with very high thresholds for temptation and provocation, and a high sensitivity for deterrence (low crime propensity), to those with very low thresholds for temptation and provocation, and a low sensitivity for deterrence (high crime propensity).

For most individuals, adolescence is a period of general increase in the criminogenic features of their activity field (e.g., in unsupervised activities), but for individuals that enter adolescence with very high thresholds for temptation and provocation, and a high sensitivity to deterrence, the impact on their crime involvement by changes in the criminogenic features of their activity fields will generally be small. They will rarely be involved in crime (regardless of the types of settings in which they take part), and if they are, it will predominantly be occasional events caused by very strong environmental inducements. This is so because their high threshold for temptation and provocation, and high sensitivity to deterrence, will act as protection against most environmental inducements. A particularly pertinent factor that may contribute to *occasional* crime involvement for individuals with a low crime propensity, who regularly take part in criminogenic settings, is *alcohol and (some types of) drug intoxication* (which may act to momentarily lower their temptation and provocation thresholds and weaken their sensitivity to deterrence). The theory predicts that it is unlikely that this group would embark on a "criminal career" (extensive periods of frequent offending) in adolescence. The theory further predicts that this is a group of adolescents that may not at all, or only on a rare occasion, get involved in crime during adolescence.

Those individuals who enter adolescence with a moderate threshold for temptation and provocation, and a moderate sensitivity to deterrence (a moderate crime propensity), may be the individuals whose crime involvement is the most likely to be affected by *environmental inducements*. This is so because this is a group whose morals and executive functions may not be strong enough to withstand strong environmental inducements. The extent to which members of this group will be involved in crime (and the extent of their involvement) will be largely dependent on the criminogenic features of their activity field. The stronger the criminogenic features of their activity field the more likely it is they will be involved in crime. For this group it is also possible that an extensive involvement in crime (fed by prolonged and frequent participation in highly criminogenic settings) may cause some *environmental habituation* that, in the longer term, may also influence the development of their morals in a direction that may increase their crime propensity. Adolescence is a period of life that is important for *life-style formation* (specific preferences for particular activities and settings, particularly leisure activities and settings). The extent to which the life-style an individual develops is linked to participating in highly criminogenic settings may influence their future course of crime involvement. Most individuals with an *adolescent onset* in crime will be found among those who enter adolescence with a moderate crime propensity and whose activity field during adolescence includes regular participation in criminogenic settings. The theory predicts that this group will vary significantly in their crime involvement depending on the criminogenic characteristics of their activity field. Some may be non-offenders or occasional offenders (as an outcome of a non-criminogenic activity field), while others (as an outcome of a highly criminogenic activity field) may risk embarking on a "criminal career."

For those who enter adolescence with low thresholds for temptation and provocation and a low sensitivity to deterrence (strong crime propensity), their criminal involvement during adolescence may be primarily driven by their (high) crime propensity. To the extent that their activity field does not change significantly in the processes of caring and nurturing, and the moral teaching and monitoring they experience, their strong crime propensity is likely to be sustained and possibly deepened during adolescence. The direct environmental impact on their crime involvement is more one of increased possibilities to *express their propensity* than motivational. They are likely to have a preference for leisure settings that have criminogenic features. Their regular involvement in crime may cause an *individual habituation* to violate laws (and moral rules) that may partly explain an increased frequency and seriousness in their crime involvement, and further contribute to the development of their crime propensity (through changes in morals). The theory predicts that individuals in this group most likely will have a criminal career during adolescence, and further that it is also likely that it will extend into adulthood. However, the theory also predicts the possibility that, for those individuals who experience substantial improvements during adolescence in caring and nurturing, and moral teaching and monitoring, concurrent with a decrease of the criminogenic features of their activity field, their crime involvement may decrease and their criminal careers may be terminated.

Adulthood and Desistance

Adulthood is a period of life when generally the criminogenic characteristics of individuals' activity fields decrease, as most individuals get established in society, for example, through entering the work-force and establishing a family life. Although most individuals will be at risk of occasional offending during adulthood (and perhaps also at risk of persistently committing minor infractions like speeding), few will start a more serious criminal career in adulthood. For most people minor offending in adulthood will be a consequence of environmental inducements. The theory predicts, with some few exceptions, that only those who already have a criminal career underway in adolescence will continue an extensive and prolonged involvement in crime into adulthood.

The group of adolescent offenders that are at the highest risk of continuing a criminal career into adulthood are those who in childhood have developed a high crime propensity that has been sustained in adolescence (through stability in the processes of poor caring and nurturing, and moral teaching and monitoring, they have experienced) and supported by a stable criminogenic activity field during childhood and adolescence. However, it is also predicted that those who entered adolescence with a moderate crime propensity, but who through frequently taking part in criminogenic settings during adolescence developed a "criminal career," due to environmental habituation and, built on this, subsequent increases in crime propensity, may risk carrying their persistent crime involvement over into adulthood. The difference between the two groups is the predicted ease with which their "criminal career" may be interrupted by external change.

The theory predicts that changes in processes of caring and nurturing, and moral teaching and monitoring in adulthood have the greatest potential of leading to a termination of a criminal career for the adolescent onset group. For the childhood onset group, however, it is more likely that such changes will act primarily to modify their crime involvement, for example, causing a decreased frequency of and de-escalation (decreased seriousness) in the acts of crime committed. These processes will be particularly strong if they concur with changes in the criminogenic features of individuals' activity fields.

Conclusion

Needless to say, what has been presented in this chapter is *a theory*, although I believe the main assumptions of the theory are in line (or at least not in conflict) with established empirical patterns of individual development and change in offending. The big unknown is the role of the activity field and its changes, an area where we have very little empirical research to support the assumptions made. To my knowledge there are no major longitudinal studies that have systematically tried to measure individuals' activity fields and their changes over the life course (or significant parts of the life course). I submit that to advance knowledge about the social causes of pathways in crime it is essential that future longitudinal studies: (1) incorporate methods aimed at measuring changes in individuals' activity fields and (2) investigate the impact of the activity field on individuals' development and change in crime involvement and its nature.

Notes

1.   Sometimes it is argued that a theory of crime involvement needs to be able to account for the key correlates of crime (Braithwaite, 1989: 44-53). However, there is no reason why this should be the case. A theory should explain why (or why not) people get involved in crime, and changes over time in their involvement, it does not necessarily need to explain all the key correlates of crime involvement and its changes (most correlates are likely to be just correlates). However, the non-random patterns of correlates is a natural starting point for, and may give good guidance where to look for explanations.

2.   In recent decades an increasing number of scholars in criminology have voiced the need to integrate individual and ecological approaches in the study of crime (e.g., Reiss, 1986; Farrington, Sampson & Wikström, 1991; Tonry, Ohlin & Farrington, 1991; Wikström, Clarke & McCord, 1993; Le Blanc, 1993; 1997; Jensen & Akers, 2003).

3.   To say that the concept of crime has to do with morals does not imply that laws are necessarily morally justified, that people have a moral obligation to follow the law, that laws are built on generally accepted morals, etc. See Hart (1961) for an instructive discussion of the concept of Law. The only implication is that the law is formal prescription of what is right and wrong to do, and that explaining why people engage (or do not engage) in particular acts of crime is to explain why they come to break (or follow) an existing law. However, this is not an argument for the position that there are no reasons for why some acts rather than others in a given society tend to be defined as crimes. This is an important but different question, and a question I shall not address in this chapter.

4.   It is possible that the breaking of certain laws (or moral rules) can become almost habitual (unreflective), particularly as regards minor infractions like speeding. However, the individual would know (if asked) that he or she was breaking a law (moral rule).

5. The logic of this argument can easily be extended to incorporate moral behavior more generally (i.e., including the adherence to or violation of moral rules that are not regulated by law). I suggest that the concept of "moral rule breaking" is better than the commonly used "antisocial behavior" because the former emphasizes that we are talking about moral rules that can change over time and vary by place.

6. The reason why, in the first place, a person smokes, hits his/her children, drives at 100 mph or engages in public sexual acts can, of course, be part of the reason why he or she breaks a law prohibiting these acts. But the key question here is why do people do it when they know it is illegal.

7. A typical example is to claim that having antisocial values is a measure of antisocial behavior. To claim this is, in my opinion, to confuse measurement and conceptual issues. For example, if there is a high correlation between having antisocial *values* and committing antisocial *acts* this does not justify the treatment of these two (values and acts) as conceptually the same. Claiming that "having antisocial values" is an *indicator* of antisocial behavior does not make things much better.

8. Crime motivation may be viewed as an individual's perception of an act of crime as an alternative, and his or her choice to carry out that action (readiness to commit an act of crime). For example, an individual that generally sees hitting other people as an action alternative when offended (propensity), and who is called an idiot by another person (provocation), is likely to consider and choose to hit that person as a response (motivation). Some people may need a strong friction to be provoked (weak propensity); others will only need a minor friction to be provoked (strong propensity).

9 . The discussion of the key aspects of settings relevant to acts of (expressive) violence is different, but this fact is not immediately important for the discussion here (see Felson, 1994).

10. Although theoretically *interaction* may be seen as the key to explaining the occurrence of crime events in routine activity theory, that is, the coming together of "motivated offenders," "suitable targets," and the "absence of capable guardians" (to use routine activity theory language), very few empirical studies in this tradition have taken interaction seriously. A likely reason for this is that, "the routine activity approach offered a thought experiment: to see how far one could go in explaining crime trends without ever discussing any of the various theories about criminal motivation" (Clarke & Felson, 1993: 2).

11. This is not to say that rational choice, self-control, and routine activity theory (as they stand in criminology) are the only, or even necessarily the best, theories of action, propensity, and ecology to be integrated.

12. Some illustrative quotes, "the routine activity and rational choice approaches, though differing in scope and purpose, are compatible and indeed, mutually supportive" (Clarke & Felson, 1993: 1); "Crime and delinquency feed on human frailty; depend on widespread situational variation in human behavior; are fed by temptations, provocations, exposure to bad company, and idleness; and are countered by the development of self-control to resist temptation and strong family life (Felson, 1994: 21); "I am confident that choice theorists could do much to sharpen the insights of control theory were they to accept the task" (Hirschi, 1986: 117); "the imagery of a hedonistic actor responding to the pleasures and pains of the moment is perfectly consistent with contemporary economic and rational choice theories of crime" (Hirschi & Gottfredson, 1988: 23).

13 . Not all individual change, or changes in settings in which an individual takes part are equally relevant to their involvement in crime. It is predominantly individual or environmental changes that have to do with whether the individual perceives crime

as an alternative, and chooses to act upon it, that are important. I shall return to this point further forward in the text.

14. Blumstein et al. (1986: 12) defines a criminal career as, "the characterization of the longitudinal sequence of crimes committed by an individual offender." Le Blanc and Loeber (1998: 117) state that, "we use the term developmental criminology to refer to temporal within-individual changes in offending." However, they also state that an additional important aspect of developmental criminology is the focus on "the identification of explicative or causal factors that predate, or co-occur with the behavioral development and have an effect on its course"(Le Blanc & Loeber, 1998: 117). Farrington (2003: 201) says that, "Developmental and life-course criminology (DLC) is concerned with three main issues: the development of offending and antisocial behavior, risk factors at different ages, and the effects of life events on the course of development."

15. I shall use the concept of "developmental mechanism" to refer to mechanisms of development and change.

16. This is not a situation particular to developmental and life-course criminology, as observed by Farrington (2003: 207-209) and many others. In fact, there are few attempts in criminological theory generally (be it individual or ecologically oriented theories) to explain what factors (processes) cause individual development and change in crime involvement over time (e.g., continuities and discontinuities).

17. Main examples of exceptions are Moffitt (1997, 2003), Sampson & Laub (1993), and Laub & Sampson (2003).

18. Other related problems of explanation from a pure risk and protective factor approach refer to (1) the vast number of established risk and protective factors (correlates) and (2) the extent to which individual action is a result of particular risk or protective factors or the specific configuration of individual characteristics and experiences (as applied to a setting). Farrington (1992: 256) has forcefully highlighted the first point. The second point refers to the discussion of variable or person-oriented approaches (e.g., Magnusson, 1988).

19. I am not suggesting that there is no discussion of causal mechanisms (processes) within the risk and protective factor approach to explanation. I am only suggesting that this is not a salient feature of this approach. In general, this is an empirically very strong, but theoretically rather weak, approach. I believe that by systematically addressing the question of causal mechanisms the risk and protective factor approach would gain much theoretically. I shall take the view that to establish a probable cause we minimally need (1) a (statistical) correlation between the suggested cause and effect, (2) a time ordering of the cause and effect (the cause preceding the effect), and (3) a plausible mechanism (process) linking the suggested cause and effect. The case for a cause may be further empirically strengthened if, when manipulated, the (hypothesized) causal factor produces the expected change in outcome. However, "controlling for" other variables may not necessarily strengthen the case for a cause. For an instructive discussion about the problems of the practice of "controlling for" other variables, see Lieberson (1985).

20. For example, if the fact that a person gets married is followed by a reduction in that person's crime involvement, marriage may be a factor that instigates a reduced crime involvement. However, this explanation is much stronger if one can also specify a credible mechanism (process) as to how marriage leads to a reduction in crime involvement. For example, through changes in the types of settings in which an individual takes part (the settings to which the individual reacts) as a consequence of living and sharing life with a spouse.

21. About mechanisms and their importance in social research, see Bunge (1999: 17-44)

22. Examples of developmental research in criminology that, at least partially, takes the role of activity fields seriously are the studies by Laub and Sampson (2003) and Horney, Osgood and Marshall (1995). Although they do not directly study activity fields and their changes, Laub and Sampson (2003: 39) stress, based on their interpretation of their research findings (Sampson & Laub, 1993; Laub & Sampson, 2003), that "life-style activities needs to be taken into account when explaining continuity and change in criminal behavior over the life-course." Horney, Osgood and Marshall (1995) studied monthly changes in "local life circumstances" among a group of felons and showed that their crime involvement was related to temporal variation in "local life circumstances." Both Sampson and Laub and Horney, Osgood and Marshall interpreted their findings as showing that variations in criminal involvement reflect variation in informal social controls. I would, however, argue that changes in informal social controls are only one part of the story, although an important one.

23. About the importance of activity field, see Hägerstrand (1953).

24. I will use *situation* as a concept that refers to the individual's perception of alternatives and process of choice in a particular setting. I will use *situational mechanism* as a summary concept for those mechanisms (processes) that link the individual (morality, self-control) and the setting (temptation, provocation, deterrence) to action (acts of crime) through their influences on whether the individual perceives crime as an alternative and chooses to act upon it. Theories of action generally pay a good deal of attention to how individuals choose among a set of alternatives, but often ignore why an individual sees a particular set of alternatives in the first place. I argue that perception of alternatives is the more basic mechanism of the two (Wikström, 2004).

25. I have argued that moral *emotions* (shame and guilt associated with breaking a moral rule) and how much the individual *cares* about following his or her moral values (related to the strength of relevant social bonds), may be the most important aspect of morals in explaining individual differences in crime involvement (Wikström, 2004: 14-15).

26. I suggested (Wikström, 2004) that most key individual risk factors relevant to crime involvement can be conceptualized as either being part of individual morals (values, emotions) or executive functions (capability of self-regulation, response inhibition). On executive functions, see, e.g., Glass & Holyoak (1986: 77-109); Barkley (1997: 51-58); Shonkoff & Phillips (2000: 93-123). I proposed that the executive function plays an important part in the individual's process of choice relevant to their involvement in acts of crime (i.e., in their capacity for moral management of individual desires and wants that if acted upon would constitute acts of crime). In other words, some individuals may have a greater capacity, in particular settings, to manage their impulses to violate *their* moral rules to get what they desire or want.

27. In my previous paper on the situational action theory (Wikström, 2004) I used the concept of morality instead of moral judgment. However, judging from feedback I got on that paper, I believe talking about morals and moral judgment (the application of morals to a setting) instead of morals and morality helps make the distinction clearer.

28. These two are linked, as should be clear in the subsequent discussion, because individuals do not only act but also develop and change in settings. In part their development and change is a consequence of their actions and others' reactions to them.

29. However, at specific points in time individual change or changes in the individual's activity field may be the dominant source of change in the individual's involvement in crime. The argument here refers to the life-course not specific points in time.

30. Rutter et al. (1995: 61) argue that, "growth takes place in a social milieu, and it will therefore, be influenced by a person's interactions and transactions with that milieu, as well as by within-the-individual organismic factors." See also for similar views, for example, Bronfenbrenner (1979); Magnusson (1988); Moen, Elder & Lucher (1995); and Magnusson & Cairns (1996).

31. This argument is different from (but not in opposition to) the argument that individuals are genetically different and that these differences, in interaction with the individual's environment, influence their development. The role of the interaction between genetics and environments is probably more relevant in the development of executive functions than in the development and change of individual morals.

32. I suggest that human agency (that varies between individuals), and that may be defined as the individual's power to make things happen the way he or she wants, is primarily based on the level of human capital (experiences, knowledge, skills) and social capital (resourceful networks the individual can draw upon in his/her daily life). Agency is context-dependent. An individual's power to make things happen varies between settings.

33. This does not imply that the individual is necessarily always aware of (conscious of) having this influence on his/her future development and change. It is probably true that the awareness of this potential influence is generally greater regarding some types of activities (education, work) than others (leisure).

34. An alternative concept for this is *social control*. I shall use the concepts of monitoring and (formal and informal) social control as interchangeable.

35. In addition to teaching and monitoring, the individual's changing capacity for moral reasoning is also likely to be important, particularly for moral developments through childhood and adolescence.

36. See, for example, Zahn-Waxler & Robinson (1995: 159-161).

37. Please note that this does not say anything about the content of their morals, only something about the strength of their morals.

38. This is not to say that all parents, friends, teachers and spouses, in any objective sense, provide good care. It is just to say that they are examples of categories of people on whom the individual is dependent for his or her emotional and physical well-being and to whom he or she therefore may develop strong attachments.

39. Please note that this is not an argument concerned with whether existing laws are morally justified or not. It is just a correspondence argument.

40. The idea that individual morals develop sequentially over the life-course (particularly during childhood and adolescence), and that different individuals reach different stages of moral reasoning is an important aspect of moral development and change, but not one I shall specifically discuss in this chapter (e.g., Colby & Kohlberg, 1987: 15-35; Kohlberg, 1973; 1984). The linking of the idea of sequential moral development and the idea of the role of socialization in formation and change of morals would probably benefit our understanding of the process of moral development.

41. For example, youths with weak (conventional) morals may *prefer* to be in settings with weak monitoring of moral rule breaking, which, in turn, may further weaken their (conventional) morals (due to less exposure to effective teaching and monitoring of conventional morals). They may also be *excluded* from or *not allowed* to take part in certain (conventional) settings due to their behavior (arising from their morals and executive function), which, in turn, for example, may put them into greater contact with criminogenic settings (that may be more open to them), which, in turn, may further weaken their (conventional) morals.

42. Although effects of ageing and specific events like frontal lobe injuries may cause later significant change in the individual's executive function.

43. I use the concept of nurturing to refer to *skill* promotion, while I use the concept of caring to refer to the promotion of physical and emotional *well-being*.

44. Perhaps with exceptions such as the effect of frontal lobe injuries (e.g., blows to the head or a stroke) on executive functions.

45. This obviously also holds, but to an absolute extent, for their prenatal development.

46 . On the link between family management strategies and neighborhood conditions see, e.g., Pratt, Turner & Piquero (2004); Furstenberg et al (1999); and Sampson (1993).

47. To be clear, I am not suggesting that they necessarily (although they sometimes may) look for settings with great opportunity and friction, and poor monitoring, just that the characteristics of the settings they look for (e.g., exciting settings) may coincidentally provide these characteristics.

48. External changes may include anything from parent's decision to move to another city to an outbreak of war. One source of external change, of particular relevance to the study of criminal careers, are those changes that happen due to actions taken by the criminal justice system, for example, imprisonment or tagging.

49. If acts of crime occurred randomly in the various settings in which a criminally active individual takes part there would be little evidence that settings played any role in the motivation to crime. However, the fact that even the most criminally active individual spends only a marginal part of his/her waking time committing acts of crime, and the fact that crime tends to cluster in certain locations, are strong indications that settings play an important role in crime motivation (e.g., Baldwin & Bottoms, 1976; Sherman, Gartin & Buerger, 1989; Wikström, 1991; Dolmen, 2002).

50. That is, whether there is something about settings, which over and above the influence of individual propensity, contributes to the motivation to offend.

51. This is, of course, also the basic idea on which so-called situational crime prevention is based.

52. In the long run, an increased participation in criminogenic settings may also (as earlier discussed) have some influence on the individual's development and change in crime propensity (e.g., influence his/her morals). Individuals' actions and others' reaction to them is an important part of what influences their individual development and change. As should be clear from the discussion so far, development and change in individual crime propensity and their exposure to criminogenic settings is a partly intertwined process.

53. The requirement that the perpetrator knows that the act is a crime (moral rule breaking) only implies that if asked retrospectively the individual would be aware that the act is a crime (moral rule breaking).

54. As previously argued, individuals with a low crime propensity need stronger environmental inducement to engage in acts of crime than thus with a high crime propensity.

55. The relationship between early development of executive functions and subsequent early development of morals is an intriguing one, for example, does the development of poor executive functions impair the development of morals (particularly moral emotions like shame and guilt)?

56. Please note that "defective" moral teaching in this context refers to a poor correspondence between the moral teaching the individual experiences and the rules of law (moral rules) that apply in the broader context (society) in which the individual operates. Please also note that moral teaching does not only refer to direct instruction but also to influences on the individual's moral development from the direct (or indirect) observation of others' behavior and people's reaction to that.

References

Aronfreed, J. (1968). *Conduct and Conscience: The Socialization of Internalized Control and Behavior.* New York: Academic Press.

Baldwin, J. & Bottoms, A. E. (1976*). The Urban Criminal.* London. Tavistock.

Barkley, R. A. (1997). *ADHD and the Nature of Self-Control.* New York: The Guilford Press.

Bloom, B. S. (1964). *Stability and Change in Human Characteristics.* New York: John Wiley.

Blumstein, A., Cohen, J., Roth, J. A. & Visher, C. A. (1986). *Criminal Careers and Career Criminals. Volume 1.* Washington, DC: National Academy Press.

Braithwaite J. (1989). *Crime, Shame and Reintegration.* Cambridge. Cambridge University Press.

Brantingham, P. J. & Brantingham, P. L. (1993). Environment, routine and situation. Toward a pattern theory of crime. In R.V. Clarke and M. Felson (Eds.), *Routine Activity and Rational Choice.* New Brunswick, NJ: Transaction Publications.

Brody, L. M., Tremblay, R. E., Brame, B., Fergusson, D., Horwood, J. L., Laird, R., Moffitt, M. E., Nagin, D. S., Bates, J. E., Dodge, K. A., Loeber, R., Lynham, D. R., Petit, G. S. & Vitaro, F. (2003). Developmental trajectories of childhood disruptive behavior and adolescent delinquency: A six-site, cross-national study. *Developmental Psychology,* 39: 222-245.

Bronfenbrenner, U. (1979). *The Ecology of Human Development.* Cambridge, MA: Harvard University Press.

Bunge, M. (1999). *The Sociology-Philosophy Connection.* New Brunswick, NJ: Transaction Publishers.

Bursik, R. J. & Grasmick, H. G. (1993). *Neighborhoods and Crime.* New York: Lexington books.

Clarke, R. V. & Felson, M. (1993). Introduction: Criminology, routine activity, and rational choice. In R. V. Clarke & M. Felson (Eds.), *Routine Activity and Rational Choice.* Advances in Criminological Theory, Vol. 5. New Brunswick, NJ: Transaction Publishers.

Cohen, L. E., & Felson, M. (1979). Social-change and crime rate trends—Routine activity approach. *American Sociological Review,* 44, 4: 588-608.

Colby, A. & Kohlberg, L. (1987).*The Measurement of Moral Judgement. Volume 1.* Cambridge: Cambridge University Press.

Coleman, J. C. (1990). *Foundations of Social Theory.* Cambridge, MA: Harvard University Press.

Dolmen, L. (2002). *Brottslighetens geografi.* Stockholm: Kriminologiska Institituionen, Stockholms universitet.

Durkheim, E. (1961). *Moral Education.* New York. Free Press.

Earls, F. & Carlson, M. (1995). Promoting human capability as an alternative to early crime prevention. In P.-O. Wikstrom, R. V. Clarke & J. McCord (Eds.), *Integrating Crime Prevention Strategies: Propensity and Opportunity.* Stockholm: Allmänna Förlaget.

Farrington, D. P. (1986). Stepping stones to adult criminal careers. In D. Olweus, J. Block & M. R. Yarrow (Eds.), *Development of Antisocial and Prosocial Behaviour: Research, Theories and Issues.* New York: Academic Press.

Farrington D. P. (1988). Studying changes within individuals: The causes of offending. In M. Rutter (Ed.), *Studies of Psychosocial Risk.* Cambridge: Cambridge University Press.

Farrington, D. P. (1992). Explaining the beginning, progress and ending of antisocial behavior from birth to adulthood. In J. McCord (Ed.), *Facts, Frameworks, and Forecasts.* Advances in Criminological Theory, Vol. 3. New Brunswick, NJ: Transaction Publishers.

Farrington, D. P. (1996). The explanation and prevention of youthful offending. In J. D. Hawkins (Ed.), *Delinquency and Crime*. Cambridge: Cambridge University Press.

Farrington, D. P. (2000). Explaining and preventing crime: The globalization of knowledge—The American Society of Criminology 1999 Presidential Address. *Criminology*, 38, 1: 1-24.

Farrington, D. P. (2002). Human development and criminal careers. In M. Maguire, R. Morgan & R. Reiner (Eds.), *The Oxford Handbook of Criminology* (3rd ed.) Oxford: Clarendon Press.

Farrington D. P. (2003). Developmental and life-course criminology: Key theoretical and empirical issues. *Criminology*, 41: 221-255.

Farrington, D. P. & Wikstrom, P. O. (1994). Criminal careers in London and Stockholm. A cross-national comparative study. In E. Weitekamp & H. J. Kerner (Eds.), *Cross-National Longitudinal Research on Human Development*. Dordrecht: Kluwer.

Farrington, D. P., Sampson, R. J., and Wikström, Per-Olof (Eds.). (1993). *Integrating Individual and Ecological Aspects of Crime*. Stockholm: Allmänna Förlaget.

Farrington, D. P., Loeber, R., Yin, Y. & Anderson, S. J. (2002). Are within-individual causes of delinquency the same as between-individual causes? *Criminal Behaviour and Mental Health*, 12: 53-68.

Felson, R. B. (1993). Predatory and dispute-related violence: A social interactionist approach. In R.V. Clarke and M. Felson (Eds.), *Routine Activity and Rational Choice*. New Brunswick, NJ: Transaction Publications.

Felson, M. (1994). *Crime and Everyday Life*. Thousand Oaks, CA: Pine Forge Press.

Furstenberg, F. F. Jr., Cook, T. D., Eccles, J. S., Elder, G. H. Jr., and Sameroff, A. (1999). *Managing to make it*. Chicago: University of Chicago Press.

Glass, A. L. & Holyoak, K. J. (1986). *Cognition* (2nd ed.) New York: Random House.

Gottfredson, D. C., & Hirschi, T. (1990). *A General Theory of Crime*. Stanford, CA: Stanford University Press.

Gottfredson, M. R. & Hirschi, T. (2003). Self-control and opportunity. In C. L. Britt & M. Gottfredson (Eds), *Control Theories of Crime and Delinquency*. Advances in Criminological Theory, Vol. 12. New Brunswick, NJ: Transaction Publishers.

Granovetter, M. (1985). Economic action and social structure: The problem of embeddedness. *American Journal of Sociology*, 91: 481-510.

Hagerstrand, T. *Innovation Diffusion as a Spatial Process*. Chicago: University of Chicago Press.

Hart, H.L.A. (1961). *The Concept of Law*. Oxford: Clarendon Press.

Hirschi, T. (1969). *Causes of Delinquency*. Berkeley: University of California Press.

Hirschi, T. (1986). On the compability of rational choice and control theories of crime. In D. B. Cornish & R. V. Clarke (Eds.), *The Reasoning Criminal*. New York: Springer-Verlag.

Hirschi, T. & Gottfredson, M. (1986). The distinction between crime and criminality. In T. F.Hartnagel & R. A.Silverman (Eds.), *Critique and Explanation: Essays in Honor of Gwynne Nettler*. New Brunswick, NJ: Transaction Publishers.

Hirschi, T. & Gottfredson, M. (1988). Towards a general theory of crime. In W. Buikhuisen &S. A. Mednick (Eds.), *Explaining Criminal Behaviour*. Leiden: E. J. Brill.

von Hirsch, A., Bottoms, A. B., Burney, E. & Wikström, P-O. (1999). *Criminal Deterrence and Sentence Severity. An Analysis of Recent Research*. Oxford: Hart publishing.

Horney, J. Osgood, D. W. & Marshall, I. H. (1995).Criminal careers in the short-term: Intra individual variability in crime and its relation to local life circumstances. *American Sociological Review*, 60: 655-673.

Ishikawa, S.S. & Raine, A. (2003). Prefrontal deficits and antisocial behavior. A causal model. In B. B. Lahey, T. E. Moffitt & A. Caspi (Eds.), *Causes of Conduct Disorder and Juvenile Delinquency*. New York:The Guilford Press.

Jensen, G. F. & Akers, R. L. (2003). Taking social learning theory global: Micro-macro transitions in criminological theory. In R. L.Akers & G. F.Jensen (Eds.), *Social Learning Theory and the Explanation of Crime*. Advances in Criminological Theory, Vol. 11. New Brunswick, NJ: Transaction Publishers.

Kohlberg, L. (1984). *Essays on Moral Development, Volume 2: The Psychology of Moral Development*. San Francisco: Harper & Row.

Kohlberg, L. (1973). Continuities in childhood and adult moral development revisited. In P. B. Baltes & K. Warner Schaie (Eds.), *Life-Span Developmental Psychology. Personality and Socialization*. New York: Academic Press.

Kornhauser, R. R. (1978). *Social Sources of Delinquency*. Chicago. University of Chicago Press.

Laub J. H. & Sampson, R. J. (2003). *Shared Beginnings, Divergent Lives. Delinquent Boys at Age 70*. Cambridge MA: Harvard University Press.

Laufer, W. S. & Adler, F. (1989). Introduction: The challenges of advances in criminological theory. In W. S. Laufer & F. Adler (Eds.), *Advances in Criminological Theory*, Vol. 1. New Brunswick, NJ. Transaction Publishers.

Le Blanc, M. (1993). Prevention of delinquency: An integrative multilayered control based perspective. In D. P. Farrington, R. J. Sampson & P.-O. Wikström (Eds.), *Integrating Individual and Ecological Aspects of Crime*. Stockholm: Allmänna Förlaget.

Le Blanc, M. (1997). A generic control theory of the criminal phenomena: The structural and dynamic statements of an integrative multilayered control theory. In T. P. Thornberry (Ed.), *Developmental Theories of Crime and Delinquency* (pp. 215-286). New Brunswick, NJ: Transaction Publishers.

Le Blanc, M., & Frechette, M. (1989). *Male Criminal Activity from Childhood Through Youth*. New York: Springer-Verlag.

Le Blanc, M. & Loeber, R. (1998). Developmental criminology updated. In M. Tonry (Ed.), *Crime and Justice*, Vol. 23 (pp. 115-198). Chicago: University of Chicago Press.

Lieberson, S. (1985). *Making It Count*. Berkeley: University of California Press.

Loeber, R. (1990). Development and risk factors of juvenile antisocial behavior and delinquency. *Clinical Psychology Review,* 10: 1-41.

Loeber, R. (1996). Development continuity, change, and pathways in male juvenile problem behaviors and delinquency. In J. D. Hawkins (Ed.), *Delinquency and Crime. Current Theories*. Cambridge: Cambridge University Press.

Loeber, R., & Le Blanc, M. (1990). Toward a developmental criminology. *Crime and Justice—A Review of Research*, 12: 375-473.

Loeber, R., & Wikström, P.-O. (1993). Individual pathways to crime in different types of neighborhoods. In D. P. Farrington, R. J. Sampson & P.-O. Wikström (Eds.), *Integrating Individual and Ecological Aspects of Crime*. Stockholm: Allmänna Förlaget.

Loeber, R., & Farrington, D. P. (1998). *Serious and Violent Juvenile Offenders: Risk Factors and Successful Interventions*. Thousand Oaks, CA: Sage.

Loeber, R., & Farrington, D. P. (2001). *Child Delinquents: Risk Factors, Interventions, and Service Needs*. Thousand Oaks, CA: Sage.

Magnusson, D. (1988). *Individual Development from an Interactional Perspective*. Hillsdale, NJ: Erlbaum.

Magnusson, D. & Cairns, R. B. (1996). Developmental Science: Towards a unified framework. In R. B. Cairns, G. H. Elder, Jr. & E. J. Costello (Eds.), *Developmental Science*. Cambridge: Cambridge University Press.

Moen, P., Elder, G. H. Jr., & Lucher, K. (1995). *Examining Lives in Context*. Washington, DC: The American Psychological Association.

Moffitt, T. E. (1993). Adolescence-limited and life-course-persistent antisocial-behavior— A developmental taxonomy. *Psychological Review*, 100, 4: 674-701.

Moffitt, T. E. (1997). Adolescent-limited and life-course persistent offending: A complementary pair of developmental theories. In T. Thornberry (Ed.), *Developmental Theories of Crime and Delinquency*. Advances in Criminological Theory, Vol. 7. New Brunswick, NJ: Transaction Publishers.

Moffitt, T. E. (2003) Life-course-persistent and adolescent-limited antisocial behavior. In B. B. Lahey, T. E. Moffitt & A. Caspi (Eds.), *Causes of Conduct Disorder and Juvenile Delinquency*. New York: The Guilford Press.

Nagin, D. S. & Paternoster, R. (1993). Enduring individual differences and rational choice theories of crime. *Law & Society Review*, 27, 3: 467-496.

Nagin, D., Farrington, D. P. & Moffitt, T. E. (1995). Life-course trajectories of different types of offenders. *Criminology*, 33: 111-139.

Osgood, D. W., Wilson, J. K., O'Malley, P. M., Bachman, J. G., & Johnston, L. D. (1996). Routine activities and individual deviant behavior. *American Sociological Review*, 61, 4: 635-655.

Piquero, A. R., Farrington D. P. & Blumstein A. (2003). The criminal career paradigm. *Crime and Justice*, 30: 359-506. Chicago. University of Chicago Press.

Pratt, T. C., Turner, M. G. & Piquero, A. (2004), Parental socialization and community context: A longitudinal analysis of the structural sources of low self-control. *Journal of Research in Crime and Delinquency*, 40: 219-243.

Reiss, A. J. (1986). Why are communities important in understanding crime? In A. J. Reiss & M. Tonry (Eds.), *Communities and Crime. Crime and Justice: A Review of Research*, Vol. 8. Chicago: University of Chicago Press.

Rutter et al. (1995). Understanding individual differences in environmental-risk exposure. In P. Moen, G. H. Elder, Jr. & K. Lucher (Eds.), *Examining Lives in Context*. Washington, DC: The American Psychological Association.

Rutter, M. (2003). Crucial paths from risk indicator to causal mechanism. In B. B. Lahey, T. E. Moffitt & A. Caspi (Eds.), *Causes of Conduct Disorder and Juvenile Delinquency*. New York: The Guilford Press.

Sampson, R. J. (1993). Family and community-level influences on crime. In D. P. Farrington, R. J. Sampson & P.-O. Wikström (Eds.), *Integrating Individual and Ecological Aspects of Crime*. Stockholm: Allmänna Förlaget.

Sampson, R. J., and Laub, J. L. (1993). *Crime in the Making*. Cambridge, MA: Harvard University Press.

Sampson, R. J., Raudenbush, S. W. & Earls, F. (1997). Neighborhoods and violent crime: A multilevel study of collective efficacy. *Science*, 277: 918-924.

Settersten Jr., R. A. & Owens, T. J. (2002). *New Frontiers in Socialization*. Advances in Life Course Research, Vol. 7. Amsterdam: JAI Press.

Sherman, L. W., P. R. Gartin & M. E. Buerger. (1989). Hot spots of predatory crime: Routine activities and the criminology of place. *Criminology*, 27: 27-55.

Shonkoff, J. P., & Phillips, D.A.E. (2000). *From Neurons to Neighborhoods. The Science of Early Childhood Development*. Washington DC: National Academy Press.

Thornberry, T. P. & Krohn M. D. (Eds.). (2003). *Taking Stock of Delinquency. An Overview of Findings from Contemporary Longitudinal Studies*. New York: Kluwer Academic/ Plenum Press.

Tonry, M., Ohlin, L. E., & Farrington, D. P. (1991). *Human Development and Criminal Behavior*. New York: Springer-Verlag.

Wikström, P.-O. (1987). *Patterns of Crime in A Birth Cohort* (Report No. 24). Stockholm: University of Stockholm, Department of Sociology.

Wikström, P-O. H. (1990). Age and crime in a Stockholm cohort. *Journal of Quantitative Criminology*, 6: 61-84.

Wikström, P.-O. (1991). *Urban Crime, Criminals and Victims*. New York: Springer-Verlag.

Wikström, P.-O. (1998). Communities and crime. In M. Tonry (Ed.), *The Handbook of Crime and Punishment* (pp. 269-301). New York: Oxford University Press.

Wikström, P-O. H. (2004). Crime as alternative. Towards a cross-level situational action theory of crime causation. In J. McCord. (Ed.), *Beyond Empiricism: Institutions and Intentions in the Study of Crime*. Advances in Criminological Theory, Vol. 13 (pp. 1-37). New Brunswick, NJ: Transaction Publishers.

Wikström, P.-O., & Loeber, R. (2000). Do disadvantaged neighborhoods cause well-adjusted children to become adolescent delinquents? *Criminology*, 38: 1109-1142.

Wikström, P-O. H., & Sampson, R. J. (2003). Social mechanisms of community influences on crime and pathways in criminality. In B. B. Lahey, T. E. Moffitt, and A. Caspi (Eds.), *Causes of Conduct Disorder and Serious Juvenile Delinquency* (pp. 118-148). New York: Guilford Press.

Wikström, P.-O., Clarke, R. V. & McCord, J. (1995). *Integrating Crime Prevention Strategies: Propensity and Opportunity*. Stockholm: Fritzes.

Wilson, J. Q. & Herrnstein, R. J. (1985). *Crime and Human Nature*. New York: Simon and Schuster.

Wolfgang, M., Figlio, R. M. & Sellin T. (1972). *Delinquency in a Birth Cohort*. Chicago: University of Chicago Press.

Wolfgang, M. E., Thornberry T. P. & Figlio, R. M. (1987) *From Boy to Man, From Delinquency to Crime*. Chicago: University of Chicago Press.

Wrong, D. H. (1994). *The Problem of Order. What Unites and Divides Society?* New York: The Free Press.

Zahn-Waxler, C. & Robinson, J. (1995). Empathy and guilt: Early origins of feelings and responsibility. In J. P. Tangney & K. W. Fischer (Eds.), *Self-Conscious Emotions. The Psychology of Shame, Guilt, Embarrassment, and Pride* (pp. 143-173). New York: The Guilford Press.

10

Conclusions about Developmental and Life-Course Theories

David P. Farrington

I will begin by summarizing the key features of the eight theories. This was easier where the theorists systematically tried to address the key questions raised in chapter 1.

Lahey and Waldman

Lahey and Waldman aim to explain the development of juvenile delinquency and child conduct problems, focusing particularly on childhood and adolescence. They do not address adult life events or attempt to explain desistance in the adult years, for example. They assume that it is desirable to distinguish different types of people, but they propose a continuum of developmental trajectories rather than only two categories of adolescence-limited and life-course-persistent offenders, for example.

Their key construct is antisocial propensity, which tends to persist over time and has a wide variety of behavioral manifestations, reflecting the versatility and comorbidity of antisocial behavior. The most important factors that contribute to antisocial propensity are low cognitive ability (especially verbal ability), and three dimensions of temperament: prosociality (including sympathy and empathy), daring (uninhibited or poorly controlled), and negative emotionality (e.g., easily frustrated, bored, or annoyed). These four factors have a genetic basis, and Lahey and Waldman discuss gene-environment interactions.

Their theory does not explicitly distinguish protective factors and does not attempt to explain why people commit offenses or address immediate situational influences on criminal events. Lahey and Waldman suggest that living in a high crime neighborhood has an influence on antisocial propensity, and that neighborhood factors interact with temperament and cognitive factors. They do not address the effect of criminal justice processing or propose any kind of labelling process. They do not incorporate strain theory postulates or address reasons for offending, but they do propose social learning and reinforcement processes in socialization.

Overall, Lahey and Waldman's theory particularly emphasizes the importance of biological and individual factors. They did not explicitly answer all the questions raised in chapter 1.

Piquero and Moffitt

Piquero and Moffitt propose that there are two qualitatively different categories of antisocial people (differing in kind rather than in degree), namely life-course-persistent (LCP) and adolescence-limited (AL) offenders. As indicated by the terms, the LCPs start offending at an early age and persist beyond their 20s, while the ALs have a short criminal career largely limited to their teenage years. The LCPs commit a wide range of offenses including violence, whereas the ALs commit predominantly "rebellious" non-violent offenses.

The main factors that encourage offending by the LCPs are cognitive deficits, an undercontrolled temperament, hyperactivity, poor parenting, disrupted families, teenage parents, poverty, and low SES. Genetic and biological factors, such as a low heart rate, are important. There is not much discussion of neighborhood factors, but it is proposed that the neuropsychological risk of the LCPs interacts multiplicatively with a disadvantaged environment. The theory does not propose that neuropsychological deficits and a disadvantaged environment influence an underlying construct such as antisocial propensity; rather, it suggests that neuropsychological and environmental factors are the key constructs underlying antisocial behavior.

The main factors that encourage offending by the ALs are the "maturity gap" (their inability to achieve adult rewards such as material goods during their teenage years—similar to strain theory ideas) and peer influence (especially from the LCPs). Consequently, the ALs stop offending when they enter legitimate adult roles and can achieve their desires legally. The ALs can easily stop because they have no neuropsychological deficits.

The theory assumes that there can be labelling effects of "snares" such as a criminal record, incarceration, drug or alcohol addiction, and (for girls) unwanted pregnancy, especially for the ALs. However, the observed continuity in offending over time is largely driven by the LCPs. The theory focuses mainly on the development of offenders and does not attempt to explain why offenses are committed. However, it suggests that the presence of delinquent peers is an important situational influence on ALs, and that the availability of opportunities and victims influences the offending of LCPs.

Decision-making in criminal opportunities is supposed to be rational for the ALs (who weigh likely costs against likely benefits) but not for the LCPs (who largely follow well-learned "automatic" behavioral repertoires without thinking). However, the LCPs are mainly influenced by utilitarian motives, whereas the ALs are influenced by teenage boredom. Adult life events such as getting a job or getting married are hypothesized to be of little importance, because the LCPs are too committed to an antisocial life-style and the ALs desist naturally as they age into adult roles.

Piquero and Moffitt also identify a third category of "abstainers" who commit no offenses, because they have personal characteristics that exclude them from peer networks (e.g., nervous and withdrawn), because they are immature (not wishing to achieve teenage status symbols) or because their environment does not provide opportunities for antisocial behavior. This is the nearest approach to a discussion of protective factors. There is also a recent fourth category of low-level offenders with mental health problems, but these are not reviewed in the chapter. No category of "late onset offenders" is proposed.

Piquero and Moffitt provide explicit answers to all of the key questions raised in chapter 1. The answers differ greatly for LCP as opposed to AL offenders. It seems that most of the well-established findings in criminology (e.g., in regard to early risk factors) are largely driven by the LCPs.

Farrington

The integrated cognitive antisocial potential (ICAP) theory is mainly intended to explain offending by lower-class males. It integrates ideas from strain, control, social learning, differential association, and labeling theories. No distinct types of offenders are proposed. The key construct underlying antisocial behavior is antisocial potential (AP), and there is continuity in offending and antisocial behavior over time because of consistency in the relative ordering of people on AP.

Long-term and short-term influences on AP are explicitly distinguished. Long-term factors encouraging offending include impulsiveness, strain, and antisocial models, while short-term (immediate situational) influences include opportunities and victims. Long-term factors inhibiting offending include attachment and socialization (based on social learning) and life events such as getting married or moving house. The theory is presented in one diagram but there should be different diagrams (with different influencing factors) for different life stages. The theory explicitly aims to explain both the development of offending and the commission of offenses. Situational factors, motives, and cognitive (thinking and decision-making) processes are included.

The ICAP theory includes neighborhood factors but does not attempt to explain individual development in different neighborhoods. It includes individual factors and could easily include biological factors. It assumes that the consequences of offending have labelling, deterrent, or learning effects on AP. Chapter 4 includes explicit answers to all the key questions raised in chapter 1.

Catalano and Hawkins

According to Catalano and Hawkins and their colleagues, the social development model (SDM) integrates social control/bonding, social learning and differential association theories, but does not include strain theory postulates. Their chapter includes an empirical test of their theory. The key construct is bonding to society (or socializing agents), consisting of attachment, commitment, and belief. The key construct underlying offending is the balance between antisocial and prosocial bonding. Continuity in antisocial behavior over time depends on continuity in this balance. The main motivation that leads to offending and antisocial behavior is the hedonistic desire to seek satisfaction and follow self-interest. This is opposed by the bond to society. Offending is essentially a rational decision in which people weigh the benefits against the costs. There is no assumption about different types of offenders.

There are two causal pathways, leading to antisocial or prosocial bonding. On the prosocial pathway, opportunities for prosocial interaction lead to involvement in prosocial behavior; involvement and skills for prosocial behavior lead to rewards for prosocial behavior, which lead to prosocial bonding (attachment, commitment, and belief). On the antisocial pathway, opportunities for antisocial interaction lead to involvement in antisocial behavior; involvement and skills for antisocial behavior lead to rewards for antisocial behavior, which lead to antisocial bonding. Hence, the antisocial pathway specifies factors encouraging offending and the prosocial pathway specifies factors inhibiting offending. Opportunities, involvement, skills, and rewards are part of a socialization process. People learn prosocial and antisocial behavior according to socialization by families, peers, schools, and communities.

The SDM specifies that demographic factors (such as age, race, gender, and social class) and biological factors (such as difficult temperament, cognitive ability, low arousal, and hyperactivity) influence opportunities and skills in the socialization process. They propose somewhat different models for different developmental periods (preschool, elementary school, middle school, high school, young adulthood). For example, in the first two periods interaction with prosocial or antisocial family members is the most important, while in the other two periods interaction with prosocial or antisocial peers is the most important.

The development of offending and the commission of offenses are not explicitly distinguished in the SDM. However, the theory includes prosocial and antisocial opportunities as situational factors and suggests that the perceived rewards and costs of antisocial behavior influence the decision to offend. Motives for offending (e.g., utilitarian or excitement) are included under the heading of perceived rewards and costs. Neighborhood factors, official labelling, and life events are important only insofar as they influence the key constructs of opportunities, involvement, skills, rewards, and bonding. For example, official labelling may increase involvement with antisocial people and marriage may increase prosocial opportunities and involvement.

The SDM is very much a social bonding theory and is noteworthy for its explicit distinction between prosocial and antisocial pathways. Catalano and Hawkins and colleagues provide explicit answers to all the key questions raised in chapter 1.

Le Blanc

Le Blanc proposes an integrative multilayered control theory that explains the development of offending, the occurrence of criminal events, and community crime rates. In his chapter, he focuses only on the first of these topics. The key construct underlying offending is general deviance, and Le Blanc discusses its structure and how it changes over time. According to his theory, the development of offending depends on four mechanisms of control: bonding to society (including family, school, peers, marriage, and work), psychological development over time (especially away from self-centeredness), modelling (prosocial or antisocial), and constraints (external, including socialization, and internal, including beliefs). He assumes that environmental factors (e.g., social class and neighborhood) influence bonding while biological capacity (including difficult temperament) influences psychological development. Bonding and psychological development influence modelling and constraints, which are proximate influences on general deviance and hence on offending. There is continuity in offending because the relative ordering of people on control mechanisms stays fairly consistent over time.

Le Blanc proposes that there are three types of offenders: persistent, transitory, and common. Persistent offenders are most extreme on weak bonding, self-centeredness, antisocial modelling, and low constraints. Common offenders are largely influenced by opportunities, while transitory offenders are in the middle (in having moderate control and being moderately influenced by opportunities). His theory includes biological and neighborhood factors, but they are assumed to have indirect effects on offending through their effects on the constructs of bonding and psychological development. Similarly, he assumes that life events have effects via the constructs and that labelling influences external constraints. The theory includes learning processes and socialization but does not include strain theory assumptions.

Le Blanc's (1997) theory of criminal events suggests that they depend on community control (e.g., social disorganization), personal control (rational choice ideas of decision-making), self-control (impulsiveness, vulnerability to temptations), opportunities, routine activities and guardianship (e.g., physical protection). People are viewed as hedonistic, and motives (e.g., excitement or utilitarian) are considered.

While Le Blanc generally espouses control theory notions, his theory also includes ideas from several other sources including social learning, differential association, and rational choice theories. He addresses key questions raised in chapter 1 and helpfully discusses and extends the well-established findings and contentious issues identified there.

Sampson and Laub

The key construct in Sampson and Laub's theory is age-graded informal social control, which means the strength of bonding to family, peers, schools, and later adult social institutions such as marriages and jobs. Sampson and Laub primarily aim to explain why people do not commit offenses, on the assumption that why people offend is unproblematic (presumably caused by hedonistic desires) and that offending is inhibited by the strength of bonding to society.

The strength of bonding depends on attachments to parents, schools, delinquent friends and delinquent siblings, and also on parental socialization processes such as discipline and supervision. Structural background variables (e.g., social class, ethnicity, large family size, criminal parents, disrupted families) and individual difference factors (e.g., low intelligence, difficult temperament, early conduct disorder) have indirect effects on offending through their effects on informal social control (attachment and socialization processes).

Sampson and Laub are concerned with the whole life course. They emphasize change over time rather than consistency, and the poor ability of early childhood risk factors to predict later life outcomes. They focus on the importance of later life events (adult turning points) such as joining the military, getting a stable job, and getting married in fostering desistance and "knifing off" the past from the present. They also suggest that neighborhood changes can cause changes in offending. Because of their emphasis on change and unpredictability, they deny the importance of types of offenders such as "life-course-persisters."

Sampson and Laub do not explicitly include immediate situational influences on criminal events in their theory, and believe that opportunities are not important because they are ubiquitous (Sampson & Laub, 1995). However, they do suggest that having few structured routine activities is conducive to offending. They focus on why people do not offend rather than on why people offend, and emphasize the importance of individual free will and purposeful choice in the decision to desist. They do not include strain theory ideas, but they propose that official labelling influences offending through its effects on job instability and unemployment. They argue that early delinquency can cause weak adult social bonds, which, in turn, fail to inhibit adult offending.

Sampson and Laub's theory is essentially a social control theory. They did not explicitly attempt to answer the questions raised in chapter 1.

Thornberry and Krohn

The interactional theory of Thornberry and Krohn particularly focuses on factors encouraging antisocial behavior at different ages. They do not propose types of offenders but suggest that the causes of antisocial behavior vary for children who start at different ages. At the earliest ages (birth to 6), the three most important factors are neuropsychological deficit and difficult temperament (e.g., impulsiveness, negative emotionality, fearlessness, poor emotion regulation), parenting deficits (e.g., poor monitoring, low affective ties, inconsistent discipline, physical punishment), and structural adversity (e.g., poverty, unemployment, welfare dependency, disorganized neighborhood). They also suggest that structural adversity might cause poor parenting.

Neuropsychological deficits are less important for children who start antisocial behavior at older ages. At ages 6-12, neighborhood and family factors are particularly salient, while at ages 12-18 school and peer factors dominate. Thornberry and Krohn also suggest that deviant opportunities, gangs, and deviant social networks are important for onset at ages 12-18. They propose that late starters (ages 18-25) have cognitive deficits such as low IQ and poor school performance but that they were protected from antisocial behavior at earlier ages by a supportive family and school environment. At ages 18-25, they find it hard to make a successful transition to adult roles such as employment and marriage.

The most distinctive feature of this interactional theory is its emphasis on reciprocal causation. For example, it is proposed that the child's antisocial behavior elicits coercive responses from parents and rejection by peers and makes antisocial behavior more likely in the future. The theory does not postulate a single key construct underlying offending but suggests that children who start early tend to persist because of the persistence of neuropsychological and parenting deficits and structural adversity. Interestingly, Thornberry and Krohn predict that late starters (ages 18-25) will show more continuity over time than earlier starters (ages 12-18) because the late starters have more cognitive deficits. In an earlier exposition of the theory (Thornberry & Krohn, 2001), they proposed that desistance was caused by changing social influences (e.g., stronger family bonding), protective factors (e.g., high IQ and school success), and intervention programs. Hence, they do think that criminal justice processing has an effect on future offending.

Generally, Thornberry and Krohn focus on social learning processes and social influences and on factors that encourage antisocial behavior. They did not provide explicit answers to all the questions raised in chapter 1. However, it seems that their theory does not include postulates about why crimes are committed (e.g., discussing situational factors or decision-making in criminal opportunities) and does not explicitly include strain theory postulates or consider motives for offending.

Wikström

Wikström proposes a developmental ecological action theory that aims to explain moral rule breaking. The key construct underlying offending is individual criminal propensity, which depends on moral judgment and self-control. In turn, moral values influence moral judgment, and executive functions influence self-control. Wikström does not propose types of offenders. The motivation to offend arises from the interaction between the individual and the setting. For example, if individual propensity is low, features of the setting (persons, objects, and events) become more important. Continuity or change in offending over time depends on continuity or change in moral values, executive functions, and settings.

Situational factors are important in Wikström's theory, which aims to explain the commission of offenses as well as the development of offenders. Opportunities cause temptation, friction produces provocation, and monitoring or the risk of sanctions has a deterrent effect. The theory emphasizes perception, choice, and human agency in deciding to offend. Learning processes are included in the theory, since it is suggested that moral values are taught by instruction and observation in a socialization process and that nurturing (the promotion of cognitive skills) influences executive functions. Life events also matter, since it is proposed that starting school, getting married (etc.) can trigger changes in constructs such as moral teaching and monitoring and hence influence moral rule breaking.

Wikström's theory emphasizes different influences at different ages and on different stages of criminal careers (e.g., onset, persistence, desistance). He does not include biological factors or strain theory postulates, or suggest that criminal justice processing or the consequences of offending have labelling effects. Also, he does not explicitly address the key questions raised in chapter 1.

Differences among DLC Theories

In comparing the eight theories, I will refer to them using the name of the person who seems to be most associated with them: Lahey, Moffitt, Farrington, Hawkins, Le Blanc, Sampson, Thornberry, and Wikström. All the theories are generally concordant with the well-established empirical findings outlined in chapter 1, but there are clearly theoretical differences between them.

First, while most theories emphasize continuity in antisocial behavior over time, Sampson emphasizes change, unpredictability, and a lack of continuity. Moffitt suggests that only the LCPs (not the ALs) show continuity, while Wikström gives equal attention to continuity and change. To some extent, this is a question about whether the glass is half full or half empty. Clearly, it is desirable that quantitative predictions from theories about the degree of continuity are compared with quantitative measures of continuity.

Second, the theories vary in how much they postulate key constructs that underlie offending. Lahey (antisocial propensity), Farrington (antisocial potential), Le Blanc (general deviance), and Wikström (individual crime propensity) clearly do, while Moffitt and Thornberry clearly do not. Hawkins (the balance of prosocial and antisocial bonding) and Sampson (informal social control) propose underlying constructs that are less directly related to antisocial behavior. It would be helpful to review the advantages and disadvantages of having an underlying construct, and how it might be operationally defined in a non-tautological way.

Third, the theories vary in how far they think it is useful to distinguish types of offenders. Moffitt, of course, distinguishes LCPs and ALs (and other categories) explicitly, while Le Blanc distinguishes three categories (persistent, transitory, and common offenders), Thornberry suggests different causal factors associated with different ages of onset, and Lahey proposes a continuum of different trajectories. The other four theories do not distinguish types of offenders. The key empirical question is: What are the advantages and disadvantages of proposing types of offenders in explaining observed results?

Fourth, the theories vary in how much they explicitly aim to explain the occurrence of offenses as well as the development of offenders. Farrington, Le Blanc, and Wikström clearly do, while Lahey, Sampson, and Thornberry clearly do not. Moffitt and Hawkins incorporate situational factors such as opportunities, victims, and rational decision-making in their theories but do not provide an explicit theory of the occurrence of criminal events. In my opinion, DLC theories should aim to explain both.

Fifth, while all the theories include individual difference factors and postulates about social influences, they vary in how much they emphasize biological as opposed to neighborhood and community factors. In this book, the theories are roughly ordered from those that give most emphasis to biological factors (Lahey and Moffitt) to those that give most emphasis to social structural factors (Sampson and Wikström). It seems desirable to include all types of causal factors in a comprehensive DLC theory.

Sixth, the theories vary in how much they emphasize the importance of life events on antisocial behavior, especially later events such as getting married and obtaining a steady job. Farrington, Sampson, and Wikström clearly do, while Lahey clearly does not, because his theory focuses very much on early childhood development. Hawkins, Le Blanc, and (I imagine) Thornberry would say that life events are important, but only to the extent that they influence key constructs in their models, but Moffitt thinks that later life events are of relatively little importance.

Seventh, the theories vary in their emphasis on explaining why people do or do not commit offenses. Farrington, Hawkins, and Wikström give equal emphasis to both questions, while Lahey, Moffitt, and Thornberry give more emphasis to factors encouraging offending, and Le Blanc and Sampson (as control theories) give more emphasis to factors inhibiting offending. Eighth, and somewhat relatedly, the theories vary in how much they include strain theory postulates and how much they focus on motives and reasons for offending. Only Moffitt and Farrington, include strain theory assumptions, although Le Blanc and Wikström explicitly consider motives for offending (in discussing the commission of offenses).

Ninth, the theories vary in how much they think that the consequences of offending (e.g., labeling or deterrence) influence future offending. Moffitt, Farrington, and Thornberry give most emphasis to this, while Hawkins, Le Blanc, and Sampson suggest that consequences are important insofar as they have an effect on their key constructs. Lahey and Wikström do not mention such effects, but Wikström proposes that the perceived risk of sanctions has a deterrent effect.

Conclusions

My hope is that this book will be viewed as useful in summarizing the "state-of-the-art" in regard to integrated developmental and life-course theories. I also hope that it will stimulate the further development of DLC theories and the further development of other theories to address key DLC issues. In particular, I hope that it will help to facilitate systematic point-by-point comparisons of DLC theories on their predictions regarding key empirical issues. From these comparisons, it should be possible to specify which elements of DLC theories are more or less advantageous. In turn, this should lead to more adequate theories and—eventually—better prediction and more effective crime reduction techniques.

References

Le Blanc, M. (1997). A generic control theory of the criminal phenomenon: The structural and dynamic statements of an integrated multilayered control theory. In T. P. Thornberry (Ed.), *Developmental Theories of Crime and Delinquency* (pp. 215-285). New Brunswick, NJ: Transaction Publishers.

Sampson, R. J. & Laub, J. H. (1995). Understanding variability in lives through time: Contributions of life-course criminology. *Studies on Crime and Crime Prevention*, 4: 143-158.

Thornberry, T. P. & Krohn, M. D. (2001). The development of delinquency: An interactional perspective. In S. O. White (Ed.), *Handbook of Youth and Justice*. New York: Plenum.

About the Authors

Robert D. Abbott is professor and chair of educational psychology at the University of Washington. His interests include teaching educational statistics and researching the use of different methods of analyzing longitudinal data. Dr. Abbott and colleagues are engaged in a research project funded by the National Institute of Child Health and Human Development that focuses on learning disabilities in children and ways in which teachers can help them learn more effectively. Dr. Abbott is a fellow of the American Psychological Association.

Marc Le Blanc, Ph.D. (Criminology) is a member of the Royal Society of Canada and emeritus professor of the School of Psychoeducation and School of Criminology, Universite de Montreal. He has published eleven books and over 200 articles in French and English on theory, longitudinal research, juvenile justice and treatment. He is best known for his prospective longitudinal surveys of Montreal adolescents and delinquents from childhood to adulthood.

Richard F. Catalano is professor and director of the Social Development Research Group, School of Social Work, University of Washington. Dr. Catalano is the principal investigator on a number of federal grants, which include family, school, and community-based prevention approaches to reduce risk while enhancing the protective factors of bonding and promotion of healthy beliefs and clear standards.

David P. Farrington, O.B.E. (Officer of the British Empire) is professor of psychological criminology at the Institute of Criminology, Cambridge University. He is a fellow of the British Academy, of the Academy of medical Sciences, of the British Psychological Society, and of the American Society of Criminology, and co-chair of the International Campbell Collaboration Crime and Justice Coordinating Group. He has been president of the American Society of Criminology (the first person from outside North America to be elected to this office), president of the European Association of Psychology and Law, president of the British Society of Criminology, president of the Academy of Experimental Criminology, chair of the Division of Forensic Psychology of the British Psychological Society, vice-chair of the U.S. National Academy Sciences Panel on Violence, and co-chair of the U.S. office of Juvenile Justice and Delinquency

Prevention Study Groups on Serious and Violent Juvenile Offenders and on Very Young Offenders. He has received the Sellin-Glueck Award of the American Society of Criminology for international contributions to criminology, and the Sutherland Award of the American Society of Criminology for outstanding contributions to criminology. His major research interest is in the longitudinal study of delinquency and crime, and he is director of the Cambridge Study in Delinquent Development, which is a prospective longitudinal survey of over 400 London males from age 8 to age 48.

Kevin P. Haggerty, MSW, is a faculty lecturer and project director of the Raising Healthy Children project at the Social Development Research Group, University of Washington. Mr. Haggerty is an international trainer and speaker in the areas of substance abuse and delinquency prevention and has written extensively in the field. He has more than two dozen articles and book chapters in print and is the developer of multiple prevention curricula.

Tracy W. Harachi received her Ph.D. in social welfare from the University of Washington in 1991. She currently is a research associate professor in the School of Social Work at the University of Washington. She is a principal and co-principal investigator for research projects funded by NIMH, NICHD, and NIDA. Her research area is the prevention of adolescent problem behaviors, understanding the developmental trajectories of children and youth, and the application of prevention science within family and school-based interventions.

J. David Hawkins is founding director of the Social Development Research Group and Kozmetsky Professor of Prevention at the School of Social Work, University of Washington. His research focuses on understanding and preventing child and adolescent health and behavior problems. He is committed to translating theory and research into effective practice and policy to improve young peoples' health and development.

Marvin D. Krohn received his Ph.D. from the School of Criminology at Florida State University. He is a professor of sociology with a joint appointment in the School of Criminal Justice at the State University of New York at Albany. His research focuses on theoretical explanations of juvenile delinquency and adolescent drug use with special attention to social network and interactional theories within a life-course perspective. He is a co-principal investigator of the Rochester Youth Development Study, which is a panel study of 1,000 high-risk youth from age 13 to their late 20s. He has published numerous articles on adolescent delinquency, drug use, gangs, and gun use and is the co-author of two books and co-editor of three collections of original articles. His recent book, *Gangs and Delinquency in Developmental Perspective,* was the recipients of the 2003 Michael J. Hindelang Award presented by the American Society of Criminology. He is also the recipient of the SUNY Chancellor's Award for Excellence in Teaching.

Benjamin B. Lahey is professor of psychiatry and chief of psychology at the University of Chicago. He is president of the Society for Child and Adolescent Clinical Psychology and past president of the International Society for Research on Child and Adolescent Psychopathology. He is the recipient of the Research Prize of the National Academy of Neuropsychology and the Distinguished Research Contributions Award of the Society for Child and Adolescent Clinical Psychology. His research focuses on the childhood origins of serious conduct problems and the evaluation of diagnostic criteria for mental health disorders of childhood.

John H. Laub is a professor of criminology and criminal justice at the University of Maryland, College Park, and an affiliated scholar at the Henry A. Murray Center at the Radcliffe Institute for Advanced Study at Harvard University. He is a past president of the American Society of Criminology, a fellow of the American Society of Criminology, and a member of the Committee on Law and Justice of the National Research Council. His areas of research include crime and deviance over the life course, juvenile delinquency and juvenile justice, and the history of criminology. He has published widely including *Crime in the Making: Pathways and Turning Points Through Life*, co-authored with Robert Sampson (1993) and *Shared Beginnings, Divergent Lives: Delinquent Boys to Age 70,* also with Robert Sampson (2003).

Rolf Loeber, Ph.D. is Distinguished Professor of Psychiatry, and professor of psychology and epidemiology at the Western Psychiatric Institute and Clinic, School of Medicine, University of Pittsburgh, Pittsburgh, Pennsylvania, and professor of juvenile delinquency and social development, Free University, Amsterdam, Netherlands. He obtained his initial degree in clinical psychology from the University of Amsterdam, and his Ph.D. in psychology from Queen's University, Kingston, Ontario, Canada. Currently, he is co-director of the Life History Program and is principal investigator of three longitudinal studies, the Pittsburgh Youth Study, the Developmental Trends Study, and the Pittsburgh Girls Study. Dr. Loeber has published widely in the fields of juvenile antisocial behavior and delinquency, substance use, and mental health problems. Books published by him include *Serious and Violent Juvenile Offenders: Risk Factors and Successful Interventions* (1998), co-edited with David P. Farrington; *Antisocial Behavior and Mental Problems: Explanatory Factors in Childhood and Adolescence* (1998), co-authored with David P. Farrington, Magda Stouthamer-Loeber, and Welmoet B. Van Kammen; *Child Delinquents: Development, Interventions, and Service Needs* (2001), co-edited with David P. Farrington; and, *Serious and Violent Juvenile Delinquency in the Netherlands,*

Prevalence, Causes, and Interventions (2001), co-authored with Wim Slot and Joseph Sergeant.

Terrie E. Moffitt researches how nature and nurture interact in the origins of human psychopathology, particularly antisocial behavior. She is a clinical psychologist, and a professor at the Institute of Psychiatry at King's College London and the University of Wisconsin-Madison. She directs the Environmental-Risk Study ("E-risk"), which follows 1,116 families with twins born in 1994, to study how family adversities and heritable risk affect children's behavior disorders. She is also associate director of the Dunedin Multidisciplinary Health and Development Study, a thirty-two-year longitudinal study of the health and behavior of 1,000 New Zealanders born in 1972. For her research, she has received the Award for Early Career Contribution from the American Psychological Association (1993) and a Royal Society-Wolfson Merit Award (2002). She is a fellow of the Academy of Medical Sciences (1999), the American Society of Criminology (2003), and the British Academy (2004).

Jisuk Park was a research analyst at the Social Development Research Group, School of Social Work, University of Washington. Her research interests while at SDRG included the longitudinal study of problem behaviors such as substance abuse and depression. Currently, she is employed as a statistician at Washington Mutual, Inc.

Alex R. Piquero is professor of criminology at the University of Florida, member of the National Consortium on Violence Research, and member of the MacArthur Foundation's Research Network on Adolescent Development and Juvenile Justice. His research interests include criminal careers, criminological theory, and quantitative research methods. He received the ASC's Cavan Young Scholar Award as well as the University of Florida College of Arts and Sciences Teacher of the Year Award.

Robert J. Sampson is the Henry Ford II Professor of the Social Sciences at Harvard University. Formerly, he was the Fairfax M. Cone Distinguished Service Professor in Sociology at the University of Chicago, a senior research fellow at the American Bar Foundation, and a fellow at the Center for Advanced Study in the Behavioral Sciences in Stanford, California (1997-1998 and 2002-2003). Professor Sampson's main research interests include crime, law, and deviance, the life course, and urban/community sociology. He is currently focusing on the study of neighborhood effects, spatial dynamics, and social processes as part of the Project on Human Development in Chicago Neighborhoods, for which he serves as scientific director. Professor Sampson is also engaged in a longitudinal study from birth to death of 1,000 disadvantaged men born in Boston during the Great Depression era. His first book from this project, *Crime in the Making: Pathways and Turning Points Through Life* (1993), written with John Laub, received the outstanding book award from the American Society of Criminology, the Academy of Criminal Justice Sciences, and the Crime, Law, and Deviance Section of the American Sociological Association. A second book from this project, *Shared Beginnings, Divergent Lives: Delinquent Boys to Age 70*, was published in 2003.

Terence P. Thornberry is director of the Research Program on Problem Behavior at the Institute of Behavioral Science and professor of sociology, University of Colorado. He is the principal investigator of the Rochester Youth Development Study, an ongoing panel study begun in 1986 to examine the causes and consequences of delinquency, drug use, and other forms of antisocial behavior. Professor Thornberry is an author of *Gangs and Delinquency in Developmental Perspective* (which received the American Society of Criminology's Michael J. Hindelang Award for the Most Outstanding Contribution to Research in Criminology in 2003) and an editor of *Taking Stock of Delinquency: An Overview of Findings from Contemporary Longitudinal Studies.* His research interests focus on understanding the development of delinquency and drug use over the life course.

Irwin D. Waldman is associate professor in the Department of Psychology of Emory University. Dr. Waldman is a clinical psychologist with developmental interests who examines the genetic and environmental etiology of disruptive behavior disorders in childhood and adolescence. His current research explores the role of candidate genes in the development of externalizing behavior problems, as well as genetic and environmental influences on comorbidity and on the links between normal variation in symptoms and in personality in the general population and extreme variants in clinical samples. He is co-author of the developmental propensity model of conduct problems.

Per-Olof H. Wikström is professor of ecological and developmental criminology, Institute of Criminology, University of Cambridge (UK). He is the director of the ESRC (Economic and Social Research Council) Cambridge Network for the Study of the Social Contexts of Pathways in Crime (ScoPiC, see www.scopic.ac.uk) and the principal investigator of the Peterborough Adolescent Development Study (PADS). Recent publications include *Do Disadvantaged Neighborhoods Cause Well-adjusted Children to Become Adolescent Delinquents?* (2000, with Rolf Loeber), *Social Mechanisms of Community Influences on Crime and Pathways in Criminality* (2003, with Robert J. Sampson), and *Crime as an Alternative* (2004). Professor Wikström was the 1994 recipient of the American Society of Criminology's Sellin-Glueck Award for international contributions to criminology, and in 2002 he was elected a fellow of the Center for Advanced Study in the Behavioral Sciences at Stanford, California.

Index

Note: Locators in italics indicate material in figures/tables.